Research Methods in Social Work

Nelson-Hall Series in Social Work

Consulting Editor: Charles Zastrow
University of Wisconsin—Whitewater

Research Methods in Social Work

Third Edition

David Royse

University of Kentucky

Nelson-Hall Publishers   Chicago

Copy editor: Rachel Schick
Designer: Jane Rae Brown
Cover painting: *Magic Landscape II* by Franz Altschuler
Typesetter: Precision Typographers, Inc.
Printer: Bang Printing

Library of Congress Cataloging-in-Publication Data

Royse, David D. (David Daniel)
    Research methods in social work / David Royse. — 3rd ed.
      p.   cm. — (Nelson-Hall series in social work)
    Includes bibliographical references and index.
    ISBN 0-8304-1533-5 (alk. paper)
    1. Social service—Research—Methodology.   I. Title.   II. Series.
HV11.R69   1999   98-44273
361.3'2'072—dc21   CIP

Manufactured in the United States of America

10 9 8 7 6 5 4 3 2 1

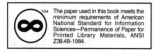 The paper used in this book meets the minimum requirements of American National Standard for Information Sciences—Permanence of Paper for Printed Library Materials, ANSI Z39.48-1984.

Contents

CHAPTER 3 / Single System Designs   42

CHAPTER 4 / Research Designs for Group Comparisons   73

CHAPTER 5 / Understanding and Using Research Instruments   100

CHAPTER 6 / Survey Research   138

CHAPTER 7 / Developing Data Collection Instruments: Scales and Questionnaires   175

CHAPTER 8 / Unobtrusive Approaches to Data Collection: Secondary Data and Content Analysis   200

CHAPTER 9 / Data Analysis   226

CHAPTER 10 / Program Evaluation   255

Preface to the Third Edition

New Features

This third edition is different from the others, and, I think, from all the other research texts, in its attempt to demonstrate that research informs our practice and that questions from practice are often the catalyst for our studies. Besides lots of social work literature built into this text, you'll see sprinkled throughout new Practice Notes that show the interrelatedness of practice and research.

Also new to this edition is the inclusion of Internet resources. This is somewhat of a risk on my part in that electronic addresses can change overnight. But there are so many wonderful sources of information on the World Wide Web; I felt it would be irresponsible to not call your attention to a few of these. Admittedly, I've been somewhat selective and some of you will wonder why I didn't list your favorite sites. If you feel strongly about it, send me an e-mail (droyse@pop.uky.edu). For those of you who have yet to discover the electronic libraries and databases available over the Internet, I hope you will take the time to do some exploring when the text points to potentially informative resources.

Lastly, students will like the text even more than the previous editions because another new feature is a Self-Review (with answers!) at the end of each chapter.

Audience

I have written this book for both undergraduate and graduate social work students. Those students who desire more information on selected topics are encouraged to consult the extensive references at the end of each chapter. By reading those books and journal articles, students can vastly expand upon their knowledge and the coverage provided in this introductory text.

Author's Perspective

I'm going to make a bold statement: Social workers can be assigned to one of three broad categories:

- Those who are confused by research
- Those who understand and can use research findings
- Those who can conduct research.

My role is not unlike that of a bus driver, and this book is a vehicle. We'll be stopping to pick up passengers all along the way. Some will initially be quite far from the destination and others quite close. You may already have a general sense of the route we will be taking; there will be grand vistas and exotic places, and interesting things to think about as we progress toward the goal of becoming competent researchers. I hope you have the curiosity of a tourist and ask questions and reflect—maybe you'll even go to the library or the Internet and do some digging yourself. There's nothing more rewarding than social work and sometimes nothing more frustrating. Prepare yourself well for this career you have chosen.

One thing is for certain: few decisions are made today without some kind of data gathering. In fact, there seems to be a hunger for research today unlike that of any other era. I believe the importance of research to society will only continue to grow. It won't go away and can't be ignored. Jump on the bus. It won't be a waste of your time!

CHAPTER 1
Introduction

Where Does Research Start?

Have you ever noticed that unanswered questions, riddles, and mysteries surround us? If we were face-to-face in a classroom, I'd ask you to take a minute or two to think about some of the questions percolating in the back of your mind that have never been satisfactorily answered. I'm not talking about questions like "I wonder what's for supper?" or "Who on earth did Jimmy go out with last night?" but larger questions like "Is heredity or environment the more powerful influence in alcoholism?" or "To what extent do most victims of child abuse recover from their trauma?"

For some of you, life's mysteries involve specific individuals and their behavior. You may wonder why a favorite cousin committed suicide in the prime of his life, or why Aunt Martha can't seem to quit drinking. Maybe you have grown up with a schizophrenic parent or sibling and wonder if you somehow unintentionally contributed to their illness.

Research seeks to provide answers to life's enigmas by exploring questions that originate from people just like yourself. You see, ideas for suitable research projects often stem from our own life experiences or observations. Allow me to give you a brief illustration of this.

Close to the end of a spring semester several years ago, I was concluding a lecture on qualitative research methods. (Qualitative research methods seek to help the investigator understand the experience or viewpoint of another person or group of persons.) As I typically do during that lecture, I introduced material from Clifford Beers's book, *A Mind That Found Itself* (1910). Beers was a college student around the turn of the century who, after breaking up with his fiancé, began losing his mind. He kept a diary of the events that occurred during this period of his life—he talks, for instance, of feeling a compulsion to jump out of a third-floor window, at the same time knowing that it was a crazy thought.

"What would it be like," I asked the class, "to feel torn between wanting to injure yourself and knowing that those thoughts were crazy? To be unable to stop obsessing about something?" I had the class's attention, but paused for a moment to switch examples.

In a recent series of articles on child abuse our local newspaper had portrayed a number of officials (judges, lawyers, and, yes, social workers) who had not done enough to protect vulnerable children. Most students probably were familiar with the newspaper accounts, but I wanted to impress upon them that knowledge of the statistics and facts about child abuse is quite different from the experience of abuse.

"What would it be like," I asked the class, "to be chained in a dark, damp basement as a child? To have your cries of hunger ignored by your parents—or worse, to be sexually abused on a filthy mattress on the cold concrete floor? Would you understand child abuse any differently than you do now? How might living in a different culture or taking on a different lifestyle provide you with knowledge that you wouldn't get just by reading a book or journal article?"

A student raised her hand and when I acknowledged her, she simply pointed to the student beside her. Even from the front of the classroom, I could see that something was unusual about Frank. As the whole class turned to look at him, he sat rigid, eyes glazed over. I walked closer and called his name several times. There was no response. Gently I reached over and tugged on his sleeve. Again, there was no indication that Frank recognized he was the focus of the class's attention. I shook Frank harder. Nothing. I checked for blink and startle reflexes ... he had none.

Never had I encountered such a problem in the classroom! My first thought was that he was having some sort of seizure, although I had never seen one like it. Someone suggested that we look in his wallet to see if it contained any emergency medical information. It did. We found the number of a clinical social worker whose office wasn't too far from campus.

With the card in my hand, I sprinted to the nearest pay phone on the next floor and dialed the number. I insisted that the receptionist immediately connect me with the therapist. A few seconds later, the social worker confirmed that Frank became temporarily catatonic from time to time; not all of his triggers had been identified. However, she assured me, Frank usually recovered on his own within twenty minutes to an hour.

I went back to the classroom and found my students anxiously gathered around Frank, watching for some blink or sigh, some indication that he was in the land of the living. The bell rang, signaling the end of class. Anticipating that another class would be coming into our classroom, I asked a student to help me lift Frank to see if we could assist him in walking out of the classroom. However, Frank was still unresponsive and unable to help. It was like lifting a 150-pound bag of potatoes. Rather than risk dropping him, we decided to leave Frank in his seat.

Several students volunteered to stay with Frank, but I encouraged them to go on to their own classes, assuring them that I would remain behind. About this time, I looked back at Frank and noticed a single tear slipping down his cheek. He blinked his eyes and turned his head as if to acquaint himself with his surroundings. "Are you okay?" I asked. Frank responded by nodding his head affirmatively. It took a few more minutes for Frank to compose himself enough to walk to my car so that I could take him to his therapist.

I saw Frank again about a week later when he took his final exam for my class. He did well, and finished in the top third of the class.

Frank had been a victim of nightmarish child abuse. Something I had said, some image I evoked, summoned a flood of memories so painful that Frank's catatonia had resulted. But Frank's experience also had an effect upon me. Maybe not that afternoon, but shortly thereafter, I began wondering about the extent to which other students of social work might have been impaired by early childhood or dysfunctional family experiences. That thought spun off others—could early childhood experiences affect the choice of social work as a career? Could unfortunate childhood experiences affect our satisfaction with life as adults? That remarkable experience with Frank fueled my curiosity about a whole set of questions I had never seriously contemplated before and was the catalyst for several research projects (see, for example, Rompf and Royse, 1994, and Royse, Rompf, and Dhooper, 1991).

Like the clinical social worker looking for clues in a client's speech, dress, or behavior to assist in making an assessment, the researcher is also in the business of collecting and interpreting data to unravel some mystery. Different experiences raise different questions. A paraplegic MSW student once remarked in class that few professionals know how to talk to persons with handicaps. He speculated that because their training had taught them not to ask questions for which they do not need answers, professionals often did not inquire as to how he lost the use of his legs. As a result, they often made erroneous assumptions—and in doing so, failed to get to know him as a person. "I would much rather," he said, "have them ask, 'What happened to you?' so that I can explain something about me as a person. As I tell them about my former career as an electronics engineer and the airplane crash, they begin to know me as a human being. I'm no longer some vegetable in a wheelchair."

As he talked, I realized that other persons with handicaps may feel as he did. And, you guessed it, a number of questions about disability and preferences for disclosure began forming in my mind. Later, the two of us combined our knowledge and conducted a study (Royse and Edwards, 1989). While our investigation was not definitive by any means, it did provide some beginning evidence suggesting that persons with disabilities are frequently open to disclosing. As a small study, it is only one piece of evidence, a starting place for other researchers interested in this issue, possibly persons like yourself, to build upon.

Unanswered questions, riddles, and mysteries surround us and provide the stimulus for research. Over the years, I've lost track of the number of students who've come to me to explore some particular research interest. Those able to conceptualize their projects clearly and those with lots of perseverance (willingness to revise and rewrite) have been rewarded by seeing their efforts published in professional journals. Who creates knowledge for social workers? Individuals like yourself. The research process can (and should) start with you.

Why Study Research?

Social work is an exciting career choice. Students select this profession because they like people and want to help families where there has been abuse, mental illness, or alcoholism and to assist such special populations as the aged and the homeless. As a consequence, social work students are often eager to soak up instruction that will assist them in becoming better counselors or practitioners. They approach practice-oriented courses with enthusiasm and vigor. All goes well until they learn that they must take a research course (sometimes two courses) as part of the requirements for a degree. Immediately some students are resentful. "Research!" they say. "Why do I have to take research?" "I don't want to do research. I want to work with the severely mentally ill." Variations of this are: "I want to work with children" and "I want to work with adolescents who have eating disorders."

Why, then, must social work students study research? Consider a few examples that will demonstrate its usefulness to practitioners of social work.

1. You are asked to direct an adolescent AIDS prevention program. The goal of the program is to supply adolescents with information about how to avoid contracting the AIDS virus. After several months you are convinced that the adolescents in your program are more knowledgeable after participation in the program. How would you convince others of the success of your intervention?

2. You are hired by an agency that provides counseling to families in which children have been sexually assaulted by a family member. You are assigned to work with the offenders. Counseling seems to go well with your first several clients, and now several want to return to their families. How would you go about providing evidence that your intervention was effective—that it was safe to reunite the family members?

3. You manage services in a community agency for persons with chronic mental illness and have approached a local foundation to provide funding for an exciting new program that matches clients with volunteers. The foundation asks how you will evaluate the success of the proposed program.

In each of these three examples, some research skills are required—skills that can be used with other problems and concerns. However, before these skills can be taught, oftentimes it is necessary to address and "neutralize" negative attitudes about research so that there is the greatest opportunity for learning to occur.

Social Work Students and Research

Although a few students are delighted to be in their first research course because they are eager to acquire the tools that will allow them to investigate some area of interest, many more do not see the necessity for the course. In fact, Epstein (1987) has observed that "no other part of the social work curriculum has been so consistently received by students with as much groaning, moaning, eye-rolling, bad-mouthing, hyperventilation, and waiver-strategizing as the research course" (p.71). Epstein has cited other studies that document social work students' disinterest in research—what he calls the "resistance phenomenon" (Rosenblatt, 1968; Kirk and Fisher, 1976; Dane and Epstein, 1985).

Briar (1980) has noted that there is a widespread belief among social workers that the same person cannot be both a good researcher and a good practitioner. He continues:

> The personal qualities believed to make a good researcher are seen as handicaps for a practitioner, and the reverse also has been said to be true. The stereotypes are familiar. Researchers are supposedly intellectual, rational, unfeeling creatures who lack the sensitivity to understand the subtle nuances that are of primary concern to practitioners. Practitioners are purported to be intuitive, sensitive, creative persons more akin to artists than scientists; they emphasize the importance of seeing clients as whole persons who should not be subjected to the categorization and atomization that research allegedly requires. It is easy, of course, to show that these stereotypes are invalid, but such beliefs, although less prevalent than they once were, continue to influence the relationship between practice and research in social work. (P. 31)

Unlike psychology, which adopted the Scientist-Professional Training Model shortly after World War II, the dual emphasis on research and practice has not received the same emphasis in social work until fairly recent times. We educators know that students are exposed to and supervised by social workers who do not conduct any research or evaluate their own practice. These individuals are not the best role models for students and, unfortunately, they perpetuate the myth that social workers do not need research skills.

Having taught the methodology course for more years than I care to remember, it is quite apparent to me that many students come into social work because they are math phobic. That is, they fear mathematical concepts and quantification. These students are math avoiders and have selected social work because of their perception that there will be fewer required courses in research and statistics here than elsewhere.

Why do students choose the career of social work? It's another one of those mysteries. As I told a class not too long ago, two things we know for sure: (1) as long as you are a social worker, you'll never run out of work, and (2) they'll never pay you all that you deserve. However, it is clear that at least some students choose this field because of their anxiety about math. A small study of our own BSW students found that they rated themselves significantly more anxious on a 24-item Mathematics Anxiety Rating Scale than did a cross-section of undergraduates (Royse and Rompf, 1992). I believe that this is a finding that could be replicated in other programs across the country.

Blame it on your high school algebra teacher or a bad experience in seventh-grade math, but for whatever reason, a sizeable proportion of students coming into this field not only want to help vulnerable populations but also want to do it with as little involvement with research and statistics as possible. We educators know this and it is our secret agenda to try and change your thinking about the need to acquire research skills. Don't say I didn't warn you.

Why Research Is Required

There are several reasons why you, as a social work student, should take at least one research course. First of all, both as a student and as a social worker you will be reading journal articles and technical articles in which research results are presented. You need to have a basic knowledge of how research is conducted, or could be conducted, to help you evaluate the strengths and weaknesses of the published research. As an informed consumer of information you ought to know if too few subjects were interviewed, if the methodology was flawed, or if the author generalized well beyond his or her findings. Research studies can be biased or flawed for a lot of different reasons, and you might not be able to detect these reasons without a basic understanding of research methodology. To make effective use of research that you encounter, whether in journals or unpublished reports produced in your agency, you need to know something about how proper research is conducted.

Like it or not, we are all consumers of research. We hear the results of studies or polls on the television and radio, and we read about studies that are reported in newspapers, magazines, and journals. How do you know if these studies are any good? Could you identify a poorly designed study? What criteria would you use? One bestseller that used thousands of questionnaires to support its conclusions has been called the "functional equivalent of malpractice for surveys." Just because something finds its way into print does not mean that it is based on good research or scholarship. Learn to be a skeptical reader. Ask questions of what you read. Do the findings seem consistent with what you know about the subject? Even a little knowledge of research will help you become a more informed consumer of the information you routinely encounter.

Being an informed consumer will lead you to evaluate the reported research and enable you to make more substantial contributions when you are called upon to disseminate knowledge in your everyday practice. Social workers are often required to prepare reports, conduct inservice training, or make workshop presentations. Information is shared not only with fellow professionals but also with clients and the community. As you make greater use of professional journals, you will find that you need an understanding of research in order to fully comprehend what is being reported.

Second, social workers are accountable for their interventions. As a professional, you must be able to determine whether the intervention you are using with a client is making any difference. Could you demonstrate that the client is improving? Or, at the very least, could you show that your intervention has not harmed the client? Even if you are not interested in conducting research on a large scale, you owe it to your clients and yourself to be able to evaluate your practice with them. A research approach discussed in this book, the single system design, will help you evaluate your practice with individual clients.

Accountability is important on another level. Social service agencies vary enormously in size and may employ several to hundreds of social workers. Taxpayers, governmental agencies, and funding sources, such as United Way organizations, often expect social service agencies to conduct or provide evaluation research on such issues as client utilization of the agency's services and the effects or outcomes of the services provided. Agencies must show that they are meeting the needs of their target populations, that their clientele feel satisfied with services, and that the agency's operation is productive and efficient.

Suppose you become a program director or manager in a social service organization, and the executive director wants you to begin a new program. The director insists that the program have a good evaluation system built into it. Would you know how to go about evaluating a social service program? Would you know a poor evaluation if you saw one? Programs are sometimes funded with the provision that they can demonstrate some impact on the problem. This usually means that research in some form or fashion is required. Faced as we are with major social problems and fairly limited amounts of monies that can be applied to these problems, it is incumbent upon us social workers to strive for implementation of programs that have the best success rates.

Even as a new social worker, fresh from the university, you might be asked to conduct research to meet some reporting or accreditation requirement. Occasionally, students tell me how surprised they were on their first jobs when they were assigned a research project—especially when it was not even discussed during the job interview. Would you be more interested in learning how to conduct research if you knew you would be responsible for conducting research sometime in the near future?

Third, the Council on Social Work Education (CSWE), a national, nongovernmental accreditation and standard-setting organization for baccalaureate and master's degree programs, requires research as one of the five required professional content areas. Each college and university that grants degrees in social work must periodically submit documentation that it conforms with curriculum policy in order for the institution's program to be accredited by CSWE.

The council's curriculum policy requires that social work students (at both the BSW and MSW levels) understand that a "spirit of inquiry" and "informed criticism" are the bases of scientific thinking and lead to the acquisition of knowledge and the application of that knowledge in practice. Research content is expected to help students learn the critical appreciation and use of research and program evaluation as they learn the methods for evaluating service delivery in all areas of practice. The clear expectation is that students will move from a position of only being able to consume research to being able to evaluate practice systematically.

A fourth reason you are in a research class is because of this language in the National Association of Social Workers Code of Ethics (1996):

> 5.02 (a) Social workers should monitor and evaluate policies, the implementation of programs, and practice interventions.
> (b) Social workers should promote and facilitate evaluation and research to contribute to the development of knowledge.
> (c) Social workers should critically examine and keep current with emerging knowledge relevant to social work and fully use evaluation and research evidence in their professional practice.

The Code of Ethics asserts that we have a responsibility for both evaluating practice and building knowledge. Research improves our practice and allows us to test new innovations.

As professional social workers, we must advocate for our clients by conducting research on social policies at the state and national levels. While it may seem unlikely that you would ever be involved in such research, consider for a moment the extent to which most social workers are affected by state and national policies. Some of these policies are good, and some could use modification. Consider, for example, how you might go about convincing legislators and government officials that cutting funds to social services will have an adverse effect upon your client population. Can you see the value of having "hard data" to show skeptics how many people depend upon a certain social service and how their lives might be affected if funds were cut? The profession needs researchers who can show that cuts in social service programs ultimately result in greater tax burdens. I am convinced that greater funding for social services will come as social workers are better able to demonstrate that adequate levels of social services are cost-effective for reducing or eliminating some of the major social problems facing us today.

Also, you need to be comfortable with both consuming and conducting research because otherwise you may not be practicing the most effective treatment available. Myers and Thyer (1997) have raised the issue: "A client sees a clinical social worker about a psychosocial disorder for which there is a treatment that has been demonstrated effective through repeated, well-designed outcome studies. Does the client have the right to receive this validated treatment, or does the social worker have the latitude to provide another, unsupported treatment?" (p.288). Most of us would probably agree that clients deserve the best intervention available, not one that is delivered simply because "that's the way I have always treated this problem" or "this is what I learned thirty years ago in graduate school."

Social workers who do not keep current on the literature and research in their fields are in danger of practicing primitive, if not incompetent, social work. Interventions are not equally effective, and social workers need to be able to inform clients why, on the basis of empirical studies, one particular treatment is recommended over another. Although Myers and Thyer (1997) list thirteen different psychosocial disorders (for examples, bulimia, chronic pain, social phobia) and the empirically validated treatments for them, it is also apparent that such knowledge has not been developed for all the problems our clients may bring. This is where you come in. As a social worker who can understand as well as conduct research, you will be able to identify those interventions that should be used with specific client groups and those that shouldn't. You have an ethical obligation to do as much.

Along this line, Gambrill (1995) argues that an empirically based social work practice exposes fraud and quackery and those who make questionable claims of effectiveness. I like that notion—that social work professionals should be consumer advocates for more than just the daily necessities of our clients.

At this point in your career, evaluating policies and attempting to build knowledge may not interest you, but once you are engaged in practice full time you may make discoveries—perhaps you will want to report on the effectiveness of some new treatment approach or exciting innovation that you have devised. There might be a conference in sunny Orlando that would be interested in your making a presentation or a journal that would like to have your article on the intervention. In other words, you need competence in research methods to help you achieve your potential as a contributing member of the social work profession. There will be times when even the most thoroughly convinced "I've-always-wanted-to-be-just-a-clinician" wishes that he or she understood a little more about research. By knowing research, you position yourself to reach higher goals and even to increase your income. For instance, some social workers become managers and interpreters of data within their agencies or districts; others develop copyrighted instruments or interventions that can be sold commercially; others become nationally recognized experts/consultants; and so on.

Desired Outcome

Every social work educator wants his or her students to be skilled, expert practitioners. We have a vested interest in your success, but we can't do it all. Our profession's future self-respect depends upon your use of research in an empirically based practice. You as a practitioner must be able to do the following (Siegel, 1984):

1. make maximum use of research findings;
2. collect data systematically to monitor the interventions;
3. demonstrate empirically whether or not interventions are effective;
4. specify problems, interventions, and outcomes in concrete, observable, measurable terms;
5. apply research skills in defining clients' problems, formulating questions for practice, evaluating the effectiveness of interventions; and
6. view research as a tool and as part of the problem-solving process.

Perhaps the best way to acquire this stance of viewing research as a tool to be used is to approach each of the new methodologies you'll be learning with a question or problem that you would like to investigate. This should be one that interests you—one that piques your curiosity. Keep this question in the back of your mind as each new chapter is presented. As you read, think about how that information could be harnessed to answer your question, to enrich your expertise as a social worker.

One of the characteristics of social work research is that it is applied; it seeks knowledge that will improve the lives of our clients and make this world a little better place. Research begins when people like you develop questions from real-life situations and observations of human nature and social problems, and become concerned about the lack of answers. In some instances, a thorough search of library resources will provide needed information. But if it does not, you may have identified a gap in our knowledge base. There is no shortage of problems needing additional investigation, and many opportunities exist for you as a researcher to make important contributions to our field. If you had the time and the funding to explore one unanswered question, what would it be?

Self-Review

(Answers at the end of the book)

1. The Scientist-Professional Training Model is closely associated with which discipline:
   a. social work
   b. psychology
   c. anthropology
   d. theology
2. List five reasons discussed in this chapter why social work students should study research methods
3. What is the purpose of the Council on Social Work Education?
   a. accreditation of social work programs
   b. peer-training of social work educators
   c. marketing of social work programs
4. T or F.   The NASW Code of Ethics requires social workers to monitor and evaluate their practice, their programs, and the policies that shape their interventions.
5. Summarize what "empirically based practice" means.
6. What is the chief characteristic of social work research?
7. Where does research start?

Questions for Class Discussion

1. What are your fears about taking a research class?
2. What do you hope to learn from this class?
3. What experiences have you had that might help in this class? Describe any research-related experiences you may have had.
4. What are the problems that might develop when a profession's knowledge base and research lag behind its practice?
5. As a class, make a list of problems and questions that you think need to be researched.
6. Have you ever come across a piece of research that you thought was worthless? Why did you have this opinion?
7. What stereotypes do you have about researchers?

8. In what ways could research be used to affect a local, state, or national policy that you think needs to be changed?
9. Discuss ways you might go about investigating the problems in the three examples at the beginning of this chapter.
10. Make a list of reasons why it is important for social workers to engage in empirically based practice.

Mini-Projects for Experiencing Research Firsthand

1. Conduct a survey to find out the most popular explanation for why social work students do not want to study research methods.
2. Design a questionnaire that will allow you to investigate whether there are major differences in the opinions of social work, psychology, and nursing majors about the importance of taking research methods and statistics courses.

Resources and References

Briar, S. (1980). Toward the integration of practice and research. In David Fanshel (Ed.), *Future of social work research*. Washington, DC: National Association of Social Workers.

Dane, E. and Epstein, I. (1985). A dark horse in continued education programming at the post-master's level: Monitoring and evaluation skills for social workers in middle management. *Journal of Continuing Social Work Education,* 3(2), 3–8.

Epstein, I. (1987). Pedagogy of the perturbed: Teaching research to the reluctants. *Journal of Teaching in Social Work,* 1(1), 71–89.

Gambrill, E. (1995). Behavioral social work: Past, present, and future. *Research on Social Work Practice,* 5, 460–484.

Kirk, S. and Fisher, J. (1976). Do social workers understand research? *Journal of Education for Social Work,* 2(1), 63–71.

Myers, L.L. and Thyer, B.A. (1997). Should social work clients have the right to effective treatment? *Social Work,* 42, 288–298.

Rompf, E. L. and Royse, D. (1994). Choice of social work as a career: Possible influences. *Journal of Social Work Education,* 30, 163–171.

Rosenblatt, A. (1968). The practitioners' use and evaluation of research. *Social Work,* 13, 53–59.

Royse, D. and Edwards, T. (1989). Communicating about disability: Attitudes and preferences of persons with physical handicaps. *Rehabilitation Counseling Bulletin,* 32(3), 203–209.

Royse, D. and Rompf, E.L. (1992). Math anxiety: A comparison of social work and non-social work students. *Journal of Social Work Education,* 28(3), 270–277.

Royse, D., Rompf, E.L., and Dhooper, S.S. (1991). Childhood trauma and adult life satisfaction in a random adult sample. *Psychological Reports,* 69, 1227–1231.

Siegel, D.H. (1984). Defining empirically based practice. *Social Work,* 29(4), 325–331.

CHAPTER 2
The Way Research Proceeds

Research in the social sciences usually results from a real problem someone has encountered. The process is logical and similar to the problem-solving model so familiar to social workers. You may be surprised to find that the research process is not much different from the way that you normally go about finding solutions. This chapter will provide an overview of the various steps.

The research process (sometimes called the scientific method) is based on the assumptions that the natural world is essentially orderly and that observed phenomena have some stimulus or cause. If the laws of nature are not haphazard in their operation, then it follows that laws that govern the phenomena can be learned. Our knowledge about the world is obtained through the use of a logical sequence of steps. It is only when we don't know very much about a phenomenon that there seem to be no discernible laws. The more we know about something, the better we can see certain laws or principles in action. Let's take an example of a problematic situation suggested by Leedy (1974) that illustrates a research-like process.

You leave your home to go to class. You are running a little bit late and are in a hurry. You put the key in your car's ignition and turn it. Nothing happens. At first you don't believe your bad luck, turning the key again and again. Nothing happens. You pull the key from the ignition and look at it to make sure that it's the right key. You try again. Nothing. At this point you almost immediately pose questions to yourself. Did I leave the lights on? Is there enough gas? You select a logical explanation and begin the "research" process. Suppose you have a notion that you left the car lights on all night. You can test the hypothesis of a weak battery by turning on the car's radio or headlights. If they work, then you can assume that the battery still has a charge, and you can move on to another hypothesis. You remember telling your brother to put gas in the car, and you wonder whether or not he did. You look at the fuel indicator and see that it registers "Full." Does the gauge work properly? Assuming it does, you move on to the next hypothesis: perhaps your ten-year-old car is in need of spark plugs, or the distributor got wet from last night's rain. Those of you who have had the experience of owning an old car could probably proceed with such hypotheses longer than anyone else would be interested. The point is that a series of questions needing investigation flows from the problematic situation. As this example reveals, research involves an orderly thought process that moves from what is known to what is not known. Numerous and varied hypotheses may be tested. Information gained leads to the consideration of other questions or hypotheses.

The Research Process

As illustrated in the example above, the research process is composed of a few relatively simple steps or stages. For instructional purposes, these steps are presented as being sequential. However, sometimes they are taken out of order. For instance, once a question is formulated, we might start thinking about how to collect the necessary data before we go to the library to start a literature search.

Step 1: Posing a Question or Stating a Hypothesis

Before you can begin conducting research you must necessarily limit yourself to one question (or at least to a small set of related questions) or one specific topic to investigate. Ideas may emerge from observations of clients, personal experiences, discussions with colleagues, or reading the literature pertinent to a certain problem.

Research questions may come about as a result of **deduction** (where knowledge of a theory or general principle allows you to make a prediction or an application to a single specific case) or from **induction** (where your observations about a case or cases seem to suggest a theory or set of principles). For instance, learning of a two-year-old child in a housing project who has been eating plaster may result in your wondering if this problem is widespread. How many other two-year-olds in the city or nation are so hungry they are eating bits of fallen plaster? Induction goes from the specific to the general. Unlike research questions in other disciplines, those in social work generally stem from problems that actually need to be solved. We tend as professionals to be inductive rather than deductive thinkers because our research tends to have more of an applied focus.

Once a question has been roughly posed or drafted, it will often need to be restated as a researchable question. Not all questions can be answered— and the purpose of research is to generate information that can be verified by others. "Why is there suffering?" is an example of a question best left to philosophers or theologians. Social scientists are interested in concrete, tangible, objective findings that can be replicated (reproduced) by others.

Sometimes, however, it is possible to give a slightly different emphasis to an expansive question like "Why is there suffering?" and thereby make it a researchable question. "How do children with leukemia explain the origin of their illnesses?" is a question that could be investigated. Often, very broad questions can be narrowed down by considering specific manifestations of the problem or how you would go about collecting data.

There is a definite knack to developing a good question. If too few words are used, the question tends to be too large to investigate. "What causes child abuse?" is an example of a research question that needs to be narrowed down. There is nothing wrong with wanting to provide answers to such questions, but practically speaking, the research needed to answer them would be well beyond the resources of most undergraduate or graduate students. As you read about child abuse, you will discover that the role of certain factors has already been demonstrated. It is usually better to ask questions that allow you to examine a specific theory or perhaps a small part of the problem. A better question might be "Were child abusers abused themselves as children?" or "Do perpetrators of child abuse tend to be chemically dependent?"

Questions that are asked in research studies are often very specific. This specificity is reflected in the titles of journal articles. Browse through an issue of *Social Work Abstracts*. The abstracts will demonstrate how precisely worded hypotheses and research questions are. The research process starts with *either* a question to be answered *or* with a hypothesis to be tested. Most students find it easier to understand the research process in terms of asking questions rather than testing hypotheses. However, a **hypothesis** is simply an assumption expressed as a statement. Hypotheses are formal versions of hunches, expectations, or speculations that make a prediction or express an assumed relationship between variables. Hypotheses and research questions are both legitimate starting points for the research process. Either one can be converted into the other; the following question and hypothesis deal with the same research.

> *Example of a hypothesis:* Adolescent female athletes are more likely to disclose an eating disorder than females not involved in athletics.

> *Example of a research question:* Are eating disorders reported more often by adolescent female athletes or adolescent females not participating in organized athletic competition?

Elaborate studies may have several major hypotheses as well as a number of minor or subhypotheses.

Occasionally **null hypotheses** are used. These state that there is no difference between the groups being compared (for example, adolescent males are no more impulsive than adolescent females). Researchers sometimes hope to find sufficient evidence to allow for rejection of the null hypothesis. The researcher does not have to believe that there is no difference or no relationship in order to state a null hypothesis.

> *Example of a null hypothesis:* Female adolescents who participate in organized sports are no more likely to report eating disorders than female adolescents who are not involved in athletics.

When you write hypotheses, aim for precision and avoid the "you" construction as in these examples:

> *Poor:* The lower the education level, the more likely you are to be unhappy. If you come from a broken family, you are less likely to be happy.

> *Better:* Adults with less than twelve years of education will have lower life satisfaction scores than adults who have completed twelve or more years of education.

Children between the ages of four and sixteen whose parents have divorced or separated will rate themselves as more depressed than children from intact families.

Hypotheses, like research questions, may be suggested from theories, the literature, or interactions with colleagues or clients. Hypotheses need not always be stated but may be the driving force behind exploratory or descriptive studies. After such studies have been conducted and more data are available, hypotheses can be tested in a more formal manner.

The Importance of Theory

Theories vary considerably in their complexity, their perspective or orientation, and the amount of evidence that can be mustered to support them. For a good example of how various theories from different disciplines might be used to explain a social phenomenon, consider the concept of altruism—why are some people more altruistic than others? According to social learning theory, altruism might be acquired by children who learn it from generous role models. However, sociobiologists might argue that there is an "altruist" gene that developed because sharing behavior promotes greater survival of the species. From a psychological standpoint, altruism might be explained because it serves some inner, egoistic motive. From this perspective, even helping others may result in some self-benefit (for example, a positive mood state).

The research you do, or at least the way you go about it, is strongly influenced by your theoretical orientation. If you assume that altruism is caused by one's genetic inheritance, then the types of questions you'll explore will be vastly different from those you'd employ if your assumption is that we learn altruism by observing others. Your theoretical orientation directs your attention to events that are assumed to be important and allows you to ignore those that are expected to be irrelevant.

A good theory explains, organizes, and predicts (Munson, 1983). It allows you to go beyond the known facts, suggesting what you might expect in the future and allowing you to integrate the facts you already have. Theories provide clues or suggestions for interventions and help explain things that we don't understand very well. For instance, remember in chapter 1 the discussion about why social work students may not look forward to their research methods class?

A good theory focuses your attention, saves energy, and builds upon existent knowledge. Theories lead to predictions about the world in which we operate and might be likened to mental maps that suggest avenues or directions.

Why is a theoretical framework so important? Let me give you an example from a practicum seminar that I led one summer. As was our custom, the students each took about ten minutes at the beginning of class to report the progress of their clients or to share something new they had learned in the previous week. When it was Marcie's turn, she reported working with an alcoholic client who was heavily into denial. He maintained that he did not have a drinking problem, although he was beginning to have some liver complications, and that he could quit drinking any time he wanted. Since she wasn't making much headway with him, Marcie, noticing that her client was a chain smoker, asked if he could give up cigarette smoking as a way of showing that he could quit drinking. She reasoned that he might be more willing to quit drinking once he realized that he could live without cigarettes.

"Marcie," I asked when she had finished her account, "what theory or whose intervention are you following?"

"What do you mean?" she asked.

"Who has suggested that asking clients to give up their cigarettes helps them give up alcohol?"

"Well," she said, looking skyward for inspiration, "no one that I can think of. I thought of this all by myself."

"What happens," I asked, "if your client tries to quit smoking but fails? Could that experience convince him that he couldn't quit drinking even if he wanted to?"

"Oh," she said, her face blushing, "I didn't think of that."

At that point, we began a discussion about the importance of theory and how it can help guide our efforts, whether we are researchers or direct service practitioners. Theories are equally valuable to both. Practitioners employ theories in their interventions, and these theories provide guidelines or suggest techniques as well as offer explanations of observed phenomena.

It should also be noted that our theories, more times than not, emerge from our value orientations. This can be seen most sharply when we look at dated, historical theories like those of Freud and the way he viewed women and children. Bettelheim's (1967) blaming autism on "cold" mothers who happened to be career-oriented is also an infamous example. It makes one wonder: What theories that we currently hold precious will be discarded twenty or thirty years from now?

Although the logical positivists (the counters, those who quantity) among us strive to be "objective" so that our science can be "value-free," in some ways it's like trying to scoop a cup of sunlight. Social and cultural values do affect our learning, the persons we become, the questions we want to explore, the explanations of phenomena that we attend to and those that we ignore. Our values affect our research at every level— theories, hypotheses, choice of methodologies and variables, data analysis strategies—whether we are conscious of our values or not.

Step 2: Reviewing the Literature

Once you have a question or hypothesis in mind, the second step is to review the professional literature to see what others have already written about the topic. There are many good reasons for learning as much as possible about your subject before beginning to conduct a study. First of all, a careful review of the literature can save you a lot of unnecessary work and prevent you from wasting your time studying a problem that has already been thoroughly investigated.

As you discover how others have studied the problem, approaches that you hadn't considered may be suggested. You may find new instruments or ways for measuring your **dependent variable**. (The dependent variable is the topic of your investigation—what you are trying to explain or predict.) And, a solid review of the literature will help you ground your research interest and possible findings within a theoretical framework. Finally, acquainting yourself with the literature can provide you with data to compare with your own findings. Particularly if you are evaluating the success of an intervention, you may want to know how successful other approaches have been.

Journals sometimes have a particular theoretical orientation that influences the articles they publish. Sometimes this "slant" is very apparent—as in this example:

> The patient was a forty-year-old male who reported at age three he had gone into his parents' bedroom and seen his father's leg draped over his mother. The memory was associated with narcissistic rage. . . . Interpretation of the erotic transference allowed the patient to work through the anxiety associated with his sexual feelings and understand the Oedipal issues surfacing in his struggle with his career choice.

One thing is for sure—oftentimes there is so much literature on a topic that you are almost always certain to have a large number of titles to choose from. In fact, the amount of literature available may be almost unmanageable. There is so much literature on schizophrenia, for instance, that it would take years to read all the relevant journal articles and books. Once again we can see the utility of having a research question that is relatively narrow in its focus. How might this topic be narrowed down? (*Hint:* by searching for explanations of etiology—genetic evidence; diagnostic criteria for different types of schizophrenia; use of specific antipsychotic drugs for treatment; psychosocial intervention and management; the history of institutional treatment of schizophrenia; relapse—by searching for partial hospitalization or day treatment programs, by limiting the search to specific populations or age groups.)

Starting a Literature Search

There are several ways to begin a literature search; you might use only one approach or many, depending upon your success in finding relevant articles of interest. If you love to browse in libraries, a laid-back approach is to check the subject index to find where the books on your topic are located. Then examine the books on those shelves. As you review these books, you may find references to other books or journals.

The method I sometimes use is to go to specific journals that I know publish articles on the subject of my literature review. For instance, *Child Abuse and Neglect: An International Journal* would be a logical place to start if one wanted to find journal articles on child abuse. You might also look at *Child Welfare* or *Social Work*, and skim the table of contents in issues of the last two years. If you find several articles of interest, they almost always direct you to additional journal articles or studies that you can use to further explore what is known about your question.

A third approach when you want to conduct a serious search of the literature is to use the various bibliographic databases available at your university. For instance, *PsycLit* is comprehensive and a good place to begin searching for just about any topic in the social sciences. You may be able to access it on CD-ROM or through the Internet. Similarly, *Social Work Abstracts* will be a good source of articles on topics that are of interest to social workers. Some libraries will carry a regular subscription to *Social Work Abstracts* and it will be kept in the periodical section. Other schools may carry it on a CD-ROM that is updated regularly. Examples of other databases that can be searched by computer are:

- ERIC   For information on education-based concerns (for example, school dropouts; adolescent pregnancies; learning disorders).
- *MEDLINE*   For articles on medical-related problems (for example, depression, autism, attention-deficit hyperactivity disorder, anorexia).
- *TRAC*   A general purpose database that incorporates both scholarly and general interest periodicals (for example, *The New York Times*).
- *INFOTRAC*   Similar to *TRAC*, except it contains abstracts and some full-text articles.
- *FIRSTSEARCH*   This is a database of databases. Your library may subscribe to all of them or a selected set. Some of those contained in *FirstSearch* include: Article1st, Contents1st, Books in Print, Dissertation Abstracts, NewsAbs, SocioAbs, SocSciAbs, and WorldCat.

Don't make the assumption that all databases are the same, that if there was nothing on "long-term care ombudsmen" in ERIC, there would be nothing in Medline. As Kemp and Brustman (1997) have noted, that while there is duplication, say, between SOCIOFILE and AgeLine, databases will vary in terms of the number of relevant matches—some producing stronger results than others. If you don't find a sufficient number of resources in one database, consult another. Another useful strategy is to search using different terms—"nursing home ombudsmen" instead of "long-term care ombudsmen," and even "ombud" might be useful.

The world of electronic databases is changing very rapidly, which is good news for you. It is becoming quicker, cheaper, and easier to search for literature by computer than ever before. Some databases allow you to order an article to be sent to you by fax or electronic mail. Computerized databases abound and there are many more than I have attempted to list. Lexis-Nexis, for example, could be useful if you are interested in a topic usually associated with the criminal justice system (for example, home incarceration or juvenile delinquency). And your reference librarian may know of other specialized databases on such topics as AIDS, child abuse, or gerontology.

If your library does not have one or more of the databases listed above, get on the Internet and search. If you've never done this, I think you'll be amazed at the number of useful scholarly and professional resources that can be found. Most branches of government have their own web pages and allow you to access information on specialized topics. Although there is a risk that some of these addresses could have changed by the time you read this, take the time to browse a few sites if you have never spent much time on the Internet:

- Library of Congress lcweb.loc.gov/z3950/gateway.html
- U.S. Census www.census.gov
- Tiger Map Service tiger.census.gov
- National Clearinghouse for Alcohol and Drug Information www.nida.nih.gov
- National Criminal Justice Reference Service www.ncjrs.org
- Government statistics on the Web www.fedstats.gov

If you have never searched by computer for professional literature, don't be intimidated. Sometimes just a few quick tips from the reference librarian are all that you need. Most of the databases operate from menus and are simple enough that even beginners can use them. Once you learn your way around, there are just two problems you are likely to encounter: (1) not finding any (or not enough) literature on your topic; and (2) finding too much.

Here are a few tips if you find barely any literature:

- Substitute synonyms (for example, try adolescent instead of teenager).
- Think categorically (for example, "parenting styles," "disciplinary techniques").
- Go further than the most recent three years (for example, five or seven years).
- Check your spelling (for example, bulimia not bulemia).
- Use fewer words ("parenting" rather than "parental disciplinary styles").
- Look in a different database.
- Try variations of the key words ("juvenile delinquent" and "juvenile delinquency").

If your search comes back with thousands of "hits," then your topic is much too broad. Here are your options:

- Add key words (for example, "suspensions high school" not "suspensions").
- Skim the most current titles to determine if there are other keywords that may eliminate some of the citations that do not interest you.
- Limit the search by language, year, or type of publication (for example, books, journals, monographs, and so on).
- Skim the titles and/or abstracts for those articles that are themselves reviews of the literature on your topic.

If you can find a recent article that has already surveyed the literature on your topic, it will save you a great deal of time. While you may still want to read the studies cited in that paper, your time will be used more effectively if you can locate a review article than if you have to review all of the literature yourself. For instance, Moote and Wodarski (1997) have authored "The Acquisition of Life Skills Through Adventure-Based Activities and Programs: A Review of the Literature." Nancy Sidell (1997) has written "Adult Adjustment to Chronic Illness: A Review of the Literature." Maria Aranda and Bob Knight (1997) have summarized studies that examined ethnic minority caregivers in their article "The Influence of Ethnicity and Culture on the Caregiver Stress and Coping Process: A Sociocultural Review and Analysis."

Even if you don't discover titles or abstracts clearly suggesting a review of the literature on your topic, most articles in professional journals will contain some survey of the literature. Whether the article contains an extensive or more restricted list of references will depend somewhat upon the journal and the nature of the article. It is likely, however, that the literature review stopped two years or more before the article was published. (It may take an article three to ten months to be examined by a journal's reviewers, and even if no revisions are required of the author, many journals have a backlog of a year or longer before a manuscript is published.) So, even if you find a rather complete review of the literature in an article published in 1998, the author's references may not include any sources published later than 1996. Odds are, however, that you won't be so lucky as to find one article that does all your library work for you. A good social worker-researcher would want to stay current and do some searching.

While some information databases may contain book titles, do not be surprised if all of the references produced from a computer search are found in journals (many of which you may not have known existed). New knowledge in a field is often first introduced or reported in that field's journals. Unlike magazines that are written largely for public entertainment, journals report studies and new thinking about old problems for students, professionals, and scholars. Journals usually lack vivid graphics and multicolor advertisements.

An information database like *Infotrac* may mix some professional journal articles with magazines like *Newsweek* and *Time*. While these magazines are useful for providing current statistics about social problems and experts' opinions, they are not considered professional literature. Many instructors will not count magazine or newspaper articles when students are given the assignment of preparing a bibliography on a special topic.

A number of social work journals are listed on the next page to help you become familiar with some of the important journals in our profession. This is by no means a comprehensive listing. There are many more journals than could conveniently be listed here, and the number of new journals has increased in recent years. Also, there are many specialized journals (for example, *Crime and Delinquency, Gerontologist, Evaluation Review*) that are not listed but may be of interest to some students.

Such journals as these and other specialized journals allow for in-depth reporting and discussion of a topic because they are written for a specific audience. Typically, a journal article starts with a literature review or a historical overview of the problem and then explains the current study. At the end, the findings are discussed in terms of implications for professionals. An article may also identify areas where future research should be directed. Contrast this with the coverage of a report in a newspaper article or a magazine; often these accounts do not explain the investigator's approach (the methodology), the sample size, and how the data were analyzed, or address implications of the findings. You should get all of this information in a journal article. At the end, you should be able to make a conclusion about the worth of a study.

As you become more familiar with the literature relevant to your research problem, you will be able to refine your question and might even decide to modify it. You may delight to discover that researchers have suggested that the study you are planning is desperately needed. Even if it is not so directly stated, you may find gaps in our knowledge about the problem that interests

---

Selected Social Work Journals

Administration in Social Work
Affilia: Journal of Women and
    Social Work
Arete
Child and Adolescent Social
    Work Journal
Child Welfare
Clinical Social Work Journal
Families in Society
Health and Social Work
International Social Work
Journal of Applied Social
    Sciences
Journal of Gerontological Social
    Work
Journal of Multicultural Social
    Work
Journal of Social Service
    Research
Journal of Social Welfare

Journal of Social Work and
    Human Sexuality
Journal of Social Work Education
Journal of Sociology and Social
    Welfare
Journal of Teaching in Social
    Work
Public Welfare
Research on Social Work Practice
School Social Work Journal
Smith College Studies in Social
    Work
Social Service Review
Social Work
Social Work Abstracts
Social Work in Education
Social Work with Groups
Social Work in Health Care
Social Work Research

---

you. These are fertile areas where you as a social worker can make an important contribution with your research.

The necessity for immersing yourself in the literature cannot be emphasized strongly enough. Research builds upon the accumulated efforts of all those laboring to expand our knowledge and correct our misconceptions. But to make a contribution in the social sciences, we first must be familiar with what is known about the problem. When you read the literature on a topic as a social work researcher, you are reading for a purpose. You are trying to discover:

- What do the majority of the studies conclude?
- What theories have attempted to explain the phenomenon?
- What interventions have been tried?
- What instruments have been used to assess the problem?
- What are the gaps in our knowledge about the problem?
- What additional research needs have been identified?

Step 3: Developing a Research Design

A research design is something like a blueprint. It outlines the approach to be used to collect the data. It describes the conditions under which the data will be collected; how the subjects or respondents will be selected; what instrument will be used; and generally provides information about the who, what, when, where, and how of the research project.

The research design should be carefully thought out to ensure that the information you obtain will be the information you need to support or reject your hypothesis. In developing a research design, ask yourself, "What do I need to know?" and then "How will I go about getting it?" The answers to these two questions will guide the development of a research design.

For now, research designs can be classified as fitting one of three broad categories:

1. Exploratory designs
2. Descriptive designs
3. Explanatory designs

Exploratory research designs are used with topics about which very little information is available. For example, the first studies on the psychosocial impact of AIDS on the lives of gay men were important even if they involved only a relatively small number of respondents. Because these exploratory studies are responsive to new concerns or to areas that have not been subjected to research, they tend to be more tentative and small-scale (small samples). Their findings are not general conclusive or definitive, and, as a consumer of the information resulting from an exploratory design, you may get ideas for further areas of inquiry. This is, in fact, the main value of exploratory studies—to generate research questions and hypotheses for additional investigation.

The idea for some exploratory research might start when you discover something about a client—say, one of your homeless street teens reports a history of childhood sexual abuse. From there you might gather data from a few more similar clients to see if they fit the same pattern. If they also affirm childhood abuse, you might then want to expand your inquiry and conduct a descriptive study to provide a profile of these clients that allows you to generalize your findings.

Descriptive studies are larger-scale efforts that attempt to characterize a population group (for example, the homeless) in a definitive way. Because the studies want to provide precise information, for instance, on what proportion of the homeless are single women, women with children, Vietnam vets, persons of color, and so on, they will be noted for the large numbers of people they survey. They report data largely in terms of percentages and proportions and will be concerned with questions like "How many clients ..." This descriptive purpose may result from an agency's need to understand its client population better, to

---

Example of an Exploratory Study

Because no prior study had investigated the extent of homelessness among those who gather aluminum cans to sell, fifty individuals were interviewed.

- Eighteen percent were homeless.
- Twenty-four percent had been hospitalized for emotional or mental health problems.
- Thirty-six percent said can collecting supplemented Social Security or some form of a disability or pension payment.
- Fifty-two percent had never held a job that provided hospitalization insurance.
- Sixty-four percent reported drinking "some" or "a lot" during the past month.
- Seventy-six percent said they couldn't find another job or that they were disabled or too old for other employment (the average age was fifty-one with a range that went from nineteen to seventy-seven).
- The average amount of money made on a "good day" was $4.00.
- Forty-four percent were judged to be impaired from alcoholism, mental retardation, or psychotism.

Source: Royse, D. (1987), Homelessness among trash pickers, *Psychological Reports,* 60, 808–810.

---

compare its caseload today with the "typical client" from five years ago, or to make comparisons with client groups in other agencies or other parts of the country. Typically, these studies are quite concerned with the issue of representativeness and go to great lengths to insure that they have adequate samples.

Explanatory studies are experiments in which hypotheses are tested and control or comparison groups are often used. In social work research, an explanatory study might seek to understand the differential effects of an intervention. Did it, for example, work as well on younger clients as on older ones? Were there differences by gender or race? Was the new intervention more effective than the more traditional one?

Often the studies we want to conduct as social workers are exploratory. We may read about or attend a workshop on some new treatment approach and want to implement it. However, because we're not entirely sure that it will work with our clients, we realize the importance of initially involving only a small group of clients—and then if it is effective, expanding the number of clients who would receive it. On other occasions, it makes sense to conduct a small-scale exploratory study because if our hunch is correct, then a foundation or other funding source might provide the resources to launch a more thorough descriptive or explanatory study.

Sometimes it is difficult to know how many subjects are required by a particular type of research design. Although this is an issue we will be discussing in more depth later (particularly in chapter 6), for now the best advice is to plan your study to be roughly comparable to similar studies being reported in the journals you have been reading. Having a small number of subjects is not likely to jeopardize the potential of your manuscript being published if your project is exploring a topic never previously investigated. If, however, you are planning a more elaborate study in an area where there has already been a good deal of research, then sample size is much more crucial.

Group research designs are discussed in chapter 4. In that chapter, you'll learn that designs employing random assignment of subjects and control groups can produce information in which we can place a great deal of confidence. You'll also learn about situations that rob us of the ability to determine if it was our intervention (or some other factor) that made a difference in the lives of our clients. Research designs are obviously important and design considerations will be discussed in practically every chapter. Your choice of a research design will be largely determined by the problem you are studying, the type and amount of data available to you, and how you choose to examine the data.

Step 4: Operationalizing

In everyday conversation we easily accept concepts that are somewhat vague because we think we understand what they mean. For instance, in most conversations we all understand the terms "heavy," "frequent," and "problem drinker" to mean the same thing. However, researchers must be precise about the concepts employed in their studies; this is called developing **operational definitions.** The way one researcher defines problem drinking for the purposes of a study may be quite different from the way another investigator defines the concept.

One study might define problem drinker as a person who drank to the point of intoxication six times or more in the past year, another may identify problem drinkers in terms of the presence of two or more negative consequences (for example, arrests for drunken driving, liver damage, loss of relationships, trouble at work or school). A third study could focus on the number of times an individual drinks per week (for example, three or four times) or on the symptoms normally associated with alcoholism (alcohol-induced memory lapses, drinking before noon). Still another study may ask significant others to rate their loved ones' drinking on a continuum with numerical values representing low and high levels of the behavior. It should be apparent to you that how you define your variables (such as "problem drinker") has considerable impact on who is included or excluded from participation in the study.

As a researcher you have the freedom to use the operational definitions employed by other researchers or you may want to revise and improve upon them. If you want to compare your results to those findings produced by another researcher, then you will want to use the same methodology, operational definitions, and data-gathering instruments. When you do, you are **replicating** (reproducing) that study for the purpose of comparison with your local clients or population.

Before you can begin to collect data, you must operationally define your variables so precisely that no one would have any problem understanding exactly what was being measured or observed. To take an example, if you are working to reduce the incidence of child abuse in a community, you must define what constitutes child abuse. There are several ways to go about this, but it might make sense to count the number of new reports of child abuse investigated by the local child protective service. We know, however, that the number of child abuse investigations only reflects the tip of the iceberg—that most acts of abuse are never reported. But other methods, such as surveying families and asking the respondent if there were fewer acts of abuse in his or her family than the year before, are problematic, too. (Those who claimed to be abusing their children less than the year before would be admitting that they were abusive in a prior year.) Even if you settle on counting the official reports of abuse processed by the child protective service in a given year or two, you still would need to define for the readers of your report whether you are counting the total number of abuse incidents or the number of *substantiated* cases of abuse. Operationally defining your variables well requires you to have a good knowledge of your subject.

The way we operationalize our variables has a direct bearing on what our research can potentially reveal and the use we can make of the data. Imagine you have designed a new intervention for persons with a gambling addiction. It would be easy to claim success if your clients had absolutely no relapses over a twenty-year period. Unfortunately, most social workers cannot wait that long to conclude that an intervention was effective. We need results much sooner than that. What if we were to use a fourteen- or thirty-day follow-up period? It is entirely possible there would be no relapses if our observation period is narrow enough. Suppose we define successful intervention as meaning no relapses within six months? Within a year? During the thirty-six months following intervention? We would very likely discover that the longer time frame we observe for relapses, the more that will be discovered. In other words, it would be possible to conclude that the intervention was a total success when it was not—if we observe for too brief a period. What is a reasonable period of time? This is where your knowledge of the subject and of the literature comes in.

Constructing operational definitions requires us to think conceptually about what we want to measure. Homelessness is a topic that often needs to be defined better. Anybody can be locked out of a house and have to sleep in a car for a night. That's not homelessness as we usually think about it. What about the sixteen-year old adolescent whose stepmother throws her out and who has to live with friends for five or six days? Are you homeless even if you have a roof over your head but have no running water or electricity?

Social workers deal with a lot of intangible concepts. We might talk about Susan's self-esteem, and we all tend to know what that means. Similarly, we may have a client who is depressed, one who has school phobia, and still another who is passive-aggressive. We have to deal with differences in intelligence and motivation, power, social status, and pathology. These abstract concepts must become operationalized if we are to employ them as variables in a research project.

Independent variables such as age, gender, race, marital status, political affiliation, and religion tend to be easier for us to operationalize than dependent variables. **Independent variables** are variables that are suspected to influence, affect, or cause the event or situation that you are studying. For example, prior hospitalizations for mental illness or alcoholism might be important independent variables to use to help explain or predict the problem of homelessness. Also, you might want to include such independent (or socio-demographic) variables as age, education, and job skills.

In experimental settings, independent variables are those that the researcher can manipulate or control. For example, in studying the effect of positive reinforcement upon the retention of research terminology, the researcher might decide to examine the usefulness of candy as a reinforcement for each new vocabulary term learned. The amount, type, and timing of the receipt of the candy are controlled by the researcher and could be considered independent variables. The number of vocabulary items retained would be the dependent variable.

Dependent variables in one study may be used as independent variables in another study. For instance, you could start off your research career by studying the level of self-esteem in ninth grade boys. In a subsequent study, you may wish to use those self-esteem scores to predict juvenile delinquency (which is now the dependent variable).

Operationalizing Involves Measurement

One of the keys to understanding social science research is the notion that if a thing can be defined, then it can be measured. If we can precisely define concepts such as depression and anxiety, for example, then we can measure how much less a client is depressed or anxious after intervention. Since problems brought to social workers are often vague and ambiguous, it is helpful to collect data in order to determine how much clients improve. Just how anxious is the client? How severe is the depression? Social workers design or use instruments to measure the extent of such problems. These instruments provide quantifiable (numerical) values for problems like depression so that we can discuss relative levels of depression and talk more precisely about those who are very depressed and those who are somewhat less depressed. Simply stated, **measurement** is the process of quantifying states, traits, attitudes, behaviors, and theoretical concepts.

The importance of measurement is revealed in two axioms of treatment formulated by social worker Walt Hudson (1978): The first states: "If you cannot measure the client's problem, it does not exist." The second, a corollary of the first, states: "If you cannot measure the client's problem, you cannot treat it" (p. 65). Clinicians and researchers alike must be able to precisely assess (measure) clients' problems. Without precise measurement, it may be impossible to show that clients have improved as a result of intervention. Researchers often attempt to obtain this precision by using scales and instruments when they operationalize their variables.

A **scale** is a cluster or group of statements or questions (items) that are designed to measure a single concept. Social scientists constantly work on and develop new scales to measure more accurately concepts of interest to them. It is not unusual for scales to be revised over time. Also, you will find that investigators may approach a concept in different ways, so scales measuring the same general concept may vary in length, in the type of item used, and in the response categories available to the subject. For example, it is possible to find a ten-item self-esteem inventory, a twenty-five-item one, and others several times that length.

Scales can be developed to measure many different kinds of problems or concepts. Social workers Joel Fischer and Kevin Corcoran (1994) have collected 320 brief scales, which they refer to as "rapid assessment instruments," for social workers to use with problems commonly encountered in clinical practice. Complete scales as well as information on the scales' availability, primary reference, scoring, and other essential information are found in their reference book, which contains many interesting and useful scales to use for research projects and for evaluating one's practice. For illustrative purposes, several examples of scales can be found in chapter 5 and in the appendices.

It is likely that sometime in your life you have been asked to complete a questionnaire that used a Likert scale (sometimes referred to as a five-point scale). In this usage of the term, the scale is the standard set of response choices typically:

5   Strongly Agree
4   Agree
3   Undecided
2   Disagree
1   Strongly Disagree

There is nothing sacred about these particular categories. For instances, you may encounter a scale where clients self-reporting on how much various symptoms bother them might use:

0 Not at all
1 Slightly
2 Somewhat
3 Very much
4 Extremely

What characterizes a Likert scale is that the categories are recognizable and hierarchical. By employing the same descriptors each time and assigning them numerical values, responses to multiple items can be summed to create a single overall score. Likert scales are not limited to only five response choices and can contain an odd or even number of categories.

When you as a researcher begin to look at scales that have been constructed to measure abstract concepts like marital satisfaction and emotional abuse, you will discover that there is an enormous variation in how well they measure the concept they were designed to assess. We'll discuss this topic further in chapter 5; however, for now you need to know that you always have the option to operationalize a concept in terms of a single-item scale. This involves naming the concept and then anchoring it at a minimum of two (three is better) points. Look at the examples in figure 2.1.

Even children can respond to single-item scales. A colleague once told me that whenever her children wanted to say home from school she asked, "On a scale from one to ten, how sick are you?" She said they soon learned that saying eight, nine, or ten would probably mean a visit to the doctor. A six or seven would probably result in their getting their temperature taken, and maybe a Tylenol or two. If they said "four" or "five," then Mom might give them some special attention or ask what was going on at school (for example, maybe the child had a special report due and was experiencing some butterflies).

Many social workers first realize that they have to operationalize certain concepts when they begin to develop a questionnaire for use within their agencies. Some early advice for when you have to operationalize such common variables as age, education, and income—try to think ahead to the use you will be making of the data. Will you need to report average age, average income? If you use categories instead of asking for actual age or income, then you are precluded from getting averages. So, if you would like to know that the average client was 26.4 years old and earned $7,585 per year, then don't set up response categories like the following example:

What is your present age?

_____ Adolescent (18 and under)
_____ Young Adult (19 to 30)
_____ Adult (31 to 44)
_____ Middle-aged Adult (45 to 65)

Figure 2.1 Examples of Single-Item Scales

Emotional Abuse

Rate show much you have felt "put down" by your partner in the last week:

| *None* | | | | *Some* | | | | *Quite a bit* | |
| 1 | 2 | 3 | 4 | 5 | 6 | 7 | 8 | 9 | 10 |

Fear of Injury

Rate the extent to which you fear injury from your partner:

| *No Fear* | | | | *Moderate* | | | | *Extremely Fearful* | |
| 1 | 2 | 3 | 4 | 5 | 6 | 7 | 8 | 9 | 10 |

Any operationalization or measurement of a concept should meet the test of clarity. It would do little good to create an age category, for instance, of "pre-middle age," or "old old" if there was confusion as to what ages went into these groupings. A concept has not been operationally well-defined (for example, emotional exhaustion) if you don't know or can't tell who is and who isn't emotionally exhausted.

Often, behaviors are very indicative of the concepts we want to measure. For instance, a racist might attend white supremacist meetings or tell ethnic jokes, a sexist might use "girls" in speech when referring to women. Some students find it helpful to think of operationalizing concepts in terms of behaviors that you could detect from watching a videotape. A "good" student might be one who studies at his or her desk at least four hours a day; an emotionally neglectful mother might be one who never touches, hugs, or kisses a young child.

You don't have to have a scale to operationally define a concept: it's just that scales tend to allow for more possibilities so that gradations (think of a continuum running from low to high) of the concept can be measured. Does it make sense to try to distinguish persons who are a little sexist from those who are profoundly sexist in their thinking?

Step 5: Collecting Data

This step is sometimes referred to as "implementation of the study." Depending upon your research design, you interview people, mail out questionnaires, or begin to procure data that have already been published (such as suicide rates, marriages, divorces, or births by county and year).

This phase of the research process is obviously important. Without data you will have nothing to analyze or report. If your choice of methodology was well-considered, it will not allow for an extreme amount of bias to influence your findings.

Researchers strive to eliminate **bias** from their studies. Bias is an outside event that tends to produce some distortion from what is actually occurring or present, causing us to make erroneous conclusions about reality. For instance, clients who fear that they might lose their services or their therapists might not be completely honest and instead tell the researcher what they think she or he wants to hear. This results in inaccuracy. Bias can be conscious or unconscious, glaring or subtle, and may creep in and affect the research process at various points. For instance, in developing a questionnaire you might inadvertently use all masculine pronouns and offend female readers. Offended respondents, if they are angry, may not respond to the questionnaire as you had intended. Complex instructions (which might be confusing to persons with less than a high school education) can also result in biased data. While we all have values and biases of our own, researchers should strive to keep their studies as free from bias as possible. A biased questionnaire can give information that does not produce a true picture or representation of the attitudes or behaviors you are investigating.

Bias can also result from the way we select interviewees or respondents. This commonly happens when not enough thought has been given to the sampling design. For example, suppose you are interested in getting social work majors to evaluate their undergraduate program. You decide, because it is convenient for you, to go to a nearby men's dormitory and interview all of the social work majors you can find. Obviously, if you base your study on just the interviews from that one dorm, you will have ignored all female social work majors. Your study, then, will be very biased, as female social work students may have different experiences and evaluations of the social work program.

The way, the time of day, and the place you collect your data can have major effects upon the outcome of your study. Suppose you go to a neighborhood supermarket to conduct a survey on attitudes about abortion. You choose to do your interviewing on Mondays, Wednesdays, and Fridays for two weeks during the hours between 9:00 A.M. and 4:00 P.M. However, a friend tells you that a better day to go is Saturday because everyone is more talkative. When should you collect your data?

Had you chosen to interview solely on Mondays, Wednesdays, and Fridays until 4:00 P.M., you may discover that your study underrepresented those persons who generally are at work during those hours. By interviewing persons who buy their groceries only on Saturday, you may collect a group of respondents who are employed Monday through Friday. The older, retired, or unemployed persons could be underrepresented. One approach would give respondents who would likely be older and possibly more conservative, while the other could result in younger, potentially more liberal respondents. If you choose to do your interviewing on Sunday mornings between 10:00 A.M. and 12:00 noon, what segment of the population would be underrepresented?

Some research questions or populations of interest determine how the data will be collected. Because homeless persons do not have telephones and may not have an address to which mail could be sent, it would be ludicrous to attempt a mail or telephone data collection procedure with this population.

Pragmatic considerations such as the amount of time available to conduct the study, the amount of money that can be spent, the availability of subjects, and the ease of locating them all have a direct bearing on the way researchers go about collecting their data and the research design chosen.

Bias is generally minimized as survey samples approach **representativeness**—that is, as samples more closely resemble the larger population being studied. Typically, we draw respondents randomly (where everyone has a chance of being selected) in order to create representative samples. There can be many sources of bias, but in the conduct of research, objectivity is the proper and necessary stance. You want your data to be as free from bias as possible.

Studies that are free from bias generally have much greater generalizability than those with overt bias. **Generalizability** means how well the findings from a specific study fit another situation. Let's say that I think that my spaghetti sauce is the greatest in the world. I invite my aunt Bessie over to try it. She agrees that it is the best she has ever tasted. My wife also agrees. Even the kids like it. I then decide that I am ready to sell it across the country. Is it reasonable to assume from a small sample of family members that enough of the American public would buy my spaghetti sauce to justify spending all my savings to market it? In this instance I would have been guilty of **overgeneralization**. In other words, I assumed too much. I went beyond what my data would support.

Suppose that you are interested in predicting an upcoming presidential election. You ask all the social work majors in your college or university how they will vote. In this instance, a much larger sample is involved, but will your findings indicate which candidate will win the national election? The answer is: probably not. Why? Because social work majors do not adequately represent a cross-sampling of American voters. For one thing, social work majors probably tend to be more liberal and younger than the average voter. Social work majors at any one school may or may not represent the opinions of other students attending the same school. Similarly, you probably could not predict a national election based upon interviews of all the residents of several retirement centers located in South Carolina. However, depending upon the size of your sample and how the retirement centers were selected, you might be able to discover the candidate most preferred by older adults living in retirement centers in South Carolina.

As a rule, you can generalize only to the specific universe of people from whom you selected your subjects. If you draw an unbiased national sample, then you can speak to the attitudes or preferences of the nation. If you draw an unbiased sample from all the adults in a given state, then you can speak about the knowledge or attitudes of adults residing in that particular state. An unbiased sample from a large city will allow you to speak only about the citizens of that city. It would not be responsible, for instance, if you had data from a sample of adults living in Las Vegas, Nevada, concerning their attitudes toward prostitution to assume that the data were representative of attitudes in other American cities.

Studies that are relatively free of bias are the wheels that allow science to move forward. By allowing us to generalize our findings to similar populations, they improve our knowledge and guide our practice. And while the ideal is to have a bias-free study representative of the population being studied from which we can generalize to similar populations, in reality our data collection methods are often compromised.

I once attended a conference that brought together researchers and chronically mentally ill who had been studied for four years as part of a special project that provided them with peer counseling and other new interventions in addition to what they normally received. The principal investigator, armed with charts and transparencies, began explaining that the battery of eight different psychological tests administered before and after the project began showed no significant changes. He was a little perplexed by this, but took the tack of justifying the findings by saying that at least the chronically mentally ill in the study weren't any worse off. There were a couple of snickers from the audience, and after a few minutes, one of the consumers revealed a possible reason why the psychological tests hadn't found any changes. He said that some in his group had been afraid that if they answered honestly they could ultimately lose their disability checks!

So while the investigators had gone to great lengths to protect their study from known sources of bias by using such procedures as random assignment of consumers to the different intervention groups and sensitive instruments, some of the subjects, acting in their own self-interest, appeared to have biased the findings. I suspect the researchers had not prepared for this turn of events. Who would have? The researchers knew that the information they were collecting from individuals in the study would not be shared with any governmental agencies. They may even have explained this to their subjects. However, to individuals who had much less education and were not informed about what researchers actually do with their data, integrity of the research was less important than preserving the few resources available to them.

Keep this story in mind as you plan your research projects. At each stage of the research process, consider how bias might creep into your study and what you could do to minimize it. If you anticipate problems, you may wish to strengthen your design or change the way you collect your data or operationalize your dependent variable.

Step 6: Analyzing and Interpreting the Data

Once you have finished collecting the data, you are ready to analyze it. One of the purposes of analysis is to express the data in a way that is "mentally digestible." It may be easy to present detailed responses from three or four individuals, but when you have more than five responses, full descriptions become very cumbersome. Further, it is awkward, if not impossible, to display information from a large number of persons (for example, fifty or more) without summarizing the data in some fashion.

Why summarize the data? Which of the following statements do you find easier to understand?

1. The ages of respondents in Group A were: 12, 14, 15, 12, 13, 14, 12, 13, and 14.
2. The average age of respondents in Group A was 13 years.

Basically, we summarize in order to comprehend the information that we have gathered. Your hypothesis may suggest ways that you can summarize, categorize, or organize your data. For instance, if your hypothesis is that women voters are more supportive than men of tax levies that directly benefit persons with low income, your data naturally suggest two divisions: male and female voters. In your analysis, you will compare and contrast the voting behavior of males and females on specific social service election issues.

Analysis is a logical process that begins with looking at the raw data. For example, you will first want to determine how many persons of each sex, race, or age grouping completed your questionnaires. More than likely, you will then order or arrange your data in some fashion. If you looked at several elections in different years, you might array the data by year of the election. You may begin to notice a trend, for example, of women being more supportive of social service issues or you may identify patterns or directions that have not been suggested in the literature. Sometimes the data are hard to interpret, and the findings are not intuitively obvious.

Interpreting the data is made easier by comparing your findings with those of other studies. Perhaps your respondents are more conservative or less knowledgeable than those in a study that you found during the literature search. Often it is helpful to brainstorm with others as to what could account for the findings that you obtained.

Occasionally, research findings portrayed as pie or bar charts (figure 2.2) or even maps shaded to indicate high or low densities of one variable or another are useful for helping others understand the results of your study. However, statistical methods may also be needed to determine if there is a significant difference between two or more groups. Statistics aid in the interpretation of data. With the advent of computer technology, the computation of statistical tests has become relatively easy.

Chapter 9 presents most of the statistics that you'll need to know to begin to analyze your data. That chapter will present a quick overview of descriptive (for example, measures of central tendency like mean and median) and inferential statistics (for example, t-tests and one-way analysis of variance). Descriptive statistics help us understand how much our variables vary (like

Figure 2.2 Example of a Pie Chart

Sample by Age

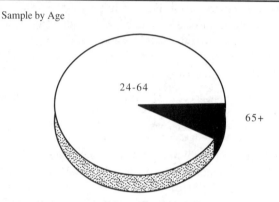

the range of years between the oldest and youngest participant). Inferential statistics are used to test hypotheses about differences between groups and to aid us in understanding the probabilities of obtaining our results by chance.

There is one statistic, however, that we need to become familiar with prior to chapter 9. A **correlation coefficient** (sometimes expressed as *r*) is a statistic that helps us understand relationships between two variables. This relationship is summarized as a numerical value that ranges between –1.00 and +1.00. For example, test grades in this research course may have a strong positive relationship (+.80) with the amount of time students spend studying. With this correlation coefficient, we would predict that as students' studying time increased, their test grades would improve. If a negative correlation (for example, –.40) had been obtained, this would indicate the ludicrous situation where test grades deteriorate the more students study.

Just because two variables are correlated, this does not mean that one variable caused the other. Not long ago I read about a study that found that nearsightedness was correlated with high intelligence. This study found that persons who do well on intelligence tests tend to be nearsighted. This does not mean, however, that all nearsighted persons are intelligent or that one could improve one's I.Q. by becoming nearsighted.

Step 7: Writing the Report

Once the data have been collected and analyzed, the final step is preparing your findings in such a way that they can be made available to others. There may be times when a memorandum to your supervisor or director summarizing the results of your study will be adequate. If you received funding for the research, it is very likely that you will be required to write a report of your findings. If what you found was especially interesting, you may want to submit your findings to a professional journal. Journals, even those in different fields, tend to be organized in the same format as research reports.

The first part of a research report, the Introduction, puts the research question or hypothesis in context (a description of the extent or severity of the problem, the length of time it has been a problem, what is generally known or believed about the problem) and reviews the important studies found in the literature.

The next section, Methods, is an explanation of the research methodology—how the data were collected, which variables were included and how they were operationalized, and who the subjects were, their characteristics, and how they were recruited. Enough information should be presented so that others can follow what you did and replicate the study.

The third section of the research report presents what was actually learned from the study. Tables and graphs may be employed to visually demonstrate differences and to help with comparisons. Statistical tests may be used.

Finally, the Discussion section addresses the implications of your findings, speculates why those particular results were obtained, and suggests how future research in this area might be conducted.

It almost goes without saying that many fine research reports are filed away or relegated to dusty shelves because the social work investigators did not exert a little extra effort and prepare the report for publication in a journal or as a paper for a professional symposium. In order to rectify this situation, the last chapter of this text will focus on writing the research report.

Social Work Research and Practice

While it is often convenient to think of social work practice and research as completely separate and distinct, they both share a logical problem-solving process. They both, for instance, start with a focus on a problem, proceed through some review of its extent and history, development of a plan, its implementation, and an evaluation of the process. See for yourself the similarities between the research process and the task-centered or problem-solving process used by social workers shown in figure 2.3.

Even the step that might seem the strangest to you, operationally defining variables, is part and parcel of what social workers must do in everyday practice. A man who could have benefited from counseling once told some friends that his wife didn't respect him. What does that mean? Unless he gives us some additional information, we are clueless as to what exactly upsets him. A skilled social worker would possibly ask such questions as, "When do you feel that you are not respected? What is your wife doing or saying?" In gathering more details, the social worker finds out how the client has defined (operationalized) the term "respect."

Figure 2.3 Comparison of the Research Process and the Task-Centered Process

Research Process	Task-Centered Process
Starts with a problem, question, or hypothesis	Starts with a client's problem
Review of the literature	History-taking, identification of resources, strengths, networks
Development of research and operationalization of variables	Negotiate a contract design
Data collection	Begin intervention
Data analysis	Evaluation of intervention
Final report	Termination/summary report

If you look for areas of overlap between research and practice, you surely will find them as they use the same general approach. The research process is no more complicated than the problem-solving model you will use as a social worker. It is not an artificial contrivance designed to make life difficult, but an orderly and logical process that should be almost second nature to you.

Self-Review

(Answers at the end of the book)

1. List the seven steps in the research process.
2. T or F. The following is a null hypothesis: Math majors do not have higher grade point averages than chemistry majors.
3. In the following hypothesis, what is the dependent variable? Men arrested for assault and battery are more impulsive than men arrested for public intoxication.
4. What is the major characteristic of descriptive studies?
5. Operationally define "good student."
6. In a study of men arrested for assault and battery, what would be some logical independent variables that would describe this group?
7. A scale is designed to measure a single _____.
8. T or F. A true/false response set on a questionnaire is not an example of a Likert scale.
9. Researchers strive to eliminate what from their studies?
   a. theories   c. bias
   b. dependent variables   d. representativeness

10. T or F.   Betsy interviewed ten students from her research methods class about the president's job performance. As a result of this study she thinks she can speak to what most Americans think about the topic. This is a case of overgeneralizing.

11. Betsy found a correlation of .35 between her research subjects' ages and their monthly income. In her own words, she says that younger subjects tend to have less money and older subjects tend to have more. Is this a correct interpretation of the correlation coefficient?

Questions for Class Discussion

1. Practice developing hypotheses and research questions on the following list of topics:

   a. alcoholism
   b. effective psychotherapy
   c. fear of open spaces
   d. depression
   e. social drinkers
   f. racist attitudes
   g. heavy cigarette smokers

2. Take a hypothesis or research question from question 1 and convert it into a null hypothesis.

3. Identify as many theories used by social work practitioners as you can.

4. Identify the dependent variables in the following studies:

   a. Relapse in Alcoholism: New Perspectives
   b. Repeat Pregnancies among Unmarried Teen Parents
   c. Increasing Child Support Payments with Two New Interventions
   d. Do All-Nighters Pay Off? An Examination of Test Scores and Cram-studying Techniques in First-Year College Students
   e. Weight Gain in a Sample of Anorexics Receiving Cognitive Therapy

5. Operationally define a "bad marriage" so that a clinical social worker could locate couples who might benefit from a new twelve-week intervention designed to help those with troubled marriages.

6. Operationally define each of the following:

   a. A humorous television program.
   b. An educational television program.
   c. An offensive television program.

7. Examine "Attitudes about Research Courses" in appendix B and discuss how many different scales it contains.

8. Make up examples of how bias could affect a study.

9. Look around the classroom. In how many different ways do your classmates vary? Make a list of as many different independent variables as may be represented by the diversity of characteristics found among your classmates.

Mini-Projects for Experiencing Research Firsthand

1. Select a social problem and state it clearly.
   a. Frame either a research question or a hypothesis suggested by what you know or would like to know about the social problem.
   b. What is the dependent variable?
   c. What data would you need to collect in order to test your hypothesis? Who would be your subjects?
   d. What independent variables would help you analyze and understand your findings? List them.
   e. Operationally define your dependent variable.
2. Select a social problem and locate ten relevant abstracts using one of the computerized databases discussed in this chapter.
3. Refer to Fischer and Corcoran's (1994) *Measures for Clinical Practice,* and find a scale that you could use in some future research. As you look at the instrument you have chosen, make a list of the questions that occur to you when you think about employing such an instrument for research or evaluation purposes. Write a brief description of the population that will be the subjects of your study. What hypothesis will you test? What will the instrument tell you?
4. Sue Fictitious is a manager of an intake unit in a state agency responsible for investigating complaints of child abuse and neglect. She also is a part-time MSW student. One day, while in the library, she came across an article in a professional journal describing the Child Abuse Potential Inventory. She began to think of applications—ways in which her office might use the instrument to identify adults who are potential abusers.
   a. What hypotheses would interest you if you were Sue?
   b. Who would be your subjects?
   c. What personal or independent variables would you like to include?
5. Browse through research articles in a professional journal until you find one where the operational definition for the dependent variable is clearly stated. In an accompanying brief paragraph, state the limitations and advantages of defining the dependent variable in this way.

Resources and References

Aranda, M.P. and Knight, B. (1997). The influence of ethnicity and culture on the caregiver stress and coping process: A socioculture review and analysis. *The Gerontologist,* 37, 342–354.

Bettelheim, B. (1967). *The empty fortress: Infantile autism and the birth of the self.* New York: Free Press.

Fischer, J. and Corcoran K. (1994). *Measures for clinical practice.* 2nd ed. New York: Free Press.

Hudson, W.W. (1978). Notes for practice: First axioms of treatment. *Social Work,* 23(1), 65–66.

Kemp, B.E. and Brustman, M.J. (1997). Social policy research: Comparison and analysis of CD-ROM resources. *Social Work Research,* 21, 111–119.

Leedy, P.D. (1974). *Practical research: Planning and design.* New York: Macmillan.

Moote, G.T. and Wodarski, J.S. (1997). The acquisition of life skills through adventure-based activities and programs: A Review of the literature. *Adolescence*, 32, 143–167.

Munson, C. (1983). *An introduction to clinical social work supervision.* New York: Haworth Press.

Sidell, N.L. (1997). Adult adjustment to chronic illness: A review of the literature. *Health and Social Work*, 22, 5–11.

CHAPTER 3
Single System Designs

Imagine my dilemma: The social work department of a Veterans Affairs (VA) hospital wanted me, over the course of three afternoon sessions (spaced a week apart) to refresh their knowledge of research—to remind them of everything that they needed to know. I was supposed to help them remember what they had forgotten and teach them what they had never learned, preparing them to meet the hospital's new emphasis on accountability and evaluation. Although I was flattered that they had confidence in my ability to condense possibly more than a semester's course into six hours of instruction, I had to think long and hard about where to start and what content to give them. Most of the social workers had been out of school for fifteen years or longer. What did they know? What would they be likely to retain and use after I left? Where should I start?

I started with single system designs since this tool can be used even with very little research expertise. In fact, these designs are attractive to social workers because they are so easy to use and understand, even with a limited understanding of research methodology. Single system designs provide practitioners with immediate, inexpensive, and practical feedback on whether their clients are improving.

Unlike the quantitative approaches that we will study later that involve groups of clients and assist us in understanding the "average" client, single system designs focus on an individual client and his or her situation. Single system designs are easiest to explain when the client has a specific behavior, like binge eating, that will be the focus of intervention. However, social work practitioners are not limited to applying these designs only to individual clients. Single system designs can be used to evaluate the progress being made by a community, an organization, a family, or even a couple receiving marital counseling.

Advocates of single system designs argue that information about specific clients is often obscured in studies where clients are grouped together, that one might learn little about an individual client—perhaps only whether a client did better or worse than average. Single system designs "personalize" the research by looking at a client's particular behavior over time. Before we learn how to develop single system designs (also known as N = 1 research, single case evaluation, and single subject designs) for our clients, let's first consider a little of the history about them.

The Origin of Single System Designs

The study of individual cases has long been a part of the richness of the social sciences. For more than a century, case studies have been conducted in behavioral research. Bromley (1986) has stated that, in fact, the case study method goes back even further, to "remote origins in human social history" (p. 39). Prior to the development of statistics for group comparisons, research in the social sciences consisted almost entirely of descriptive case studies and reflections upon them. Case studies were useful for illustrating to one's colleagues and students how problems requiring remedial action could be approached with specific theories or interventions.

Although these studies seldom employed any quantification of dependent variables, a number of important discoveries have come from the observations of individuals. Several examples will serve to demonstrate this. Using nonsense syllables and himself as the subject, Ebbinghaus made major discoveries regarding principles of human learning. (We learn more efficiently in the morning than in the evening, for instance.) Pavlov's basic findings were obtained from single organisms and later reproduced (replicated) with other organisms. Piaget's theories derived from observations of his own children. From Freud's discussion of specific cases to eleven-month-old little Albert becoming conditioned to fear a white rat, generalizations from single subjects have played significant roles in helping us understand human behavior.

Individual case studies have appeared with some frequency all through the social science literature, and case examples or vignettes of cases are not uncommon today in medical and law journals. However, case studies have tended to vary greatly in their format, content, and organization. As statistical tests of comparison were developed and widely accepted, case studies fell out of favor with researchers in the social sciences. The use of control groups and group statistical comparisons is now firmly established in the social sciences, and the objective or quantitative methods of measurement used with these studies have led to changes among those conducting case studies.

The emergence of single system designs in the 1960s and 1970s has been attributed to their use by B. F. Skinner and other practitioners of behavior modification. With a focus on a specific target behavior, single system designs were well-suited for practitioners interested in demonstrating that their interventions were effective. Unlike the descriptive case studies of prior years, which relied heavily upon subjective assessments of change, single system studies today use objective measures to document that change has occurred. In fact, they may be very quantitative in appearance, and do not resemble the heavily narrative case studies of previous years except for the fact that they focus on one individual.

Single system designs were developed primarily in response to dissatisfaction with group research designs for clinical practice situations and provide an alternative to the group designs usually associated with the conduct of research in the social sciences.

Single System Designs and Practice

Single system designs can be thought of as a bridge between research and practice. How is this possible? Imagine for a moment that it is sometime in the future. You have made it through the social work program and are now employed as a therapist in a mental health agency. Your next appointment is a college student in her twenties. As she explains why she has sought counseling, you begin to see a pattern of symptoms suggestive of depression. You have worked with depressed persons before and feel that you can help this woman. Go forward in time another ten weeks. The young woman is now interested in terminating treatment. How would you determine whether your counseling was successful? Would you calculate the number of times she smiled during your last several sessions? Would her body posture indicate her level of depression? Her plans for the future? While you might have an intuition that you had helped her, could you empirically document this for a supervisor or program director? How would you go about evaluating your own practice?

This example of the depressed young woman comes from Berlin's (1983) description of a practitioner involved in both research and practice with the same client. In her article, Berlin describes how a single system design was employed by the practitioner to evaluate intervention with a twenty-two-year-old part-time graduate student with overwhelming feelings of sadness and despair.

Because the client's symptoms suggested depression, the therapist asked the client to complete a short, twenty-item standardized scale (the CES-D) that measured depression. The client scored forty-five on this scale, suggesting that she was clinically depressed. Treatment goals were then developed. Berlin was able to track the client's progress by administering the CES-D each time she met with the client. When one views these test results on a graph over the several weeks of treatment, it is easy to see that the client's level of depression fell dramatically during this time and remained low one month after termination. Figure 3.1 demonstrates this visually in the graph used by Berlin.

Figure 3.1 A Graph from a Single System Study

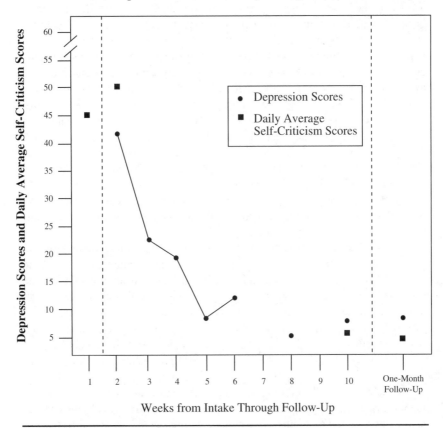

CES-D Depression Scores and Daily Average Self-Criticism Scores

Weeks from Intake Through Follow-Up

Source: Berlin, S. (1983), Single-case evaluation: Another version, *Social Work Research and Abstracts,* 19(1), 9. Copyright © National Association of Social Workers, Inc. Reprinted with permission.

Even a cursory glimpse at this graph or at the others in this chapter will convince you that single system graphs are often easy to comprehend. This is the essence of single system designs—the visual presentation of a client's progress.

A Closer Look at the Single System Design

If you look closely at figure 3.1, the several component parts needed for a single subject design can be detected. Note that a single **target behavior** (the dependent variable) was identified. In this instance, the problem was the client's depression, and the practitioner's interventions were oriented toward reducing that depression. Berlin chose an objective instrument to measure the level of depression being experienced by the client but it would also have been possible to monitor improvement with behavioral measures of depression. For instance, the client may have had crying spells, restless sleep, poor appetite, and loneliness. The selection of a target behavior, such as frequent crying spells, could have been used had there been no objective instrument available for detecting changes in the depression.

Note that no complicated statistical procedures were used—just a simple graph to record (with repeated measurements) the client's improvement over time. (Although it is possible to use statistical procedures to check for statistically significant differences in improvement, this is not a requirement or a necessity for most single system designs.) The arrangement of the data chronologically on the graph is easy to interpret and follows from the research design. Ideally, data are collected before the intervention begins. The preinterventive data are called the **baseline** and allow for comparisons to be made with the behavior during and after intervention.

Retrospective (or reconstructed) baselines are estimates of the severity of a problem based upon memory, or in some instances upon prior data that already exist, such as a report card indicating grades or absences from school. Concurrent baselines are measurements of the problem that are begun sometime after intake assessment.

Starting a Single System Study

The first step in developing a single system study is to choose a behavior to monitor. This may be a difficult decision, but sometimes it is obvious which behavior needs to be targeted: If you have a client who has been arrested for driving while intoxicated and this is the second arrest in six months, it is clear that you have a client who needs to change his or her drinking behavior. Similarly, it would be apparent that a child with school phobia needs to decrease the number of days absent from school. Some clients need to demonstrate greater assertiveness; others need to learn to handle their destructive anger. Generally speaking, you will be working with clients to either increase or decrease certain behaviors. However, there can be as many as five different ways to think about how to modify behavior. Sundel and Sundel (1993) have suggested that we can help the client: (1) acquire a behavior; (2) increase the strength or frequency of a behavior; (3) maintain a behavior; or (4) decrease a behavior.

There will not be one target behavior that can be selected for all your clients. Suggestions of behaviors that can be monitored include:

- Increasing a child's positive interactions with peers.
- Reducing a child's fear of the dark.
- Helping a shy adult become more assertive.
- Reducing amount of time spent watching television.
- Improving reading comprehension.
- Decreasing a compulsive behavior.
- Managing anger outbursts better.
- Overcoming a fear of flying.
- Losing excess weight.
- Managing money better.
- Procrastinating less.

Behaviors to be monitored in a single system study must necessarily follow from the treatment plan prepared for that individual client. Even though most social workers are not behaviorists, and the goals for their clients are fairly global or long-range, single system designs can be used in nonbehavioral treatment providing that the client's final goals can be stated in measurable terms.

The selection of the appropriate problem to be influenced by the intervention is obviously very important. When choosing a target behavior, there are several considerations that should be kept in mind:

1. *Target behaviors should come from the client.* To select problems that are not attuned to clients' perceptions of their problems risks premature termination. Although some clients may have a secret agenda for seeking help or other problems that may be revealed after a trusting relationship has been established, the best place to start is with the problem the client has identified as being most significant. This may require some prioritizing of the client's problems.

Along this line, it may be helpful to use the following criteria to help rank the problems mentioned by clients: (1) problems that are the most immediate expressed concern of the client; (2) problems that have the most negative consequence for the client, significant others, or society if not handled immediately; (3) problems that have the highest probability of being corrected quickly, thus providing an experience of success; and (4) problems that require handling before other problems can be dealt with (Sundel and Sundel, 1993). Ideally, there should be mutual agreement between the social worker and the client regarding the major concern and focus of the intervention.

2. *Vaguely stated problems are difficult to measure.* Select behaviors that are concrete and observable. Avoid any behavior that might be difficult to detect or about which there might be disagreement as to whether it was happening or not.

Choose behaviors that can be counted, observed, or quantified. You may have to help your client move from an ambiguous description of the problem to a more precise definition. For instance, "nervousness" is a vague complaint, but associated with it may be several observable behaviors such as nail biting, overeating, stuttering, episodes of gastro-intestinal attacks, or excessive use of antacids, that could be used as surrogate measures of the nervousness. One could count the number of antacids consumed in a day, the number of stuttering episodes, or the number of calories ingested per day. Whenever possible, target behaviors should be so well defined that others would have little difficulty in observing or recording them.

Start with the presenting problem, and then explore how that problem manifests itself. Let's say that a woman tells you that her husband doesn't respect her. You cannot use "lack of respect" as a target behavior, because the term is too broad and not immediately associated with any specific behaviors. You need to find how this problem is expressed or detected by the client. What specific behaviors illustrate the problem of lack of respect? It could mean that her husband walks away while she is talking. Is he having an affair? You want to identify the actions that indicate to the woman that her husband does not respect her. From these specific behaviors, choose one or two to focus on during the intervention.

In Berlin's example, a short standardized instrument was available for use. What happens if the therapist knows of no instrument suitable for measuring a problem like depression, anxiety, or other vaguely stated concerns? The therapist has only two choices: review the literature and attempt to find such an instrument or select specific target behaviors suggested by the client's particular set of problems.

For instance, suppose a married couple comes to you because they are arguing almost daily. They are interested in saving their marriage; however, both are assertive, strong-willed individuals. The obvious target behavior is the number of arguments that they have. What led the couple to therapy? The wife (who happens to be a bookkeeper) kept a record of the number of arguments that the couple had over the past fourteen days. The frequency of these arguments was disturbing to both of them, and they agreed to seek help.

In this instance, the baseline was readily available to the therapist, and the couple were in agreement that they wanted to reduce the number of arguments that had been occurring. While an instrument would not be needed, one that measured marital satisfaction could be used. If the marital counseling is successful, then it is reasonable to assume that a graph illustrating the number of arguments would show fewer arguments after intervention than during the baseline period.

Sometimes clients describe problems like fear of dying or loneliness that seem to be more of a mental state, more attitudinal than behavioral. In instances like these, you may want to consult Fischer and Corcoran's (1994) *Measures for Clinical Practice* to obtain scales to objectively measure their death anxiety or loneliness. However, even these conditions are likely to be associated with problem behaviors. The person who is afraid of dying may be having panic attacks or insomnia or be unable to concentrate at work or school. The individual who is experiencing loneliness may need to change introverted, reclusive behaviors and increase social contacts by joining clubs, bowling leagues, co-ed volleyball teams, hobby groups, and so on. As a practitioner you have to decide what behaviors to monitor and how to monitor improvement. The challenge is always to operationalize so specifically that there is little doubt when change or improvement is occurring.

Not only will vaguely stated problems create difficulties when you attempt to measure them, but so can rather specific events (for example, hearing voices or having delusions) if your client doesn't always report these and if they are not observable by others. Certainly, clients are able to self-report on behaviors or problems that are not noticeable to others, but I would not select these for measurement with a single system design unless the client was strongly motivated to alleviate the problem and could be trusted to report with accuracy. The easiest problems to measure are those that are easily recognized by others and repetitive. (For instance, I once heard of a client in a residential treatment program who took ten or more showers a day.)

Frequency of an event is not the only way of measuring problem behavior like a couple's arguments. In a different situation the therapist might have suggested that the length (or duration) of the arguments be monitored. Or the intensity (magnitude) of the arguments might have been recorded. Minor verbal disagreements might not be counted; only those of the foot-stomping, door-slamming variety would qualify. Residents of a group home who live with someone showering ten times a day might be just as unhappy if "Mr. Clean" took fewer showers but stayed in thirty-five minutes each time, using up all the hot water.

The practitioner has quite a bit of freedom in choosing what to measure, how to measure, and even who should do the recording. However, the target behavior should suggest itself from the client's description of the problem. The behavior should be an activity that a client agrees is important to count or record. Clients should be able to see how change in the target behavior contributes to improving their problem situation.

3. *Target behaviors are monitored over time.* Graphs are useful tools to portray changes in behavior. Graphs need not be drawn on engineering or graph paper; you can draw vertical and horizontal lines that intersect at a right angle and calibrate or demarcate the lines in a way that has meaning and indicates how much of the activity is occurring during the observation period (see figure 3.2).

On the vertical line (or axis), plot the number of times (frequency) the target behavior occurs. You need to have a rough idea how often the behavior is occurring in order to devise a scale to show its pattern.

For instance, if little Pablo misses his morning bus three times in one

Figure 3.2 Incomplete Single System Graph

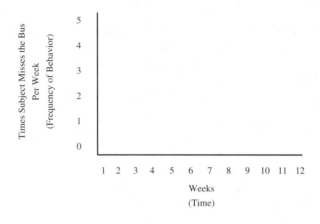

week, the vertical axis should be constructed to record the lowest and greatest number of these incidents. It is likely that he couldn't miss his bus more than five mornings a week, so the range would be 0 to 5.

Some thought needs to go into the selection of the behavior or the problem being counted on the vertical axis. Because missing a bus might be a matter of oversleeping, you might want to target the number of times that little Pablo gets to bed on time the night before. Or, if he is a little older and sets his own alarm clock, the number of times that he oversleeps. Both of these could be legitimate target behaviors for intervention.

Notice the emphasis on counting behaviors. It would be less useful to chart the actual times (for example, 7:04 A.M.) that little Pablo awakens since his problem might be one of procrastination and not oversleeping. On the other hand, if his difficulty is getting to bed on time, the vertical axis might be constructed to show the number of minutes past his bedtime that he is late each evening. Counting intervals of time such as minutes past bedtime and hours spent doing homework are also appropriate for the vertical axis.

The horizontal line is used to portray the behavior as it occurs over time. Whether you decide to use hours, days, or weeks as the unit of time is dependent upon the behavior itself. If you were working with a twelve-year-old who was having stomachaches because of school phobia and this tended to happen once a day (ten minutes before the school bus arrived), it would be better to count the number of times a week that the stomachaches occurred than to keep hourly records. A baseline graph of the stomachaches in a month prior to the intervention might resemble the one in figure 3.3.

Figure 3.3 An Example of Developing a Baseline

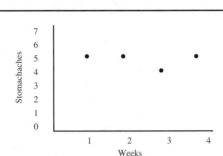

This graph shows that the child had stomach problems five times (corresponding to the five school days) the first week that a record was kept, five times the second and fourth weeks, but only four times in the third week when there was a school holiday. In this example, we know that the symptoms are occurring every schoolday. The child missed having a stomachache only once on a schoolday during a twenty-eight-day period. This is a well-established or *stable pattern* of behavior. If intervention is effective, a pattern of improvement will be readily observable. Contrast this with a target behavior that is unpredictable (where there is no discernible pattern). Suppose that the child had one stomachache the first week, none the second week, five stomachaches during the third week, and none during the fourth week. This would be an erratic pattern where we might want a longer baseline to help us understand what is going on. Instead of school phobia, the child's stomach problems might be due to food allergies that are triggered by specific foods that are not eaten every week.

It is difficult to provide a rule about how long the baseline period should be. Much depends on how often the behavior is occurring and how stable this pattern is. A behavior that occurs relatively infrequently probably is not a useful behavior to choose for monitoring because it will be hard to see any patterns. Similarly, behavior that varies a great deal will not make a good target behavior. Choose a behavior that is fairly dependable in its occurrence. There can be some variation in the frequency of the behavior, but this variation should not have "wild swings."

Here are several guidelines concerning the length of the baseline (Bloom, Fischer and Orme, 1995):

- It should be long enough to be useful in assessing the client's problems.
- It should be stable enough to allow you to make some estimates about its frequency if there were no intervention.

- Three observations during baseline are considered a minimum, but this number is often insufficient and ten baseline points is recommended if it is ethically and practically possible.

Stable patterns are characterized by little variability in the data—for instance, the absence of big peaks and valleys. However, the length of the baseline should be tempered by the availability of data and concern for not unduly delaying intervention.

You don't have to wait five or six weeks to construct a baseline. Suppose a mother comes to you because she is concerned that her five-year-old is still wetting the bed. You ask, "About how often does this happen?" If the mother says,"About every night" or "Almost every night," then the baseline is established and you can begin with the assumption that bed wetting is occurring about thirty times a month. Even if it is actually happening only twenty-seven or twenty-five times a month, the obvious goal is to decrease these incidents to zero times a month.

Baseline data can come from various sources. You might find that there is ample reference to the occurrence of the target behavior in progress notes, the client may have kept some informal records or have a good memory, or there may be official records (for example, elementary school absences). In our society, documentation is often readily available. A baseline for a spouse whose drinking behavior results in days missed from work, for example, might be obtained by looking at paycheck stubs. In some instances, clients can keep logs or self-report on the occurrence of the target behavior. In other situations, someone else will need to monitor the behavior. These are individually determined by a knowledge of the client's abilities and situation.

The argument for using existing records or data for the baseline is that the very act of counting or measuring a behavior during the baseline phase may begin to change the client's behavior (especially if the client is self-reporting and motivated to improve) even before the intervention is implemented. Self-reporting, though generally regarded as reliable, does have a reactive effect in that clients' behavior might change when they know they are being observed. (See Kopp, 1988, for a thorough discussion of the self-monitoring literature.) Needless to say, self-monitoring data will give a false picture if the client is motivated to misrepresent the extent or severity of the problem.

As can be seen in figure 3.4, the behavior during the baseline period is usually separated from the behavior during the intervention phase by a vertical dotted line.

4. *The last step in developing a single system study is selecting a design.* Of the many single system designs from which to choose, only a few of those judged to be the most useful to practitioners are presented here. As you read the balance of this chapter, you may find yourself liking some designs because you feel that you could comfortably use them. Other designs may strike you

Figure 3.4 Essential Components of a Single Subject Design

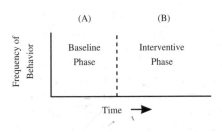

as impractical (or worse) because they seem more suited for experimental labs and require greater control over the client system than you feel that you have or ought to have. One design (the AB) is likely to meet most of your needs. But other designs may be more appropriate for specific cases or when you want greater assurance that it was your intervention that had the desired effect.

Types of Designs

The Case Study or B Design

The case study, as we have already mentioned, is familiar to students. Case studies are sometimes called uncontrolled case studies because they lack baseline measures and use anecdotal information rather than objective measures of the target behavior. These designs are therefore seriously limited in that they do not permit conclusions that the intervention caused the change in the client's behavior. (There may have been other forces or influences at work in addition to the intervention.) What's more, there is no guarantee that the findings from a case study will fit any other cases (Gilgun, 1994).

However, these designs are simple to conceptualize, don't require pre-planning, and are possible to start once intervention has begun. Although they can't ascribe causation or rule out competing explanations, they can describe client progress.

The practitioner begins keeping records with the beginning of intervention regarding how the client changes or improves. No attempt is made to compare the behavior at the end of the intervention with its baseline (because there was none). This design can be used with any theoretical orientation, and its value is the feedback it provides. However, there are a number of serious limitations to the case study: Lack of systematic observation and standardization of assessment, no baseline measures, and little control of the treatment variable (the intervention may involve several simultaneous procedures). Further, case studies rely heavily upon anecdotal information that may rest on

---

Practice Note: Sudden Infant Death Syndrome

In 1972, five case reports of Sudden Infant Death Syndrome (SIDS) occurring in only three families were described by a physician, Alfred Steinschneider, in the journal *Pediatrics*. Twenty-five years later, a book *The Death of Innocents: A True Story of Murder* by Richard Firstman and Jamie Talan (1997) raised important questions about how a seriously flawed study could have shaped medical thinking all those years. Even today, Steinschneider's theories about sleep apnea are considered influential, although the editor of *Pediatrics*, Jerold Lucey, noted in the journal, "We never should have published this article. . . . The patients studied were murdered. They were not SIDS patients . . . some physicians still believe SIDS runs in families. It doesn't—murder does" (1997, p. A77).

In one of the families Steinschneider included in his case reports, the mother was convicted recently of smothering all five of her children. The impact of this book and Dr. Lucey's apology (he was the editor in 1972 also) will likely result in medical examiners becoming much more resistant to concluding that SIDS was responsible for an infant's death—particularly when it is the second one within a family.

SIDS now kills about 3,500 infants a year, about 2,000 a year fewer than in the years before 1992, when doctors began recommending that parents put babies on their backs to sleep. The overwhelming majority of SIDS deaths are not thought to be infanticide. However, a recent study in Massachusetts found evidence of parental abuse in more than one-third of 155 babies treated for "near-SIDS" episodes or studied because siblings had died of SIDS. Of those who died from SIDS in 1996, about 3 percent had siblings who also reportedly died from it (*USA Today*, 26 September 1997, 28 October 1997).

This terrible tragedy points out the necessity for researchers to not allow themselves to become blinded by their theories and the importance of continuing to search for other explanations. It cautions us against concluding too much from a small amount of data.

---

a heavily biased presentation, and because of the focus on one individual, the results cannot be generalized to other situations.

Though they lack scientific rigor, case studies are useful for several reasons: They are a source of hypotheses about human behavior and techniques for working with clients, they have a strong persuasive appeal in illustrating well a particular point, and they stimulate us to examine rare phenomena (Kazdin, 1992).

A fascinating case study is found in Russ Rymer's *Genie: An Abused*

Child's Flight from Silence (1993). This book reveals a great deal about the effects of extreme childhood neglect and abuse on personality and language. It narrates the discovery of a thirteen-year-old girl who, weighing fifty-nine pounds, was incontinent, could not chew solid food, could not cry or focus her eyes beyond twelve feet, and had no perception of heat and cold. Her productive vocabulary was limited to "Stopit," "Nomore," and several other shorter negatives. And yet she was described as having incredible curiosity, energy, and personality. For most of her life, Genie had been confined alone in a small bedroom, harnessed to an infant's potty chair and beaten if she made any noise. Case studies like this can be riveting to read because of their rich description. However, oftentimes they are devoid of pertinent information that would give us a basis for comparison. In this case, the child's father was convinced that she was mentally retarded and would die before the age of twelve, but what was her her I.Q. before she was socially and physically deprived? Although she was making good progress, how much was she capable of achieving?

While case studies may be educational and useful from a pedagogic standpoint, they generally are not considered to be formal research methodologies. When we are responsible for the intervention for a complex, difficult, or particularly puzzling client or family, it is often beneficial to build upon the simple case study model by constructing a baseline and observing target behaviors. When we add these features, the simple case study becomes a single system design, capable of providing objective evidence that our treatment did or did not benefit the client.

The AB Design

The basic **AB design** is the single system design most often used by social work practitioners and researchers. The A portion of the design is the baseline measurement (for example, the client's scores on a scale assessing depression). The B part of the design is the data collected during the treatment phase. Because of its simplicity, the AB design is virtually unlimited in its applicability in social work. This is perhaps its greatest strength. It reveals changes in behavior—if they occur. Unfortunately, changes in behavior that are detected with this design do not "prove" that the intervention was responsible. There could be alternative explanations such as the occurrence of other events during intervention (for example, leaving a stressful job, the birth of a child, over-the-fence counseling by a neighbor, or maturation of the client) that account for changes in the client's behavior. These alternative or rival explanations are difficult to rule out with the basic AB design. Most practitioners, however, would be happy with the client's success and would not worry about alternative explanations. While the AB design may not adequately control for competing explanations, it provides a useful way of examining whether there has been an improvement since intervention began.

Figure 3.5 Illustration of an AB Design Graph

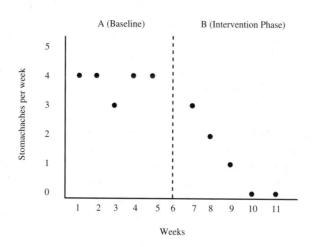

The ABA and ABAB Designs

These two designs are sometimes called withdrawal, reversal, or experimental single system designs because they employ a second period of nonintervention, another baseline condition in order to show that the intervention was responsible for the observed effect on the target behavior. These designs are concerned with whether the effect of the intervention will continue or be maintained. After the intervention (B) has been completed or substantially delivered, treatment is withdrawn or stopped, and the target problem is monitored to see what direction it takes.

The second (A) phase in an **ABA design** is like the first A phase in that behavior is recorded during a period of no intervention. This is not to suggest that you as a practitioner should purposely withdraw treatment for "research" purposes; that would be an unethical practice. The second A phase could legitimately come about following termination (Berlin mailed a depression scale to the client as a follow-up measure one month after treatment. Look back to figure 3.1 for an example of this graph).

Because of practice-related concerns about ending client contact during a nonintervention phase, Bloom and Fischer (1995) do not recommend this design for most practice situations. However, if the second A phase comes about as a follow-up to intervention, or for other therapeutically sound reasons, this design might be useful and ought not be overlooked.

Each phase of the classical single system design (AB) is repeated twice in the **ABAB design**. As in the ABA design, treatment is withdrawn or removed in the second baseline (A phase) in order to see if the target behavior will return to its original level (prior to intervention). There may be valid reasons for a second period of nonintervention, both practical—for example, the therapist's vacation—and therapeutic—for example, a trial period of three weeks between appointments to wean a "dependent" client away from intervention. After the second baseline period, the treatment is reintroduced. Unlike the ABA design, the study ends during an intervention phase, which makes it more appealing from an ethical standpoint.

Because the client serves as his or her own control, the ABAB design is an experimental design and provides some assurance that the intervention actually was responsible for any changes in behavior. In this sense, the ABAB design is a stronger and more powerful design than the AB and ABA designs. If the same effects are shown during the second AB (replication) phase, then there is less likelihood that outside influences (alternative explanations) were responsible. The ABAB is a strong design for those who are interested in contributing to our knowledge base by experimentally demonstrating that some intervention is effective.

However, use of the ABAB design is not always practical. In fact, if the first treatment phase reduced the behavior to acceptable levels for the client and others concerned, it is likely that all involved persons would feel that the intervention was a success. Termination would occur, and the therapist would be given a new client to add to his or her caseload. There would be little reason to introduce intervention again unless the client made another request. In fact, the more successful the intervention, the less likely it will be that the behavior would return to its initial baseline (A) level.

The ABAB design may not feel comfortable to many practitioners because they are painfully aware of the shortage of staff or the long lists of clients patiently waiting for help with their problems. Even though the second baseline could come about naturally (vacations, hospitalizations, and so on), the ABAB design may still seem excessive or a luxury unavailable to many practitioners.

The ABAB design is best thought of as a design to be used for knowledge-building. It is a design that enables thorough testing of an intervention and reduction of alternative explanations for the client's improvement. This design is what you would use if you were sure that a given intervention worked and you wanted to document or publish your success in some sort of formal way.

The ABC and ABCD Designs

Practitioners know well that sometimes the intervention that you start with doesn't work, is not valued by the client, or does not appear to be working as fast as it should. In these situations, major changes are made in the treatment plan. Another intervention might be started or multiple modalities employed.

The **ABC or "successive interventions" design** permits the practitioner to respond with different interventions when needed and still allows for monitoring the effects of these interventions. In this scheme, the effects of the second intervention are identified as (C). The effects of the third intervention are (D), and so on.

Since there is no return to a baseline between the second and third (or even fourth) interventions, these successive intervention designs do not allow the practitioner to determine which interventions caused the changes in the behavior. Even though it might appear that the first intervention (B) didn't work, but that the second intervention (C) did, it could be that the accumulative or interactive effects of both B and C resulted in the change. Although one's colleagues and the client may be duly impressed with these changes, strictly speaking, conditions were not controlled enough for any sort of formal statement of causality.

Even if this design tends to fall short of the experimenter's expectations, it is appealing to practitioners because intervention is often modified in practice and different techniques are used in the course of therapy. If everyone is happy that the behavior has changed in the desired direction, and success is in the air, neither client nor practitioner may need greater "proof" that the interventions worked. Figure 3.6 shows an example of an **ABCD design** found in the social work literature.

Multiple Baseline Designs

Single system designs known as **multiple baseline designs** may be used when you are working with several clients who have the same problem and who receive the same intervention. For instance, suppose you are employed as a social worker in a nursing home and the staff begin to complain about a problem of urinary incontinence with three wheelchair-bound residents who have organic brain disorders. You've recently read an article describing the use of an intervention involving praise and cookies for patients like this that resulted in a decrease in urinary accidents. The staff are eager to participate and soon begin collecting baseline data.

Keeping true to the standards on which single system designs are based, the intervention starts first with Mr. Smith. Only when there is clear indication of improvement is the intervention applied to the second resident, Mrs. Wright. And then only when she shows improvement can the intervention be applied to the third resident. When success is achieved with all three residents, this becomes the basis for inferring that the intervention caused the observed changes following the "principle of unlikely successive coincidences" (Bloom, Fischer, and Orme, 1995). The shorthand notation for a **multiple baseline across subjects design** is A1A2A3B.

You can see in figure 3.7 that multiple baseline designs have baselines of

**Figure 3.6 Treatment Progress of a Businesswoman with
            Early-Phase Alcoholism**

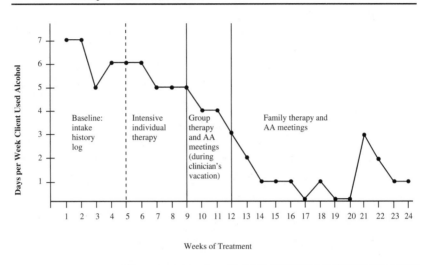

Source: Nuehring, E.M. and Pascone, A.B. (1986), Single-subject evaluation: A tool for quality assurance, *Social Work,* 31(5), 361. Copyright © National Association of Social Workers, Inc. Reprinted with permission.

unequal length and that intervention does not begin in the second graph until change has been shown with the first client.

A **multiple baseline across behaviors design** can be employed if a single client has two, three, or more problems that are likely to respond to the same intervention. If the client has three target problems, then the notation would reflect the three separate baselines and one intervention and would be **A1A2A3B**.

For instance, suppose you are working with a fifteen-year-old in a residential treatment facility for youth. Alberto has been abused by a stepfather, is not doing well in school, and has poor impulse control, which gets him into frequent fights. He defies authority, is uncooperative with staff, and boasts of several instances of grand theft auto as well as smoking marijuana for the past two years. Alberto is bright and personable, capable of finishing high school, and possibly able to succeed in college. But where do you start?

Following the principles we learned earlier, baselines need to be started on all of the targeted behaviors. Let's say that his social worker and Alberto first attempt to reduce the incidence of fighting with residents at the treatment center. When there is progress there, then another behavior like being less defi-

Figure 3.7 Illustration of Multiple Baselines Across Subjects

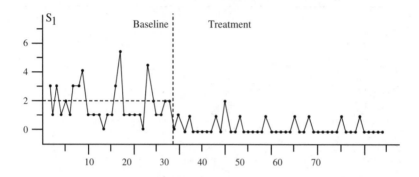

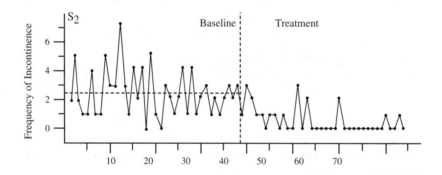

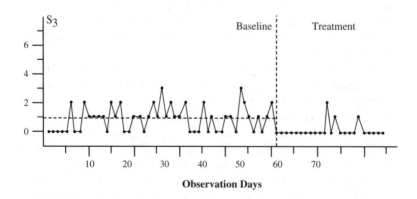

Observation Days

Source: Pinkston, E.M., Howe, M.W., and Blackman, D.K. (1987), Medical social work management of urinary incontinence in the elderly: A behavioral approach, *Journal of Social Service Research,* 10 (2,3,4), 188. Copyright © Haworth Press, Inc. Reprinted with permission.

ant of authority might be attempted, and then when there is progress with that one, getting Alberto to apply greater effort toward his schoolwork.

Practitioners may want to consider the multiple baseline designs because of the inferences that can be made about the effectiveness of treatment. An intervention that produces strong rates of change across various behaviors or with different clients is showing generalizability or external validity (which we'll talk more about in the next chapter). In other words, these designs provide evidence that the intervention was responsible for the improvement. The assumption is then that other social workers who employ this intervention should also expect to find the same beneficial effects with their clients.

However, it is also possible that a multiple baseline across behaviors design could seem too impractical or unwieldy to use. Oftentimes, social workers find it necessary to begin working on several of the client's problems at once. There simply is not the luxury of time to address problems sequentially with an adequate baseline for each that began with the monitoring of the first behavior. In real life, Alberto would likely receive more than one intervention (for example, individual therapy, group therapy for impulse control, twelve-step group, as well as token economy or other various treatments). Given the multiple interventions, it may make more sense to think of monitoring Alberto's behavior with a series of AB designs. Teachers in the school program would probably keep their own graphs, as would Alberto's probation officer, his social worker at the treatment center, and the social worker managing his case for the state.

Statistical Analysis

Cooper (1990) has demonstrated the use of one of the simplest statistical approaches in analyzing data from a client with obsessive-compulsive disorder. The client was a young woman with pervasive ritualistic behavior, such as rinsing in the shower for forty-five minutes and counting gulps of liquid when swallowing. Figure 3.8 shows how Cooper used a celeration line to understand the behavior was accelerating and to reveal where it would have been without intervention.

You can construct a celeration line easily once an adequate baseline is obtained (there are ten baseline points in figure 3.8). Begin by dividing the baseline in half, and then divide each of these in half so that the baseline has four equal quarters. If you have an even number of baseline points you will need to draw your lines between data points. If there is an odd number, draw through the middle point.

Once this is done, compute an average or mean frequency for each half of the baseline. These means are then marked on the one-quarter and third-

**Figure 3.8 Number of Twists, Presses, and Clicks of Make-Up Case
by Client Each Morning at Baseline (7/2 to 7/15) and
After Intervention (7/17 to 8/21)**

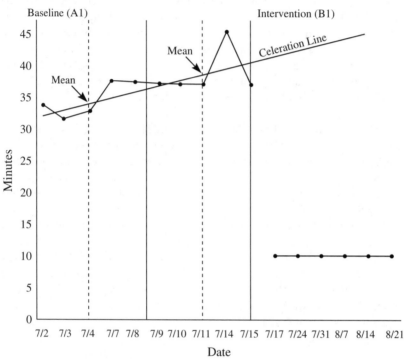

Source: Cooper, M. (1990), Treatment of a client with obsessive-compulsive disorder, *Social Work Research and Abstracts*, 24(2), 29. Copyright © National Association of Social Workers, Inc. Reprinted with permission.

quarter indicator lines and a line is drawn connecting them and extending in both directions.

The celeration line that crosses the line indicating when intervention begins shows what you could expect of the behavior or event if there were no intervention. Bloom, Fischer, and Orme (1995) explain further procedures so that interested practitioners can determine if a statistically significant change has occurred.

Statistics usually are not needed with single system designs. Because these designs rely upon graphs and visual inspection, "eyeballing" and clinical significance are all that is usually needed to establish that improvement occurred.

Figure 3.9 Example of an Ambiguous Graph

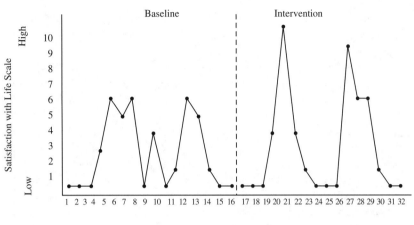

Days Satisfaction Rated

However, the results from these tests at best only rule out a chance occurrence and do not eliminate rival explanations or permit conclusive causal inferences. Sometimes unusually high or low data points affect these statistical techniques and can produce results that are contradictory. Clearly, the ideal situation would be a single system graph in which an intervention's success (or not) was visually obvious.

Rubin and Knox (1996) caution us about ambiguity in single system designs. They found ambiguous outcomes in seven of twenty-three graphs where male adolescent sex offenders were self-monitoring on pro-social behaviors and in seven of sixteen graphs where parents were reporting on their sons' antisocial behaviors. The point is this: You should be prepared for the possibility of obtaining unstable, indistinct baselines. These might be recognized by improvement that begins during the baseline, and by cyclical periods of no problematic behaviors during the intervention phase except for a few high spikes. An example is provided in figure 3.9 of an ambiguous single system graph.

If you look closely at figure 3.9, you'll note that although the spikes are higher during the intervention period, the client actually experiences only one more day than in baseline when his satisfaction with life was self-reported as either two or lower. Also, during the sixteen days after baseline, the client experienced only one day more when he rated his satisfaction with life as six or higher.

Practice Note: Gender and Ethnicity

There is a strong possibility that the clients chosen and even the target behaviors selected for single system design research may be influenced by gender and ethnicity considerations. Nelsen (1994) has suggested that female clients may be more likely to be asked to participate in single system designs than males. Do you expect females in this society to be more compliant? To be less assertive and more in touch with their feelings?

Conversely, social workers not of the same ethnic background probably are less likely to involve minority clients in this type of research because of concern that they may be accused of being insensitive to cultural issues. Nelsen (1994) observes, "The practitioner who avoids asking out of anxiety about practitioner-client ethnic differences also misses an opportunity to address differences that should be discussed at some point in treatment" (p. 146).

Evaluation is intrinsic to good practice (Bloom and Orme, 1993), and single systems designs are perhaps the most practical means for monitoring client improvement. Because there is always the possibility that our interventions can have iatrogenic effects, there is no ethical alternative to monitoring what is happening with our clients (Mattaini, 1996). (An iatrogenic disorder is any adverse mental or physical condition induced in a patient by the effects of treatment.) Competent practice demands that we make every effort to be aware of our biases that may affect clients, and to inform ourselves about those who differ from us in ethnicity, national origin, race, color, gender, and sexual orientation. And insofar as it is possible, we ought to involve the client in defining the problem and assisting with the data collection (Bloom and Orme, 1993).

Advantages and Disadvantages of Single System Designs

Single system designs are popular with social workers for several reasons. First of all, single system designs readily lend themselves to clinical practice situations. If a social worker wants to objectively evaluate his or her practice, single system designs do not require either control groups or large groups of clients in order to demonstrate that the intervention is working.

Secondly, single system designs are not disruptive to the treatment process.

Practice Note: Impediments to Using Single System Designs

Corcoran (1993) has identified the following practical impediments to using single system designs:

- Lack of time to do single system designs.
- Availability of suitable measures.
- Settings (for example, acute care hospitals) not amenable to single system designs.

In fact, they support and complement practice nicely by focusing on specific treatment goals or problems. Often, they serve to clarify or confirm a worker's initial assessment of a client. Further, these designs are constructive in that they provide continuous feedback to the practitioner as well as the client. There is no need to wait until the treatment has ended to determine progress. Many clients have "failure" identities and need to be reassured that they are progressing. Single system designs can visually demonstrate the progress that has been made.

Thirdly, single system designs do not normally require computers, knowledge of statistics, or clerical help in compiling data. These designs do not require that you develop a hypothesis to test. In short, they are not burdensome to one's practice. They are easy to use and understand. Lastly, they are theory-free. That is, they can be applied regardless of the worker's theoretical application. For social workers who are interested in some form of accountability, but not able to undertake large-scale research projects, there is much to recommend single system studies.

On the other hand, these designs have some major limitations. A considerable one is the problem of generalization. Even though one uses a rigorous single system design and clearly demonstrates that the intervention worked, there will still be those skeptics who say, "So? Maybe you worked well with this one client. Show me that your approach works with lots of clients." A social worker or counselor could be very effective with a single client and yet ineffective with the rest of the caseload.

A number of practical problems sometimes emerge during the use of single system designs. Ideally, all phases should be of equal length, yet realistically an intervention might be longer than the baseline or longer in one phase (the B phase) than another phase (the C phase). In actual practice, it is unlikely that all phases would be the same length. Other problems are encountered when we know the baseline behavior is not stable but must start intervention immediately or when several interventive techniques have to be applied simultaneously. Another problem is that even experienced practitioners may be hard-pressed to think of situations in which they would deliberately withdraw or remove an intervention that is working just to show that it is the intervention that was responsible for the change in behavior. As a consequence, some of the more experimental single system designs (for example, ABAB) may be viewed by practitioners with disdain or lack of interest.

The Choice and Use of Single System Designs

There are many more single system designs that could be practically presented in this chapter. For instance, Kazi and Wilson (1996) discuss the **ABBC design** where the intervention B is discovered to be relatively feeble and is combined with another intervention C. Bloom, Fischer, and Orme (1995) have identified many more varieties of designs. Single system designs allow for the creative adaptation and changes in intervention that occur naturally in social work practice. One cannot employ the excuse "I can't find the 'right' design for my client." They are out there, whether simple, or complex, waiting to be used.

The single system design that is "best" to use depends upon how much evidence you feel that you need to rule out alternative explanations for improvement; it is also dictated by the target behaviors or problems identified in the treatment plan. Knowledge of the client and his or her problems is an important consideration in the choice of a design. For instance, you wouldn't want to attempt an ABAB design with a client who agrees to a maximum of three contacts. With another client, you may feel that it is important to monitor three or more target behaviors. Sometimes you might combine such behaviors as hitting and fighting and refer to the commission of either as "assaultive acts"; then you could use only one graph instead of two. With single subject designs, you have a great deal of flexibility. As a general guideline, however, let your knowledge of the client dictate the design rather than choosing a design and attempting to find a client who conforms to it. If we were all to wait for the "ideal" client to come along before beginning to evaluate our practice, not much evaluation would get done.

It is important not to forget that the purpose and best use of single system designs is to identify whether a client is progressing. These designs cannot explain why an intervention isn't working. Their purpose is only to inform you whether the intervention is working.

Recent developments in the creation of objective measures to document the severity of our clients' problems make the use of single subject designs even more exciting. Besides the over three hundred scales available in the

Fischer and Corcoran (1994) book, you'll find other useful instruments to use in Nurius and Hudson's book (1993). Some of the scales contained in their book are:

Index of Self-Esteem
Clinical Anxiety Scale
Index of Peer Relations
Index of Alcohol Involvement
Index of Marital Satisfaction
Partner Abuse Scale (Nonphysical abuse)
Partner Abuse Scale (Physical abuse)
Generalized Contentment Scale

Each of these scales is twenty-five items and is constructed so that a score of thirty or higher indicates a clinically significant problem. Further, these and other scales can be purchased relatively inexpensively in pads of fifty or you can buy the computer software so that clients can complete the scales you select for them on a computer in your agency. The software allows data to be stored so that single subject graphs can be created.

It requires a certain amount of self-discipline to conduct research. One has to be conscientious about keeping records or monitoring changes in behavior. For many practitioners whose agencies do not require formal evaluation, it is easier to use subjective determinations ("I think the client is doing better"; "The client is acting more appropriately"; "I feel that the couple is getting along better.") However, subjective determinations do not advance the profession or build practice knowledge. Single system designs can help you to discover what works under which circumstances. A study by Campbell (1988) indicates that clients prefer the use of some single system evaluation procedure over practitioners' opinions of effectiveness of treatment. Campbell went on to note that "concern over client reactions to the use of single system evaluation procedures does not appear to be a valid reason for not using them" (p. 22).

Single system designs have practical value and can benefit you and your clients. You may find that if you make use of them, you gain an appreciation for empirical research and are more willing to engage in it. As a practicing social worker, you will surely find that you are too busy to attempt a single system design for every client. That's understood. However, unless you make an effort to evaluate some clients, you'll soon forget how to go about it. What do I recommend? Simply that you use a single system design with your most difficult clients. You'll keep your skills fresh and your supervisor happy, and you'll be able to determine objectively whether or not these clients are making progress.

Self-Review

(Answers at the end of the book)

1   T or F.   A Single system design *must* contain a baseline.
2. T or F.   In a single system design, time is recorded on the vertical axis.
3. How many baselines does the design ABA contain?
4. Which design is better for knowledge-building, the ABCD or the ABAB?
5. Which design was used in the management of incontinence among the elderly in a nursing home?
    a. ABA
    b. ABAB
    c. ABCD
    d. $A_1A_2A_3B$
6. What makes for an ambiguous graph on either the baseline or intervention side?
7   List the advantages of using a single system design.
8. What is the major limitation of single system designs?
9. Besides the fact that it involves more than one client, how is the multiple baseline across subjects design different from the traditional AB design?
10. Why should social workers use single system designs?

Questions for Class Discussion

1. Think again about the discussion of the twelve-year-old who had stomachaches. Why wouldn't you want to graph the behavior in terms of times per day? (*Hint:* make a graph on the blackboard showing the reduction from one episode a day to none per day at the end of the intervention.)
2. Is there more than one way graphs can show lack of improvement? Choose a target behavior and draw suggestions from the class that demonstrate lack of improvement.
3. Why is the ability to operationalize target behaviors important for single subject designs?
4. What would be a good argument for monitoring more than one target behavior with a client?
5. Think about how to set up a graph for a particular target behavior. Would there be advantages in graphing positive behaviors (for exam-

ple, number of days on the job) rather than negative behaviors (for example, days of work missed)?

6. A coworker tells you that she has just completed a single system design on a family that has received intervention for seven months. She is pleased with what she has done and brings a graph to show you.
   a. What would be your initial reactions about her competence?
   b. Can the single subject design "prove" that your co-worker is an excellent social worker? Why not?

7. With a multiple baseline across subjects design, what is the reason for waiting for a change in the behavior of the first subject before beginning intervention on the second? Can you think of any reasons why intervention shouldn't be started on all three subjects at the same time?

8. Odette is failing the ninth grade. At a conference with her mother, Odette's teachers said that she simply was not studying or turning in any homework. The family's social worker wants to develop a single subject design to monitor the effect of requiring Odette to study two hours every afternoon before the television could be turned on. The social worker is planning to have the vertical axis show "yes" or "no" regarding the completion of two hours of study time every afternoon. Could this design be improved? How?

9. What is wrong with this single subject design?

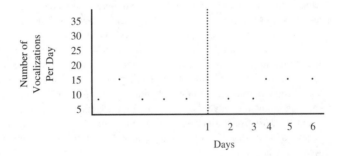

Mini-Projects for Experiencing Research Firsthand

1. Choose a client with whom you have worked or are working. (Or make up a fictitious client.) Describe the presenting problem, and then select a target behavior that follows from the client's description of major concerns. Construct a graph for a single system design to monitor the client's progress. Be sure to address the following:

    a. What is the target behavior?

    b. How long a baseline will you need? What units will you use to measure the time intervals? How will you measure the target behavior (for example, frequency of the behavior)?

    c. What design would you use? It should be apparent on the graph.

    d. Have the graph show that the intervention was successful.

    e. What other explanations for the change could there be?

2   Find an article that reports the use of a single system design.

    a. What additional information do you think should have been included? Do you have enough information to replicate the study?

    b. Could another design have been used? If so, what design?

    c. How convincing were the findings? Do you think replication should be attempted?

    d. Were alternative explanations adequately discussed?

    e. What are the implications for social work practice?

3. Using the scenario below, construct a graph or graphs to use with a single system design to monitor the couple's progress.

Mr. and Mrs. Jones have been having terrible arguments. Mrs. Jones, a college graduate, has quite a bit more education than her husband (a high school graduate). He has been spending time away from home, and often finds excuses to work late and on weekends. They are not having meaningful discussions. Generally, the arguments start when Mr. Jones finds fault with something that Mrs. Jones has either done or not done. Sometimes she doesn't get up when the alarm clock rings, and he must fix breakfast for their kids. She does not like to do housework, and clutter greatly bothers Mr. Jones.

    On the other hand, Mr. Jones does not often sit down and listen when his wife is talking. Mr. Jones is very conscious of time and most often will be doing something else while she is talking. She complains that he doesn't spend enough time with the family, but Mr. Jones feels that it is more stressful than enjoyable when they do something together. When she complains about this, Mr. Jones finds some problem with her housekeeping. The zip seems to have gone out of this marriage, and the number of arguments each week is escalating.

With your single system design, be sure to address:

a. the target behavior(s)

b. the design

c. the baseline

Briefly summarize the intervention and the client's progress after eight weeks.

4. Particularly for students interested in working with populations where behavior modification techniques are commonly employed

(for example, clients with serious behavioral and mental challenges), *The Journal of Applied Behavior Analysis* provides a plethora of articles containing single subject designs. Choose an article from this journal to read and then write a one-page summary of what you learned.

Resources and References

Berlin, S.B. (1983). Single-case evaluation: Another version. *Social Work Research and Abstracts*, 19, 3–11.

Bloom, M., Fischer, J., and Orme, J.G. (1995). *Evaluating practice: Guidelines for the accountable professional*. Englewood Cliffs, NJ: Prentice-Hall.

Bloom, M. and Orme, J. (1993). Ethics and the single-system design. *Journal of Social Service Research*, 19, 161–180.

Bromley, D.B. (1986). *The case-study method in psychology and related disciplines*. New York: Wiley.

Campbell, J.A. (1988). Client acceptance of single-system evaluation procedures. *Social Work Research and Abstracts*, 24(2), 21–22.

Carillo, D.F., DeWeaver, K.L., Kilpatrick, A.C., and Smith, M.L. (1993). Single-system research design content in the doctoral curriculum. *Research on Social Work Practice*, 3, 414–419.

Cooper, M. (1990). Treatment of a client with obsessive-compulsive disorder. *Social Work Research and Abstracts,* 26(2), 26–32.

Corcoran, K.J. (1993). Practice evaluation: Problems and promises of single-system designs in clinical practice. *Journal of Social Service Research*, 18, 147–160.

Firstman, R. and Talan, J. (1997). *The death of innocents: A true story of murder*. New York: Bantam Books.

Fischer, J. and Corcoran, K. (1994) *Measures for clinical practice.* New York: Free Press.

Gilgun, J.F. (1994). A case for case studies in social work research. *Social Work*, 39, 371–380.

Kazdin, A.E. (1992). *Research design in clinical psychology*. Boston: Allyn and Bacon.

Kazi, M. and Wilson, J.T. (1996). Applying single-case evaluation methodology in a British social work agency. *Research on Social Work Practice*, 6, 5–26.

Kopp, J. (1988). Self-monitoring: A literature review of research and practice. *Social Work Research and Abstracts,* 24(4), 8–20.

Lucy, J.F. (1997) Editorial. *Pediatrics*, 100, A76–A77.

Mattaini, M. (1996). The abuse and neglect of single-case designs. *Research on Social Work Practice*, 6, 83–90.

Nelsen, J. (1994). Ethics, gender, and ethnicity in single-case research and evaluation. *Journal of Social Service Research*, 18, 139–152.

Nurius, P.S., and Hudson, W.W. (1993). *Human services practice, evaluation, and computers.* Pacific Grove, CA: Brooks/Cole.

Rubin, A. and Knox, K.S. (1996). Data and analysis problems in single-case evalua-
    tion: Issues for research on social work practice. *Research on Social Work
    Practice*, 6, 40–65.

Rymer, R. (1993). *Genie: An abused child's flight from silence*. New York:
    HarperCollins.

Slonim-Nevo, V. (1997). Evaluating practice: The dual roles of clinician and evalua-
    tor. *Families in Society*, 78, 232–239.

Steinschneider, A. (1972). Prolonged apnea and the sudden infant death syndrome:
    Clinical and laboratory observations. *Pediatrics*, 50, 646–654.

Sundel, M., and Sundel, S.S. (1993). *Behavior modification in the human services: A
    systematic introduction to concepts and applications*. Newbury Park, CA: Sage.

Thyer, B.A. and Thyer, K.B. (1992). Single-system designs in social work practice: A
    bibliography from 1965 to 1990. *Research on Social Work Practice,* 2(1), 99–116.

Tripodi, T. (1994). *A primer on single-subject design for clinician social workers*.
    Washington, DC: NASW Press.

CHAPTER 4
Research Designs for Group Comparisons

Single subject designs (SSDs) are impractical on a large scale. If you are the director of a community agency that provided a recreational program to seven hundred fifty young people last summer, you probably would not want to look at more than seven hundred SSDs in order to evaluate the program's success. The problems of possible ambiguity and your staff's selection of diverse and wildly different target behaviors aside, single subject designs in this instance would be the wrong research tool because the focus is no longer on a particular client but on the larger group.

The research designs contained in this chapter are the approaches commonly used for program evaluation and basic research in the social sciences. The results they report are concerned with group averages, not with an individual client's success. In the stronger group designs, one group is provided with an intervention, and these results are compared to a control group that does not receive any treatment. The essence of these designs, in many respects, is an evaluation based upon comparison to another group.

Few of us would want to hire a carpenter who is skilled only with the use of a hammer. While this is important knowledge, it is also essential to know something about the other tools that carpenters need. Similarly, single system designs will not always be the right tool for every research occasion. There are many times when we need to aggregate data in order to understand to what extent a group, program, or community benefited from our services. Group research designs are particularly appropriate for those who work with various systems, agencies, and communities and are involved with administration of programs, community development, and social policy analysis. Direct service social workers often find that they need a knowledge of group research designs in order to develop evaluation procedures when they apply for grants or wish to test hypotheses about specific interventions.

Choosing the Right Design

Numerous research designs can be used to guide research projects, and choosing the right one is somewhat analogous to picking out a new car. The primary consideration may be how much money you have or how big a monthly payment you can manage. The researcher must also consider how much has been budgeted for the research. Design issues related to finances are: use of staff time (for example, making follow-up contacts with clients in person or by phone); postage, telephone, or travel expenses; purchase of copyrighted instruments or scales; computer processing of the data; use of consultants; and so on. These and other variables contribute to the cost of the project.

While the car buyer considers what optional equipment is really necessary, the researcher decides which facets of the study are essential. For instance, the researcher may believe that the success of the intervention should be determined by expensive in-home personal interviews instead of mailed questionnaires.

Besides the issue of cost, car buyers and researchers must simultaneously consider other variables. Both are presented with decisions about no-frills, low-prestige models. The experimental designs that we will talk about are highly respected, but there are other less rigorous designs that are often adequate. Sometimes automobiles are chosen because their styling or color will turn heads; researchers desire good response rates and instruments that produce reliable findings. And while the car buyer may consider how long a particular vehicle might be expected to last, the researcher must give thought to the amount of time that he or she wishes the study to run.

In summary, various motives or considerations have a bearing on the choice of a research design. No one design will be applicable or correct in every situation. The design is dependent upon the nature of the problem being investigated, the availability of clients or other data, monetary and staff resources, the amount of time one has to complete the project, and the purpose of the research (is it for internal agency use or do you need to convince skeptical colleagues outside of the agency?).

Research strategies are most often developed from the specific objectives of the study and the nature of the presenting problem. Social work researchers generally move from interest in a problem to the selection of a design. Seldom would one choose a design and then look for a problem to investigate.

Experimental Research

The classic experimental design is the "ideal," the model to which other research designs are compared. Even though the opportunities to conduct true experiments may not often come your way, the experimental design remains the standard when it is important to be as scientific as possible. Other designs in this chapter are discussed in terms of how close they come to the "ideal."

For many social workers, the notion of experimentation involving human subjects brings to mind misconceptions about unethical, painful, or presumably painful stimuli (for example, the controversial Milgram experiments) being inflicted upon unsuspecting persons in a climate-controlled laboratory. These notions are best forgotten. Today there is much greater concern for and widespread protection of the rights of persons participating in research than in the past.

The federal government requires institutional review boards to oversee research being funded with federal money and involving human subjects. These committees (sometimes called human subject committees) often go to great lengths to insure that potential research participants know that their participation is completely voluntary. Even more safeguards must be in place when subjects are considered vulnerable (for example, children, prisoners, clients of counseling services) or when deception is required. We'll discuss these procedures and ethical guidelines for researchers in chapter 12.

What is an experiment? Simply stated, it is a controlled study where clients or subjects are randomly assigned to a group (sometimes called a condition) where they will receive a new (or different) intervention from those designated to be in the control group. Individuals in the control condition may receive the customary or usual treatment for comparison with the new one. The notion of random assignment is crucial—it prevents a number of **extraneous** (unwanted, confounding) **variables** and biases from interfering with the researcher's ability to make a conclusion about the strength or weakness of the intervention.

It may be helpful at this point to briefly discuss an example of relevant experimental research. Barber and Gilbertson (1996) conducted a study examining the effectiveness of three different interventions for partners of heavy drinkers. The Pressures to Change approach coached partners in how to assist drinkers in changing their drinking behavior; some clients were assigned to receive this instruction by individual counseling and others by group instruction. A third group was involved with Al-Anon, which places primary emphasis on improving the quality of life for those living with the drinker. A fourth group, the control, was placed on a waiting list until the conclusion of the study.

Clients recruited through a newspaper were screened for eligibility. To be eligible, drinkers had to score above the threshold for dependence on the family form of the Short Michigan Alcoholism Screening Test. At the conclusion of the study, Barber and Gilbertson found that none of the drinkers whose partners had been assigned to Al-Anon or to the control group had sought help, cut down, or quit drinking. This was in contrast with four partners each in the individual and group interventions who reported drinkers who sought help. The authors concluded the Pressures to Change approach was an effective intervention to help resistant drinkers. However, Al-Anon as well as the individual presentation of the intervention produced substantive reductions in the number of personal problems reported by clients whose partners were drinking.

The Classic Experimental Research Design

True experiments are the most rigorous of research designs and the ones that best permit casual inferences to be made. These designs have two main features that distinguish them from other designs: clients (or subjects) who participate in the experiment are randomly selected (defined as the absence of bias; allowing chance to play the role of selecting clients) and assigned to either the group that gets the intervention (the *experimental group)* or the group that gets no intervention (the *control group*).

The shorthand notation for the classic **pretest-posttest control group design** is often written as follows:

$$R \quad O_1 \quad X \quad O_2$$
$$R \quad O_3 \quad \quad O_4$$

The R in this notation scheme stands for the random assignment of clients to either the experimental or the control group; the X represents the intervention. Observations, measurements, or assessments of each group are made twice. The first observation (O_1) is called the **pretest,** and the second observation (O_2) is called the **posttest.** This design provides information not only about changes in the group that receives the intervention, but also comparable information from the group that does not get intervention. What kind of changes would the true experiment pick up? This depends entirely on the dependent variable or variables the researcher has chosen and the way they have been operationalized. Random assignment *must* occur prior to the intervention. One should never begin a treatment and then if clients are not improving, assign them to the control group.

As an example of this design, suppose you are a medical social worker assigned to a dialysis clinic. Let's further assume that the management of anxiety is a major problem for patients in the clinic. You decide to start a support group for anxious patients because you believe it will help alleviate some of their health concerns. Because you are limited in the amount of time you can allocate for this project, you want to start small with about twenty-five patients. Since this is a large dialysis clinic with hundreds of patients, there is no problem in finding willing participants. In keeping with the experimental pretest-posttest control group design, you randomly select twenty-five dialysis patients for the support group and randomly assign an approximate number to the control group. Next, you use a standardized measure like the Clinical Anxiety Scale (Thyer, 1984) to determine the anxiety level of both groups prior to the start of the intervention. The support group begins and runs its normal course (six to eight weeks). Afterwards, you administer the instrument a second time to both groups and make comparisons. Has the average level of anxiety in the experimental group decreased? Has the average amount of anxiety in the control group remained about the same or increased? Finally, is the level of anxiety in the experimental group less than in the control group? If so, then you have some evidence that the intervention was effective.

This is a strong design because the group that receives no intervention provides a "control" for possible alternative explanations for the effect on the experimental group. (Random selection of subjects makes the group equivalent before the intervention begins. For instance, if clients tend to make better decisions because they grow wiser with the passage of time (maturation) and not because of the intervention, then the control group would also show similar improvement or outcome. There would be little reason to believe that the intervention was responsible for any changers if the same changes were also found in the control group.)

The Posttest Only Control Group Design

A second true experiment design, the **posttest only control group design,** is handy for those situations where a pretest might affect the posttest results or when it is not possible to conduct a pretest. This design is also useful in situations where anonymity is paramount—so it would not be possible to compare an individual's pretest and posttest scores.

Campbell and Stanley (1963) note that there is a common misconception that pretests are always needed in an experimental design. Not so, they say. Early experimental designs in agriculture did not make much use of pretests. As with the previous design, random selection and assignment of subjects establish the initial equivalence between the experimental and control groups. Measurement of the control group (O_2) then serves as a pretest measure for comparison with the experimental group's posttest (O_1).

$$R \quad X \quad O_1$$
$$R \qquad\;\; O_2$$

As an example of this design, consider the following problem. Counseling agencies often find that 30 percent or more of scheduled appointments result in "no-shows" or last minute cancellations. Productive or "billable" time is lost, which can seriously affect the revenue needed to operate an agency. Suppose you have a hypothesis that the 30 percent no-show rate could be reduced by the agency's receptionist calling clients to remind them of their

---

Practice Note: Cancer Prevention

Colorectal cancer is health concern for middle-aged and older adults and their loved ones. More than 50,000 Americans die from this disease each year although it is treatable. Screening with a fecal occult blood test detects the cancer in its early stages when treatment is most effective and is recommended for persons over the age of fifty, those with a history of polyps or inflammatory bowel disease, those who have a close relative with the disease, a change in bowel habits, or weight loss. Historically, persons with low education and income, the elderly, and those with inadequate medical insurance have low participation rates in colorectal screening.

Plaskon and Fadden (1995) designed a posttest only experiment to test if a combination of a physician talking about the benefits of screening and provision of a free test kit would increase participation in screening. In a rural area known for high rates of colorectal cancer, experimental and control group assignment were determined by the contents of an envelope given from the top of a stack left with the receptionist. Both the experimental and the control group received educational materials and a talk by the physician on the importance of screening. The control group was informed that they could pick up a test kit at the desk. The intervention group was given the test kit in their envelopes.

Within a week of their appointment, all subjects were called or mailed a questionnaire to ask whether they had used the fecal occult blood test. The findings: very few of the control group had asked for a test kit and none of them had actually used it while 51 percent of the intervention group had utilized their screening kit.

---

scheduled appointments. The group receiving the phone calls would constitute the experimental group. Those clients who do not receive a reminder constitute the control group. Membership in either the experimental or control group would be randomly determined. (For instance, even-numbered clients scheduled for an appointment during the first week of March would be assigned to the experimental group and would get a reminder. Odd-numbered clients would be assigned to the control group.) At the end of the study period, the cancellation rates for the two groups could be compared.

The Solomon Four-Group Design

The third true experiment design is called the Solomon four-group design. As you can see from the notation below, it is composed of the basic experimental design plus the posttest only control group design. This is an elaborate, sophisticated design that social workers may not often have the opportunity to utilize because of the logistics involved with the creation and maintaining of four different groups.

$$R \quad O_1 \quad X \quad O_2$$
$$R \quad O_3 \quad \quad O_4$$
$$R \quad \quad X \quad O_5$$
$$R \quad \quad \quad O_6$$

This design provides two opportunities for the treatment effect to be demonstrated. The design's strong point, however, is that the investigator can maximally control for alternative explanations and thus increase the confidence that can be placed in the findings. While this is a rigorous design and provides greater confidence that the intervention produced any observed changes, the tradeoff for this certainty is greater difficulty in coordinating and implementing the design.

Reid and Finchilescu (1995) have reported an interesting application of a Solomon four-group design to measure the effects on women of violence against women as portrayed in film. Female college students in Group 1 completed a disempowerment scale, watched film clips from such films as *The Burning Bed* (which showed a woman being assaulted by her husband), and completed the disempowerment scale. Group 2 was the same as Group 1 except that they saw film clips of violence against men (from such movies as *Point Break*). Group 3 saw the violence against women clips and completed a posttest. Group 4 saw the violence against men clips and completed the disempowerment posttest scale.

The researchers found that completing the disempowerment scale before the viewing did not sensitize the group who were shown violence against women, and that the experimental group revealed significantly more feelings of disempowerment than did the group who watched clips of violence against men. In other words, female participants experienced an increase in feelings of disempowerment after viewing film depicting women as victims of violence. If this research is confirmed by additional studies, what implications do you see concerning the media's portrayal of violence?

Internal and External Validity

To keep the explanation of the single system design in chapter 3 uncomplicated, I used the terms *alternative explanations* and *competing explanations* to refer to those unplanned or unexpected variables that might have had an effect upon the observed outcome. However, now we need to discuss the internal and external validity of studies to more fully understand the strengths and weaknesses of the various research designs for group comparisons. The following section is presented to help you think about the variables that can influence your study and make it difficult to determine if your intervention was effective. As you learn more about research, you will develop an appreciation for factors (not limited to those below) that can interfere with your study. Keep in mind that this discussion of internal and external validity is equally applicable to the single system designs.

Campbell and Stanley (1963) and Cook and Campbell (1979) are prominent in social science research because of their conceptualization of research designs. Their books are classic texts on the topic, and few research methodology texts have not cited their work. Besides identifying a host of experimental, quasi-experimental, and pre-experimental research designs (more about these a little later), these authors contributed much to our understanding of internal and external validity.

Threats to the **internal validity** of a study (that is, whether the intervention was truly responsible for the observed differences in the dependent variable) come from **extraneous variables** (those not purposely incorporated into the experiment). Studies with greater interval validity allow the researcher to rule out alternative explanations and rival hypotheses. Studies with less interval validity cannot control (account for) the effect of extraneous variables on the experimental group.

Major Threats to Internal Validity

1. *Maturation.* Growing older or different rates of growth within two comparison groups are examples of an influence that researchers should be cognizant of and attempt to control as much as possible. Certainly, there is a lot of difference between kindergarteners at the beginning of the school year and at its end. Why? Because they have grown older and been socialized into the culture of "student." Similarly, anyone who has been hurt when a relationship breaks up knows that there is a lot of truth to the adage, "Time heals all wounds." The simple passage of time is an alternative explanation that should not be discounted when gauging the effects of an intervention that runs over several weeks or months. The longer the intervention, the more likely that maturation (the passage of time) may play a role. Another example: sometimes our clients cease certain long-established behaviors not because of any special intervention they received but because they become too old to hustle, or they are not as fleet-footed and no longer have the athletic quickness to avoid arrest. Clients sometimes change for reasons independent of the intervention they've received.

2. *History.* This refers to the specific events that occur between the pretest and posttest that were not part of the researcher's design and that could

influence the results (for example, national crises, tragedies, or historical events; or, on a local level, a large factory laying off hundreds of employees—including some of those in your study). For instance, if you were trying to evaluate the impact of an AIDS prevention program, and a national celebrity made his public announcement during the study period, this would constitute a threat to the internal validity.

History is not an event like a personal history of abuse, and not usually considered a threat when something happens to a single client in a group. However, if a treatment group is well established (there is a strong sense of "the group"), and one of the members commits suicide—then history is a viable threat to the internal validity of the study. Group members may be adversely affected and lose the progress they had made. Or, they might pull together in a way that was completely unexpected and make gigantic strides—more than they would have made without the suicide. History is an internal threat because once it happens, the investigator doesn't know whether it was the intervention or the event that caused the improvement. If there is no improvement, was it because of the suicide or because the intervention was ineffective? There is no good way to know when a study has weak internal validity.

3. *Testing.* Taking a test on more than one occasion can affect later test scores. Repeated testing provides practice and in itself can improve test scores. If clients' scores improve over time, but they were measured six times with the same scale, was the improvement because they figured out what you were measuring or because interventions made a difference? The threat of testing is sometimes known as the practice effect. The influence of testing can also be a factor when pretests sensitize subjects to issues or attitudes and cause some reflection so that subjects' responses change as a result of measurement and not intervention. Instruments can also be too difficult or too lengthy; subjects can get bored (test fatigue) and may not pay careful attention to how they respond. If it is anticipated that testing may be a problem, then researchers can choose designs to assess it (Solomon four-group) or eliminate the pretests (posttest only control group design).

4. *Instrumentation.* This refers to changes in the use of the measuring instrument, in the way the instrument is scored, in procedures during the study, or in the way the dependent variable is counted or measured. Suppose you administer a timed test to some students, and because you are not paying attention, you give them five fewer minutes at the posttest than they had at the pretest. You have created a situation where the intervention will likely look less powerful than it really is. (Because they had fewer minutes to complete the test, double-check their answers, and so forth, their scores will be lower.) Conversely, if you accidentally give them too much time—maybe you were interrupted by a phone call—then you might conclude that the intervention was more effective that it actually is. Not administering the instruments

according to directions and not training staff on how to collect the data can result in inaccurate reporting. Another instrumentation problem would be to change instruments and use different ones at posttest than were used at pretest.

5. *Selection of respondents.* This threat to internal validity stems from any bias that causes the experimental and control groups to be different from each other or to be different from those individuals in the larger population that they should represent. For instance, suppose you have come up with a new intervention for parents who are having difficulty getting along with their teenagers. You purchase an advertisement in the paper that says: "Having trouble communicating with your teenager? Call 321-6543 for information on a free parents' group at Shiloh Baptist Church on Wednesday evenings." How does the ad create a selection problem? First of all, some parents who are having trouble with their teens may not respond because they can't read, or don't subscribe to the newspaper. Other parents needing the intervention may not respond because they don't like the idea of discussing their problems in a group. So who would be most likely to respond to the ad? Possibly better educated, more assertive people; individuals who may be somewhat outgoing or at least comfortable in social situations—certainly, *motivated* parents. A researcher who uses such an ad has to remain cognizant that the parents in his or her study may not represent all parents who are having trouble communicating with their teens. If the intervention works well, then the researcher may want to find a group of less motivated parents (for example, parents who were court-ordered to participate) to see if the intervention works equally well with them. Selection is nearly always a concern because of self-selection when clients choose one agency over another or this treatment modality and not that one. This threat to the internal validity of a study is best handled by random sampling from the population of interest. However, this is not always possible, and researchers quite often have to admit that their studies have limitations (may not generalize well to the larger population or other geographical areas) because of the way their subjects were chosen or selected.

6. *Statistical regression.* This refers to the selection of subjects who were chosen because of extreme scores. There is a tendency for extreme scores to move toward the group average on a second testing. For instance, think about a situation where you scored a perfect 100 percent on your first test in research methods. Even though you may be a very bright individual, it will be a lot easier for you to do not as well on the second test than it will be to score 100 again. So even if you obtain a 95 on the second test, your score will have regressed. Similarly, if you score 15 on the first test, it is likely that you will improve on the second test. Statistical regression as an internal threat to the validity of a study means this: subjects who were chosen because of low pretest scores can be expected to have higher scores at posttest because of statistical regression. As a researcher, you can't prevent this occurrence, but you can measure it when there is random assignment and a control group. (The

amount of improvement that the control group shows is likely to be due to statistical regression. This can then be subtracted from the amount of improvement shown by the experimental group in order to understand the impact of the intervention.

7. *Mortality.* Also known as attrition, this threat to internal validity refers to the loss of respondents (for example, they terminate services, move out of town, get sick, or simply just drop out of the study). The loss of subjects may change the overall group complexion and may produce differences in the data at the posttest that have nothing to do with the intervention.

Think about a scenario where you are running a group for nine sixth-grade boys who are behavior problems in the classroom. The intervention is going well, but for one reason or another the group dwindles to four participants by the end of the school year. While all four showed definite improvement, what about the five who dropped out or moved to other school districts? Had they been present at the posttest, would you still have been able to conclude the intervention was a success? A major loss of subjects from a study can undermine whatever conclusion the researcher is prepared to make regarding the effectiveness of the intervention. Social work researchers have to be aware that individuals in the control group are at risk for dropping out of the study or may be unavailable at posttest. Because they are less involved with the study by nature of the fact that they are receiving no intervention, they may be less motivated to participate in posttesting. Especially when testing procedures are lengthy or demanding, incentives like coupons or small gifts may be necessary to keep subject mortality from being a problem. Here's another tip that might help: some researchers have discovered that mailing out birthday and holiday cards is a useful way to stay in contact with study participants when attrition might be a problem. Since the post office will forward mail for only one year, mailing twice a year keeps addresses current.

8. *Interaction effects.* This occurs when any of the extraneous variables interact with one another. In a selection and maturation interaction, the subjects in one group may mature at a faster rate than those in the comparison group. In a selection and mortality interaction, there could be differences in motivational level or severity of psychiatric illness between the groups, with resulting differential dropout rates. By the study's end, the groups could look vastly different—and not because of the intervention. Another example could be that the demands on subjects at pretest could force many to reconsider their participation—forcing a selection and mortality interaction. There are many possible interactions with extraneous variables that complicate the investigator's ability to understand the true impact of the intervention.

Threats to the internal validity of a study are like viruses that can infect and weaken it. They sap the confidence that you as a researcher have in the finding that it was the intervention, and only the intervention, that was responsible for any improvement in clients' lives.

The use of any experimental design will help you gauge the extent of any of these threats to the internal validity of your study. It is the use of randomization and a control group that allows the investigator to determine if any extraneous variable has exerted an unexpected influence. For instance, if you notice an unexpected improvement in the control group, you might suspect that an extraneous variable (such as history, maturation, or testing) had an effect upon the study.

When you have considered these eight threats and ruled them out as having produced an effect, then you have established that your study has internal validity. You can now conclude with some confidence that the intervention was responsible for (caused) the observed changes. Then, if you want to ensure that the findings from your study can be generalized to different subjects or settings, you should consider the threats to the external validity of the study.

Campbell and Stanley (1963) must also be given credit for identifying several ways in which the **external validity** (the generalizability or representativeness of the study) can be threatened. External validity is important if you want to convince others that your study or experiment has produced a major scientific discovery.

In those situations where you are evaluating a local or specific program, it might *not* be important to you to demonstrate external validity. In this instance, you are concerned only with whether treatment worked in a specific program—you may not be interested in generalizing your results to their communities or subjects because your program is not like any others.

On the other hand, if you are concerned with generalization and obtaining maximum credibility, you'll want to use an experimental design and attempt to anticipate all the potential threats to the internal and external validity of your study. In particular, you will want to pay attention to:

1. *Reactive or interactive effect of testing.* This occurs when a pretest affects the respondent's sensitivity or awareness to important variables associated with the study. The pretest could make the subjects unrepresentative of the population from which they were drawn by raising their consciousness or by stimulating new learning, or simply because they realize that they are involved in a study. This threat should seem familiar to you because it is the same as the internal validity threat of testing.

2. *Interaction effects of selection biases and any research stimulus.* These occur when there are problems getting a random sample. If you are conducting a study that requires in-depth interviews of two or three hours in duration, the majority of persons you contact might turn you down and not participate. Those who agree to the interview may not be representative of the larger population—they have volunteered when most others have not. They may have some traits or

characteristics (for example, they are lonely) that make them less representative and therefore affect the generalizability of the study.

3. *Reactive effects of arrangements.* This has to do with the experiment being conducted in a setting that is different from the subject's usual experience. Subjects' behavior may change because of the different environment. Subjects may be more productive or more wary and nervous. They may behave in a way not indicative of their normal style. (Would your behavior change if you knew that you were being videotaped or observed through a two-way mirror?)

4. *Multiple-treatment interaction.* This becomes a problem when there is more than one intervention. The researcher needs to be sure that the same timing, sequence, or order is followed for each subject. Multiple treatments may have a cumulative effect, which could make reaching conclusions about a specific intervention difficult.

Researchers who want to generalize their findings beyond the setting in which they conducted the study need to be concerned that: (a) subjects in the study are representative of other clients with the problem or the population to which they are being compared; (b) the intervention is not vague but well-defined and structured (as in a psychoeducational group with a definite curriculum to be followed); and (c) staff uniformly deliver the intervention in the same way using the same approaches, theoretical orientations, and emphases.

Those who will read your research and want to implement the intervention must be given sufficient detail to replicate the study. Without critical information about the characteristics of your clients (for example, are they first-time or multi-offenders?), your staff (were they MSWs with at least five years of experience or graduate students?), and the nature of your intervention (did the group meet twice a week for a total of three hours weekly or once a month?), those who attempt to replicate your study may not achieve the same results. This would be most unfortunate if you had a successful intervention, but because you failed to provide sufficient explanation about it, the staff, or the clients, assumptions were made that resulted in another researcher using a weaker or diluted version of the intervention or choosing a tougher client population and then encountering a lack of success.

In summary, there are always distinct threats to a study's internal and external validity. Experimental research designs use random selection and assignment of subjects to comparison groups to help the researcher monitor and understand the threats to internal validity. As a rule, the more control you have over the situation or experiment, the greater the internal validity. However, there is a corresponding cost in terms of external validity.

As greater effort is made to control for possible influences upon the subjects or in the experimental setting, the investigator runs the risk of creating a situation that is vastly different from the way most programs of a similar type would be run in real life. Sometimes it is comforting to realize that all studies have some limitations or weaknesses. Research with actual clients and in real social service agencies often means that compromises have to be made.

Not too long ago, I learned of an evaluation being conducted of a family preservation program. Families in crisis were randomly assigned to the special intensive intervention or to a control group that received the usual services provided by the agency. After the death of a child whose family was receiving the customary (not intensive) services, a decision was made to end the random assignment. The control group from that point on consisted of persons who refused or dropped out of the family preservation services. While this is better than having no control group at all, the obvious and discernable differences in the two client groups makes it much more difficult to gauge the actual impact of family preservation services. These are the kinds of things that can happen when research is conducted not in the laboratory but in the "field."

Pre-Experimental Designs

Suppose you are a counselor in an agency and are working with a group of shy individuals. You have developed an approach that, over the course of ten meetings, significantly alleviates shyness. You administer a shyness inventory to the group on its first meeting, and the average score for the group is 135. From the scores and your clinical impressions, you know that this group is extremely shy. Your group meets ten times, and you administer a posttest on the last session. You find that the group's average score has gone down to 62, which indicates major improvement.

This type of design does not have the complexity of an experiment. Since subjects are not randomly selected or assigned to either a treatment or a control group, this design is popular and often used in evaluations of social service programs. This design (which is similar to the AB design) is called the **one-group pretest-posttest design** and can be designated with the notation:

$$O_1 \quad X \quad O_2$$

Here, again, the O_1 represents the pretest measurement or observation and the O_2 the posttest.

Even though you, as a clinician, have seen major improvement in the individuals of the group, this design cannot rule out alternative explanations for the changes. It cannot rule out the internal validity threats of history, maturation, testing, instrumentation, statistical regression or the interaction of selection and maturation. Any of these extraneous variables may have produced the changes in the shyness inventory. Without a control group, it is impossible to say that these threats did not have an effect. The researcher, however, may be able to rule out some of these threats because of the particular situation or context within which the study occurred. Although this is a weak design, it serves a purpose when no control group is available for comparison.

If there were no pretest data associated with the earlier study of shy individuals, the resulting design would be the **one-group posttest only design.**

$$X \quad O_1$$

With this design, an intervention is delivered, and later, observations are recorded in order to determine the intervention's outcome. This design stipulates only that you make an observation after the intervention. If you were working with the group of shy individuals described above, this design would require only a posttest after the intervention. Since there would have been no pretest for comparison, the average posttest score of 62 does not provide much information. With no data available for comparison, any perceptions of a reduction in shyness are unsubstantiated. Instead of the intervention having an effect on shyness, extraneous variables such as selection, history, maturation, or mortality may have contributed to any perceived effect after treatment.

With the one-group posttest only design there is the presumption of an effect. Sometimes, however, you can see an effect more clearly—especially if you are conducting a study of a problem that is behavioral (for example, you have a group of clients who are trying to quit drinking). If the group reported after ten weeks that they weren't drinking, you would be pleased and willing to take the credit. Indeed, your colleagues probably would have no difficulty attributing the cessation of drinking to the intervention. However, the "success" might have been due to spouses or mates threatening to leave if loved ones didn't stop drinking, bosses threatening to fire inebriated employees, court appearances for driving while intoxicated, or a combination of several factors. Again, without a control group, it is difficult to know the extent to which extraneous factors are influencing the outcome.

A third pre-experimental design is called the **posttest only design with nonequivalent groups.** It is expressed:

$$X \quad O_1$$
$$O_2$$

This design is an improvement over the previous two in that the control group functions as a pretest condition and can be compared with the group that receives the intervention. While it may seem logical to infer that any observed differences are due to the intervention, this is debatable, since we cannot assume that the two groups were similar prior to the intervention (there was no random assignment to the groups). As a consequence, differences between O_1 and O_2 may be due to their nonequivalence in the beginning and not to the effect of intervention.

By way of example, think of the population of women who have been battered by their partners. Assume we want to know if service programs connected with a shelter for battered women are instrumental in helping these women avoid returning to abusive situations. Of the battered women who contact the shelter, some request shelter services, while others request information about child custody, jobs, and police protection, and soon attempt to leave abusive situations on their own without spending time in the shelter. There are, then, two groups of women with the same basic problem. One group gets the intervention (the shelter) and its counseling services, while the other group does not. For the purpose of follow-up research to determine how many women were living in abusive situations one year later, would these two groups be equivalent? I think not. They may differ in the amount of financial resources at their disposal (those who don't stay at the shelter may have more money), in the extent of family or social support systems, and possibly with regard to the severity of the abuse experienced.

These two groups of women may be convenient groupings in terms of trying to determine the impact of a battered women's shelter but if it were later found that a greater proportion of the women who used the shelter's services than of women who didn't were still in abusive situations, what does this say about the shelter's services? It would be risky to conclude that the shelter was in some way responsible for its clients returning to abusive situations. While it may appear that women who avoid the shelter are more successful in not returning to abusive situations, we must keep in mind that the two groups of women may not have been equivalent even though they shared a common problem. In fact, we might expect differences in the two groups even before our data are aggregated. Of course, the more similar (or homogeneous) the two groups are, the more comfortable everyone will be that the intervention did have an effect. The absence of randomization makes this design weak; we are unable to rule out such internal validity threats as those of selection, mortality, and interaction among variables (such as selection and maturation).

Kidder and Judd (1986) say that these three pre-experimental designs are examples of *how not to do research* if there are alternatives. Fortunately, alternatives exist—they are called quasi-experimental designs.

Quasi-Experimental Designs

Quasi-experimental designs are those that fall a little short of the "ideal." Often in agency settings, it is not acceptable or possible to randomly assign clients to one of several treatment modalities (or to a control group receiving no intervention). When randomization cannot be done, the researcher should consider quasi-experimental designs.

> **Practice Note: Group Work with Survivors of
> Child Sexual Abuse**
>
> Studies on adults who experienced childhood sexual abuse show
> that depression, low self-esteem, and a host of other problems (alcohol
> and drug abuse, relationship problems) are common. Therapeutic
> groups combat isolation and stigmatization by allowing survivors to
> safely share their histories in a milieu where what they say is valued and
> beneficial to others. Richter, Snider, and Gorey (1997) used a *quasi-
> experimental design* to evaluate the results of intervention. One hundred
> and fifteen women volunteered. Thirty-five of these went immediately
> to groups facilitated by an experienced MSW, which met weekly for fif-
> teen consecutive sessions of one-and-a-half to two hours. The other
> eighty women were placed on a waiting list and waited an average of
> four weeks to get service. These women served as a nonrandomized
> comparison group.
>
> The authors found that survivors who completed the group work
> intervention were significantly less depressed as measured by the Beck
> Depression Inventory and Generalized Contentment Scale and had sig-
> nificantly improved self-esteem compared with their counterparts on
> the waiting list. At a six-month follow-up, more than 80 percent of the
> intervention group had lower levels of depression and higher self-
> esteem than the average for those on the waiting list.

The **nonequivalent control group design** has been called the "arche-
typal quasi-experimental design" because it is the most internally valid design
that can be implemented in most applied settings (Judd and Kenny, 1981). It
is also one of the most commonly used quasi-experimental designs.

The notation for nonequivalent control group design is:

$$O_1 \quad X \quad O_2$$
$$O_3 \qquad O_4$$

In this design, a control group is used, just as with the experimental
design. However, there is no randomization. Usually a convenient natural
group (for example, another class of fifth graders, another AA group, another
group of shy clients) is selected that is similar but may not be equivalent to
the group receiving the intervention. Just as with the previous design, the control group consists of clients who have been chosen because they possess certain characteristics. The control group can come from those clients on a waiting list for service, clients receiving alternative services from the same agency
or from another similar agency, or even from nonclients.

Researchers often attempt to match the two groups on important variables (such as, age, socio-economic status, drug use history). As you can imagine, matching is difficult because of the number of variables that could be involved. A major problem with matching is that observed differences between the control and intervention groups at the end of the experiment may have been due to the influence of unmatched variables. When you must match, the best advice is to match the groups on as many of the relevant variables as possible. Equivalence is not guaranteed with matching, but it does serve to approximate equivalency. When random assignment is not possible, matching is a good alternative.

With this design, it is usually plausible to assume that the treatment produced the effect. Like the experiment, this design does provide the investigator with the ability to monitor internal validity threats such as those from testing, maturation, instrumentation, history, and mortality. The main threat to this design's internal validity comes from interaction of selection with maturation, with history, or with testing, since random assignment wasn't used (so there was no guarantee of equivalency). Still, this design is better than the pre-experimental designs because of the use of a control group. The more similar the control and the experimental groups, the more confidence you can have in your findings.

As an example of this design, consider the problem of relapse among the chronically mentally ill. You want to know whether those patients who are served by your state-run hospital stay as long in the community as those in a similar institution in a different part of the state. With the cooperation of both hospital administrators, you make comparisons of such variables as staff-to-patient ratios, percentage of first-time admissions, and average age of patients in order to establish that the patients and the facilities are roughly equivalent.

Suppose you find out that the patients from your hospital do seem to have longer stays in the community than patients of the other hospital. You might conclude that the programming or staff at your hospital is better. However, this design cannot unequivocally demonstrate this. It could be that more of the clients in the other hospital return to rural areas, where there is not the same level of community support services (aftercare) as is available to the patients from your hospital (who tend to remain in an urban area). There could be differences in staff morale at the two hospitals (which might affect the treatment received by patients) or in the ease of readmission or screening procedures. Could differences in the physical facilities be a factor? So, while you can be bolstered by your patients' success, the dissimilarities in the hospitals prevent you from *conclusively* determining that the intervention obtained there is the main reason for the patients' longer stays in the community.

Another quasi-experimental design is called **time-series** or **interrupted time series.** This design is one of the older designs used in the natural sciences, but it has not been utilized extensively in the social sciences. The time-series design is an extension of the one-group pretest-posttest design, where there are a series of measurements taken before and after an intervention. This allows the researcher to understand trends and patterns in the data before the intervention is applied and then provides for continued monitoring for major changes. Notation for a time-series design is:

$$O_1 \quad O_2 \quad O_3 \quad X \quad O_4 \quad O_5 \quad O_6$$

With this design, the researcher is able to get a grasp on incremental changes (if any) in the study group's behavior prior to the intervention and then to determine if the change after intervention is greater or not. When possible, an equal number of measurements should be made before and after the intervention. Also, the period of time between the measurements should be comparable. Note that the period of time between intervals is determined by the researcher; it is not imposed from the design. The amount of time between O_1, O_2, and the other observations could be seven days, two weeks, or three months. This design is particularly well-suited for research in social policy when historical or archival data are available. Each observation could then represent a year's data. For instance, you might monitor the number of suicides or homicides from handguns in a city three years before and three years after passage of a new ordinance requiring a five-day "cooling off" period before purchase of a handgun.

On a smaller scale, one might use the time-series design to look at staff productivity before and after the executive director implements a new four-day, forty-hour workweek. When using the time-series design in this way, it is important to watch for seasonal variations. Would it be all right to compare January (O_1), February (O_2), and March (O_3) with June (O_4), July (O_5), and August (O_6)? This wouldn't be a fair comparison if there were lower productivity in the summer months. To protect against making a conclusion influenced by seasonal or other natural fluctuations in data, include enough observation periods to get a stable baseline. This may require getting more than just the three observation points suggested by the design.

When the data from time series are graphed (recall the AB designs in the last chapter), the slope of the line is often of assistance in understanding whether the observed effect was caused by the intervention. On a graph, you can readily determine if the magnitude or frequency of a behavior is increasing prior to and after an intervention. Because the measurements are obtained over an extended period of time, history is the chief threat to the internal validity of this design. A threat from testing might also be apparent in some instances.

This time-series design provides even better information if a corresponding control group can be added:

$$O_1 \quad O_2 \quad O_3 \quad X \quad O_4 \quad O_5 \quad O_6$$
$$O_1 \quad O_2 \quad O_3 \qquad O_4 \quad O_5 \quad O_6$$

This new design with a control group is called the **multiple time-series design.** It resembles a stretched out nonequivalent control group design. Campbell and Stanley (1963) recommend this design for research in school settings. It is a strong quasi-experimental design with no serious internal validity threats. The investigator can use the control group to check for the influence of history and to understand the effects of testing, maturation, mortality, and instrumentation.

For instance, prior to the passage of the Brady Law, which requires a five-day "cooling off" period before purchase of a handgun, an investigator could examine the number of homicides in a sample of cities or states with such legislation and compare this data to a control group of cities or states that did not have such legislation. You would expect fewer homicides, over time, in the sample having the greater regulation of handgun sales. Use of a control group allows the investigator to determine whether a decrease in homicides is part of a national trend toward less violence or whether it could be attributed to the legislation.

Advanced Designs

There are even more sophisticated designs that the social work researcher may want to use. **Factorial designs** are often employed when Intervention A is being compared to Intervention B and both vary along some other dimension (for example, frequency, intensity, or duration). In the factorial design below, the researcher is able to determine not only whether Intervention A is more effective than Intervention B, but also whether the factor of meeting more frequently results in even greater improvement than the weekly sessions. In figure 4.1, there are two treatments and two levels of frequency, making this a 2 x 2 factorial design. If clients could have been randomly assigned to groups that met every day, five days a week, then this would have been a 2 x 3 design. Although it is not shown in figure 4.1, random assignment is understood.

Figure 4.1 Factorial Design (2 x 2)

	Interventions	
Frequency	Intervention A Once Weekly	Intervention B Once Weekly
	Intervention A Twice Weekly	Intervention B Twice Weekly

Figure 4.2 A Crossover Design

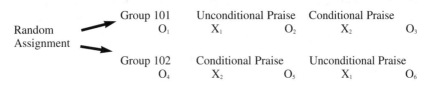

A major reason for using this design is so the investigator can look at the combined effect of two or more variables of interest (Kazdin, 1992). Within the same study, the investigator can assess the effects of separate factors (dependent variables) under different conditions—resulting in a savings of time and effort (compared to doing two different studies).

Crossover Designs

When clients are receiving more than one experimental treatment, the investigator may want to have the subjects switch places at a given point. In figure 4.2, men who have been arrested for battering their partners are randomly assigned to participate in either Group 101 or Group 102. Those in Group 101 receive praise and encouragement for every comment, vocalization, or question they raise. After four weeks, their counselors begin to reward with their verbal praise only those questions or comments where clients make an empathetic response regarding victims of abuse or express remorse. Facilitators in Group 102 start with the rewarding of empathetic and remorseful statements only and after four weeks they "cross over" and begin giving verbal praise for any comment, question, or vocalization. Assuming the goal was to increase the level of empathy in these men and that the investigator would be using a standardized instrument for her observations, this design lets the researcher determine which sequence produces the best overall results.

You can see in the example above that each group experiences three assessments. O_2 and O_5 do double duty, functioning both as posttests and as pretests at the beginning the second treatment.

There are many other variations of group research designs (such as a Latin Square for randomly ordering the sequence of multiple interventions) that some day you may want to use as a social work researcher. If you are feeling overwhelmed—that there are too many different designs to learn—it might be helpful to sort them into the three broad categories of pre-experimental, quasi-experimental, and experimental designs. And if that doesn't help remember this: Having many designs to choose from is certainly a better situation than having fewer models that don't fit your particular application. By analogy, you wouldn't want to be baking pizza and have only a muffin tin to bake it on.

Design and Validity Considerations

The main reason that researchers often choose experimental over pre-experimental or quasi-experimental designs is that they make causal inference easier. As a social work practitioner, you may have a notion that a certain intervention employed by you or your agency is more effective with clients than others. To test this hypothesis, you would probably choose one of the designs described in this chapter. Sometimes, however, social workers have questions like "Are parents of disabled children more likely to abuse their children than other parents?" Or, "Is alcoholism primarily responsible for the problem of homelessness?" Such basic research questions as these do not require experimental research designs. Rather, they are more likely to be explored using secondary data analysis (chapter 8) or a survey research design (chapter 6). The designs in this chapter are used to determine the impact or effect of an intervention used with groups.

As previously discussed, pre-experimental and quasi-experimental designs are susceptible to problems of internal validity. Yet, useful information and valuable studies can come from designs that are not truly experimental.

For example, if you are hired as a school social worker in an alternative school providing group therapy and support groups for adolescents with chemical dependency problems, random assignment may not be possible—the groups were started at the beginning of the school year. If you want to evaluate the success of these groups, the best design remaining might be the nonequivalent control group design. Even though experimental designs are the best, quasi-experimental designs should not be summarily dismissed, particularly when you are engaged in what I call "salvage" research (when you're trying to rescue data that otherwise might be lost).

In order to make your study as strong as possible, careful planning is required. Some threats to the internal validity of your study can be eliminated or minimized by following the suggestions of Mitchell and Jolley (1988):

1. Keep the time between the start and the end of the study short. This helps minimize the threat of *history*. (Note that this suggestion does not apply to time-series designs.) Also, keeping the study period short can help minimize the threat of *maturation* (especially a problem when studying children and youth), as well as any interaction of maturation with selection.

2. Test subjects only once or use different versions of the same test at posttest to minimize the threat of *testing.*

3. Train your assistants and administer the instrument the same way every time. (This helps minimize the threat of *instrumentation.*)

4. Use innocuous or placebo treatments, brief treatments, or mild incentives so that subjects do not drop out of the study. Keep in touch with those participating in your study—especially with those in the control group when there is a long period between observations. (This helps minimize the threat of *mortality.*)

5. Be careful with choosing subjects on the basis of one extreme test score. (This helps minimize the threat of *statistical regression.*)

6. Randomly assign where possible. If you must match, match on as many key variables as is practical. (This helps minimize the threat of *selection.*)

Thinking about ways of preventing extraneous variables from influencing (or explaining away) the effect of your intervention will result in a stronger study. While the selection of a good research design is important, it is no substitute for good planning. Even a strong design can be poorly implemented and go awry when little attention is paid to details. If, for instance, you lose most of your control group through neglect, even an experimental design will be of little assistance in helping you infer that the intervention caused the observed changes in the treatment group.

Research designs are only guides to the research process. They structure a problem-solving process and provide an outline for how data will be collected. Choice of a particular design is a complex decision often hinging upon feasibility considerations. Should you be faced with having to use a group research design sometime in the future, remember that there are numerous other designs (and multiple variations of the designs in this chapter) available to you. Regardless of the design you choose, devote time to considering how extraneous variables may affect the internal and external validity of your study.

Finally, we need to address the concerns that some social workers have about experimental designs that randomly relegate clients to control groups. Denying clients needed services would be unethical—no disagreement there. However, most often programs are evaluated by comparing them against another program such that clients in the experimental group would be getting a new or more intense intervention, while those in the control group would still receive the traditional treatment. The experimental intervention may not, in fact, be any better than the usual and customary treatment. It might even be less effective. In other words, there doesn't have to be a definite disadvantage to being in the control group.

Another way to think about this is that many agencies have waiting lists, and these form natural control groups. Those on the waiting lists can be administered pretests at the point of application for service and a posttest the same day they arrive for their first appointment. That posttest, by the way, is actually a second pretest or observation (O_2) and a third observation (the real posttest) would actually be taken toward the end of treatment to assess improvement. Additionally, persons on a waiting list might be given some mild form of intervention (such as educational pamphlets or videotapes) while they are waiting their turn for service. People naturally form themselves into control groups. Some men who batter would rather go to jail than attend a psycho-educational treatment program. Some men are released with community service, fined, or put on probation. Even if random assignment is not possible, comparison to some of these other groups, such as those who drop out of treatment, can still reveal cogent and compelling information.

Social work researchers are no less ethical than their colleagues who provide direct services. And, as you'll learn in chapter 12, a safeguard exists in that institutional review boards must approve human subject research if the agency or investigator has received federal funding. One of the key guidelines to which all approved research must abide is to cause no harm to those participating. Although it occurs in medical and pharmacological research much more often than in the social sciences, occasionally experiments are stopped when the early data convincingly show that the experimental approach is remarkably superior to the traditional method. When this happens, the control group is provided with the new intervention.

Randomization is not always possible even in the most research-friendly agencies. And when it is not feasible, comparison groups from other agencies or populations can be useful. Even the lowly pre-experimental designs have a role. As exploratory or pilot studies, they attempt to expand our knowledge about the interventions we use and their effects upon our clients. They may not be great studies, but they have the potential of providing some new knowledge that can be explored in greater depth and precision with a more powerful and rigorous design. In some instances, they provide all the evidence necessary to convince a foundation or funding source to underwrite a more extensive and scientific study.

Self-Review

(Answers at the end of the book)

1. Marsha has eighty clients meeting in grief counseling groups at a large hospice. At the end of each session she wants to administer a depression inventory. She's planning to evaluate these participants with eighty single system designs (AB). Is this an appropriate design?

2. What two features must a true experiment contain?
3. _____ variables are those that confound the researcher's ability to interpret the data.
4. T or F.   A posttest only design with random assignment meets the requirements for an experiment.
5. T or F.   Maturation is a possible threat to the interval validity of any study where the passage of time between pretest and subsequent observations is one or more years.
6. T or F.   Instrumentation is the name of the threat to internal validity where subjects are administered the same instrument on six different occasions.
7. T or F.   The use of volunteers, especially paid volunteers, should always suggest the possible threat to internal validity of selection.
8. T or F.   Statistical regression is where subjects at posttest score lower than they do at pretest *and* they were selected originally on the basis of their high pretest scores.
9. The following design is a true experiment:

$$O_1 \quad X \quad O_4$$
$$O_2 \quad\quad\quad O_3$$

10. What design in this chapter was said to be well-suited for social policy research?
11. T or F.   Both the factorial and crossover designs require randomization.
12. What would be the major problem with using an O X O design?

Questions for Class Discussion

1. What are the different pretest-posttest comparisons that can be made with the Solomon four-group design?
2. What kinds of experimental research do you think are needed or would you like to see conducted? Make a list of these.
3. Consider the threats to internal validity as presented in this chapter and discuss how they also may pose threats to single system designs.
4. Discuss how pragmatic considerations (the agency setting, its clientele) influence the choice of a research design. How do the possible implications or findings of the study affect the choice of a design?
5. Which two designs discussed in this chapter are identical except for the use of randomization?
6. How might the use of experimental designs in social service agencies involve ethical considerations?

7. Do you think practitioners who want to do research start with a spe-cific research design that they want to use or start with an interven-tion they want to evaluate and then seek a research design that fits the situation?
8. Discuss the arguments for choosing an experimental design over a quasi-experimental design to evaluate an intervention.

Mini-Projects for Experiencing Research Firsthand

1. Briefly describe a feasible study that could be conducted in a social service agency using one of the designs in this chapter. Be sure to identify it and to address each of the following:
   a. your hypothesis
   b. how you will acquire your subjects and how they will be ran-domly assigned
   c. your intervention
   d. your dependent variable (How would you operationalize it?)
2. Think about some controversial social problem (e.g., homelessness, teen pregnancy, drug abuse) and describe a grand social experiment that might test a hypothesis or a notion you have about how to ame-liorate the social problem. Specify a hypothesis, the research design, and threats to the internal validity of your study.
3. Identify some recent legislation and describe how a time-series quasi-experimental design could be used to study the effects of the legislation. Be sure to identify the type and source of the data that you would need for the study.
4. Read the reports of the Milgram (1963, 1965) experiments and write a brief report arguing why you think the experiments were or were not important and whether they were ethical.

Resources and References

Barber, J.G. and Gilbertson, R. (1996). An experimental study of brief unilateral inter-vention for the partners of heavy drinkers. *Research on Social Work Practice,* 6, 325–336.

Campbell, D.T. and Stanley, J.C. (1963). *Experimental and quasi-experimental designs for research.* Skokie, IL: Rand McNally.

Cook, T.D. and Campbell, D.T. (1979). *Quasi-experimentation: Design and analysis issues for field settings.* Skokie, IL: Rand McNally.

Girden, E.R. (1996) *Evaluating research articles from start to finish.* Thousand Oaks, CA: Sage.

Judd, C.M. and Kenny, D.A. (1981). *Estimating the effects of social interventions.* Cambridge: University Press.

Kazdin, A.E. (1992). *Research design in clinical psychology.* Boston: Allyn and Bacon.

Kidder, L.H. and Judd, C.M. (1986). *Research methods in social relations.* New York: Holt, Rinehart and Winston.

Milgram, S. (1963). Behavioral study of obedience. *Journal of Abnormal and Social Psychology,* 67, 371–378.

Milgram, S. (1965). Some conditions of obedience and disobedience to authority. *Human Relations,* 18, 57–76.

Mitchell, M. and Jolley, J. (1988). *Research design explained.* New York: Holt, Rinehart and Winston.

Plaskon, P.P. and Fadden, M.J. (1995). Cancer screening utilization: Is there a role for social work in cancer prevention? *Social Work in Health Care,* 21, 59–70.

Reid, P. and Finchilescu, G. (1995). The disempowering effects of media violence against women on college women. *Psychology of Women Quarterly.* 19, 397–411.

Richter, N.L., Snider, E., and Gorey, K.M. (1997). Group work intervention with female survivors of childhood sexual abuse. *Research on Social Work Practice* 7, 53–69.

Thyer, B. (1984). The clinical anxiety scale. In K. Corcoran and J. Fischer (Eds.), *Measures for clinical practice.* New York: Free Press.

CHAPTER 5

Understanding and Using Research Instruments

Social work researchers design and use scales to measure concepts that concern them. For instance, take the problem of determining if a drug prevention program had the effect intended upon its seventh, eighth, and ninth grade target population. Assume that the intervention and curriculum are already established. The presenters are ready, the school administrators are eager for the program to start. What happens next?

Let's further assume that the goals of the intervention can be clearly established and all that is needed is some sort of instrument to measure any changes that occur from the pretest to the posttest. When I was presented with this problem several years ago, I immediately thought about going to the literature and trying to find an instrument to help me gauge the results of the intervention.

One of my first dilemmas was how to operationalize the success of the program. Ideally, the best test of the program's success would be if these middle schoolers didn't abuse drugs or alcohol as adults. Since we would be unable to lurk in the shadows and follow over one thousand participants over that span of time, success had to be viewed a little differently.

We could have chosen to ask students about their current drug use prior to the intervention and then some time later (for example, six months after the program ended). However, school administrators tend not to be very comfortable with asking about current drug use. Plus, there was come concern that students might be prone to falsify statements of their drug use in order to appear "cool."

Maybe we could have envisioned success as improvement in knowledge on a test of different drugs and their effects. However, the presenters would not be teaching that red pills do this and that blue pills have this other effect.

Having considered and rejected students' current *behavior* (drug usage) and *knowledge* about drugs and alcohol, we decided to measure changes in students' *attitudes* about drugs. (These are the three domains available to you as a researcher.) And as a first step, we quickly surveyed the literature. Not finding any instrument that excited us, we had to design our own.

Now, assuming that you've approached this task after thoroughly studying the previous chapter, how would you know if the instrument you have created is any good?

Instruments and scales are evaluated along two primary dimensions: reliability and validity.

Reliability

Reliability is an easy term to understand because its usage by researchers is very close to its use in the everyday world. When a watch keeps time accurately, it is said to be reliable. If, on the other hand, your watch gained a half hour in one week, lost seventeen minutes the second week, and gained three hours at the end of the third week, you would suspect that something is wrong with it—that it is not reliable. Similarly, a scale or instrument that consistently measures some phenomenon with accuracy is said to be **reliable.** When an instrument is reliable and has a certain amount of predictability, then administering it to similar groups under comparable conditions should yield similar measurements.

One of the ways we evaluate standardized instruments is by their reliability. Generally this information resembles a correlation coefficient and is reported in a journal article or in a manual describing the characteristics of the instrument. Reliability coefficients are numeric values between 0 and 1. Nunnally (1994) says that in the early stages of research one can work with instruments having modest reliability, by which he means .70 or higher; that .80 is needed for basic research; and that a reliability of .90 is the minimum when important decisions are going to be made with respect to specific test scores. If there is no reliability data on a scale and it is not well known, reliability cannot be assumed—the scale could have poor reliability. Data produced from a scale with poor or unknown reliability should always be suspect.

Researchers want their instruments to have a form of reliability known as **internal consistency.** This means that individual items correlate well with the full scale. If this doesn't happen, the items have very little in common. For example, say you were constructing a scale to measure assertiveness. You write the following items:

The Slap-Together Assertiveness Scale

Agree   **Disagree**

Agree	Disagree	
_____	_____	1. I always speak my mind.
_____	_____	2. I am frank about my feelings.
_____	_____	3. I take care of myself.

After creating these three items, you develop writer's block. As you try to think of additional items to include, you recall your friend Henry, who was the most assertive individual you have ever known. You ponder Henry's distinctiveness and remember how fanatical he was about baseball. Maybe knowledge of baseball and assertiveness are somehow related, you think. So, you write a new item:

4. I believe professional baseball is superior to all other sports.

These four items complete our scale, and we administer the Slap-Together Assertiveness Scale to a large cross section of adults. One of the ways we can obtain information about our scale is by running the Reliability procedure available through the *Statistical Package for the Social Sciences* (SPSS). SPSS is computer software available at most universities.

After you've entered the way each individual responded to the items on the scale, the computer program will produce a reliability coefficient and indicate those items that do not correlate well with the rest. By dropping these items, it is often possible to improve a scale's internal consistency. For example, a simplified printout might show something like this:

	Item-Total Correlation	Alpha if Item Deleted
Item 1	.5350	−.3501
Item 2	.5103	−.2894
Item 3	.2556	.1150
Item 4	−.5383	.7165

The software program shows us how strong our items are individually and the contribution they make to the scale. In the first column, item 1 has the highest correlation with the group of four items in the tentative scale, followed by item 2. Item 3 has a weak correlation and item 4 has a negative correlation suggesting that it is not measuring the same concept, but something different. The second column of information also shows the relative contribution of each item. The negative .35 and negative .2894 indicate that the scale's reliability suffers tremendously if either of these two items are deleted. In fact, the scale's internal consistency would be in the hole, and it would have miserable reliability if item 3 were deleted. What the second column is saying is that all of the first three items are necessary for there to

---

Other Terms for Instruments

- Scales
- Indexes
- Questionnaires
- Checklists
- Rating Scales
- Inventories
- Tests

---

be a scale with acceptable reliability. We see this when it reports that by deleting item 4 the overall scale's internal consistency is .7165. Dropping this item would be a good decision and would leave us with a three-item scale.

What if we wanted even higher reliability? Since internal consistency is based both on the number of items and their intercorrelations, it is reasonable to assume that writing a few more new items might increase our reliability. The Spearman-Brown Prophesy Formula indicates that by doubling the number of items we could likely increase our reliability to .83. (This formula can be found in Appendix A.) Tripling the number of items would likely produce a reliability of .88. When a true/false response format has been used, another strategy is to adopt a five-point Likert scale (Strongly Agree, Agree, Undecided, Disagree, Strongly Disagree).

Sometimes researchers measure internal consistency by dividing their longer scales in half (either top and bottom or even versus odd items) and examining how well the two halves correlate with each other. This is known as the *split-half* technique. Another approach is to devise *parallel or alternate versions* of the scale and administer both forms to similar groups. The researcher hopes that both versions will correlate with each other—the higher the correlation coefficient, the stronger the reliability.

Once a scale has been shown to have internal consistency, researchers next want to demonstrate that its capability is not impaired by differences in space and time. Would those individuals who were identified as being assertive on the fifteenth of October still be assertive two weeks later? What about in January? To determine stability, researchers will often administer a scale to the same group on more than one occasion (*test-retest reliability*) to see if persons with high test scores at the first administration maintain high scores at the second administration.

Over short periods of time, scores (of assertiveness or whatever) should remain fairly consistent. While it is expected that some individuals will increase or decrease in assertiveness, possibly as a result of an intervention or some personal event that happened only to them, there would be no logical explanation for why the majority of a large group should experience extreme changes in their assertiveness scores. Should this happen, and if the researcher can find no other explanation, it is reasonable to assume that there is some problem with the instrument.

With the example of the Slap-Together Assertiveness Scale, there could be too few items to give it stability over time. Similarly, it would have reliability problems if it showed internal consistency with subjects from one part of the United States but not from another geographical area. What good would such an instrument be?

Internal consistency cannot be computed on a single item. As a general rule, fewer items usually equate to lower reliability. All else being equal, adding relevant items usually improves reliability, as does expanding the number of response choices—as in going from two to five.

Reliability of Procedures

Even if you don't use an instrument but depend upon observation of some behavior (such as how many times a special education child pops out of his seat during class), you must make every effort to standardize your procedures for counting the phenomenon of interest. Similarly, there should be a uniformity of procedures whenever instruments are administered and scored. An interviewer related an account recently that illustrates the importance of standardized conditions. She had been going into homes of rural families on welfare in a southern state. Much of their housing was dilapidated with substandard fixtures. Many often had only one or two electrical outlets per room. In fact, sometimes she had to ask those she was interviewing to unplug the TV, fan, or air conditioner in order for her to use a tape recorder. It stands to reason that if the interviewees are hot and uncomfortable, they may abbreviate their responses, become impatient, or even terminate the interview quicker than if they were not forced to sit in stifling heat. In short, the quality of the data could be affected.

When more than one person is involved in rating clients' behavior, it is desirable to compute **interrater reliability** to determine the percent of time the raters are in agreement. A correlation between their independent ratings may also be computed. If the correlation is low, then the criteria are not well defined and subjective rules are a large influence. If the obtained correlation is high (.70 or above), then the researcher has evidence that her rating scale has succeeded in providing sufficiently reliable measurements.

Measurement Validity

An instrument is said to be **valid** when it measures the construct it was designed to measure. An intelligence test should measure intelligence. An instrument designed to measure anxiety should provide an accurate assessment of anxiety but not social responsibility, dogmatism, or paranoia. Validity research demonstrates how well a scale performs—identifying its limitations and its strengths. Because the same instrument may be valid in one situation but not in another, validity research seeks to gather evidence to document that the instrument is a good method for assessing the construct in question. For instance, a self-esteem scale that you developed initially for use in a school system might be heavily influenced by what might be thought of as "academic self-esteem"—students' perceptions of their worth based upon the grades they were making. Students who were having trouble with algebra or chemistry might score very low on such a scale. This would be a rather limited way of thinking about self-esteem, which may not accurately assess a young person's "real" self-esteem when he or she is away from school or during the summer months. And, the use of your scale, even if it were valid for a school population, might not be the best tool for assessing overall self-esteem or the self-esteem of a different group of subjects—an incarcerated population, for example.

These are the situations when a researcher ought to conduct validity research:

1. When an instrument is new and unproven.
2. When an instrument designed for one age group is going to be used with another.
3. When an instrument designed for one culture is going to be used in another.
4. When an instrument is being adopted for a different use than what it was intended.
5. Whenever a researcher wants to improve his or her instrument.

There are numerous ways to go about establishing the validity of an instrument. Research texts generally discuss the types of validity efforts in terms of the three major categories listed below. However, as Koeske (1994) has noted, there is no absolute consensus or uniform taxonomy of measurement validity terms.

1. Content validity
2. Criterion validity
   a. concurrent approaches
   b. predictive approaches
3. Construct validity
   a. convergent
   b. discriminant
   c. factorial (structural)

In order to have **content validity**, an instrument needs to sample from the entire range of the concept that it was designed to measure. For instance, it could be difficult for a scale measuring anger in children under the age of eight to be valid if the scale did not consider pouting, hitting, or temper tantrums as manifestations of anger. Likewise, a scale measuring anxiety in adolescents might not have content validity if it did not include such behavior as nail-biting, crying, stomachaches, and sleeplessness. To the extent that an instrument contains a representative sampling of the universe of behaviors, attitudes, or characteristics that are believed to be associated with the concept, then it is said to have content validity. Content validity is established when a panel of experts examines the scale and agrees that the items selected are representative of the range of items associated with the concept to be measured. However, there are no standardized procedures for assessing content validity and no computed coefficient of validity is produced.

While the terms *content* and *face validity* are sometimes used interchangeably, they do not have the same meaning. An instrument is said to have **face validity** when it appears to measure the intended construct. It has never been accepted as a legitimate form of validity because appearances can be deceptive. Neither face nor content validity is sufficient for establishing that a scale will allow generalizability.

Once the researcher is reasonably confident that the scale has content validity, then the next step is to plan a strategy to demonstrate that the collection of items possesses other, more substantial, forms of validity. One begins to establish **criterion validity** when positive correlations are obtained between the test or scale values and some external criteria that are assumed to be indicators of the concept. Criterion validity, the second major category of validity research activities, is based upon the scale's ability to correspond with other test results that are thought to be indicative of the attitude, trait, or behavior being measured. There are several ways to establish criterion validity. We will quickly discuss two approaches.

Concurrent validity is demonstrated by administering your scale simultaneously along with another scale that has documented validity to the same subjects. If the two scales correlate well in the direction expected, then your scale has demonstrated one form of concurrent validity. As an example, suppose you had developed the Drug Attitude Questionnaire (Appendix C). How would you go about showing that it had concurrent validity? One way would be to administer it along with another "proven" instrument that also measures attitudes about drugs. In fact, this is what we did. We correlated the Drug Attitude Questionnaire (DAQ) with a similar but shorter (fourteen-item) instrument. This meant that some students in our study had to complete both instruments.

We found that the DAQ correlated .76 with the shorter instrument at posttest using a sample of ninth grade students and correlated .79 using a sample of college students. These relatively high correlations show that low scores on one test correspond to low scores on the other and vice versa. When high correlations are obtained between two tests presumed to be measuring the same concept, then concurrent validity is demonstrated. When groups are selected because the researcher has a good notion of how they will respond, this is sometimes called known-groups validity.

Predictive validity is another subtype of criterion validity and is demonstrated when scores on a test or scale predict future behavior or attitudes. The Drug Attitude Questionnaire would have predictive validity if, years later, you find that within your study group of middle school students, those who had pro-drug attitudes were suspended from school or arrested for drug possession, while those with anti-drug attitudes were not suspended or arrested for drug possession.

The third major category in validity research is **construct validity**. A well-constructed scale ought to be able to discriminate among groups of individuals along the lines you would expect. The scale should correlate with independent observations and behavioral reports that measure the same construct. Children who report a fear of playground bullies on an instrument you designed might be expected to stay in their classrooms more and to spend less time outside during recess. The framework of theory that gives rise to the instrument also contributes various hypotheses and independent variables for testing how well the instrument's measurements conform to expectations.

The Drug Attitude Questionnaire should show statistically significant differences in scores, say, between regular members of conservative churches and clients of an outpatient treatment agency, or persons in jail for substance abuse. Construct validity is the fundamental type of validity on which other types depend (Meier, 1994). It is the ability of an instrument to distinguish among individuals who have a lot of, some of, or none of the characteristic being measured that makes the instrument useful. When it can discriminate along the lines you hypothesize it should, then you have evidence that it can do what it was constructed to do.

Convergent validation is obtained when theoretically relevant variables demonstrate a relationship with the measure. An instrument that you developed to measure children's self-report of fear of playground bullies could, for instance, be correlated with teachers' or parents' rankings of children's fears. If the different assessment approaches yield scores that are strongly correlated, the researcher can rule out alternative explanations for the validity findings because there was no variance attributable to using a shared method of measurement.

In *discriminant validity*, the researcher hopes to find no relationship between the instrument's measurements and variables that should not, in theory, be related to the construct. Self-report instruments of children who are fearful of playground bullies should not correlate with other self-reports indicating that these same children are best friends with the bullies.

Factor analysis is still another way of establishing construct validity. When a large number of items have been created or can be drawn upon to compose a scale, factor analysis can be used to reduce the number of items to a smaller group that are statistically related. Factor analysis also helps researchers to explore inner structure, and reveals the number of dimensions that instruments may contain.

To illustrate, let's go back to our earlier example of developing a self-esteem scale. Let's say that we write eighty-five different items that seem to have face and content validity. After administering the instrument to 150 high schoolers, we then enter this data into a statistical software program and run the factor analysis program. In our hypothetical example, the computer print-out reveals that instead of one simple scale, we have items that group together in four different areas: academic self-esteem, social competence, satisfaction with personal appearance, and assertiveness. We might decide that these four factors are "the essence" of self-esteem and keep all of them, or perhaps we would pare out a factor or items that don't conform. Nonconforming items could be understood if one of the group of items clustering together seemed to measure selfishness or self-centeredness.

Depending on what we want from our instrument, we might choose to combine the original four subscales into a new summated index that provides a global measure of self-esteem. Many times researchers hope that factor analysis will produce only a single unidimensional scale like the Rosenberg Self-Esteem Scale shown later in this chapter. Factor analysis is a fascinating but somewhat sophisticated procedure and beyond the level of this introductory text. You may encounter the term as you read professional journal articles about the development or refinement of scales. The term "loads" is used to indicate that a scale item correlates well with the collection of items that cluster together to form a factor—as in "Item 3 loads higher on assertiveness than on social competence." Factor loadings are interpreted the same way as correlation coefficients.

Establishing validity is not a one-time or a single-shot deal, but rather an ongoing process. Different uses of the instrument become opportunities to show its ability to discriminate among different populations, which adds to the accumulative evidence of its validity. For example, even though the DAQ was designed for middle school students, it might be employed with inpatients or outpatients in drug treatment programs to determine if attitudes about drugs changed as a result of intervention. Instruments that have been around a long time often have extensive bibliographies associated with them as various researchers report the results of their use of the instrument in different settings and with diverse populations.

For the purpose of instruction, reliability and validity are usually presented as separate concepts. However, these two concepts are interrelated in a complex fashion. On the one hand, when we can empirically demonstrate that an instrument is valid, it can generally be assumed to have adequate reliability. On the other hand, a reliable instrument may not be valid. That is, an instrument may provide dependable measurements but of some concept unrelated to

Examples from Social Work Literature

O'Hare and Collins (1997) have developed an instrument designed to measure the frequency with which certain practice skills (such as making referrals, employing empathy, and providing emotional support) are employed with clients. They started off with a pool of ninety-seven items that was reduced to seventy-five; from that group, thirty-three of the strongest were kept that supported four factors: therapeutic, case management, supportive, and treatment planning/evaluation skills. Their article describes the theoretical framework for the Practice Skills Inventory, the sample of students, and the factor analysis procedures and results.

Hudson and McMurtry (1997) have reported on the procedures they used to gather psychometric information on the Multi-Problem Screening Inventory, a 334-item paper-and-pencil instrument with twenty-seven different subscales measuring such client problems as depression, suicidal intent, physical abuse, self-esteem, personal stress, phobias, disturbing thoughts, aggression, guilt, sexual discord, and drug use. Their article contains a good description of how they tested the MPSI for reliability, content, factorial, and construct validity. This article provides a "cookbook" example of how to go about demonstrating that a newly created instrument scale has good psychometrics.

what we thought we were measuring. Both reliability and validity ought to be demonstrated as evidence that an instrument is psychometrically strong.

As you come across various instruments in practice or in your reading, it is important to realize that if you know nothing about the reliability and validity of a scale, then any results that are obtained from its use may have very little meaning. The scale may not provide consistent results (poor reliability) or it may measure something quite different from what was intended (poor validity). The importance of knowing a scale's reliability and validity cannot be emphasized enough.

Locating Research Instruments

While complete scales are sometimes reproduced in journal articles, this is a fairly rare occurrence because of space limitations. Commonly what is found are examples of items from the scale and information about the scale's reliability and validity. This usually means that the reader will have to consult the bibliography and may have to search through several other articles to find the actual scale or more specific information about where to obtain it.

Some instruments may be protected by copyright. More than likely, you will have to purchase copies of these instruments before you can use them. Other instruments are in the public domain. That means that they belong to you, the public, and can be used without special permission.

Instruments that you find in journal articles are not likely to be protected by copyright. However, good research etiquette dictates that you contact the author anyway and request permission to use the instrument. This can be a useful contact to make. Most authors want to keep informed of research conducted with their instruments. They'll be interested in yours. As you discuss your proposed research with them, they may be able to help in ways that you didn't expect. Sometimes they have prepared shorter or newer versions of old instruments or may share a bibliography of recent applications and findings with the instrument.

Finding an appropriate instrument without immersing yourself completely in the literature can be a bit like chasing a rainbow. However, there are several good sources for scales that may contain just the instrument you require. Probably the first place to start is with the *Test Locator*, which is a computerized database accessible from the Internet (http://ericae.net/testcol.htm#ETSTF). The Test Locator is a joint project of several organizations, including the Buros Institute of Mental Measurements, the Educational Testing Service, and the ERIC Clearinghouse on Assessment and Evaluation at Catholic University. Enter the subject area or specific test you are trying to locate in the search engine and it will return a set of relevant references that should help you to find the instrument.

Other printed resources that may be of some use are:

Fischer, J. and Corcoran, K. (1994). *Measures for clinical practice: A sourcebook.* (2nd edition). New York: Free Press.

Goldman, B.A. and Busch, J.C. (1997). *Directory of unpublished experimental mental measures.* Washington, DC: American Psychological Association.

Hamill, D.D. (1992). *A consumer's guide to tests in print.* Austin, TX: Pro-ED.

Jordan, C. and Franklin, C. (1995). *Clinical assessment for social workers.* Chicago: Lyceum.

Keyser, D.J. and Sweetland, R.C. (1992). *Test critiques.* Austin, TX: Pro-ED.

Maddox, T. (1997). *Tests: A comprehensive reference for assessments in psychology, education, and business.* N.p.: N.p.

McDowell, I. and Newell, C. (1996). *Measuring health: A guide to rating scales and questionnaires.* New York: Oxford University Press.

Miller, D.C. (1991). *Handbook of research design and social measurement.* Newbury Park, CA: Sage.

Nurius, P.S. and Hudson, W.W. (1993). *Human services practice, evaluation, and computers.* Pacific Grove, CA: Brooks/Cole.

Robinson, J.P., Shaver, P., and Wrightsman, L.S. (1991). *Measures of personality and social psychological attitudes.* San Diego: Academic Press.

Touliatos, J., Perlmutter, B.F., and Straus, M.A. (1990). *Handbook of family measurement techniques.* Newbury Park, CA: Sage.

Other references, although somewhat dated, may help you to locate a specific test or instrument:

Chun, Ki-Taek, Cobb, S., and French, J.R., Jr. (1975). *Measures for psychological assessment: A guide to 3000 original sources and their applications.* Ann Arbor, MI: Institute for Social Research.

Fredman, N. and Sherman, R. (1987). *Handbook of measurements for marriage and family therapy.* New York: Brunner/Mazel.

Keyser, D.J. and Sweetland, R.C. (1987). *Test critiques compendium: Reviews of major tests from the test critiques series.* Kansas City, MO: Test Corporation of America.

Lake, D.G., Miles, M.B., and Earle, R.B., Jr. (1973). *Measuring human behavior: Tools for the assessment of social functioning.* New York: Teachers College Press.

Robinson, J.P., Athanasiou, R., and Head, K.B. (1969). *Measures of occupational attitudes and occupational characteristics.* Ann Arbor, MI: Institute for Social Research.

When You Can't Find the Instrument You Want

Most often when students complain that they can't find an instrument they need, they've had a problem narrowing down exactly what they want to measure. Not too long ago, a student told me she had spent hours in the library without finding the kind of instrument she was looking for. As we talked more, she revealed that she'd been searching under "children" and "families" when it would have been more profitable for her to look for literature on parenting programs. At times, a switch to a different database can also be beneficial.

If, however, you have conducted an exhaustive literature search and consulted with knowledgeable people and still can't find the instrument you want, two avenues lie before you. First, you can take an existing instrument and modify it to meet your needs. It is reasonable to take such drastic action if, for instance, you've found a potentially useful scale developed for adults that is too long to use with children.

In such a situation, write to the author of the instrument to ask if any short forms have been developed, and if they have not, if you may have permission to create a brief version. Most authors, particularly if their scales have appeared in professional journals and are not copyrighted, will likely be interested in your research and grant you permission. The only caution here is that anytime you modify an existing instrument, the burden is upon you to prove that the resulting instrument is reliable and valid. Because the longer instrument was psychometrically sound does not guarantee that the shorter instrument will be.

It is not at all unusual for researchers to take a scale developed by someone else and to adapt it for a different purpose. A colleague and I once modified the social distance scale created by E.S. Bogardus in 1925. To measure acceptance of different nationalities or races, Bogardus asked respondents if they would admit someone different from themselves into such situations as:

1. Kinship by marriage
2. Club membership
3. Neighbors
4. Employment in one's occupation
5. Citizenship in one's country
6. Visitors to one's country

Our social distance scale asked some of these same questions, providing *Strongly Agree, Agree, Undecided, Disagree,* and *Strongly Disagree* as response choices:

SA A U D SD   I would be opposed to a person having AIDS living on the same street with me.

SA A U D SD   I would be uncomfortable if I had to work in the same department or office as a person having AIDS.

SA A U D SD   I would allow a person having AIDS to become a citizen of the United States.

SA A U D SD   I would exclude a person having AIDS from visiting my country.

Even with just these four items, the reliability was quite strong (.82). Since this was an exploratory study, we didn't attempt to establish the validity of the instrument, but we did find that our Social Distance Scale correlated .67 with our Fear of Aids Scale and –.68 with our Empathy for AIDS Victims Scale, which at least suggests that our measure might have more than just face or content validity.

If you find no instruments you want to modify, a second option is to create your own scale. Once again, it will be your responsibility to establish that the instrument measures what was intended and does so reliably. Just because you think it has content or face validity does not make it a good instrument. Take, for example, questions 7 through 15 of the Attitudes about Research Courses Questionnaire (from Appendix B).

7. T or F   I dread speaking before a large group of people more than taking a research course.

8. T or F   I would rather take a research course than ask a waitress to return an improperly cooked meal to the chef.

9. T or F   My fear of snakes is greater than my fear of taking a research course.
10. T or F   My fear of spiders is less than my fear of taking a research course.
11. T or F   I would rather take a research course than ask a total stranger to do a favor for me.
12. T or F   My fear of research is such that I would rather the university require an additional two courses of my choosing than require one research course.
13. T or F   I dread going to the dentist more than taking a research course.
14. T or F   I fear a statistics course more than a research methodology course.
15. T or F   I have always "hated math."

Can you guess what I was trying to measure with this scale? Although I had high hopes for it, the scale's reliability was so poor that I've never attempted any further research with it. What struck me as a clever way to measure fear of research simply didn't work. I suspect that individual responses to such things as spiders and dentists interfered with rather than facilitated the concept I was trying to measure. Oh, well, this is the way research moves forward. Sometimes there's considerable trial and error involved.

How does one go about constructing a scale? Normally, you begin with creating a pool of items that you think will measure different dimensions or degrees of the behavior, knowledge, or attitude that you have in mind. Sometimes experts in the field are invited to contribute items. Then some weeding out of items occurs, and a draft of an instrument is prepared. This version is then administered to a large group. From the data the group supplies, the evaluator uses computer software to identify which items correlate well. The items that correlate most poorly are thrown out.

Depending on the reliability coefficient obtained, the researcher might, at that point, decide that the refined list of items is adequate. If the reliability coefficient is lower than desired, the researcher will add new items and administer the second version to another set of people, dropping and adding new items until he or she is satisfied with the internal consistency of the instrument.

When would it be important to establish that a scale has validity? This would be something you would want to do if you were planning further research with the instrument or if you were thinking about getting a copyright in order to market it. Perhaps your scale could help social service employers screen out applicants who have the least empathy for clients or who would be too fearful to work with AIDS patients. Or, if your responsibility with an organization is to provide in-service training, you might want a valid scale to help you evaluate what the participants acquired from the in-service training. It is necessary to determine the validity of a scale any time that important decisions may result from it.

Practice Note: Ethnicity and Measurement Issues

- The term race and ethnicity are frequently confused and mis-leading. Many Hispanics, for instance, may identify their race as White. Persons who are biracial may not always be classified accurately.
- Many, if not most, of the measurement tools currently in existence have been developed by European Americans. Further, these tests are often interpreted based on scores obtained mostly from European American subjects.
- Socio-economic status (SES) can be a confounding variable when investigators are looking at differences in their dependent variables by ethnicity.
- Instruments designed for one cultural group may contain substantial measurement bias when applied to another ethnic group. The ethnicity of the rater may affect those being rated.
- There has not been a great deal of study of bias or lack of it in cross-cultural studies pertaining to validity issues and psychological assessment.

Source: Foster, S.L. and Martinez, C.R. (1995), Ethnicity: Conceptual and methodological issues in child clinical research, *Journal of Clinical Child Psychology,* 24, 214–226; Malgady, R.G. (1996), The question of cultural bias in assessment and diagnosis of ethnic minority clients: Let's reject the null hypothesis, *Professional Psychology, Research and Practice,* 27, 73–77.

Evaluating Instruments for Use in Practice

Before adopting an assessment instrument for use in practice, social workers should consider several important questions:

1. Practicality. Is the instrument:
   a. affordable?
   b. easy for clients to read and understand?
   c. easy to administer?
   d. easy to score and interpret?
   e. not too long?
2. Psychometrics. Does the instrument have:
   a. good reliability (.70 for research and at least .90 for clinical decision making)?

      b. the necessary sensitivity to detect small increments of improvement?

      c. validity established through multiple studies and usages?

3. Theoretical application. Will the instrument:

      a. measure the concept that is the best indicator of client improvement in the particular population? Is the concept understandable to clients? Policymakers? Funding sources?

      b. allow you to make predictions consistent with the theory underlying your intervention?

      c. allow you to compare your findings with other practitioners working with similar populations?

      d. provide useful information to service providers?

If there are several instruments to choose from, then considering such questions as those identified above can help a researcher or committee to make better decisions about the assessment instruments under consideration.

A Sampling of Instruments

Throughout this chapter we've been talking about instruments and scales. For the section that follows, I've secured the permission of several authors to reproduce all or portions of their instruments. Even with this small sample, you'll see some of the great variety of instruments that have been created by social workers. Instruments contained in this section are:

- The Community Living Skills Scale.
- The Children's Motivation Scale.
- The Quality of Life Questionnaire.
- The Job Satisfaction Scale.
- RAGE—Rating Scale for Aggressive Behavior in the Elderly.
- The Adult Children of Alcoholics Tool.
- The CES-D.
- The Rosenberg Self-Esteem Scale.

The Community Living Skills Scale (CLSS)

Description

The CLSS is a scale designed to measure level of functioning within a psychiatric population. This self-rating scale is distinctive in that the consumers of a psychosocial rehabilitation agency played a major role in helping develop it. Using the Denver Community Mental Health Questionnaire

Figure 5.1 The Community Living Skills Scale

Please mark an X on the answer that is the closest to how often you accomplish each act.

	Almost Always	Usually	Some-times	Hardly Ever
Personal Care				
1. I (can) do (food) shopping	___	___	___	___
2. I bathe enough to keep myself clean.	___	___	___	___
3. I (can) do my own laundry.	___	___	___	___
4. I eat balanced meals.	___	___	___	___
5. I get dressed daily.	___	___	___	___
6. I am capable of finding ways to solve my own problems.	___	___	___	___
7. I have difficulty in getting up daily.	___	___	___	___
8. I get to the dentist when I need to.	___	___	___	___
9. I keep my appearance presentable.	___	___	___	___
10. I fight depression when it comes.	___	___	___	___
11. I get to the doctor when I need to.	___	___	___	___
12. I go to bed at a reasonable hour.	___	___	___	___
13. I keep my hair neat.	___	___	___	___
14. I manage my money.	___	___	___	___
15. I get the amount of sleep I need.	___	___	___	___
16. I keep my living quarters decent.	___	___	___	___
17. I control my alcohol/drug problems.	___	___	___	___
18. I take my medications (if any) as prescribed.	___	___	___	___
19. I find transportation as needed.	___	___	___	___
Socialization/Relationships				
20. I am afraid of being with others.	___	___	___	___
21. I avoid meeting new people.	___	___	___	___
22. I devote time to my family.	___	___	___	___
23. I get along with the people I live with.	___	___	___	___
24. I control my anger.	___	___	___	___
25. I cope with my anxiety.	___	___	___	___
26. I show consideration for others.	___	___	___	___
27. I am respectful of other people's rights.	___	___	___	___
28. My relationship with my child(ren) interferes with my life.	___	___	___	___
29. I get along with my neighbors.	___	___	___	___
30. I have trusting relationships.	___	___	___	___
31. My relationship with my spouse interferes with my life.	___	___	___	___
32. I behave in an acceptable manner.	___	___	___	___
33. I have difficulty in listening to others.	___	___	___	___
34. My relationship with my parent(s) interferes with my life.	___	___	___	___
35. I get into trouble with people in authority (parents, bosses, teachers, doctors, etc.).	___	___	___	___
Activities/Leisure Skills				
36. I participate in activities with others.	___	___	___	___
37. I do things I enjoy.	___	___	___	___
38. I walk or do some other exercise.	___	___	___	___
39. I do things that make me feel good about myself.	___	___	___	___
40. I find emotional support when I need it.	___	___	___	___
Vocational Skills				
41. I organize my tasks daily.	___	___	___	___
42. I am thorough when I work.	___	___	___	___
43. I have difficulty completing tasks as required.	___	___	___	___
44. I manage my time successfully.	___	___	___	___
45. I learn skills required to do my work.	___	___	___	___
46. I have difficulty in concentrating on the task at hand.	___	___	___	___

Source: Smith, M.K. and Ford, J. (1990) A client-developed functional level scale:The Community Living Skills Scale (CLSS), *Journal of Social Service Research*, 13(3), 73-75.Copyright © Haworth Press, Inc. Reprinted with permission.

as a model, a group of consumers participated in brainstorming sessions that identified activities within the broad areas of personal care, social relations, and activities/vocational skills in which a mental health consumer living in the community would be engaged. Later, these were restated in behavioral terms and a pretest was conducted with fifty clients. It has been proposed that the CLSS could be used to measure community living skills of individuals in psychiatric hospitals or residential facilities and for outcome evaluation.

Psychometric Data

Internal consistency (Cronbach's Alpha) ranged from .79 to .84 on four retained subscales, showing them to have adequate reliability. Validity of the scale was examined by comparing CLSS scores from consumers in the pretest group with ratings on the Global Assessment Scale (GAS). Results were mixed. The Personal Care subscale was significantly correlated ($r = .41$) with the GAS scores, but none of the other three subscales were significantly correlated. The authors explain this by stating that the GAS is geared more toward appearances and behaviors usually associated with psychosis, whereas the CLSS does a better job of measuring subjective distress.

In terms of discriminant validity, the CLSS was administered to a comparison group of fifty social work graduate students. As was expected, the student group had significantly higher (more functional) scores and smaller standard deviations on all the subscales.

Availability

Smith, M.K. and Ford, J. (1990). A client-developed functional level scale: The Community Living Skills Scale (CLSS). *Journal of Social Service Research,* 13(3), 61–84.

For further information about the instrument, contact Mieko K. Smith, Ph.D., Dept. of Social Work, Cleveland State University, Euclid Ave. at E. 24th Street, Cleveland, OH 44115, or Janet Ford, Ph.D., College of Social Work, University of Kentucky, Lexington, KY 40506-0027.

Scoring

Responses are scored as follows: "Almost always" (4), "Usually" (3), "Sometimes" (2), "Hardly ever" (1). However, reverse scoring must be used for items 7, 20, 21, 28, 31, 33, 34, 35, and 46. Additionally, some items (particularly in the socialization/relationship area) were not applicable to everyone—for example, those who are not married. For the "Not applicable" responses, the authors used an average of the other items from that subscale to replace the missing value.

The Children's Motivation Scale (CMS)

Description

The sixteen-item Children's Motivation Scale (see figure 5.2) is a rating scale that measures apathy—often a symptom of depression, PTSD, schizophrenia, or substance abuse in adults. The title of the scale does not reflects its focus, although apathy is conceptually linked with the absence of motivation. The CMS was developed as part of an ongoing investigation of brain-behavior relationships in children with closed head injuries.

Psychometric Data

Data on the CMS were provided by parents of: 290 students in regular classes, grades one through twelve in suburban Maryland; 127 consecutive inpatient admissions to a university-affiliated child and adolescent psychiatry unit in Baltimore; and thirty-eight consecutive admissions to an outpatient university-affiliated affective disorders clinic in Baltimore.

Temporal stability was demonstrated for the normal samples in a two-week test-retest design ($r = .88$). The internal consistency estimate obtained by a split-half reliability coefficient was .79. Apathy did not vary as a function of age or grade.

Evidence for construct validity is found in the scale's convergence with similar measures. The CMS was inversely correlated (–.38) with the withdrawn factor from the Child Behavior Checklist. Evidence for discriminant validity is found in the lack of correlation with scores on the Johns Hopkins Depression Scale—an indicator that depression and apathy are discriminable constructs.

Availability

Gerring, J.P., Freund, L., Gerson, A.C., Joshi, P.T., Capozzoli, J., Frosch, E., Brady, K., Marin, R.S. and Denckla, M.B. (1996). Psychometric characteristics of the Children's Motivation Scale. *Psychiatry Research*, 63, 205–217.

Scoring

The normative sample had a mean of 49.83; this compares to 30.67 for the inpatient sample and 30.58 for the outpatients.

Figure 5.2 The Children's Motivation Scale

Directions: Circle the number on the scale below each question which best describes your child's motivation.

1. Starts playing (games, activities) on his/her own. For example, gathering materials for a game, cooking.

0	1	2	3	4
Never or rarely occurs	1-3 times during the month	1-3 times a week	4-6 times a week	1 or more times a day

2. Seems to put little effort into anything. For example, choosing clothing, getting ready for school, cleaning up.

0	1	2	3	4
Never or rarely occurs	1-3 times during the month	1-3 times a week	4-6 times a week	1 or more times a day

3. Does things on his/her own. For example, household chores, homework, getting ready for a trip.

0	1	2	3	4
Never or rarely occurs	1-3 times during the month	1-3 times a week	4-6 times a week	1 or more times a day

4. Finishes projects he/she starts. For example, coloring a picture, earning a scout badge, or pursuing a hobby.

0	1	2	3	4
Never or rarely occurs	1-3 times during the month	1-3 times a week	4-6 times a week	1 or more times a day

5. Approaches activities with intensity, energy, or enthusiasm. For example, wants to be best at a sport, excited about visiting a new place.

0	1	2	3	4
Never or rarely occurs	1-3 times during the month	1-3 times a week	4-6 times a week	1 or more times a day

6. Is interested in things. For example, new TV shows, new toys, new clothes, new books.

0	1	2	3	4
Never or rarely occurs	1-3 times during the month	1-3 times a week	4-6 times a week	1 or more times a day

7. Makes plans, asks to do things in the future. For example, taking a trip, having a party, getting a new toy.

0	1	2	3	4
Never or rarely occurs	1-3 times during the month	1-3 times a week	4-6 times a week	1 or more times a day

8. Is curious. For example, wants to understand, to know about different people, places, activities, or how things work.

0	1	2	3	4
Never or rarely occurs	1-3 times during the month	1-3 times a week	4-6 times a week	1 or more times a day

Figure 5.2 continued

9. Is interested in learning new things. For example, learning the alphabet, learning a new sport, taking drivers' education.

0	1	2	3	4
Never or rarely occurs	1-3 times during the month	1-3 times a week	4-6 times a week	1 or more times a day

10. Shows expected emotional responses. For example, happy when rewarded or surprised, sad when hurt, angry when insulted.

0	1	2	3	4
Never or rarely occurs	1-3 times during the month	1-3 times a week	4-6 times a week	1 or more times a day

11. Has to be told what to do in his/her free time. For example, playing with a toy or game, or making a phone call to a friend.

0	1	2	3	4
Never or rarely occurs	1-3 times during the month	1-3 times a week	4-6 times a week	1 or more times a day

12. Wants to be with friends. For example, invites friends to play, calls on the phone, or arranges social events.

0	1	2	3	4
Never or rarely occurs	1-3 times during the month	1-3 times a week	4-6 times a week	1 or more times a day

13. Talks freely, sharing his/her ideas with those present. For example, likes to talk on the phone, talks a lot with family and friends, likes to express his/her ideas on a topic.

0	1	2	3	4
Never or rarely occurs	1-3 times during the month	1-3 times a week	4-6 times a week	1 or more times a day

14. Does not appear interested or concerned about his/her own problems. For example, being silly at school, not doing homework, lying.

0	1	2	3	4
Never or rarely occurs	1-3 times during the month	1-3 times a week	4-6 times a week	1 or more times a day

15. Lacks energy and often appears fatigued. For example, when important activities occur, when requests are made.

0	1	2	3	4
Never or rarely occurs	1-3 times during the month	1-3 times a week	4-6 times a week	1 or more times a day

16. Does not appear interested or concerned about his/her family or friends. For example, illness of a family member, being rejected or ignored by a close friend, being included in social events.

0	1	2	3	4
Never or rarely occurs	1-3 times during the month	1-3 times a week	4-6 times a week	1 or more times a day

The Quality of Life Questionnaire (QLQ)

Description

The twenty-four-item QLQ (see figure 5.3) is a self-administered instrument used for assessing subjective quality of life in persons with severe mental illness. Quality of life is one component in the assessment of quality of care and is being increasingly recognized as an important outcome indicator for improving services for people with severe mental illness.

Psychometric Data

Data on the QLQ comes from a large cross-sectional study of Wisconsin clients with serious mental illness who were receiving publicly funded mental health services—most from a community support program. Based on 971 complete and usable questionnaires, the alpha reliability was .96. Reliabilities for each of the six separate scales (dimensions) of the QLQ ranged from .81 to .89.

Construct validity was shown by correlations to evaluate hypothesized differences between groups. As expected, better client functioning as assessed by the case manager's rating of the client on the Global Assessment Functioning Scale was positively related to the QLQ (r = .16). Clients who reported that they were in the program against their will had lower QLQ levels than clients who were in the program of their own volition. Clients who were employed reported significantly higher overall quality of life than clients who were unemployed.

Availability

Greenley, J.R., Greenberg, J.S. and Brown, R. (1997). Measuring quality of life: A new and practical survey instrument. *Social Work,* 42, 244–254.

Dr. Greenberg can be contacted at the School of Social Work, University of Wisconsin-Madison, 1350 University Ave., Madison, WI 53706-1510.

Scoring

In this study, the overall mean score was 4.8. Men had higher mean scores (4.7) than women (4.5). Clients who were above the median on satisfaction with the treatment program had an overall mean score of 5.1; those who reported being in the program against their will had a mean score of 4.4.

Figure 5.3 Quality of Life Questionnaire

Instructions: below are some questions about how satisfied you are with various aspects of your life. For each question, circle the answer that best corresponds to how you feel.

Concerning your living arrangements, how do you feel about:

1. **The living arrangements where you live?**

   Terrible Unhappy Mostly Dis-Satisfied Equally Satisfied/Dissatisfied Mostly Satisfied Pleased Delighted

2. **The rules there?**

   Terrible Unhappy Mostly Dis-Satisfied Equally Satisfied/Dissatisfied Mostly Satisfied Pleased Delighted

3. **The privacy you have there?**

   Terrible Unhappy Mostly Dis-Satisfied Equally Satisfied/Dissatisfied Mostly Satisfied Pleased Delighted

4. **The amount of freedom you have there?**

   Terrible Unhappy Mostly Dis-Satisfied Equally Satisfied/Dissatisfied Mostly Satisfied Pleased Delighted

5. **The prospect of staying on where you currently live for a long period of time?**

   Terrible Unhappy Mostly Dis-Satisfied Equally Satisfied/Dissatisfied Mostly Satisfied Pleased Delighted

Here are some questions about money. How do you feel about:

6. **The amount of money you get?**

   Terrible Unhappy Mostly Dis-Satisfied Equally Satisfied/Dissatisfied Mostly Satisfied Pleased Delighted

7. **How comfortable and well-off you are financially?**

   Terrible Unhappy Mostly Dis-Satisfied Equally Satisfied/Dissatisfied Mostly Satisfied Pleased Delighted

8. **How much money you have to spend for fun?**

   Terrible Unhappy Mostly Dis-Satisfied Equally Satisfied/Dissatisfied Mostly Satisfied Pleased Delighted

Figure 5.3 continued

Here are some questions about how you spend your spare time. How do you feel about:

9. **The way you spend your spare time?**

| Terrible | Unhappy | Mostly Dis- Satisfied | Equally Satisfied/ Dissatisfied | Mostly Satisfied | Pleased | Delighted |

10. **The chance you have to enjoy pleasant or beautiful things?**

| Terrible | Unhappy | Mostly Dis- Satisfied | Equally Satisfied/ Dissatisfied | Mostly Satisfied | Pleased | Delighted |

11. **The amount of relaxation in your life?**

| Terrible | Unhappy | Mostly Dis- Satisfied | Equally Satisfied/ Dissatisfied | Mostly Satisfied | Pleased | Delighted |

12. **The pleasure you get from the TV or radio?**

| Terrible | Unhappy | Mostly Dis- Satisfied | Equally Satisfied/ Dissatisfied | Mostly Satisfied | Pleased | Delighted |

Here are some questions about your family. How do you feel about:

13. **Your family in general?**

| Terrible | Unhappy | Mostly Dis- Satisfied | Equally Satisfied/ Dissatisfied | Mostly Satisfied | Pleased | Delighted |

14. **The way you and your family act toward each other?**

| Terrible | Unhappy | Mostly Dis- Satisfied | Equally Satisfied/ Dissatisfied | Mostly Satisfied | Pleased | Delighted |

15. **The way things are in general between you and your family?**

| Terrible | Unhappy | Mostly Dis- Satisfied | Equally Satisfied/ Dissatisfied | Mostly Satisfied | Pleased | Delighted |

Here are some questions about your social life. How do you feel about:

16. **The things you do with other people?**

| Terrible | Unhappy | Mostly Dis- Satisfied | Equally Satisfied/ Dissatisfied | Mostly Satisfied | Pleased | Delighted |

Figure 5.3 continued

17. **The amount of time you spend with other people?**

| Terrible | Unhappy | Mostly Dis-Satisfied | Equally Satisfied/ Dissatisfied | Mostly Satisfied | Pleased | Delighted |

18. **The people you see socially?**

| Terrible | Unhappy | Mostly Dis-Satisfied | Equally Satisfied/ Dissatisfied | Mostly Satisfied | Pleased | Delighted |

19. **The chance you have to know people with whom you feel really comfortable?**

| Terrible | Unhappy | Mostly Dis-Satisfied | Equally Satisfied/ Dissatisfied | Mostly Satisfied | Pleased | Delighted |

20. **The amount of friendship in your life?**

| Terrible | Unhappy | Mostly Dis-Satisfied | Equally Satisfied/ Dissatisfied | Mostly Satisfied | Pleased | Delighted |

Here are some questions about your health. How do you feel about:

21. **Your health in general?**

| Terrible | Unhappy | Mostly Dis-Satisfied | Equally Satisfied/ Dissatisfied | Mostly Satisfied | Pleased | Delighted |

22. **Your physical condition?**

| Terrible | Unhappy | Mostly Dis-Satisfied | Equally Satisfied/ Dissatisfied | Mostly Satisfied | Pleased | Delighted |

23. **The medical care available to you if you need it?**

| Terrible | Unhappy | Mostly Dis-Satisfied | Equally Satisfied/ Dissatisfied | Mostly Satisfied | Pleased | Delighted |

24. **How often do you see a doctor?**

| Terrible | Unhappy | Mostly Dis-Satisfied | Equally Satisfied/ Dissatisfied | Mostly Satisfied | Pleased | Delighted |

Job Satisfaction Scale (JSS)

Description

The authors began using measures of job satisfaction in 1980 while exploring the antecedents and consequences of job stress and strain. The preliminary measure was a short seven-item scale, which has evolved over the years and is now made up of fourteen items. The Job Satisfaction Scale, in one form or another, has been used with more than six hundred social service professionals in diverse human service settings.

Psychometric Data

Several studies reveal the JSS to have good internal consistency, ranging from .83 to .91. From factor analysis of the fourteen job satisfaction items, three different dimensions were found. The first was called Intrinsic Job Satisfaction and reflected intrinsic qualities of the work role. The second dimension was called Organizational Job Satisfaction and depicted satisfaction with supervision and other elements of agency operation. The third factor contained two extrinsic items dealing with salary and promotion. Internal consistency of these subscales ranges from .75 to .90. Test-retest reliabilities on the full scale ranged from .80 (nine months) to .64 (fifteen months).

In terms of predictive validity, a study of intensive case managers found that JSS scores were inversely related to later depression and emotional exhaustion scores, and were positively related to intention to quit the job. Supportive findings suggest convergent and construct validity. In one study, the Moos Work Environment Scale correlated .61 with the Job Satisfaction Scale, and the JSS correlated .76 with a global item that asked, "All things considered, how satisfied or dissatisfied are you with your job?" The authors found that this instrument was significantly correlated with each of the widely used Maslach Burnout Inventory dimensions (for example, –.59 with emotional exhaustion). In a 1984 study the authors found that job satisfaction was inversely related to the percentage of "difficult" clients in one's active caseload. The JSS appears to be a short, reliable, and valid measure of job satisfaction in the human services.

Availability

The Job Satisfaction Scale is available for use without securing special permission. A description of the development of this scale can be found in Koeske, G.F., Kirk, S.A., Koeske, R.D., and Rauktis, M.B. (1994), Measuring the monday blues: Validation of a job satisfaction scale for the human services, *Social Work Research,* 29(4), 27–35.

For additional information contact Gary Koeske, Ph.D., School of Social Work, University of Pittsburgh, 2217H, Pittsburgh, PA 15260.

Figure 5.4 Job Satisfaction Scale

Instructions: Please rate each of the aspects of your work listed below according to the **degree of satisfaction or dissatisfaction** it provides you. Circle a number between 1 (Very Dissatisfied) and 11 (Very Satisfied) for each aspect.

	Very Dissatisfied							Very Satisfied			
1. Working with your clients	1	2	3	4	5	6	7	8	9	10	11
2. The amount of authority you have been given to do your job	1	2	3	4	5	6	7	8	9	10	11
3. Your salary and benefits	1	2	3	4	5	6	7	8	9	10	11
4. Opportunities for promotion	1	2	3	4	5	6	7	8	9	10	11
5. The challenge your job provides you	1	2	3	4	5	6	7	8	9	10	11
6. The quality of supervision you receive	1	2	3	4	5	6	7	8	9	10	11
7. Chances for acquiring new skills	1	2	3	4	5	6	7	8	9	10	11
8. Amount of client contact	1	2	3	4	5	6	7	8	9	10	11
9. Opportunities for really helping people	1	2	3	4	5	6	7	8	9	10	11
10. Clarity of guidelines for doing your job	1	2	3	4	5	6	7	8	9	10	11
11. Opportunity for involvement in decision making	1	2	3	4	5	6	7	8	9	10	11
12. The recognition given your work by your supervisor	1	2	3	4	5	6	7	8	9	10	11
13. Your feeling of success as a social worker	1	2	3	4	5	6	7	8	9	10	11
14. Field of specialization you are in	1	2	3	4	5	6	7	8	9	10	11

Source: Courtesy of Gary F. Koeske.

Scoring

Overall and subscale scores are simple sums, corrected for missing and any "not applicable" responses. The author has used seven- and nine-step responses scales in the past with similar results for reliability and validity. He prefers 3.5 through 0 to +5 scaling, but notes that it complicates coding and probably introduces coding error. The numerical values used, however, do not affect reliability or validity.

RAGE—A Rating Scale for Aggressive Behavior in the Elderly

Description

The RAGE is a twenty-one-item rating scale designed for the use of ward staff to measure aggressive behavior in psychogeriatric inpatients. The scale enables researchers to examine the effectiveness of treatment and the relationships between aggressive behavior and other variables.

Figure 5.5 Rating Scale for Aggressive Behavior in the Elderly (RAGE)

Be totally objective. Do not interpret motives.

Instructions: Most items are rated on a frequency basis, i.e., how often the individual
behavior occurred over the past 3 days, as follows:
0 =never;
1= at least once in the past 3 days,
2= at least once every day in the past 3 days,
3= more than once every day in the past 3 days.

Has the patient in the past 3 days . . .

1. been demanding or argumentative?	0	1	2	3
2. shouted, yelled, or screamed?	0	1	2	3
3. sworn or used abusive language?	0	1	2	3
4. disobeyed ward rules, e.g., deliberately passed urine outside the commode?	0	1	2	3
5. been uncooperative or resisted help, e.g., whilst being given a bath or medication?	0	1	2	3
6. been generally in a bad mood, irritable or quick to fly off the handle?	0	1	2	3
7. been critical, sarcastic or derogatory, e.g., saying someone is stupid or incompetent?	0	1	2	3
8. been impatient or got angry if something does not suit him/her?	0	1	2	3
9. threatened to harm or made statements to scare others?	0	1	2	3
10. indulged in antisocial acts, e.g., deliberately stealing food or tripping someone?	0	1	2	3
11. pushed or shoved others?	0	1	2	3
12. destroyed property or thrown things around angrily, e.g., towels, medicines?	0	1	2	3
13. been angry with him/herself?	0	1	2	3
14. attempted to kick anyone?	0	1	2	3
15. attempted to hit others?	0	1	2	3
16. attempted to bite, scratch, spit at or pinch others?	0	1	2	3
17. used an object (such as a towel or walking stick) to lash out or hurt someone?	0	1	2	3

In the past 3 days has the patient inflicted any injury . . .

18. on himself/herself?	0	1	2	3
19. on others?	0	1	2	3

   0= no
   1= mild, e.g., a scratch
   2= moderate, e.g., a bruise
   3= severe, e.g., a fracture

20. Has the patient in the past 3 days been required to be placed under sedation or in isolation or in physical restraints, in order to control his/her aggressiveness?	0	1	2	3
21. Taking all factors into consideration, do you consider the patient's behavior in the last 3 days to have been aggressive?	0	1	2	3

   0= not all, 1= mildly, 2= moderately, 3= severely

Psychometric Data

Test-retest reliability at six hours was computed on thirty-five patients and found to be .91. When patients were rated at an interval of seven days, the correlation was .84. And when fourteen days lapsed between ratings, the correlation was .88. Split-half reliability was computed to be .88. External validation of the scale was made possible by independent observers who recorded every occurrence of aggressive behavior in sixteen patients during a time-sampling study. The rating scores from ward nurses correlated .84 with the total number of recorded occurrences of aggressive behavior.

Availability

Vikram Patel and R.A. Hope (1992). A rating scale for aggressive behavior in the elderly—the RAGE. *Psychological Medicine*, 22, 211–221.

Dr. Hope would like to be informed of anyone using the RAGE. Contact him at: Ethox, Institute of Health Sciences, Old Road, Headington, Oxford OX3 7LF, Great Britain.

Scoring

Responses are scored as follows: "never" (0); "at least once in the past three days" (1); "at least once every day in the past 3 days" (2); "more than once every day in the past 3 days" (3).

Adult Children of Alcoholics Tool (ACAT)

Description

Although alcoholism counselors find *adult children of alcoholics* to be a useful clinical term, there exist few scales that can assess this syndrome—generally thought to be characterized by low self-esteem, substance abuse, eating disorders, depression, and anxiety. Unlike the Children of Alcoholics Screen Test, none of the items in the ACAT mentions a drinking problem or alcoholism in the family origin. Each item is designed to tape one of the ACA characteristics described by Black and Woititz. The ACAT is a measure of the internalization of alcohol-related traumas as emotional and interpersonal self-attributes.

Psychometric Data

The ACAT was administered to 365 college undergraduates at the University of Texas at Austin and 109 psychiatric outpatients. For a thirty-two-item pilot scale, the ACAT's internal consistency was computed to be .84, and its one-month test-retest stability .74. Based on individual item comparisons and exploratory factor analysis, the ACAT was shortened to twenty-five items that differentiated the ACAs from the controls and the internal consistency of the revised ACAT was .84 with a test-retest stability of .78. A replication produced a Cronbach's alpha of .89.

Figure 5.6 Adult Children of Alcoholics Tool (ACAT)

Directions: The following questions refer to your family of origin, the family with which you spent the most time when you were growing up. Indicate how strongly you agree, or disagree, with each statement by choosing the appropriate letter. Fill in the blank preceding each statement with the letter A, B, C, D, or E, depending on your choice: A = Strongly Agree; B = Somewhat Agree; C = Neutral; D = Somewhat Disagree; E Strongly Disagree.

Part 1:

_____ 1. When there is a problem in my family we talk about it.
_____ 2. The idea of loss of control is intolerable to me.
_____ 3. It is hard to share problems with people I love.
_____ 4. It is easy to trust members of my family.
_____ 5. It is difficult for me to set aside responsibilities for awhile and enjoy play.
_____ 6. When I have a problem with someone I care about I am reluctant to discuss it, for fear of "rocking the boat."
_____ 7. I find it easier to avoid situations where I have to take control in my family or personal relationships.
_____ 8. Consistency and predictability are usually the rule in my family.
_____ 9. I usually look out for others' needs before my own.
_____ 10. There is very little predictability in my family.
_____ 11. I have always felt comfortable bringing my friends home to meet my family.
_____ 12. Ever since I was young I have learned to be tough and not cry.
_____ 13. If I can just ignore a problem it will not hurt so bad and I can handle it easier later.
_____ 14. I want to trust others, but it is so much easier just to rely on myself.
_____ 15. I have trouble following a project from beginning to end.
_____ 16. I tend to overreact to changes over which I have no control.
_____ 17. It doesn't matter much to me whether others approve of my actions or not.
_____ 18. When I start a new project I usually have no difficulty finishing it.
_____ 19. I have difficulty forming intimate relationships with others.
_____ 20. I have a strong need for others' approval and affirmation of my actions.
_____ 21. It's hard for me to decide when to get close to people and when to back off.
_____ 22. Telling the truth about problems is encouraged in my family.
_____ 23. Sometimes I find it hard to draw a line between my feelings and the feelings of people who are close to me.
_____ 24. I have a tough time being honest about my feelings toward others.
_____ 25. There are times when I think that anyone who could love me is stupid or worthless.

Evidence of construct validation was found when the ACAT strongly correlated with the Beck Depression Inventory ($r = .57$), the Internalized Shame Scale ($r = .69$), the Children of Alcoholics Screening Test ($r = .38$), and inversely related to the Family Routines Inventory ($r = -.47$) and frequency of family rituals as measured by the Ritual Scale ($-.37$). The ACAT was also correlated ($.24$) with the Drinking Restraint Scale. A third study found a correlation coefficient of $.62$ between the ACAT and scores on the Adult Children of Alcoholics Index.

Availability

Hawkins, C.A. and Hawkins, R.C. (1995). Development and validation of an Adult Children of Alcoholics Tool. *Research on Social Work Practice*, 5, 317–339. There are no restrictions on the use of this scale.

Scoring

Individuals scoring 30 or above on the ACAT when informally interviewed most often report that they have shame or current mental health problems.

CES-D Scale

Description

Developed by the staff at the Center for Epidemiologic Studies, National Institute of Mental Health, the CES-D is a brief self-report scale designed to measure depressive symptomatology in the general population (Radloff, 1977). It was developed from previously existing scales and was designed not to distinguish primary depressive disorders from secondary depression or sub-types of depression but to identify the presence and severity of depressive symptomatology for epidemiologic research, needs assessment, and screening (Radloff and Locke, 1986).

Psychometric Data

This depression scale has been found to have high internal consistency (.85 in the general population and .90 in the patient sample) and acceptable test-retest stability. The CES-D scores discriminate well between psychiatric inpatient and general population samples and moderately well among patient groups with varying levels of severity. The scale has excellent concurrent validity, and substantial evidence exists of its construct validity (Radloff, 1977).

Availability

The CES-D Scale is in the public domain and may be used without copyright permission. The Epidemiology and Psychopathology Research Branch is interested, however, in receiving copies of research reports that have utilized the instrument.

Scoring

Because the CES-D is a twenty-item scale, it is easily scored. Responses are weighted 0 for "Rarely or none of the time" to 3 for "Most of the time." Items 4, 8, 12, and 16 are reverse-scored (given a 3 for "Rarely" and 0 for "Most"). The range of possible scores is 0 to 60. High scores indicate high levels of depression symptomatology, with scores of 17 or greater identified as "at-risk cases" and scores of 23 or above as "probable cases" of depression.

Figure 5.7 The CES-D Scale

CES-D Scale

Circle the number for each statement which best describes how often you felt
or behaved this way during the past week.

	Rarely or None of the Time	Some or a Little of the Time	Occasionally or a Moderate Amount of Time	Most or All of the Time
	(Less than 1 day)	(1-2 days)	(3-4 days)	(5-7 Days)

During the past week:

1. I was bothered by things that usually don't bother me.	_____	_____	_____	_____
2. I did not feel like eating; my appetite was poor.	_____	_____	_____	_____
3. I felt that I could not shake off the blues even with help from my family or friends.	_____	_____	_____	_____
4. I felt that I was just as good as other people.	_____	_____	_____	_____
5. I had trouble keeping my mind on what I was doing.	_____	_____	_____	_____
6. I felt depressed.	_____	_____	_____	_____
7. I felt that everything I did was an effort.	_____	_____	_____	_____
8. I felt hopeful about the future.	_____	_____	_____	_____
9. I thought my life had been failure.	_____	_____	_____	_____
10. I felt fearful.	_____	_____	_____	_____
11. My sleep was restless.	_____	_____	_____	_____
12. I was happy.	_____	_____	_____	_____
13. I talked less than usual.	_____	_____	_____	_____
14. I felt lonely.	_____	_____	_____	_____
15. People were unfriendly.	_____	_____	_____	_____
16. I enjoyed life.	_____	_____	_____	_____
17. I had crying spells.	_____	_____	_____	_____
18. I felt sad.	_____	_____	_____	_____
19. I felt that people disliked me.	_____	_____	_____	_____
20. I could not get "going."	_____	_____	_____	_____

Source: Courtesy U.S. Department of Health and Human Services.

Rosenberg Self-Esteem Scale

Description

The Rosenberg Self-Esteem Scale was originally developed on a sample of over five thousand high school juniors and seniors from ten randomly selected schools in New York state. A recent query in *Social Science Citation Index* produced close to 1,300 citations for Rosenberg's instrument—making it the most popular measure of global self-esteem and prompting Blascovich and Tomaka (1991) to observe that "it is the standard with which developers of other measures usually seek convergence" (p. 120).

Figure 5.8 Rosenberg Self-Esteem Scale

Instructions: Below is a list of statements dealing with your general feelings about yourself. If you <u>agree</u> with the statement, circle <u>A</u>. If you <u>strongly agree</u>, circle <u>SA</u>. If you <u>disagree</u>, circle <u>D</u>. If you <u>strongly disagree</u>, circle <u>SD</u>.

	Strongly Agree	Agree	Disagree	Strongly Disagree
1. On the whole, I am satisfied with myself.	SA	A	S	SD
2. At times I think I am no good at all.	SA	A	S	SD
3. I feel that I have a number of good qualities.	SA	A	S	SD
4. I am able to do things as well as most other people.	SA	A	S	SD
5. I feel I do not have much to be proud of.	SA	A	S	SD
6. I certainly feel useless at times.	SA	A	S	SD
7. I feel that I'm a person of worth, at least on an equal plane with others.	SA	A	S	SD
8. I wish I could have more respect for myself.	SA	A	S	SD
9. All in all, I am inclined to feel that I am a failure.	SA	A	S	SD
10. I take a positive attitude toward myself.	SA	A	S	SD

Source: Courtesy Morris Rosenberg.

Psychometric Data

Fleming and Courtney (1984) have reported a Cronbach alpha of .8' and test-retest correlations of .82 with a one-week interval. Rosenberg (1965) presented a great deal of data on the construct validity of this measure. Demo (1985) reported self-esteem scores correlating .55 with the Coopersmith SEI.

Availability

This scale is in the public domain and may be used without securing permission.

Scoring

Using the Likert procedure, responses are assigned a score ranging from 1 to 4. Items 1, 3, 4, 7, and 10 are reverse scored. (For example, item 1, "On the whole I am satisfied with myself," the "strongly agree" response is assigned a score of 4 and "strongly disagree" is assigned a score of 1.) This procedure yields possible total scores ranging from 10 to 40. The higher the score, the higher the self-esteem.

Final Notes

In reading about various scales, students often encounter terminology that needs a note of explanation. Some authors use the term *index* instead of scale. An index is a set of items that produce a summated score—in effect, a scale. *Scale* and *index* are terms that can usually be used interchangeably. Instruments that contain a number of different scales may also be referred to as multidimensional inventories—for instance, the Multi-Problem Screening Inventory contains scales measuring depression, self-esteem, aggression, fearfulness, guilt, confused thinking, and a number of others (Hudson and McMurty, 1997). Typically, the items are intermixed in a random order. This allows researchers to check for inconsistency in subjects' responses. For example, the same item (for example, "My partner calls me hurtful names") may be asked in a slightly different form ("My partner belittles me") to see if a client is responding in the same way to both items.

Students occasionally wonder about clients who deliberately misrepresent the truth on assessment instruments. They may know of an actual incident (a beating by a partner that required medical attention) that is not reported on the scale. All self-reports are based on the assumption that some error is involved but that respondents are usually honest. Further, an inaccurate response to any one item on a scale generally does not create a measurement problem. Persons who live with emotionally abusive partners would still have higher scores than persons who don't live with abusive partners even if they are dishonest on a few items. What matters most is a consistency (such as reporting abuse) across the many items contained in the scale. Of course, clients may be motivated to lie and this might not always be detected—particularly in shorter scales that don't contain inconsistency scales.

These are the ways that subjects can bias their responses:

- Social desirability—putting the "best foot forward," not reporting behavior or attitudes that might meet with social disapproval.
- Faking good—creating a false positive impression.
- Faking bad—creating a false negative impression.
- End-aversion—avoiding extreme categories like "never" and "always" and consistently choosing a middle response on a scale.
- Acquiescence—tending to agree with, to give positive responses to items.

On rating instruments, there's another response bias possibility. Because of an overall or previously formed impression about someone (such as a "chronic" patient who is manipulative or an employee who is thought to be unethical), raters may find it difficult to objectively rate their progress in different areas—generalizing instead with a *halo effect*. Thus, there may be a tendency to rate a client who is well liked and personable as higher functioning than he or she really is, and, conversely, a client who has caused trouble or complained a great deal may be viewed as having made less progress. The use of behaviorally anchored scales may help to reduce this expectancy effect.

Self-Review

(Answers at the end of the book)

1. Pam has created a scale and administered it to the same group of her chronically mentally ill clients on two occasions, a week apart. It is likely she is trying to determine:
   a. construct validity.
   b. test-retest reliability.
   c. a correlation coefficient with all the extraneous variables.
   d. content validity.
2. If an item correlates strongly with the other items on a scale, would Pam want to throw it out and create a new item, or keep it because it would add to the scale's internal consistency?

3. If you and another school social worker were observing children with suspected attention deficit disorder and each of you is using a rating scale, what would you call the effort to determine the correlation between your two ratings?

4. _____ is when an instrument measures the construct it was designed to measure.

5. T or F.   Pam shares her newly created instrument with several co-workers and they agree it appears to possess face validity. Pam doesn't need to conduct any other validity studies before using her scale in a large project involving 300 clients over a two-year study period.

6. T or F.   Factor analysis is the approved way of establishing concurrent validity.

7. T or F.   Predictive validity is when the researcher finds no relationship between the scale's measurements and variables that should not be correlated with the construct.

8. T or F.   A scale with an internal validity of .60 could be said to be "quite strong."

9. T or F.   Once a scale is determined to be valid, say, with a group of clients with chronic mental illness, no additional validity studies would be needed if the scale was then used with a group of high school underachievers.

10. T or F.   The problem with designing a new instrument each time you need one is that it always has unknown psychometrics until studies establish its reliability and validity.

Questions for Class Discussion

1. Why would a researcher prefer to measure a concept like depression or self-esteem with an instrument rather than just by observation?

2. Does it make sense to debate whether reliability is more important than validity? Why or why not?

3. Do you think it is important to disguise from research subjects the title of the scale they are completing? Under what circumstances might it make sense to cloak the title or purpose of a study?

4. The term *discrimination* usually has a negative connotation, such as when it is associated with sexism or racism. However, does the term have a positive or negative connotation when we think about a scale with construct validity being able to discriminate well?

5. What type of validity were Smith and Ford trying to demonstrate with the Community Living Skills Scale by correlating it with the Global Assessment Scale?

Mini-Projects for Experiencing Research Firsthand

1. Read one of the articles on the development and validation of a scale referenced in this chapter. Summarize, in a short paper, all the steps the authors went through.
2. With a partner, attempt to create a scale measuring some concept of your choice. Then present the scale to the class for a discussion of its face and content validity.
3. Using either a scale that you've developed or one with known psychometrics, collect a small sample of data. Enter the data into a computer with statistical analysis software so that you can compute the scale's internal consistency. Discuss what you found and possible explanations.
4. Skim one of the reference books containing scales or search on the Internet. Make a list of at least five scales that you might be able to use sometime in the future as a social work practitioner. Explain how each could be used. For extra credit, discuss their reliability and validity.

References and Resources

Abell, Neil. (1991). The index of clinical stress: A brief measure of subjective stress for practice and research. *Social Work Research and Abstracts,* 27(2), 12–15.

Camasso, M.J. and Geismar, L.L. (1992). A multivariate approach to construct reliability and validity assessment: The case of family functioning. *Social Work Research and Abstracts,* 28(4), 16–26.

Combs-Orme, T.D., Orme, J.G., and Guidry, C.J. (1991). Reliability and validity of the Protective Services Questionnaire (PSQ). *Journal of Social Service Research,* 14(1/2), 1–20.

Comrey, A.L. (1988). Factor analytic methods in scale development in personality and clinical psychology. *Journal of Consulting and Clinical Psychology,* 56, 754–761.

Congdon, D.C. and Holland, T.P. (1988). Measuring the effectiveness of substance abuse treatment: Toward a theory-based index. *Journal of Social Service Research,* 12(1/2), 23–48.

Cummings, S.M., Kelly, T.B., Holland, T.P., and Peterson-Hazan, X. (1997). Development and validation of the Needs Inventory for Caregivers of the Hospitalized Elderly. *Research on Social Work Practice,* 8, 120–132.

DeVellis, R.F. (1993). *Scale development: Theory and applications.* Newbury Park, CA: Sage.

Demo, D.H. (1985). The measurement of self-esteem: Refining our methods. *Journal of Personality and Social Psychology*, 48, 1490–1502.

Fleming, J.S. and Courtney, B.E. (1984). The dimensionality of self-esteem. II. Hierarchical facet model for revised measurement scales. *Journal of Personality and Social Psychology*, 46, 404–421.

Foster, S.L. and Martinez, C.R. (1995). Ethnicity: Conceptual and methodological issues in child clinical research. *Journal of Clinical Child Psychology,* 24, 214–226.

Harrison, D.F. and Westhuis, D.J. (1990). Rating scales for sexual adjustment. *Journal of Social Service Research,* 13(3), 85–100.

Holden, G., Cuzzi, L., Rutter, S., Chernack, P., and Rosenberg, G. (1997). The Hospital Social Work Self-Efficacy Scale. *Research on Social Work Practice,* 7, 490–499.

Hudson, W.W. and McMurtry, S.L. (1997). Comprehensive assessment in social work practice. *Research on Social Work Practice,* 7, 78–98.

Klein, W.C. (1992). Measuring caregiver attitude toward the provision of long-term care. *Journal of Social Service Research,* 16(3/4), 147–161.

Koeske, G.F. (1994). Some recommendations for improving measurement validation in social work research. *Journal of Social Work Research,* 18, 43–72.

Koeske, G.F. and Koeske, R.D. (1992). Parenting locus of control: Measurement, construct validation, and a proposed conceptual model. *Social Work Research and Abstracts,* 28(3), 37–46.

MacNeil, G. (1991). A short-form scale to measure alcohol abuse. *Research on Social Work Practice,* 1(1), 68–75.

Malgady, R.G. (1996). The question of cultural bias in assessment and diagnosis of ethnic minority clients: Let's reject the null hypothesis. *Professional Psychology, Research, and Practice,* 27, 73–77.

Meier, S.T. (1994). *The chronic crisis in psychological measurement and assessment: A historical survey.* New York: Academic Press.

Nasuti, J.P. and Pecora, P.J. (1993). Risk assessment scales in child protection: A test of the internal consistency and interrater reliability of one statewide system. *Social Work Research and Abstracts,* 29(2), 28–33.

Nugent, W.R. and Thomas, J.W. (1993). Validation of a clinical measure of self-esteem. *Research on Social Work Practice,* 3(2), 191–207.

Nunnally, J.C. (1994). *Psychometric theory.* New York: McGraw-Hill.

O'Hare, T. and Collins, P. (1997). Development and validation of a scale for measuring social work practice skills. *Research on Social Work Practice,* 7, 228–238.

Polansky, N.A., Gaudin, J.M., and Kilpatrick, A.C. (1992). The Maternal Characteristics Scale: A cross validation. *Child Welfare,* 71(3), 271–282.

Radloff, L.S. (1977). The CES-D Scale: A self-report depression scale for research in the general population. *Applied Psychological Measurement,* 3, 385–401.

Radloff, L.S. and Locke, B.Z. (1986). The Community Mental Health Assessment Survey and the CES-D Scale. In Weissman, M.M. Myers, J.K., and Ross, C.E. (Eds.), *Community surveys of psychiatric disorders.* New Brunswick, NJ: Rutgers University Press.

Rosenberg, M. (1965). *Society and the adolescent self-image.* Princeton, NJ: Princeton University Press.

Schondel, C., Shields, G., and Orel, N. (1992). Development of an instrument to measure volunteers' motivation in working with people with AIDS. *Social Work in Health Care,* 17(2), 53–71.

Shields, J.J. (1992). Evaluating community organization projects: The development of an empirically based measure. *Social Work Research and Abstracts,* 28(2), 15–20.

Spector, P.E. (1992). *Summated rating scale construction: An introduction.* Newbury Park, CA: Sage.

Streiner, D.L. and Norman, G.R. (1995). *Health measurement scales: A practical guide to their development and use.* New York: Oxford University Press.

CHAPTER 6
Survey Research

If the topic of experimental design seemed foreign to you, survey research should be familiar. We see results of surveys in our newspapers and magazines almost every day. Social work literature abounds with surveys. They are the research methodology most commonly used by social workers. Surveys have been conducted to explore such issues as job burnout, values and ethical dilemmas, client satisfaction with services, and drug use among high school students. Pick up any social work journal and you are likely to find some type of a survey. Surveys have been called "the single most important information gathering invention of the social sciences" and it is essential that social workers, both as consumers and producers of research, understand them well.

Surveys can be thought of as snapshots of attitudes, beliefs, or behaviors at one point in time. Using a predetermined set of questions or issues, they reveal what a group of respondents is thinking, feeling, or doing. Social workers might use surveys to uncover special needs within their communities or within special populations of clients. Often called **needs assessments,** these surveys might try to determine the prenatal care needs of low-income clients, understand transportation barriers, or help agencies respond after a natural disaster like a hurricane or tornado. These surveys provide information about what the targeted population knows or perceives about the availability and accessibility of services and can also identify unmet needs—gaps in services. Needs assessments may involve prepared questionnaires or personal interviewing and may solicit information from clients, their caseworkers, other professionals such as parole officers or physicians, or citizens randomly selected from the community. Needs assessments are sometimes used to provide evaluative information, such as when a program director wants to know if the clients or community view the agency as providing acceptable service. In this vein, the program director would be trying to identify problems that need correcting in order for the program to be viewed more positively.

Social service agencies can also use these surveys internally to identify areas where staff feel that they need additional training or continuing education. Following a situation where an intoxicated client punched the receptionist and broke her jaw, the administration might conduct a needs assessment of staff to identify ideas about how to provide greater security in the workplace.

Needs assessments may involve surveys of **key informants**—individuals in the community who are likely to know about special needs as a result of their positions. They may be physicians, social service providers, clergy, public officials, and so on.

Another type of needs assessment involves **community forums**—public meetings or hearings where members of a community state their preferences or present their demands. These meetings can be loud and boisterous, or they may be poorly attended. For the most part, clients typically seen by social workers seldom attend such meetings. A conceptual weakness with this approach is that those who attend and express their views may not be representative of the community or even familiar with its needs.

Rates under treatment is a type of needs assessment that usually relies upon existing agency data. By looking at the profiles of an agency's clients and comparing this data with census information, one can tell which population groups are being over- or underserved. Agency data can also inform as to trends—perhaps indicating that a problem in the community is getting worse. (More on this topic in chapter 10). Akin to this method would be the use of social indicators (such as high school dropout rates, delinquency cases, teen pregnancies) and existing data from other available sources.

Possibly the most popular form of needs assessment would involve some sort of community survey. These surveys can range from those hastily conceived and executed to those based on scientifically selected samples that provide a good deal of confidence in the findings.

Surveys appeal to us, I think, because they are rooted in the democratic process of asking people about their opinions. We like to know how our attitudes compare with those of others—to learn whether we are in the mainstream or not. But also, surveys invite participation. Designing a questionnaire can be great fun, almost like a game. If this task is being done by committee, practically everyone can participate either by suggesting items or by pointing out ways specific items might be misinterpreted or could be improved. Other reasons for the popularity of surveys are that they are quickly implemented and convenient to administer. Once the survey instrument has been chosen or designed and a sample identified, the survey can often be handled by a clerical person (for instance, with a mail survey), thus freeing the researcher to attend to other matters until a sufficient number of survey questionnaires have come in for analysis. Sometimes, the investigator can coordinate the collection of data from personal or telephone interviews. Each of these approaches has its own set of advantages and disadvantages that we'll discuss later in the chapter.

Surveys come in many different varieties. It is common in social work literature for authors to note that they have conducted an **exploratory survey**.

These are generally recognized by their small samples. Exploratory studies are sometimes conducted prior to applying for federal grant dollars to allow investigators to test out hypotheses or instruments on a small scale. Since science is built by small, incremental steps, exploratory surveys are legitimate even though the knowledge they produce is often seriously limited.

When investigators are ready to define a phenomenon definitively, they must increase their sample sizes and address the problems of acquiring representative samples. While an exploratory survey of teens involved in Satan worship may consist only of four individuals arrested in a local cemetery, a **descriptive survey** must be concerned with obtaining a representative sample. As you might imagine, this can be difficult to do, and so descriptive surveys often try to compensate by constructing very large samples. These surveys may involve four hundred, twenty-five hundred, or even more research subjects. To change examples, a descriptive survey of the homeless in Illinois might involve having every shelter in the state collect data each night for a week during a winter month. Even though you may gather information on five thousand different homeless persons, many would still be missed because they don't stay in shelters even in cold weather. However, the large sample size probably does accurately reflect the characteristics of most of the homeless and would allow the researcher to create a profile of the homeless and to generalize about the homeless population in Illinois.

When we conduct a survey, there are four different means by which we collect the data. These are:

- Mail surveys
- Telephone surveys
- Personal interviews
- E-mail surveys

Each of these approaches will be discussed in turn.

The Mail Questionnaire

The advantages of the mail questionnaire have been noted by Mangione (1995):

- Relatively inexpensive
- Large numbers of respondents can be surveyed in a relatively short period
- Respondents can look up information if they need to
- Privacy is maximized
- Visual presentation

- Can be completed when convenient for the respondent
- Respondents can see the context of a series of questions
- Insulate respondents from the expectations of the researcher

A final advantage of the mail questionnaire is that it reduces errors that might occur in the process of interviewing. Not all interviewers are equally skilled, and some may have traits that annoy, offend, or cause those being interviewed to be less than honest.

On the other hand, there are a number of specific disadvantages to the mail questionnaire: first of all, unlike with personal or telephone interviews, researchers experience some loss of control over the survey process once the questionnaire has been mailed. Although the questionnaire may be delivered to the proper address, there is no guarantee that the intended recipient will be the one who completes the questionnaire. An eleven-year-old child could respond for his or her mother or father even though the researcher intended the survey form to go to adults. A related problem is that the survey could be completed under less than optimal conditions (for example, when the respondent is ill or intoxicated, or completes the questionnaire while the television is blaring or a party is going on in the living room).

Second, investigators cannot assume that all recipients of the survey will be literate or will be able to comprehend complex issues. While college students are accustomed to questionnaires and multiple choice response sets, individuals with lower levels of educational attainment may find structured response sets (such as "Strongly Agree," "Agree," "Undecided," "Disagree," "Strongly Disagree") confusing or too confining for the responses they want to give.

Third, mail questionnaires tend to be highly structured and relatively short. These questionnaires may not provide the detail that could emerge from a face-to-face contact. In personal interview situations, the interviewer is able to ask for additional information (to **probe**) if the respondent says something exceptionally interesting or if the interviewer is not sure of the response or thinks the respondent did not understand the question.

Mail questionnaires have become a popular gimmick with some businesses (for example, an official-looking survey form arrives asking information about how much you travel or take vacations, but its real purpose is to sell real estate or vacation time-sharing plans). Consequently, some Americans see surveys as a form of soliciting or as junk mail. Even if a survey form arrives in an envelope carrying first-class postage, it can be seen as an invasion of privacy and thrown away. Individuals with good intentions can put the survey form aside until "later" with the result that questionnaires get lost, thrown out, or put in the parakeet's cage.

Another problem is that Americans are a highly mobile population and are constantly changing addresses, last names, and places of employment.

Your survey will be seriously disadvantaged if your mailing list is inaccurate or out of date. The post office may not be able to deliver or to forward mail—especially if the intended respondent is trying to avoid creditors or legal authorities.

These factors directly affect the number of people who complete and return survey questionnaires. It is not uncommon for only 25 to 35 percent of those who were mailed a questionnaire to return it. The response rates for mail surveys are often only 5 to 10 percent, and response rates over 30 percent are rare. Of course, if your addresses are recent and the topic is one that interests the respondents, response rates will improve, but will seldom reach response rates of telephone or face-to-face interviews. However, these rates apply only to those who receive one mailing. With a reminder postcard and the mailing of a second questionnaire to those who did not initially respond, these rates can be improved quite a bit—to 50 percent or more. This is discussed in the next section.

Getting a Good Response Rate

Designing a mail questionnaire is not so simple as it may first appear. Extensive research exists on all aspects of the mail survey. It is known, for instance, that using first-class postage results in better response rates. Similarly, increasing the perceived personalization of each letter seems to pay dividends. In addition to the use of first-class stamps (versus meter or bulk mail), Ransdell (1996) recommends handwritten addresses and signatures. Personalized notes at the bottom of cover letters also seem to increase the response rate. Other successful tactics include prenotifying the potential participants that they will be asked to participate in a survey, having a university or "official" sponsorship, and sending reminder postcards or making phone call follow-ups to those who have forgotten to return their surveys.

Dillman (1983) has provided an overview of steps that contribute to what he calls the "Total Design Method." He suggests that long questionnaires be photo-reduced and designed as a booklet to make it more appealing and less imposing (preferable size is 6.5 inches by 8.25 inches). The first page is designed as a cover with an interesting title and illustration; the back page is left blank for additional comments. The booklet should be printed on white paper (preferably sixteen-pound weight) and arranged so that the most interesting questions appear first. The whole questionnaire should be designed so that lowercase letters are used for questions and uppercase letters for responses. Visual clues (arrows, indentations, and spacing) are used to their fullest advantage to help respondents answer in a straight vertical line rather than going back and forth across the page (see figure 6.1).

Figure 6.1: An Example of Items from a Questionnaire

Child Abuse Survey

1. How serious a problem is child abuse and neglect in our community?

_____ VERY SERIOUS
_____ SOMEWHAT SERIOUS
_____ NOT VERY SERIOUS
_____ NOT A PROBLEM AT ALL

2. Have you ever had reason to suspect that a child living in your neighborhood has been emotionally abused?

_____ NO
_____ YES ⌐

        2a. Have you ever reported a case of suspected emotional abuse?

           _____ YES
           _____ NO

3. Compared to ten years ago, do you think there is now more, less, or about the same amount of child abuse?

_____ MORE
_____ LESS
_____ ABOUT THE SAME

Considerable thought and research have also gone into the implementation of the survey procedures. Dillman (1983) suggests a one-page cover letter on letterhead stationery explaining that a socially useful study is being conducted and why each respondent is important. Individual names and addresses are typed on the cover letter and the envelope. One week after the first mail-out, a reminder postcard is sent to all recipients. Three weeks after the first mail-out, a second cover letter, questionnaire, and return envelope are sent to all those who have not responded. Seven weeks after the first mail-out, another cover letter and questionnaire are sent by certified mail to all those who have not responded.

The total design method greatly improves the response rates ordinarily found with mail surveys. Dillman (1978) states that the average response rate for forty-eight surveys using his procedures was 74 percent, with no survey receiving less than a 50 percent response.

Incentives are sometimes necessary to increase response rates. The good news, however, is that monetary inducements don't have to be very large. One study (James and Bolstein, 1992) found that a prepaid incentive of $1 almost doubled the response rate. Further, a $5 check produced almost the same response rate (52 percent) as a $40 check (54 percent). Promising even as much as $50 did not improve response rates over providing no incentive at all.

Wilk (1993) reported a systematic random survey of four hundred names chosen from the NASW *Register of Clinical Social Workers.* She found that a $1 incentive improved her response rate from 43 percent to 63 percent. Lotteries are another way to reward participation.

Nonmonetary incentives such as pens, refrigerator magnets, book marks, and the like can also be effectively used. I once bought a large five hundred-piece jigsaw puzzle and taped a piece of it to each questionnaire being sent a second time to nonresponders. My cover letter started off, "I'm puzzled. About two weeks ago, we mailed you a questionnaire, but we've not heard from you . . ." While the puzzle pieces weren't exactly an incentive, the novelty of the idea was effective and a number of respondents actually mailed the pieces back. Occasionally, I've seen companies use bright new pennies ("A penny for your thoughts . . .") to engage the reader's interest. A penny isn't enough compensation to function as a monetary incentive—the point here is to be creative in your thinking. Remember, respondents don't *have* to cooperate, each one who does is doing you a favor!

Dillman's approach greatly improves response rates over a single mailing. Researchers who follow his method can expect to obtain response rates of 70 percent or higher. Of course, the nature of the survey—how well it holds the reader's interest and its complexity and length—has direct effects. Your cover letter should grab the potential respondents and keep them reading. If it is dry and dull, odds are the questionnaire will be ignored. Ask questions to stimulate thinking, even in the cover letter. In a study of social workers one might start with, "What do the next generation of social workers need to know? What advice do you have for them? We'd like to draw upon your professional experience if you can spare just ten minutes."

When designing a survey questionnaire, follow these steps:

- Make it interesting and easy to read.
- Keep the questionnaire as short as possible (response rates and length of questionnaires are inversely related).
- Pilot test it (to make sure the questions provide you with the information you seek).

Additionally, take the time to ensure that the mailing list is current and as accurate as possible. Also, plan on mailing at least a second letter and questionnaire to all nonrespondents. You may want to include a toll-free number for respondents to use if they have questions about the survey, how they were selected, and that sort of thing. Some institutional review boards require that researchers routinely provide such a phone number for potential respondents to inquire about their rights as research subjects. (Clients of an agency, for instance, might worry that they might be in jeopardy of losing their services if they refuse to participate.)

The Telephone Survey

The chief advantage of the telephone survey over the face-to-face interview is that it is less expensive (one avoids all expenses associated with traveling to the respondent). Telephone surveys can also be conveniently run from an office. Bulk user rates help reduce the costs of numerous calls. Telephone surveys allow the interviewer to have control over the choice of the respondent and give the interviewer the ability to probe when questions or responses are not understood.

Telephone surveys allow interviewers access to individuals who cannot or will not open their doors to strangers for the purpose of an interview (such as, persons confined to bed because of illness or injury). Another advantage is that when timeliness is important, special issues can be explored and data gathered almost overnight. A final advantage is that telephone interviewers can be closely monitored and the quality of their work frequently evaluated to ensure that questions are asked correctly and responses are coded satisfactorily.

A disadvantage of the telephone survey is that the interviewer cannot see the respondent. This means that some items such as the person's race or the condition of the house cannot be observed. If these are important to the investigator, they must be asked of the respondent. When the phone is used, the interviewer misses facial expressions, which indicate such states as confusion or the beginning of an emotion like anger or sadness. Not everyone can be a successful telephone interviewer; he or she must be articulate, personable, and a good conversationalist. The quality of the interviewer's voice is also important. An interviewer must quickly interest the potential respondent in cooperating and establish rapport before the respondent loses interest. If open-ended questions are used, the interviewer must be able to record the responses quickly and accurately.

Another disadvantage of telephone surveys is that they must be kept short. Telephone interviews should be under twenty minutes long, and the shorter the better. There are exceptions—much longer surveys have been successfully completed by phone, but respondent fatigue can cause hang-ups and incompletions. As a general rule, the more interesting the topic is for the respondent, the greater the probability that the respondent will complete the interview even if it is lengthy.

Some believe that interviewing by telephone is unacceptable because of built-in bias associated with the inability to interview persons who do not have telephones. While it is true that telephone surveys will underrepresent the poorest of the poor, it is estimated that about 80 percent of households with annual incomes of less than $10,000 in central cities have telephones (cited in Gwiasda, Taluc, and Popkin, 1997). Nationally, about 94 percent of all American households have telephones (U.S. Department of Commerce,

1997). Except when the most economically disadvantaged are being targeted, telephone surveys are generally thought to be adequate and representative of "most" Americans. Professional market survey and polling organizations do not simply accept the responses of just anyone who answers the phone, rather they often go to great lengths to find individuals who fit a specific category (for example, African-American males with incomes under $20,000). They may reject some households where they already have too many respondents (for example, white females thirty to forty-five years of age) in their quest to make their samples representative of the larger population.

If as a social worker you want to survey persons with low income who may not have phones, you need to think about where they may be found. Many of the homeless, for instance, could be located in shelters or at soup kitchens. Those slightly better off might be interviewed in public housing projects, low-income neighborhoods, or as they patronize such businesses as laundromats.

The use of a telephone directory to produce samples for telephone surveys can lead to biased data. Police officers, celebrities, single and divorced women, mental health professionals, and public officials often do not have listed phone numbers. And the number of unlisted phones varies markedly by geographical area. In Lexington, Kentucky, about 11 percent of phones are unlisted, compared with 43 percent in Philadelphia, 61 percent in Los Angeles, and 62 percent in Las Vegas. Nationally, about a third of all phone numbers are unlisted (*Lexington Herald-Leader,* May 9, 1990). To compensate for unlisted numbers, most large-scale telephone surveys use such procedures as random-digit or added-digit dialing. In random-digit dialing, there is intentional selection of the first three digits for the desired local exchanges, and the last four digits are randomly generated by a computer. In added-digit dialing, a legitimate "seed number" is provided for those local exchanges from which the samples are to be drawn, and then consecutive digits are added to the last digit or the last two or three digits. While these procedures result in some phone calls to businesses or others who are not target respondents, it provides a good way of accessing households with unlisted numbers and thus getting a representative sample of all households with phones.

Although telephone response rates are often much better than those obtained from mailed surveys, recent advances in electronic technology have expanded the use of computers in telephone solicitation, resulting in many more "nuisance" calls to households with phones. As a defensive measure, many Americans have resorted to screening their calls with telephone answering machines or with "Caller-ID" services. As many as two-thirds or more of Americans may own telephone answering machines. The use of these technologies and new products still being developed is going to create interesting challenges for those who use telephone surveying techniques. Already the Gallup organization, one of the better-known survey companies in the United

States, has noted a decline in response rates from 80 percent when they first began interviewing by phone in the 1970s to approximately 60 percent (Farhi, 1992).

Getting the Most Out of Telephone Surveys

Interviewers need to be trained in the conduct of the survey. This training should include role-plays and interviewing other trainees to ensure that the purpose of each question is well understood. All interviewers should be given standardized introductory statements that move quickly to the survey questions and are often advised against asking the respondents permission to interview them or if they have a few minutes to answer some questions. A brief introduction might go something like this:

> Hello. My name is _____. I'm calling from the _____ Survey Research Center. We're conducting a survey this month of people randomly selected from across the state. The survey will take about fifteen minutes. We have only a phone number and not any names, so all of your responses will be anonymous. If I have your permission, let me begin by asking how many years you have lived in this state . . . .

It is strongly recommended that the questionnaire and interview procedures be pilot-tested with a small sample to determine if there are any unforeseen problems.

Personal Interviews

The personal interview provides the interviewer with more control than either mail or telephone surveys. The interviewer can read facial expressions and moods, monitor environmental distractions, and determine if the interview should move to a quieter room or be continued at a later date. See, for example, the following report from an interviewer:

> It was a three-ring circus—the respondent had five children ranging from one to eight years and they all had a great time climbing all over the furniture. One child stood on her head on the couch next to me. I managed to hang onto my pencil, the questionnaire, my purse—but it wasn't easy! (Converse and Schuman, 1974, p. 3)

Observational data (such as the respondent's race or affect) can also be determined from the personal interview without requiring questions to be asked of the respondent. Further, visual aids can be used to help a respondent. This is particularly advantageous if there is a need for a complex response set.

In such situations, the respondent can be handed a card from which to choose a response. Another advantage is that the personal interview usually achieves a higher response rate than either mail or telephone surveys.

The prime disadvantage of the interview is that it is much more expensive than the two other approaches. While interviewers can be paid either by the hour or by the number of interviews completed, there must be allowances for travel time to the respondents' homes. Occasionally, multiple trips must be made when appointments are broken (because they have been forgotten, friends drop in, or minor emergencies arise). Interviewers can get lost, find it difficult to locate the respondent's residence, or have car trouble. Further, comments hurriedly scrawled in the margin of the questionnaire can become difficult to discern hours later in the office. The safety of interviewers can also be a major concern, and sometimes interviewers must be assigned in teams of two. Supervision and quality control of the interview process can be more difficult to assure than with the telephone survey.

In order to avoid the great expense of selecting a random sample of households, going door-to-door, and then personally interviewing those selected, another approach is called intercept surveying. Typically, these surveyors position themselves in malls or on busy streets and attempt to interview those persons who are willing to stop and talk to them.

Intercept surveys utilize convenience samples (we'll discuss these more fully later in the chapter) where surveyors seek to fulfill certain quotas or to capture information from persons with certain apparent characteristics (for example, executives carrying briefcases). Even if they strive to reach a cross-section of persons, there's always a problem with self-selection (some people don't like to be stopped on the street). These surveys are limited by the location and times chosen to do the interviewing.

Because they draw nonprobability samples, there is no way to tell whether the data they obtain is representative of the larger population. On the other hand, interviewing convenience samples can be accomplished a lot faster and cheaper than going door to door.

Getting the Most from Personal Interviews

The Survey Research Center at the University of Michigan is one of several well-known institutions that have many years of experience in conducting surveys. Another is the National Opinion Research Center at the University of Chicago. Anyone seriously considering conducting a large number of personal interviews for research purposes should start by reading the Survey Research Center's *Interviewer's Manual: Revised Edition*. This very practical publication outlines, in a step-by-step format, what the interviewer

Practice Note: Interviewing Children

Interviewing young children presents special problems for researchers. They are, for instance, assumed to be highly suggestible. Particularly when children are being interviewed in connection with sexual or physical abuse, the interviewer needs to be extremely cautious about using any leading questions. However, if the interviewer suspects the child's responding indicates a susceptibility to suggestion, several leading questions might be used as a test. In such a situation, the interviewer may want to ask questions that he or she knows to be false— such as: "You came here by taxi, didn't you?" (Yuille, Hunter, Joffe, and Zaparniuk, 1993). Having detailed information about some past event (such as a shopping trip, a prior interview) allows the interviewer to assess the accuracy of the child's recall.

While it is important to establish rapport with children before beginning and this may lengthen the investigatory or research process, most experts feel that children should be interviewed as few times as possible. Yuille, Hunter, Joffe, and Zaparniuk (1993) note one study where the average number of interviews of child victims by police was seven per child.

Here are several guidelines for interviewing young children suggested by Boat and Everson (1988):

1. Limit the number of words used in sentences.
2. To check for a child's understanding, do not say "Do you understand what I said?" but ask the child to repeat what was said.
3. When children do not understand a question, rephrase it rather than repeating it.
4. Interviewers should avoid asking questions involving a time sequence (for example, "When was the first time this happened?")
5. Repeat a person's name instead of using pronouns.

should and should not do. Suggestions are provided for such concerns as securing the interview and responding to such questions as "How did you pick me?" and "What good will all this do?" With regard to the first question, the interviewer briefly explains the sampling process. To answer the second question, it is helpful to pull out newspaper or periodical clippings to show the respondent how information from surveys is used.

The Survey Research Center also recommends that the interviewer ask

---

Practice Note: Safety Concerns

On occasion, researchers need to conduct interviews in dangerous neighborhoods. Telephone surveys in public housing projects are notably inadequate because of the large proportion of residents who may not have phones. Gwiasda, Taluc, and Popkin (1997) have reported on their experiences in surveying for the Chicago Housing Authority's anti-drug and crime prevention program.

Among the steps that they took were to hire indigenous interviewers who had familiarity with the residents and neighborhoods and to avoid interviewing during evenings and weekends. Similarly, they interviewed during months when school was in session. Further, they worked in teams of two and were instructed to complete the interviews in the hallway and to never enter an apartment or building alone. Interviewers had to be continually aware of threats to their personal safety and observed gang meetings, drug sales, and gunfire. However, none of the interviewers or field staff was harmed.

Surveyors going into risky neighborhoods need to inform residents by letter or newsletters, even by TV or radio announcements, and by using existing formal and informal networks so that residents can "be on the lookout" for surveyors and possible perils. Certainly, advising the police of the surveyors' presence in the neighborhood is important, and it may be necessary to request additional patrols or to postpone the survey altogether when conditions are too threatening (such as warring gangs). Giving each interviewer a mobile phone might also afford a measure of safety.

---

questions exactly as they are worded and in the order in which they appear on the questionnaire. Interviewers are not to assume that they know the respondent's position or response. Every question should be asked, even if a preface is needed ("I know that we have already touched on this, but . . ."). The Center recommends that the interviewer repeat questions that are misunderstood or misinterpreted, and probe when necessary. (You can probe by repeating the question, by being silent for a few seconds and giving the respondent time to expand on his or her thoughts, by repeating the respondent's reply, by making a neutral comment such as "Can you tell me a little more?" "Anything else?" or by simply stating that you do not understand.)

Training should assist interviewers in becoming familiar with the survey instrument so that there is no stumbling over words or questions. Taking turns interviewing each other is a good way to achieve a degree of comfort and knowledge of the procedures as well as to identify possible problems with the recording of responses. How to dress should also be covered—interviewers need to look neat and professional but should not dress in a way that calls attention to themselves. If you are a supervisor of interviewers, it is a good idea to review closely the first several completed interviews and then randomly sample the interviews later to ensure that all interviewers are capturing the same type of information.

Electronic Mail Surveys

The popularity of the Internet and e-mail has made it possible for researchers to gather information with less cost than mailed surveys and less obtrusiveness than a telephone call or personal interview. Although computers are standard equipment at most places of business, those who send and receive e-mail from home are not a cross-section of Americans but a slice of the more affluent segment of the population. Their knowledge and use of the computer may, however, make them an interesting group for research. For instance, how many of them have heard about or received counseling from a professional over the Internet? How many know about or have joined an Internet support group? Would they be more likely to participate in an Internet support group than to seek out a "live" one?

Mehta and Sivadas (1995) have noted these advantages of e-mail surveys: (1) speed of delivery, (2) virtually no cost, (3) greater control over who may read the e-mail, and (4) convenience of sending and receiving responses. On the other hand, respondents may not feel they have complete anonymity, and it is not as easy to provide incentives as it is when a questionnaire is mailed in an envelope. Mehta and Sivadas's experiment compared response content and response rates when mail and e-mail surveys were used. They found that e-mail respondents wrote more comments than the mail respondents and that the best response rates (83 percent) were obtained when they used prenotification of the mailed survey along with an incentive of $1. Roughly two-thirds of the e-mailed groups with prenotification responded. However, 40 percent of the e-mail sample without prenotification responded, which was roughly comparable to the 45 percent return rate from those receiving their questionnaire from the U.S. Postal Service without prenotification or incentive.

The authors caution that sending out long, unsolicited e-mail surveys may result in complaints from those who have to pay for the amount of time they are logged on to the Internet. Given the higher response rates that were obtained by using prenotification of the impending survey, it makes good sense to give potential respondents some information about the questionnaire (such as the topic, the number of items, how long it might take to complete it, and, if possible, the benefit or value of the study).

Comparison of the Approaches

All of the approaches we have discussed have something to recommend them. Lengthy surveys and complicated questions are sometimes more easily handled by a personal interview. Mailed responses allow the respondent to feel anonymity is protected. E-mail and telephone surveys can be implemented quickly when results are needed fast. Which is the best method? Researchers have to weigh such variables as costs, response rates, the type of questions being asked, the need for confidentiality, the length of the questionnaire, the characteristics of the targeted population in making a decision, how fast the data are needed, and issues as to who is included and excluded by that technique. Given all the considerations and limitations, however, surveying via the U.S. mail is likely to remain a favorite method employed by social scientists for the forseeable future.

Sampling Theory

Virtually every day you are involved in sampling. On cold winter days you may stick your foot out from under the covers and decide that it is too cold to get up right then. Later on, you test your bath or shower water to see if the temperature is right. You might take a sip of coffee and decide it is too strong. You sometimes walk into a clothing store, glance at a few price tags, and decide the store has items more expensive than you can afford. If you donate blood, a tiny sample of your blood is tested to see if it has sufficient iron content.

In each of these instances sufficient information came from sampling. It was not necessary to experience the *whole* of the phenomenon. You didn't have to drink the whole cup of coffee to realize it was too strong. One sip served as a sample of the whole cup. You didn't have to examine every article of apparel in the clothing store to know that the store catered to an exclusive clientele. The people at the blood center didn't have to draw blood from every part of your body, because your blood is pretty much the same regardless of whether it is in your arm or foot or ear.

The notion behind sampling theory is that a small set of observations (**sampling units**) can tell you something about the larger population. Let's say that you have been elected to a school board in a town with 50,000 registered voters. If there is a movement to raise taxes to build a new high school, you wouldn't have to talk to all 50,000 registered voters to get an accurate notion of whether the majority of the adults in the community were in favor of this tax. A telephone poll of several hundred randomly selected registered voters could provide you with an accurate assessment of support for a new tax. Polling 50,000 individuals is impractical, if not impossible. But more importantly, it is unnecessary.

> **Practice Note: The Reliability of Drug Use Reporting**
> **Obtained from Telephone Interviewers**
>
> Students and investigators often are concerned about the reliability of sensitive information obtained from telephone interviewers. Aktan, Calkins, Ribisl, Kroliczak, and Kasim (1997) have reported that when one-hundred respondents, fifty-five of whom were receiving alcohol and other drug treatment and forty-five of whom were randomly selected, were interviewed a second time one week later, the test-retest reliability for all categories of lifetime dependence (for example, alcohol, cocaine, marijuana) exceeded 93 percent. They concluded that psychoactive substance abuse diagnoses can be obtained reliably over the phone by trained lay interviewers.

Sampling works because trends or tendencies within a large population can be discovered from a small number of individuals. For instance, if 90 percent of the registered voters in the above example were going to vote for an increase in their taxes, an indication of support for the tax issue should be apparent whether you sample one-hundred or five-hundred of the registered voters (if these voters were randomly selected). The larger sample merely allows for greater confidence and precision in estimating the "true" level of support or nonsupport for the tax issue. It is possible that if you sample only a handful of individuals, these few may not feel, act, or believe as the majority of the larger population. But if the sample is large enough (something akin to a critical mass), and there is no bias in the selection of the individual sampling units, then the pattern or characteristics found in the sample should match what you would find if you could contact everyone in the total population.

Surveyors employing scientifically selected samples (known as **probability samples**) are meticulous about how their respondents are selected. Their attention to random selection and sample size gives these surveys a great deal of accuracy in their findings.

The Accuracy of Probability Samples

The Gallup organization is one of several nationally recognized professional survey research organizations. Even though the population of the United States is in excess of 200 million, Gallup is able to develop representative samples of the U.S. adult civilian population with interviews of approximately fifteen hundred respondents. That sample size allows them to be 95 percent confident that the results they obtain are accurate within plus or minus 3 percentage points. Their accuracy is impressive. As can be seen in table 6.1, in twenty-eight national elections, their samples differed from the actual election results by an average of only 2 percentage points.

Although there may be times when a researcher would want to interview every person in a given population, it rarely would be necessary. If sampling is conducted without bias, then smaller representative samples can be used quite adequately to gauge or predict the larger population.

With probability sampling the investigator has a good idea of both the number of people or units in the target population and their characteristics. With these parameters the researcher can determine if a sample is representative. There are several probability sampling designs to consider. The first one we will examine is the **simple random sampling design**, where each sampling unit in the population has the same probability (an equal chance) of being chosen.

Suppose the president of your university is retiring, and the board of trustees is interested in selecting a former governor for the new president. You think it is a good idea, but you want to know what the rest of the student body thinks. You find out from the registrar that there are 19,787 students enrolled in the university. Knowing the population of university students, you can begin to make some decisions about how many to contact and which survey approach to use.

If the registrar provides you with a listing of all the enrolled students as well as their phone numbers and addresses, you could use a table of random numbers (see Appendix D) to find a starting place and randomly select a sample of students to contact. This listing would be known as the **sampling frame.** Let's say you decide to contact a sample of one-hundred students. If you have a good list and you randomly select from it, the names you draw for your sample should be representative of the population enrolled at the university. Your sample should be a microcosm of the population of university students. The proportion of males and females in the sample should reflect their proportion at the university, as should the proportion of freshmen, sophomores, juniors, and seniors. (For example, if you find that 42 percent of your sample are seniors and yet seniors make up only 18 percent of the student body as a whole, then you should suspect something is wrong with either your sampling procedure or your list of students.)

Sometimes researchers talk about **systematic sampling.** What they mean by this is best explained by way of example. Let's say that you plan to take a 10 percent sample of the 19,787 university students. However, a quick calculation shows that this would require almost two-thousand interviews. Since you plan to conduct the telephone survey in a week's time, you decide that this would be far too many students to attempt to contact. As you think about the realistic constraints on your time, you decide that 200 interviews is much

Table 6.1 Gallup Poll Accuracy Record

Year	Gallup Final Survey		Election Results		Deviation
1996	52.0%	CLINTON	50.1%	CLINTON	+1.9%
1994	53.5	Republican	53.5	Republican*	±0.0
1992**	49.0	CLINTON	43.2	CLINTON	+5.8
1990	54.0	Democratic	54.1	Democratic	-0.1
1988	56.0	BUSH	53.9	BUSH	-2.1
1984	59.0	REAGAN	59.1	REAGAN	-0.1
1982	55.0	Democratic	56.1	Democratic	-1.1
1980	47.0	REAGAN	50.8	REAGAN	-3.8
1978	55.0	Democratic	54.6	Democratic	+0.4
1976	48.0	CARTER	50.0	CARTER	-2.0
1974	60.0	Democratic	58.9	Democratic	+1.1
1972	62.0	NIXON	61.8	NIXON	+0.2
1970	53.0	Democratic	54.3	Democratic	-1.3
1968	43.0	NIXON	43.5	NIXON	-0.5
1966	52.5	Democratic	51.9	Democratic	+0.6
1964	64.0	JOHNSON	61.3	JOHNSON	+2.7
1962	55.5	Democratic	52.7	Democratic	+2.8
1960	51.0	KENNEDY	50.1	KENNEDY	+0.9
1958	57.0	Democratic	56.5	Democratic	+0.5
1956	59.5	EISENHOWER	57.8	EISENHOWER	+1.7
1954	51.5	Democratic	52.7	Democratic	-1.2
1952	51.0	EISENHOWER	55.4	EISENHOWER	-4.4
1950	51.0	Democratic	50.3	Democratic	+0.7
1948	44.5	TRUMAN	49.9	TRUMAN	-5.4
1946	58.0	Republican	54.3	Republican	+3.7
1944	51.5	ROOSEVELT	53.3	ROOSEVELT	-1.8
1942	52.0	Democratic	48.0	Democratic	+4.0
1940	52.0	ROOSEVELT	55.0	ROOSEVELT	-3,0
1938	54.0	Democratic	50.8	Democratic	+3.2
1936	55.7	ROOSEVELT	62.5	ROOSEVELT	-6.8

Note: No congressional poll done in 1986.

* Based on national aggregate vote estimate computed by The Roper Center. With votes cast for minor party candidates removed.

**The Ross Perot candidacy created an additional source of error in estimating the 1992 presidential vote. There was no historical precedent for Perot, an independent candidate who was accorded equal status to the major party nominees in the presidential debates and had a record advertising budget. Gallup's decision to allocate none of the undecided vote to Perot based on past performance of third party and independent candidates resulted in the overestimation of Clinton's vote.

Trend in Deviation

Elections	Average error
1936-1996	2.1
1936-1948	4.0
1950-1964	1.9
1966-1996	1.4

Average deviation for 30 national elections: 2.1 percent

Source: www.gallup.com/Gallup_Poll_Data/elecpoll/accuracy.htm

more feasible. If you divide the proposed sample size of 200 by the university's population of 19,787, you get a **sampling ratio** of .01—which means that your sample will draw one name for every hundred students enrolled in the university.

In this example of systematic sampling, the next thing you need to do is to number all of the students on the listing you received from the registrar. Then you refer to the random number table (Appendix D) and find a random starting place (any number between 1 and 19,787), for example 6. The first student selected from the list would be 6, followed by 106, 206, 306, 406, 506, 606, 706, 806, 906, 1,006, 1,106, 1,206, and so on through the entire list of 19,787 students. If the list was not numbered and since numbering all 19,787 students would be very time-consuming, you could count out the first 100 names, measure that distance with a ruler, and then use that distance to locate the next name to be selected.

Why is it important to get a random starting place? Because lists are often organized in some way. The list you get from the registrar might place seniors first and then juniors, or it might be organized by grade point average or by whether students are undergraduates or working on a graduate degree. If you are going to sample a few individuals from a large population and start your systematic sampling with the first or last name on your list, you are likely to get a sample that is not representative of the whole population. The size of your sample is critical, too, and we'll discuss this in some depth in the next section.

While probability sampling is the best insurance against a sample being unrepresentative, it is no guarantee that every group will be well represented. Sometimes bad luck or some form of unexpected bias will produce a random sample that is not representative. For example, 48 percent of the university population may be female, but 54 percent of those drawn for your sample could be female. If you play cards, you understand how this could happen. Even though the deck is shuffled many times, luck (chance) plays a role in which cards you are dealt—it is possible to get all hearts or four aces. Similarly, any sample from a population is by definition only an approximation of the total population. Numerically large samples are the best guarantee against obtaining unrepresentative samples.

Some researchers try to guard against a freak or fluke sample by using **stratified random sampling.** When certain important characteristics of the population (for example, the percentage of men and women) are known, exact proportions are obtained by dividing the study population into subgroups or subsets called **strata** and sampling the appropriate proportion from each stratum.

For instance, suppose that instead of sampling from the whole student body, you want to interview only seniors and freshmen. You already know that there are twice as many freshmen as seniors and that you want to interview two-hundred students. You again approach the registrar and ask for a listing of just freshmen and seniors. Once again you number each of the freshmen and seniors, choose a random starting place, and begin selecting from each strata. Since there are twice as many freshmen as seniors, you decide to select sixty-five seniors to interview and one-hundred thirty freshmen. This keeps the proportion of seniors to freshmen in your sample the same as it is in the university, and you have retained the sample size that you think is manageable. This is not simple random sampling because sampling was done within each strata.

When it is not possible to obtain or feasible to construct a sample frame of all the individuals who make up a population, (for example, the names and addresses of all social work majors in the United States), researchers sometimes employ a **cluster sampling design.**

Used primarily for convenience and economy, cluster sampling randomly selects individuals from natural groupings or clusters. Because human beings are social creatures, we tend to belong to numerous groups like civic organizations, clubs, fraternities, sororities, and churches.

For example, if you want to know how the parents of children with emotional, mental, or learning problems view helping professionals, you might go to your local mental health center and ask for their cooperation. If you wanted a more geographically diverse sample, it might occur to you to contact such national organizations as the National Alliance for the Mentally Ill, Children with Attention Deficit Disorder, and the Learning Disabilities Association of America. Once you obtain a list of their chapters, you could then call, write, or e-mail for permission to survey their membership. Such organizations could be very supportive of your research and eager to assist.

An example of a **one-stage cluster sampling** is dividing the population of a town into households (households would be the clusters because they usually contain more than one individual) and then taking a sample of households and obtaining information from *all* the members of the household. **Two-stage cluster sampling** involves dividing the population into households or clusters and then taking a *sample* of members from each selected household.

A **multistage cluster sampling design** contains several steps prior to sampling the population of interest. For example, suppose you want to conduct a survey of hospital social workers who regularly are involved with crack babies and their mothers. You might start by identifying which states have the highest birth rates of crack babies. From that cluster of states you could identify those with cities having a million or more population and from that cluster of cities list all hospitals with neonatal care units. Depending on the size of that list (since large cities can have many hospitals), you could randomly select hospitals or take all of them. The last stage could involve writing the directors of the departments of social work and asking them to identify social workers who had worked with ten or more crack babies in the past year. From this listing you could mail questionnaires to the social workers with the most experience with crack babies.

Professional survey organizations often use multistage cluster samples simply because there is no sample frame of all American citizens. Typically, they randomly draw from large geographic tracts that would include metropolitan and nonmetropolitan areas, and once those have been chosen, cities, towns, and rural areas could be selected. The next stage would involve drawing from those cities, towns, and so forth even smaller units, such as census tracts or blocks, and from those, clusters of dwellings from which respondents would be selected.

One of my students used a multistage cluster sampling design in connection with a research project. She had been reading about transracial adoption and found that there was little information about blacks' attitudes toward this topic. Since she was not interested in whites' attitudes, but only in blacks' attitudes, a random community survey would have been inefficient. Instead, a multistage cluster sampling design was selected.

We first identified the nine census tracts in the city containing the highest concentrations of blacks. From these nine tracts, three were randomly selected (since she was doing the interviewing all by herself, there was no need to walk her legs off). From these three tracts, forty city blocks were randomly chosen. Finally, every sixth household was selected from these blocks (after getting a random starting place) until one-hundred fifty interviews had been completed (Howard, Royse, and Skerl, 1977).

Because the individuals within a cluster tend to be more homogeneous than individuals in different clusters, the researcher typically should maximize the number of clusters for greater representativeness. Sampling error is reduced when researchers take fewer individuals from more clusters rather than more individuals from fewer clusters. This may mean that few individuals are selected from any one cluster. However, because of the efficiency permitted with random sampling, there is no obligation to sample from each cluster.

Determining Sample Size

How big a sample is necessary for a good survey? This is a major question in the minds of many would-be researchers. Unfortunately, there is no simple response to this question. Sample size is related to the researcher's objectives, monetary and personnel resources, and the amount of time available in which to conduct the research. A precise sample size cannot be determined until you are able to state your expectations in terms of the accuracy you need and the confidence that you would like to have in the data.

You may have heard that a minimum sample size is 10 percent of the population. But the accuracy of your survey is much more dependent upon the size of the sample than on the population size. In order to be confident that your findings are reasonably accurate, you need to interview proportionately more of those who compose small populations than of those making up large populations.

Before you determine sample size for a study where statistical probability statements can be made about the findings, you must understand several terms. **Margin of error** refers to the precision needed by the researcher, that is, the amount of sampling error that can be tolerated. A margin of error of 5 percent means that the actual findings could vary by as much as five points either positively or negatively. A consumer satisfaction survey, for instance, with a 5 percent margin of error associated with a finding of 65 percent of clients "highly satisfied" with services would mean that the true value in the population could be as low as 60 percent (65 –5 = 60) or as high as 70 percent (65 + 5 = 70). If you believe that greater precision is needed (for example, plus or minus two points), then you must plan on obtaining a larger sample to support that precision. This can be seen in table 6.2 by comparing the sample sizes in the .05 column with those in the .02 column.

The other term that is important to understand is **confidence level.** A confidence level (or level of confidence) is a statement of how often you could expect to find similar results if the survey were to be repeated. Since every survey varies slightly (depending upon who is selected to be in the sample), the confidence level informs about how often the findings will fall outside the margin of error. For example, in a sample developed to have a 95 percent confidence level with a 5 percent margin of error, the findings could be expected to miss the actual values in the population by more than 5 percent only five times in one hundred surveys. (In the example above, findings that less than 60 percent or more than 70 percent of the clients were "highly satisfied" would be expected to occur no more than five times in one hundred surveys.) The use of a 95 percent confidence level and 5 percent margin of error is pretty standard in the social sciences.

Table 6.2 will help you decide how large a sample to select in your own surveys. This table is used when you do not have a firm notion about the proportion of a population that would be in favor of or opposed to a specific issue. In order to be confident that the same findings would have occurred in ninety-five surveys out of one-hundred, and to be accurate to within plus or minus 5 percentage points, you would need to interview 79 persons in a population of one-hundred. However, in a population of 1 million, you would have to interview only 384 persons. The greater the precision you require, the larger your sample must be. Note that for a permissible error of 1 percent with the same population of 1 million, you would need a sample of 9,513. Few issues are worth the increase in sample size necessary when one goes from plus or minus 5 percentage points to plus or minus 1 point. For example, if

**Table 6.2 Appropriate Sizes of Simple Random Samples for
Specific Permissible Errors Expressed as Absolute
Proportions When the True Proportion in the Population
Is 0.50 and the Confidence Level Is 95 Percent**

Population Size	Sample Size for Permissible Error (Proportion)				
	0.05	0.04	0.03	0.02	0.01
100	79	86	91	96	99
200	132	150	168	185	196
300	168	200	234	267	291
400	196	240	291	343	384
500	217	273	340	414	475
600	234	300	384	480	565
700	248	323	423	542	652
800	260	343	457	600	738
900	269	360	488	655	823
1,000	278	375	516	706	906
2,000	322	462	696	1,091	1,655
3,000	341	500	787	1,334	2,286
4,000	350	522	842	1,500	2,824
5,000	357	536	879	1,622	3,288
6,000	361	546	906	1,715	3,693
7,000	364	553	926	1,788	4,049
8,000	367	558	942	1,847	4,364
9,000	368	563	954	1,895	4,646
10,000	370	566	964	1,936	4,899
15,000	375	577	996	2,070	5,855
20,000	377	583	1,013	2,144	6,488
25,000	378	586	1,023	2,191	6,938
30,000	379	588	1,030	2,223	7,275
40,000	381	591	1,039	2,265	7,745
50,000	381	593	1,045	2,291	8,056
75,000	382	595	1,052	2,327	8,514
100,000	383	597	1,056	2,345	8,762
500,000	384	600	1,065	2,390	9,423
1,000,000	384	600	1,066	2,395	9,513
2,000,000	384	600	1,067	2,398	9,558

Source: Sampling and Statistics Handbook for Research in Education (Washington, DC: National Education Assn., 1980). Copyright by Chester McCall. Reprinted with permission.

you are 95 percent confident, plus or minus five percentage points, that 80 percent of the sample supports a tax increase, then it really doesn't matter whether the "true" level of support is 75 percent or 85 percent. The tax issue would pass comfortably with anything over a 51 percent majority.

If you can accept less confidence, say a 90 percent confidence level, it is possible to conduct your survey with even smaller samples than those stated in table 6.2. There are numerous other tables that can be consulted or computed, too. If you had conducted prior studies and had a good idea of what the survey would likely reveal (for example, 90 percent favoring the tax increase) in the way of proportions, then there are tables that will allow you to get by with smaller sample sizes. In the example of a 90/10 split, then you could get by with a sample of approximately 150 individuals (95 percent level of confidence, 5 percent margin of error). With an expected 80/20 split, a sample of 256 would be needed (95 percent level of confidence, 5 percent margin of error). Because a pattern is more easily detected as the proportions move away from a fifty/fifty mix, smaller samples can be used. You can test this for yourself by putting one red and nine blue marbles in one pocket and five yellow and five green ones in the other pocket. The predominance of the blue marbles is quite apparent early on even when you draw a sample of one marble at a time. The pattern of yellow to green can take a lot longer to discern unless your sampling yields one yellow to one green each time you draw out two marbles.

Table 6.2 furnishes sample size guidelines only when you don't know how those surveyed will respond but you want to be reasonably confident in the findings (95 percent). Both level of confidence and margin of error can be adjusted (by you) up or down in the planning stages of your survey. Each adjustment has implications for sample size.

Sample size is obviously much more of a concern if you are planning a probability sampling design than if you are planning a sample of convenience. With a probability design, you will need to consult a table to arrive at the appropriate sample size. In nonprobability studies, sample size is dictated more by considerations of convenience and appearance.

Here's a small example to demonstrate sampling: Katie's mother complained that Katie, a seventh grader, watched too much television. "But Mom," Katie protested, "my grades are good. And besides, all my friends watch more than me." Katie's mother got on the phone that afternoon and began calling other mothers of seventh grade students. This is what she learned:

	Amount of TV Watched Daily	**GPA**
Katie	4 hours	3.0
Jake	3 hours	2.5
Rochelle	3 hours	2.0
Martha	1 hours	4.0
Tim	5 hours	2.8
Shawna	2 hours	3.3
John	3 hours	3.0
Susie	0 hours	3.4
Glenna	1 hours	2.6
Matthew	5 hours	2.0

Using the Internet to Locate Survey Databases

The Institute for Research in Social Science (IRSS) at the University of North Carolina operates the oldest and largest archives of machine-readable survey data in the United States. It is the national repository for Louis Harris public opinion data and contains more than 1,000 Harris polls dating back to 1958 with more than 60,000 questions asked of more than 900,000 respondents. Additionally, the IRSS is also a depository for the National Center for Health Statistics, the General Social Survey Data, and others such as the World Fertility Surveys. A convenient search engine allows you to display questions that have been asked over the years and the responses received to them (http://www.irss.unc.edu:80/ data_archive/pollsearch.html). The IRSS also maintains a computer-searchable catalog of more than 2,800 studies in its datafiles (http://www.irss.unc.edu:80/data_archive/catsearch.html).

Recent press releases from the Gallup Poll can be found at http://www.gallup.com/). These releases present the findings from surveys of national samples and explore issues currently affecting Americans. A brief statement about methodology is contained as well as the exact wording of the questions asked and responses obtained.

The average amount of television watched by this sample of students was 2.7 hours (total of 27 hours divided by 10). Katie's mother concluded that Katie was watching more television than her peers. However, would she have come to the same conclusion if she had taken a smaller sample of one or two students? Suppose she called only Matthew's mother. What if she contacted the mothers of Jake, Tim, John, and Matthew? Does Katie watch as much television as the other honor roll students? From this exercise, you can see that many different samples could be selected. Some smaller samples would not be very representative of the larger group. However, as the sample size increases, values obtained from the sample begin to look much more like the average of the larger group.

Nonprobability Sampling Designs

Nonprobability sampling designs are generally regarded as unscientific because there is no way of knowing how accurate or representative their findings are. At the same time, these designs are often employed as straw polls—unofficial estimates of opinions or concerns about issues. In actual practice, it is likely that social workers employ more of the nonprobability than probability designs because they are generally cheaper, faster, and more easily conducted. If you were, for instance, to poll ten friends about some matter instead of randomly selecting a sample from the 50,000 registered voters in your town, you would be taking a **sample of convenience**. When we draw a convenience sample, we do so because it is easy or quick, and we think it will provide us with some information as to what the larger population might think. But this type of sampling is prone to error. Your friends, for example, knowing how strongly you feel on an issue such as the tax for a new high school, may not be completely honest in telling you how they would vote. Since there is some reason they are your friends, the common interests you have (your friends may all be social workers, have about the same income, and have children in school) may also influence how they would vote. In other words, your ten friends may not be representative of the other 49,990 voters in your town who are not social workers, who make more or less than you do annually, and who may or may not have children.

If you were to skim a wide variety of professional journals, you would find that many surveys with college students are conducted each year. Why do you think that is? Could it have anything to do with the convenience with which researchers might access them? At the same time, how well do college students represent the other adults in our population? Could they be younger, more educated, more liberal in their views? Although college students may not be representative of our adult population, often researchers are willing to assume that patterns or relationships found with convenience samples of college students might also be discovered within more scientific probability samples. In this sense, they may use convenience samples as exploratory studies before they commit to a larger-scale investigation.

Nonprobability sampling is often done when the extent of the population is not known. For instance, in my exploratory research to find out how much money trash pickers make each day from gathering and selling aluminum beverage cans (Royse, 1987), I did not know the actual number of trash pickers, so I arbitrarily chose a nonprobability sample of fifty. This group may have been somewhat unrepresentative of the larger population of all trash pickers, but there was no way of knowing this. (I tried, however, to make the study a little more representative by interviewing trash pickers in two different cities.) This type of sampling is also known as **purposive sampling**, because the respondents had to have certain characteristics in common in order to be selected for an interview (in my study, they all had to be trash pickers).

There is a good reason that samples of convenience are also known as **accidental** and **available samples**. I once watched a television camera crew approach different individuals for "person-in-the-street" interviews. What was of interest to me was the number (perhaps the majority) of individuals who, seeing the camera, crossed to the other side of the street to avoid it. While the process of indiscriminately stopping people and asking for their opinions seemed random, actually there was a severe bias in that everyone did not have an equal chance of being chosen. Some deliberately avoided giving their opinions. Did the more vocal individuals represent the views of the shy ones? This cannot be determined in a sample of convenience.

Similarly, if you stand outside of a supermarket at 4:00 A.M. on Friday your respondents may be quite different from those who show up at 10:00 A.M. or even 8:00 P.M. Might there be a difference in the supermarket shoppers at 11:00 A.M. on Sunday and those at 3:00 P.M. on the same day?

Snowball Sampling

When one respondent leads you to another, and that one refers you to another, the approach is known as **snowball sampling.** Suppose as a school social worker you encounter a high school student who, for all practical purposes, is homeless. He stays with first this friend and then that one, sometimes sleeping in his car or in an abandoned building. When you talk with him, he indicates that he has several friends in the same predicament. If he leads you to them and they lead you to others, then you have created a snowball sampling design. This type of nonprobability sampling design grows by referrals to other potential responders. Remember, just because you don't know the respondents does not mean that you are selecting them randomly—you are not. They are all linked, in some way, to the one or two individuals you started with. They could be expected to be more homogeneous than if a sample frame of all the persons in that population could be selected and then a sample drawn. This approach is used when it is difficult to locate respondents by any other means.

Quota Samples

Quota sampling involves knowing certain characteristics of a population (for example, the proportion of an agency's clientele who are under thirty, middle aged, and eighty or older) and then striving to obtain the same proportions in the selected sample. With this approach, screening is often done early in the interview so that interviewers will not have to continue with those who do not have the desired characteristics. Although the final sample may match the population in terms of the proportions of respondents having certain characteristics, the sample may be unrepresentative in other areas because of characteristics for which they were not screened. That is, a quota sample may resemble the population by containing an identical proportion of those who are over the age of eighty, yet because they aren't probability surveys the results possibly may not accurately reflect "the real picture"—depending on how the respondents were chosen. In quota samples, interviewers and data gatherers have a great deal of freedom to find respondents any way they can. Potential respondents might be sought in shopping malls, in front of grocery stores, at the airport. Using such an approach, might not the healthiest and more affluent stand a better chance of being chosen? To take a more ludicrous example, one could get his or her quota of persons over the age of eighty fairly easily by going to the nearest nursing home or respite care center for senior citizens. If the survey were to report later that all of those eighty and older were impaired in some way, that finding could be entirely true but not at all representative of the population of persons eighty and older who lived on their own in the community. Quota samples are convenience samples with specifications regarding a certain number or proportion of respondents.

The problem with all nonprobability sampling designs is not knowing how representative the sample is or how closely it resembles the "true" population. The nonprobability sample could be very biased, yet it would be difficult for the investigator to know this without drawing additional samples.

Additional Survey Designs

In addition to the probability and nonprobability survey designs, several other designs may be useful. The term **cross-sectional survey design** is used to refer to the probability sampling designs. The term indicates that a one-time survey is made with a randomly selected sample. The cross-sectional design allows a broad representation of the population and thus involves persons of all ages, incomes, and educational levels.

In contrast, **longitudinal surveys** may not be representative of the population. These surveys are conducted on multiple occasions over an extended period of time. Change is measured through a succession of surveys. There are three types of longitudinal surveys: **trend surveys, cohort surveys,** and **panel surveys.** Trend studies require multiple samplings from the same population over months or years in order to monitor changes or trends. The same individuals are not repeatedly interviewed. For good examples of trend survey research, see *Trends in Public Opinion: A Compendium of Survey Data* (Niemi, Mueller, and Smith, 1989) or Young, Savola, and Phelps (1991).

A cohort is a group of persons who have some critical or significant experience in common (for example, Vietnam veterans). Cohort studies involve only persons who fit into these subgroups. Persons who are born, married, or graduated from high school in a given year could be used to form cohorts by birth, marriage, or graduation, respectively. Cohort studies involve multiple samples from the cohort(s) of interest. Comparisons by cohorts are most commonly found in sociological studies of the population.

Panel studies are studies of the *same* group of persons over an extended period (for example, the survivors of Hiroshima). Panel studies are used to detect changes in individuals over time.

Table 6.3 shows the three types of longitudinal surveys. Each study began

Table 6.3 Comparison Trend, Cohort, and Panel Longitudinal Surveys

Type	Subjects' Ages in 1995	Subjects' Ages in 2000	Subjects' Ages in 2005
Trend	15 yrs. old	15 yrs. old	15 yrs. old
Cohort	15 yrs. old	20 yrs. old	25 yrs. old
Panel	15 yrs. old	20 yrs. old	25 yrs. old

with interviewing fifteen-year-old runaways in Chicago. In a trend survey, the investigator is interested in differences in fifteen-year-old runaways over time. Do their characteristics change? Do the reasons they run away change? An investigator using a cohort survey would want to interview any person who was fifteen years old and a runaway in 1990. The panel surveyor would want to interview the 1990 runaways in 1995 and 2000.

Mistakes to Avoid

If you have the time and resources, choose a probability design over a nonprobability sampling design. Even then, be alert to any limitations that could result in your sampling frame being less inclusive than you had planned. Be particularly alert to sample selection bias that could occur because of the order in which the sample units are listed, incomplete listings (for example, the omission of employees who work fewer than forty hours per week), and the tendency of respondents to self-select.

Interviewer bias—the often unconscious biases and stereotypes that lead us to approach people like us, to avoid those we fear or dislike, and to attribute positive or negative attributes based on such traits as gender, race, or age—is a serious concern when interviewers and telephone callers have few guidelines regarding whom to reject or include for a survey. Grumpy people need to be included in your surveys just the same as the attractive, patient, and clever individuals who are a joy to interview.

If you need to employ interviewers, train them well to prevent careless errors in the field or in the recording of responses. Let them know that you will be recontacting a portion of their respondents to validate their answers. A nationally prominent sociologist once told me that as a student he sat in a coffee shop and made up information for a community directory when he should have been going door-to-door to obtain accurate data. However, falsification of data is not a major difficulty with most surveys, particularly if you screen your interviewers well.

Allow sufficient time to follow up on nonrespondents. Reminder postcards and mailing second and third questionnaires to nonrespondents greatly increase response rates. In telephone and face-to-face interviewing, unless you follow up on those who are not home when you call, you run the risk of having a bias against those who work during the hours that you attempt to reach them.

A low response rate is just as problematic as too small a sample. If less than a majority of the respondents reply, one is left wondering about the attitudes or characteristics of those who chose not to respond. Are the data biased when only 20 percent respond? Would a different pattern of findings emerge if the response rate could be raised from 35 percent to 70 percent by following up on the nonresponders? There is no way of knowing. With a terribly low response rate of 20 or 30 percent, the analogy that comes to mind is the old story of three blind men who encounter an elephant for the first time. One fellow standing beside a massive leg says, "An elephant is like a tree trunk."

"No," the second one says, feeling the elephant's trunk, "it is more like a boa constrictor."

The third man touches the elephant's tail and says, "It has a tail like a pig."

Low response rates don't enable you to get the whole picture—you may hear from the most satisfied or the most dissatisfied clients, the most compulsive or educated, but you can't be sure of what you've got until you have 55 percent or more of the responses. The more you have, the better you can understand your "elephant."

Here's another interesting tidbit: Barkley and Furse (1996) examined patient satisfaction data from 76 hospitals and compared the first 30 percent responding with the total number of respondents for which the average response rate was 58 percent. They found that "there is a 50–50 chance that decisions made on the basis of low-response data will not match decisions that would be made using higher response-rate data" (p. 431). In other words, those who respond early are not similar to those who respond later.

Unless a new scale is being developed, designers of surveys don't often worry about calculating the internal consistency of their questionnaires. But they do worry about response rates because response rates are good indicators of how much faith can be put in the resulting data. With less than 50 percent responding, keep your fingers crossed whenever you are drawing conclusions.

No matter which approach you select to conduct your survey, it is important to **pilot test** (or pretest) your procedures and instrument. Generally, pilot testing is informal and can involve giving the survey instrument to a few friends or co-workers to see if they understand the questions and respond in the ways you anticipate. Even better, administer the survey instrument to a group of persons as similar as possible to the population that you will be surveying. The major purpose of the pilot test is to determine if the type of information you want is supplied by the respondents. Pilot testing need not involve

---

Practice Note: Creating an Asian-American Sampling Frame

Although some Asian-Americans live in "ethnic conclaves" known by such names as "Chinatown" and "Little Saigon," most do not. Because of their geographical dispersal, it is not easy to obtain a representative sample of Asian-Americans using random methodologies such as random digit dialing. As a result, much of the research with this population has come from convenience samples. However, in order to obtain prevalence estimates regarding health and mental health issues, survey methodologies with greater external validity have been sought. Sasao (1994) reports an effort that created lists of persons with unequivocally Asian surnames from telephone directories—a process that was more cost-efficient than "true" random sampling and that seemed to produce reliable data when compared to focus group interviews in three different cities.

---

more than twenty persons if the respondents have no problems understanding the questions or recording their responses. Pilot testing provides estimates of the time required to complete the questionnaire and, in the case of telephone and face-to-face interviews, provides useful data for estimating the cost of the survey.

A Final Note about Surveys

Surveys are versatile and powerful sources of information about the world. However, they can also be flawed—that is to say, in error, even though there was no intent to deceive. In this chapter we have discussed many of the ways that surveys can be misleading if certain key elements are ignored. Whenever you are reading the results of a survey or preparing to conduct one, these considerations will help you to evaluate its worth. Knowledge of these factors can help you understand how seemingly similar survey efforts can produce dissimilar conclusions:

- *How the sample was drawn:*
  Does the survey employ a probability or a nonprobability design?
  If the sample is representative, is the margin of error and level of confidence adequate?
  Does the sample appear to be reasonable, to have been constructed without bias?

- *Sample size:*
  Is the sample adequate for the level of generalization the authors want to make?
- *Response rate:*
  Is the response rate greater than 55 percent?
- *Recency:*
  When was the survey conducted?
- *Item construction:*
  Are the questions straightforward and clear? Vague? Leading?

Surveys, particularly political polls, may appear to be at odds with one another when in fact they were conducted at different times or used different questions or incompatible sampling procedures. Attitudes can and do change over time—sometimes on a national level almost overnight when a president or other important person does something decisive or unpopular.

You shouldn't necessarily be persuaded by a large sample size. I recently read an article in our newspaper about a survey that had been mailed to five thousand families. "Interesting," I thought to myself. "I wonder how they arrived at that number? Don't they know about random sampling?" As I read further into the article, I became convinced that the researchers didn't know much at all about survey methodology. What were the clues? The researchers got back less than half (43 percent) of their questionnaires (was the questionnaire too long or uninteresting, or maybe they didn't follow up with the non-responders?), 78 percent of the respondents were women (what happened to the men?), and they used telephone books to construct their sample frame (we already know what bias that interjects into a study).

"Happy Families Abundant in State, Survey Says" proclaimed the headline. "Yeah, right," I thought to myself again. "How happy are the 57 percent of the sample who didn't respond? And how about those who weren't included because they were too poor to own a phone or because they had an unlisted number?"

Remember our discussion of the internal threat of testing in chapter 4? The designer of surveys also has to worry about how attitudes are measured. Questions can be too complex or too long, resulting in respondents forgetting the response choices available to them or causing premature termination of the survey. We'll discuss the effect that wording can have on the responses obtained in more detail in the next chapter, but you might already have some ideas about how the very act of raising a question can influence a respondent.

One last thing: sometime you may encounter a study in which the authors survey all of a population. For instance, Vissing and Diament (1997) wanted to know how many teenagers were homeless or at risk of homelessness in the seacoast area of New Hampshire and southwestern Maine. They distributed surveys to 100 percent of those in attendance at nine high schools and 3,676 students responded. Since the whole population was surveyed, there is no statement about margin of error or level of confidence. Unlike the situation when one draws small samples from a large population, the results obtained from contacting the whole population represent "reality." There is no need to try and estimate **sampling error** (another way of saying margin of error) because no sampling was done.

Self-Review

(Answers at the end of the book)

1. Which approach would be the most labor-intensive?
   a. telephone interview
   b. personal interview
   c. e-mail survey
   d. mail survey
2. T or F.   Incentives seem to increase response rates.
3. T or F.   It is not uncommon for mail surveys to have response rates of less than 30 percent.
4. T or F.   The use of a telephone directory produces biased samples.
5. T or F.   The notion on which sampling is based is that a much smaller randomly selected sample can yield approximately the same findings as one would obtain with interviewing every person in that population.
6. _____ surveys are not noted for their generalizability.
7. _____ is the list of every person or unit eligible to be contacted in a survey.
8. The accuracy of the Gallup Poll in predicting the results in the last thirty national elections is:
   a. extremely accurate (less than 3 percent error)
   b. somewhat accurate (7–12 percent error)
   c. slightly accurate (15–20 percent error)
   d. not accurate (more than 25 percent error)
9 T or F.   Systematic random sampling is recognized by the ratio of the sample to the population—as in contacting every fourth client.
10. If you were implementing a probability sampling design and wanted to make sure that the exact proportions of BSWs, MSWs, and Ph.D. social workers were represented in the sample, the type of design would be _____.
11. T or F.   Margin of error and confidence interval are independent. One could select, for example, a 90 percent confidence level and a 3 percent margin of error.

12. T or F.   The relation of sample size to population is this: generally, greater accuracy requires larger samples.

13. T or F.   Sample size is more of a consideration with samples of convenience than with probability surveys.

14. Other terms for convenience samples are: _____ and _____ samples.

15. T or F.   A quota sample is a type of probability sampling.

16. T or F.   Panel surveys are different from cohort and trend surveys in that the same individuals are contacted at different points in time.

17. Nelson Flake constructs a sample of two-hundred African-American, two-hundred Hispanic, two-hundred Asian-American, and two-hundred white students at a large state university. Can he generalize his findings to all college students in America? Why or why not?

18. One major advantage of a personal interview over a mailed survey is _____.

19. Exploratory surveys are generally noted by their _____.

20. T or F.   Once one has a randomly selected sample of about 385 persons, that sample can adequately represent a population of 100,000 or 1 million—assuming a 95 percent level of confidence, 5 percent margin of error, and a fifty/fifty split in response proportions.

Questions for Class Discussion

1. You want to conduct a national survey of social workers. What are three ways in which you might stratify the sample? Why might you want to stratify the sample?

2. Assume that you have a budget of $3,500 (exclusive of your own time) with which to conduct a national survey of social workers. What survey approach would you use? Why?

3. Give an example of a topic that might best be explored with the following:
   a. Snowball sampling
   b. Cluster sampling
   c. A longitudinal design

4. How have surveys advanced our understanding of human nature or improved our lives? Cite examples if possible.

5. Cite examples of surveys in which you have participated or personal encounters you have had with surveys.

6. Your agency has asked you to conduct a random sampling of clients to determine how satisfied they are with the agency's services. After some discussion, it is decided that a telephone survey is the most

sensible approach. If the agency closed approximately three thousand cases last year, how big a sample would be needed in order to have 95 percent confidence in the findings, plus or minus 5 percent? If the agency decides to use a mail approach, how many persons would you have to contact in order to get the same level of confidence and accuracy? (Keep in mind that about 30 percent of the respondents in a mail survey respond on the first mailing.)

7. Let's pretend that *Money* magazine prints a questionnaire in a recent issued mailed to subscribers. One of the questions asked is "What do you think about most—money or sex?" Can the findings from this study be considered to represent the thinking of most American adults? If you wanted to investigate that question, what would be a better way to do it? Would you expect the findings from the *Money* magazine survey to be different from findings from the same questionnaire in an issue of *Playboy*?

8. In his book *The Superpollsters*, David Moore discusses criticisms of books written by Shere Hite. He mentions that for one book she distributed approximately 100,000 questionnaires through women's organizations and got back approximately 3 percent. Further, she instructed respondents that they didn't have to answer every single question but only those that interested them. And she didn't standardize her questionnaire, but used multiple versions. Could she claim a representative sample? Did her methodology deserve criticism?

Mini-Projects for Experiencing Research Firsthand

1. List the steps you would go through to draw a random sample of 50 from a population of 350 using the table of random numbers. Draw the sample of 50 and record the numbers of those who would be selected.

2. Look through past issues of the *Gallup Poll Monthly* and find a topic of interest. Respond to the following questions:
   a. What does the survey data show?
   b. What period of time is covered?
   c. What was the sample size?
   d. How much confidence do you have in the findings? Why?

3. Browse through back issues of *Social Work* and find five articles that report the use of a survey methodology. What is the average size of

the samples reported? In how many instances did the sample size seem to be too small to allow 95 percent confidence and plus or minus 5 percent accuracy? Were most of these studies exploratory studies?

Resources and References

Aktan, G.B., Calkins, R.F., Ribisl, K.M. Kroliczak, A. and Kasim, R.M. (1997) Test-retest reliability of psychoactive substance abuse and dependence diagnoses in telephone interviews using a modified Diagnostic Interview Schedule-Substance Abuse Module. *American Journal of Drug and Alcohol Abuse*, 23, 229–248.

Barkley, W.M. and Furse, D.H. (1996). Changing priorities for improvement: The impact of low response rates in patient satisfaction. *Journal on Quality Improvement*, 22, 427–433.

Boat, B.W. and Everson, M.D. (1988). Interviewing young children with anatomical dolls. *Child Welfare*, 67, 337–352.

Bradburn, N.M. and Sudman, S. (1988). *Polls and surveys: Understanding what they tell us.* San Francisco: Jossey-Bass.

Converse, J.M. and Schuman, H. (1974). *Conversations at random: Survey research as interviewers see it.* New York: Wiley.

Corwin, D. and Faller, K. (1995). Children's interview statements and behaviors: Role in identifying sexually abused children. *Child Abuse and Neglect*, 19, 71–80.

Dillman, D.A. (1978). *Mail and telephone surveys: The total design method.* New York: Wiley.

Dillman, D.A. (1983). Mail and other self-administered questionnaires. In P.H. Rossi, J.D. Wright, and A.B. Anderson (Eds.), *Handbook of survey research.* New York: Academic Press.

Dillman, D.A. (1991). The design and administration of mail surveys. In W. Richard Scott and Judith Blake (Eds.) *Annal reviews of sociology.* Palo Alto, CA: Annual Reviews.

Farhi, P. (1992). Pollsters looking at who's not talking. *Lexington Herald-Leader.* April 15, p. A3.

Gwiasda, V., Taluc, N., and Popkin, S.J. (1997). Data collection in dangerous neighborhoods: Lessons from a survey of public housing residents in Chicago. *Evaluation Review*, 21, 77–93.

Hartman, G. and Hibbard, R. (1993). Components of child and parent interviews in cases of alleged sexual abuse. *Child Abuse and Neglect*, 17, 495–499.

Howard, A., Royse, D., and Skerl, J.A. (1977). Transracial adoption: The black community perspective. *Social Work,* 22(3), 184–189.

Institute for Social Research, Survey Research Center. (1976). *Interviewer's manual.* Rev. ed. Ann Arbor: University of Michigan Press.

James, J.M. and Bolstein, R. (1992). Large monetary incentives and their effect on mail survey response rates. *Public Opinion Quarterly,* 56(4), 442–453.

Lavrakas, P.J. (1993). *Telephone survey methods: Sampling, selection, and supervision.* Newbury Park, CA: Sage.

Mangione, T.W. (1995). *Mail surveys: Improving the quality.* Thousand Oaks, CA: Sage.

Mehta, R. and Sivadas, E. (1995). Comparing response rates and response content in mail versus electronic mail surveys. *Journal of the Market Research Society*, 37, 429–439.

Moore, D.W. (1992). *The superpollsters: How they measure and manipulate public opinion in America.* New York: Four Walls Eight Windows.

Niemi, R.G., Mueller, J. and Smith, T. (1989). *Trends in public opinion: A compendium of survey data.* New York: Greenwood Press.

Ransdell, L.B. (1996). Maximizing response rates in questionnaire research. *American Journal of Health Behavior*, 20, 50–56.

Rosenberg, A.S. (1990). 'The number you have dialed' . . . is often unlisted. *Lexington Herald-Leader.* May 9, p. A2.

Royse, D. (1987). Homelessness among trash pickers. *Psychological Reports,* 60, 808–810.

Sasao, T. (1994). Using surname-based telephone survey methodology in Asian-American communities: Practical issues and caveats. *Journal of Community Psychology*, 22, 283–295.

Schwarz, N. and Sudman, S. (1995). *Answering questions: Methodology for determining cognitive and communicative processes in survey research.* San Francisco: Jossey-Bass.

Soriano, F.I. (1995). *Conducting needs assessments: A multidisciplinary approach.* Thousand Oaks, CA: Sage.

Sudman, S. Bradburn, N.M. and Schwarz, N. (1995). *Thinking about answers: The application of cognitive processes to survey methodology.* San Francisco: Jossey-Bass.

U.S. Department of Commerce, Bureau of the Census. (1997). *Statistical abstract of the United States: 1997.* Washington, DC: U.S. Government Printing Office.

Vissing, V.M. and Diament, J. (1997). Housing distress among high school students. *Social Work*, 42, 31–40.

Wentland, E.J. and Smith, K.W. (1993). *Survey responses: An evaluation of their validity.* San Diego: Academic Press.

Wilk, R. (1993). Research note: The use of monetary incentives to increase survey response rates. *Social Work Research and Abstracts*, 29(1), 33–34.

Xu, M., Batu, B.J., and Schweitzer, J.C. (1993) The impact of messages on survey participation in answering machine households. *Public Opinion Quarterly*, 57(2), 232–237.

Young, C.H., Savola, K.L., and Phelps, E. (1991). *Inventory of longitudinal studies in the social sciences.* Newbury Park, CA: Sage.

Yuille, J.C., Hunter, R., Joffe, R., and Zaparniuk, J. (1993). Interviewing children in sexual abuse cases. In Gail Goodman and Bette Bottoms (Eds.) *Child victims, child witnesses: Understanding and improving testimony.* New York: Guilford.

CHAPTER 7

Developing Data Collection Instruments: Scales and Questionnaires

Social workers are familiar with the use of questionnaires. In almost every social service agency, initial data collection is conducted before new clients are admitted for services. This process is called "intake," "screening," completing the "face sheet," or "taking the client's history." To collect data, social workers follow a set of previously determined questions in an established order and sequence. Although most agencies' admission forms may not have been designed for research purposes, they have enough in common with research questionnaires that we can use them to increase our knowledge about questionnaires.

Think for a moment about an agency's admission form (or any other questionnaire with which you are familiar). Someone (or perhaps a committee) may have spent a considerable number of hours in deciding which questions were important to ask and which ones were not. One of the purposes of the questionnaire is to ensure that the same set of questions is asked each time information is required. From the agency's perspective, this standard set of questions provides the minimal level of information required of each client. The social worker does not have to guess or anticipate what information the agency needs, because it has already been predetermined on the printed form. The social worker is also freed from worrying about wording the question the same way each time. If the social worker had to decide with each new client how to phrase the questions, there is the possibility that these questions might not generate the same type of information each time. With a standard set of pretested questions in a carefully designed admission form, problems are minimized.

Similarly, research questionnaires use a set of carefully selected questions that standardize the way the information is asked for and structure the respondents' responses (for example, instead of asking the respondent to state his or her age, the questionnaire asks for year of birth). Through careful wording and attention to such matters as the sequence and order of questions, researchers attempt to remove opportunities for collecting inaccurate data.

Questionnaire design requires more precise statements and questions than we use in ordinary conversation. In casual conversation, one person may say to another, "I've noticed that Martha has a pretty low self-esteem." Seldom will the other party say, "How are you operationalizing self-esteem?" However, in the conduct of research the concepts we use must be operationalized and focused. Ambiguities and vague terms in questionnaires can cause problems for respondent and researcher alike. Such problems will be discovered and eliminated during pretests of the questionnaire. The resulting final product should provide each respondent with a clear notion of what is being asked.

DeVaus (1986) articulates well the importance of specificity in developing useful items for questionnaires:

> It is not enough to say, "I'm interested in getting some answers about inequality." What answers to what questions? Do you want to know the extent of inequality, its distribution, its causes, its effects, or what? What sort of inequality are you interested in? Over what period? (P. 27)

Designing research questions that are clear and concise and that result in data that can be used by the researcher is not an easy task. Questions that seem to be straightforward to their developers might be described as confusing or circuitous by others. In an effort to become precise, it is possible to become too wordy so that the intent of the question is hard to comprehend. Questions may also inadvertently omit important response choices or contain overlapping response choices. And there is always the problem of unconsciously biasing the responses simply by the way the questions are phrased.

Even professionals can slip. After the movie *Schindler's List* was released, a Roper poll seemed to suggest that 34 percent of Americans were uncertain about whether the Holocaust actually occurred. However, the Roper question was not worded as well as it might have been. It asked, "Does it seem possible or does it seem impossible to you that the Nazi extermination of the Jews never happened?" A subsequent Gallup poll used this wording: " . . . in your opinion did the Holocaust definitely happen, probably happen, probably not happen, or definitely not happen?" When asked this way, seventy-nine percent said it definitely happened and another 17 percent said it probably happened for a total of 96 percent of Americans expressing belief that the Holocaust did occur (Moore and Gallup, 1994). This just shows how seriously we have to take item construction for our survey questionnaires, needs assessments, and scales.

The Importance of Appearance

The vast majority of this chapter discusses phrasing of items in the construction of questionnaires and scales. However, before we move to that discussion, here are a few thoughts about the appearance of the instruments you prepare.

In real estate there is an expression about the three most important considerations when buying or selling a house. They are: location, location, location. In the preparation of data gathering instruments, a similar aphorism might guide us: appearance, appearance, appearance. Saying that the success of our research rests solely on the physical attractiveness of questionnaires and scales is, of course, putting it much too strongly. But remember, more times than not our research subjects are *voluntarily* providing us with data they may not be eager to share. *They don't have to cooperate!*

As a social work researcher, you are more likely to get a higher rate of completed forms if they are visually appealing—when they don't appear that they will take too long or be too difficult. They also should not look amateurish as in the two examples provided in figures 7.1 and 7.2. Once you polish the appearance *and* the phrasing, then you have it made! Well, almost.

In figure 7.1 the response categories jump out so powerfully that the questions are lost. The reader shouldn't have to look so hard for them. In figure 7.2 there are probably too many choices. If there is no other way around that, then some verbiage could be eliminated by just listing the problem (such as housing, transportation, child care). That would result in a set of responses that could be read faster and require less effort.

Developing a Data Collection Instrument

First and foremost, you must have a clear idea of what data are needed. What is it that you want to find out? What are the specific content areas to be covered? If you are designing a questionnaire for a survey, then you must concurrently decide which survey modality will be used to present the questions to the respondents. Some formats (for example, questions requiring many response options) work better in mail surveys than in telephone surveys. In mail surveys, respondents can simultaneously view all of the response categories (such as, "Strongly agree," "Agree," "Undecided," "Disagree," "Strongly disagree") before choosing one. In telephone surveys, respondents find it difficult to keep the question as well as all of the response options in mind. Even five categories can stretch a respondent's ability to keep a whole scale in mind at once. Consequently, respondents may remember some but not all of the responses, and their responses may have a narrower range of variation ("Agree" or "Disagree"). When recall and recogni-

Figure 7.1 Illustration of an Unattractive Questionnaire

WHAT IS YOUR OPINION???

DO YOU AGREE OR DISAGREE WITH THESE COMMENTS???

11. When he comes to an agency for help, a person usually knows what he needs.
- ☐ Strongly agree
- ☐ Somewhat agree
- ☐ Don't know
- ☐ Somewhat disagree
- ☐ Strongly disagree

12. Most workers don't know what it's really like to need help.
- ☐ Strongly agree
- ☐ Somewhat agree
- ☐ Don't know
- ☐ Somewhat disagree
- ☐ Strongly disagree

13. The worker always knows what's best for the client.
- ☐ Strongly agree
- ☐ Somewhat agree
- ☐ Don't know
- ☐ Somewhat disagree
- ☐ Strongly disagree

14. People who ask for help should do as they're told and not complain.
- ☐ Strongly agree
- ☐ Somewhat agree
- ☐ Don't know
- ☐ Somewhat disagree
- ☐ Strongly disagree

15. Most people can choose their own services if they know where to go.
- ☐ Strongly agree
- ☐ Somewhat agree
- ☐ Don't know
- ☐ Somewhat disagree
- ☐ Strongly disagree

16. Most people who come to an agency don't really know what they need.
- ☐ Strongly agree
- ☐ Somewhat agree
- ☐ Don't know
- ☐ Somewhat disagree
- ☐ Strongly disagree

Figure 7.2 Illustration of an Uninviting Questionnaire

```
RECENTLY YOU WENT TO _____

FOR HELP THEY SENT YOU TO ANOTHER AGENCY. WE WANT TO KNOW YOUR
FEELINGS ABOUT WHAT HAPPENED TO YOU.
1. Why did you go to _____?
   ▱ Wanted to obtain food or clothing.
   ▱ Wanted better housing.
   ▱ Wanted to talk about money (Social Security, unemployment,
emergency aid, etc.).
   ▱ Wanted a job.
   ▱ Wanted to know about going to school.
   ▱ Wanted to know about medical or dental help.
   ▱ Wanted to talk about family problems.
   ▱ Wanted to know about day care or child care.
   ▱ Wanted to get transportation.
   ▱ Wanted to talk to a lawyer.
   ▱ Wanted to know about budgeting or credit.
   ▱ Wanted to work on a personal problem not listed above.
   ▱ Other:  _____
            _____
            _____
```

tion questions are vital to the survey, interviews seem to work better than mail surveys.

The nature of the content, the intended survey approach, the nature of the population, and their reading level being surveyed affect the final form that the questionnaire takes. Only after consideration has been given to these areas should further conceptualizing of the questionnaire begin.

A review of the literature can provide questions or examples of ways that researchers have approached the topic of interest. It is not unethical, but rather good research practice, to use questions that have worked well for other researchers (Sudman and Bradburn, 1982). Do not, however, "borrow" items that are protected by copyright without the author's permission. Customarily, one writes the author of the instrument for permission to use it and requests any additional information that the author may have on the instrument. Sometimes the author can refer you to other researchers who have recently modified or used the instrument with interesting results. Besides the possibility of saving time in questionnaire design, another advantage of using questions that have already been employed by other researchers is that you can then compare your findings to those from existing studies. The literature review may also reveal methods or approaches that were not successful.

As you begin selecting and composing questions for the first draft of a questionnaire, you will have to give some thought to whether your research topic requires **closed-ended questions** (multiple choice type responses) or **open-ended questions** (unstructured responses).

Closed-Ended Questions

Closed-ended questions are those that have their own predetermined response set. The major advantage of closed-ended questions is that a great deal of time is saved in the tabulation of the data and coding it for computer analysis. Since the response choices are supplied (for example, "Yes," "No," or "Strongly agree," "Agree," and so on) the person who is tabulating the responses does not have the problem of deciphering lengthy, illegible responses. Virtually no interpretation is required of what the respondent intended or whether a response is more like an existing set of responses or deserves a whole new category. Another advantage is that closed-ended questions with their response options communicate the same frame of reference to all respondents.

Closed-ended questions are used when it is known how respondents might reply. If their responses are difficult to anticipate, open-ended questions can be used in a pilot study to find out what terms or language respondents tend to use in responding. It is then possible to identify frequent or common responses as well as the range of responses so that closed-ended questions can be developed.

Closed-ended questions can be used effectively in practically all areas of interest to social workers. For example, perhaps you are interested in specific dimensions of nursing home life. One area that you feel is important is how the residents evaluate the food prepared by the nursing home. You might construct a closed-ended question that allows for ratings of "Excellent," "Good," "Fair," or "Poor." However, a "fair" rating does not provide a wealth of information about the food. It doesn't tell you, for instance, whether oatmeal is served every day for breakfast, whether it arrives cold or warm, or if there is a variety of breakfast foods available. Other closed-ended questions might be used to follow the initial question and to further help assess the quality of meals provided at the nursing home.

Open-Ended Questions

Open-ended questions have no prepared response choices. This form of question allows respondents to communicate without having to choose from a set of prepared response categories. Open-ended questions are best suited for those occasions when the researcher intends that direct interviewing be employed. Few respondents take the time to elaborate on their thoughts or feelings when they must write them out on paper, and as a result, mailed ques-

---

Practice Note: Open-Ended Questions

The best argument for why open-ended questions should be included in most questionnaires comes from a student who was interning in a state social service agency. Foster children were routinely given questionnaires on which they could evaluate their placement.

On one particular form completed by a female adolescent the girl indicated that the placement was satisfactory on all the criteria used by the agency. The last question on the back of the form asked simply, "Is there anything about this placement you don't like?" The teen wrote in response, "One thing I didn't like was that Jim [the foster father] came into my bedroom every night about the time I started getting ready for bed."

Obviously, the foster father's behavior was inappropriate. He had no business trying to make conversation in the foster child's bedroom when she was changing into pajamas. As a result, this foster home was viewed as not being acceptable for future placements of young women.

---

tionnaires that rely heavily on open-ended questions have a poorer response rate than those that use closed-ended questions. There is some evidence that open-ended questions result in greater reporting of sensitive or socially disapproved behavior than closed-ended questions. One possible explanation for this is that respondents will avoid placing themselves in categories that include high levels of socially unacceptable behavior when they can choose categories with more acceptable levels of behavior.

There are times when the researcher wants greater detail than closed-ended questions typically provide. For example, if you wanted to know more about the quality of life in a nursing home as the residents experience it, closed-ended questions are not likely to provide you with much insight into their personal reflections. Open-ended questions supply you with quotes from residents—their experiences in their own words. On the other hand, a respondent can ramble; it requires a skillful interviewer to bring the respondent back to the topic of interest.

In any given survey, it is possible to combine both closed-ended and open-ended questions. In the example of an evaluation of a nursing home, one could rely chiefly upon closed-ended questions for rating various facets of the nursing home (for example, courteousness of the staff, noise level, social and recreational opportunities) and still employ an open-ended question such as: "Is there anything else you would like to tell us about how it feels to live in this nursing home?" Alternatively, you could use these open-ended questions: "What is the *best* thing about living in this nursing home?"

and "What is the *worst* thing about living in this nursing home?" Your use of open- or closed-ended questions (or a mixture of the two) is dependent upon the goals of your research and the type of information you require. Keep in mind that open-ended questions are easier to develop than closed-ended ones, but they are harder to analyze. For instance, suppose you ask a group of volunteers this question: "What kinds of things did you do as a Big Brother or Big Sister?" You might get back a list of such activities as:

Went out to eat
Played basketball
Went to movies
Tutored
Visited the mall
Visited the zoo
Went shopping
Built model planes
Talked on the phone
Played Monopoly and board games
Worked on my car
Went fishing
Watched television
Went bicycling
Visited friends
Went to the library
Baked cookies
Took a walk

Now suppose you want to summarize these into one or two categories to understand what kinds of activities Big Brothers and Big Sisters favored. Would you use the category of athletic/nonathletic activity? If so, is fishing athletic? Would you create categories for those activities that required spending money (such as, going to a movie or to a restaurant) versus those that didn't (such as, watching television)? But then, couldn't making cookies involve an expense (if you had to buy chocolate chips and sugar)? Does fishing involve an expense? A visit to the mall doesn't have to be expensive, but would you know if the Big Brother bought soft drinks and tacos?

Take my word for it, closed-ended questions are a great deal easier to analyze. The only problem is that with them you have to anticipate how the respondents would answer. However, a small pilot test with open-ended questions can often suggest the categories or response set that you need for the same item to be converted to a closed-ended question.

Whether you adopt questions that have been used by other researchers or write your own, circulate a rough draft of the proposed questionnaire among your colleagues for comments and suggestions. Use their responses to revise the questionnaire before it goes out for a pilot test. After the pilot test, scrutinize the questionnaire again for questions that might have been misunderstood, biased items that suggest responses, insufficient response categories, typographical errors, and similar problems. Only after several revisions should the questionnaire be printed and distributed.

To assist you in developing good questionnaires, a number of specific guidelines have been elaborated. These guidelines will help you recognize the ways in which item construction can affect the data you obtain. Ill-conceived questions can produce error. Hastily constructed questions can result in worthless data. Examples of poorly phrased or constructed questions appear in this chapter; consider each of the examples and decide for yourself why it is flawed before reading the discussion accompanying it.

Pitfalls in Writing Good Questions

Double-Barreled Questions

Example: Have you donated blood or gone to the dentist this month?

( )   Yes
( )   No
( )   Don't know

This question is poorly constructed because it asks about two different behaviors but is structured so that only one response is expected. In the minds of most people, these two events are not connected in any way. A response of "Yes" could mean that the respondent had donated blood and been to the dentist. It is also possible that some respondents might respond "Yes" when they had visited the dentist but not donated blood, and vice versa. Some respondents will indicate "No" when they have done one but not the other. Some "No" responses will mean that the respondent has neither donated blood nor gone to the dentist. If it is impossible to interpret what any response means, then the item is not a good one.

As a rule, a question should ask about one issue, thought, or event at a time. If more information is desired, additional questions should be asked. In this example, two separate questions should be constructed—each one focusing upon a single issue. Avoid asking two questions in one item.

However, sometimes a single item might be used when the focus is on the similarity of two different events. For instance, if we were interviewing abuse victims it could be acceptable to ask, "Were you threatened with a gun or a knife?" If the intent was to discover how often abuse victims were threatened with weapons, there may not be any reason to break this item into two different questions.

On the other hand, a question like "Have you ever been called names or threatened with harm?" is poorly constructed because being called names is a fairly common occurrence and doesn't imply the same order of danger as being threatened with harm.

Leading Questions

Example: Don't you agree with the president that the federal government should not overspend?

( ) Agree
( ) Disagree
( ) Don't know

This question clearly leads the respondent into thinking along certain lines. Most of us want to be agreeable and to get along with others. And most Americans believe it is important to respect the president and would generally want to support that office (by agreeing with the president when possible). This example is a leading question because it suggests the desired response.

The question "Don't you agree that the federal government should spend more on social services and less on biological warfare research?" is both leading and double-barreled. Besides begging for an "Agree" response, it also asks for information about two different things. First, it wants to know if the government should spend more money on social services. Second, it wants to know if the respondent thinks the government should spend less on biological warfare. Again, the respondent could agree with one of these two thoughts and disagree with the other and be confused about how to respond.

Unavailable Information

Example: How many hours of television did you watch last year?

Respondents should not be asked for information that would not normally be available to them. Since most of us do not keep records regarding how much television we watch, any response that we might give to a question like this one would be no more than a wild estimate. A much better way to get at this kind of information would be to ask about the average number of hours of television watched daily or weekly.

Possibly the best (worst?) example of a question asking for unavailable information was in a questionnaire actually used in an agency. The respondent was asked, "Describe your mother's pregnancy with you; for example, were there complications?" While it is true that a few individuals may have acquired this information because they were born prematurely, my hunch is that the vast majority of Americans would have no information at all about their mother's health status during pregnancy.

Practice Note: Human Memory

Alcohol and drug use impair one's ability to accurately recall information. This includes prescription drugs such as Valium. Further, the more time that elapses after an event, the less accurate will be the recall of details associated with that event. In a study based on reports of traffic accidents where one or more persons were injured, when subjects were interviewed three months after their accident, 97 percent said they had reported the accident. Only 70 percent said they had filed a report when interviewed nine to twelve months after their accident. In a study of concentration camp survivors, most of the people had forgotten the names of guards although they had been reported in earlier interviews. In a third study, professors were asked to recall the faces of former pupils. Their accuracy was only slightly above chance after four years. Human memory is affected not only by the passage of time, but also by our own internal motivations, so that our memories tend to take a self-advantageous direction—we're not all that objective in remembering our actions and contributions. Finally, our recollections can be reconstructed, supplemented, and even alerted by post-event information (Loftus and Doyle, 1992).

The recall of distant events is always problematic and increased error is associated with the passage of time (see Practice Note: Human Memory). As a rule, it is better to ask about events and activities that have happened recently, say, within the past thirty days or twelve months. However, sometimes it is necessary to ask what is known as "lifetime" questions, such as, "Have you ever been arrested?" or "How many times have you been in any kind of treatment program for alcohol or drug problems?"

Asking for information that might not be available to *all* respondents can present another problem. Consider the following question: "Do you agree or disagree with the philosophy of the state's Commission on Literacy?" This question is a poor one *if* the philosophy of the state's Commission on Literacy is not well known. If, on the other hand, the Commission has recently been in the news because of some unusual or controversial philosophy, then it would be quite reasonable to ask this question. However, it might be better to ask in one question if there is a Commission on Literacy; then ask those respondents who answer "Yes" to describe the Commission's philosophy. A third question in this series might ask if they agree or disagree with the Commission's philosophy. This approach involves the use of **contingency questions** (branching questions). Those respondents who answer "Yes" to the first question are

**Figure 7.3 Illustration of a Contingency Question in a Personal or
Telephone Interview Schedule**

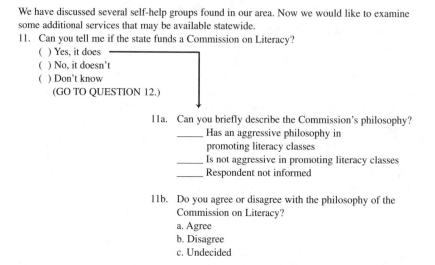

We have discussed several self-help groups found in our area. Now we would like to examine some additional services that may be available statewide.

11. Can you tell me if the state funds a Commission on Literacy?
     ( ) Yes, it does
     ( ) No, it doesn't
     ( ) Don't know
         (GO TO QUESTION 12.)

11a. Can you briefly describe the Commission's philosophy?
      _____ Has an aggressive philosophy in
              promoting literacy classes
      _____ Is not aggressive in promoting literacy classes
      _____ Respondent not informed

11b. Do you agree or disagree with the philosophy of the
      Commission on Literacy?
      a. Agree
      b. Disagree
      c. Undecided

directed to the second and third subquestions. Those who respond "No" to the first question are guided to another set of questions. See figure 7.3 for an example of a contingency question. Contingency questions might also be called filter questions, because the investigator may want to study a certain subgroup of subjects with particular characteristics.

Use of Jargon and Technical Terms

Example: Do you feel that Freud's structural hypothesis is an improvement over his topographic hypothesis?

Even those who are familiar with psychoanalytic theory may not know how to respond to this question. It is too technical, using jargon not known to most Americans. Your goal as a designer of questionnaire or scale items is to use familiar rather than unfamiliar language. Being cognizant of the reading level and vocabularies of your possible subjects, you would not want to use professional terms that might not be understood by everyone. For example, if you were surveying teens about their use of birth control methods, would you want to use the word *prophylactic*? Probably not. Even terms that you think everyone should understand can be too sophisticated. A study of patients at the Primary Care Center of Yale New Haven Hospital found that one in four believed that "orally" referred to "how often" medication should be taken (Gibbs and Gibbs, 1987).

Use the simplest terms and vocabulary possible—the language that we use in everyday speech (sometimes called Standard English). Avoid colloquialisms, abbreviations (t.i.d., TIA), foreign phrases, and terminology like "borderline personality." The general rule is to aim for a seventh or eighth grade comprehension level—unless, of course, you are dealing with younger children. Keep sentences short and simple. Avoid compound sentences if possible.

Insensitive Language

Example: How do you people feel about Jesse Jackson?

You may be interested in discovering how a certain ethnic or racial group feels about an issue. But a question like this may make some people uneasy because it is suggestive of racial bias. It accentuates differences among respondents by saying, in effect, that the respondent is a member of a group that is dissimilar from others (possibly the majority of Americans). Instead of asking questions in the format of "How do *you blacks* (or *you Indians*) feel about . . .?" simply ask "How do *you* feel about . . .?" Or, present a statement and ask the respondent to choose a response that reflects his or her feelings about the subject. Later, when analyzing the data, you will be able to determine if racial groups differ in their attitudes (if you collect data on the respondent's racial group as part of your questionnaire). Avoid using any language in a questionnaire that is suggestive of racism, sexism, or insensitivity.

Inflammatory or "Loaded" Terms

Example: Are you a religious fanatic?

Social desirability is a term used to describe the tendency of people to want their behavior to be perceived as socially acceptable. It is a strong motivation, and response bias can easily occur as respondents avoid categories or labels that are stigmatizing. Few of us want to be labeled fanatic, zealot, or any other term that has socially undesirable connotations. Even though a respondent may have very strong convictions, he or she would likely deny having tendencies toward fanaticism. Examples of loaded terms that should be replaced with more neutral terms include *crisis, innocent, victim, forced,* and *coerced.*

Just as the word *fanatic* is loaded, few people would want to be labeled a drunk or alcoholic. Questions that get the information without labeling or stigmatization should be employed. A better way to explore the extent of problem drinking is to ask respondents about specific behaviors, for example, "How many times a week do you have a drink in the morning?" You want to provide a series of categories that give a respondent an opportunity to describe his or her pattern of drinking as objectively as possible.

Mutually Exclusive Response Choices

Example: "Teetotaler," "Social Drinker," "I occasionally drink to excess," "I frequently drink to excess."

In our quest to avoid socially unacceptable labels, we might create another problem. Consider the two response choices of "social drinker" and "I occasionally drink to excess." Are they mutually exclusive? Is it possible to be a social drinker and to occasionally drink to excess? If you agree, then this response set will not provide "clean" data.

Some respondents will think of themselves as social drinkers even though they drink to excess. Being a social drinker is a more attractive response to some individuals than revealing how often they drink to excess. Measuring the number of times a person drinks in an average week is a more precise way of separating light drinkers from moderate or heavy drinkers. Behavioral measures such as these are much more useful than stigmatizing or labeling terms.

The problems of overlapping response categories and finding good behavioral measures are obvious examples of why you need to refer to the literature as part of the research process. It is very likely that other researchers have struggled with these problems and have developed response sets or categories (if not whole questionnaires) that you could use in your research. If your literature review is thorough, you may find that someone has already done the very research that you are proposing. This being the case, you may decide to go no further, or you may make modifications to pursue a slightly different hypothesis.

We're not always aware of overlapping response choices. Can you detect any problems with the responses in the following example?

How often do you date?

a. almost every night   d. three to four times a week
b. once or twice a week   e. once every two weeks
c. a few times a month   f. a few times a year

Other classic examples of overlapping response options include:

What is your income?
1. 0–$5,000
2. $5,000–$10,000
3. $10,000–$15,000
4. $15,000 or higher

What is your grade-point average?
1. Below 2.00
2. 2.00 to 2.50
3. 2.50 to 3.00
4. 3.00 to 3.50
5. 3.50 to 4.00

Vague and Ambiguous Terms

Example: How many times in the past year have you seen a social worker?

The problem with this question is that it contains language that is vague. Is the intent of this question to find out how many social workers are observed (seen)? Or, is it to learn the number of appointments or sessions the respondent had with a social worker last year? To rephrase the question to "How many times in the past year have you talked with a social worker?" is not an improvement, since one can talk informally or socially with social workers (for instance, in the hallway). Would it be better to ask, "How many appointments have you made with your social worker in the last thirty days?" Or, since it is possible to make appointments but not keep them, "How many office visits have you had with your social worker in the last thirty days?" Even these two questions could be refined since an office visit could last ten minutes or two and a half hours. Both of these questions omit the whole dimension of home visits. A more exact approach would be to ask, "In the past thirty days, about how many hours have you spent talking about your problems face-to-face with your social worker?"

The following question also uses a vague term that may cause problems: "Do you attend Alcoholics Anonymous (AA) meetings regularly?" The problem with this sentence is that "regularly" is one of those terms that means different things to different individuals. Some respondents may attend AA regularly three times a year. Other respondents may attend regularly the first Wednesday of the month. Some respondents may attend twice a day every day. A better way to ask for information of this type would be: "How many times a month do you attend Alcoholics Anonymous meetings?"

Another example of the use of vague terms is the question: "What is your income?" This question is problematic because the respondent must figure out whether the information sought has a yearly, monthly, or weekly referent. It also is unclear whether the respondent should report annual salary (gross income) or the amount after all the deductions have been made (net income). A further problem is that the question does not indicate whether combined family income is expected or whether the respondent should report only his or her personal income (even though others in the household may be working).

Similarly, "Are you employed?" may be difficult to answer because there are several responses that can be made in addition to "Yes" or "No." The status of being employed usually includes full-time and part-time workers. Also, respondents could be employed seasonally (for example, migrant workers or college students who work full time in the summer but not at all when school is in session). Finally, there are those who help with a family business (such as, a spouse who keeps the books) but who do not receive a paycheck.

Vague and ambiguous terms do not convey the same frame of reference to all respondents. For instance, some respondents will read "Has your child missed a lot of school?" and think in terms of the whole school year. Other parents may think only about absences in the past month or week. Parents may also respond to this question in terms of their own experience in missing school or compare one child to another so that even though Hugh has missed fourteen days of school in the first grading period, that's not a "lot" compared to his sister Edna who missed six weeks due to illness. It is better practice to provide the same frame of reference for everyone—for example, by asking, "How many days of school did your child miss during the first grading period?"

Even when we think an item is not vague, pretesting or reliability scaling may show that respondents have different impressions of what it is asking. Agreeing to the item "I have difficulty getting up in the morning" may mean either that the respondent needs assistance because of a physical disability or that the individual tends to oversleep, perhaps because of not hearing the alarm clock. It would be a mistake to plan a large-scale survey without pilot testing your questionnaire to eliminate confusing and vague items.

All-Inclusive Terms

Example: Are you always in bed by 11:00 P.M.?

The use of such words as *always* and *never* creates problems for the respondent and for the researcher attempting to interpret the data. Does *always* allow for exceptions? For instance, what if you are in bed by 11:00 P.M every night of the year except for New Year's Eve, when you stay up until 12:01 A.M? Does that mean that you should respond with a "No" to the above question? *Always* and *never* imply that there are no exceptions. Researchers are more concerned with general patterns; for example, "On most week nights, about what time do you usually go to bed?"

Negatively Constructed Items

Example: Marijuana should not be decriminalized.

This item, borrowed from DeVaus (1986), is a good example of how the word "not" confuses the meaning of the statement. In this instance, it reverses the meaning of decriminalized so that a person agreeing to the statement is saying in effect that marijuana usage should be illegal. A respondent disagreeing with the statement is saying that marijuana use should be made legal. It is much more clear and straightforward to ask, "Should the private use of marijuana be made legal?" Where possible, the term *not* should be avoided in questionnaires.

Figure 7.4 Phrasing Questions to Avoid Acquiescence

	Strongly Agree	Agree	Undecided	Disagree	Strongly Disagree
1. Children who are HIV+ should be allowed to attend school.	( )	( )	( )	( )	( )
2. Persons who are HIV+ should be quarantined.	( )	( )	( )	( )	( )
3. Persons who are HIV+ should be allowed to eat in public restaurants.	( )	( )	( )	( )	( )
4. Persons who are HIV+ deserve what they get.	( )	( )	( )	( )	( )

Acquiescence, a tendency some respondents have to agree with items regardless of their content, can be countered by constructing items so that the respondent will respond positively (for example, "Agree") and negatively (for example, "Disagree") in roughly equal proportions. With a little creativity, items can be prepared so that the respondent does not know which response is the one desired by the researcher. Figure 7.4 provides an example of wording questions so that a respondent sympathetic to people who are HIV positive could not respond either "Strongly Agree" or "Agree" to all four questions.

Sequence of Questions

There is general agreement that the first questions to be asked should be of interest to the respondent. Respondents need to "warm up" to the survey process and establish a sense of trust or rapport with the researcher or the researcher's representative (which could be the mailed questionnaire). Accordingly, the first several questions should be applicable to all respondents. Respondents seem to prefer closed-ended questions at the start of mailed questionnaires but open-ended questions when interviewed in person or over the phone. Information about potentially sensitive areas such as age and income should occur at the end of the questionnaire. Such information, if asked at the beginning of the interview or questionnaire, may result in refusals to participate and a lower response rate. More important questions should be asked earlier than less important ones in case the respondent decides to terminate the interview or stop working on the questionnaire before all questions have been completed. Respondent fatigue can be a problem with especially long questionnaires.

There also seems to be consensus that topically related questions should follow one another in some sort of recognizable sequence as opposed to being interposed and spread throughout the questionnaire. Usually, some sort of "funnel sequence" is used, in which general questions are followed by more narrowly focused questions. A problem may occur if a question has an effect on subsequent responses because it creates some sort of expectancy or "mind-set." Some topics seem to be immune to this sort of problem, and others are sensitive to it. The best advice that can be offered regarding order effects is to be alert to the possibility that earlier questions can affect later responses.

Thinking about Guidelines

The problem with guidelines is that sometimes it makes sense to violate them. There are times when one might use a loaded question to try to determine the extent of some socially undesirable behavior. For instance, the implication that "everyone does it" may be useful in reducing the threat of reporting some behaviors. This approach is illustrated in the following example:

> All parents get angry when their children misbehave. About how many times in the past month did you scream at your children?

Another instance comes to mind of when guidelines are best ignored. If you are interviewing members of a street gang, you may want to use terms that they commonly use instead of those terms common to Standard English.

Besides these guidelines, there are other concerns, too. It has been shown, for example, that crowded, cluttered, or difficult-appearing questionnaires result in lower response rates than those that appear interesting, inviting, or simple to complete. Mailed questionnaires should be visually attractive. Blank or white space should be used to full advantage. The responses should appear in the same area of the questionnaire so that the respondent can easily locate them. Instructions, questions, and response categories should be kept brief, and diagrams used to visually direct the respondent where necessary. Numbering the questions is also useful to both respondents and those who must process the data. Where there are various components or parts to the study, a sentence or two to indicate that a shift is occurring smoothes the transition (for example, "Now we would like to change the subject just a bit and ask some health related questions").

In Appendix C of this book you'll find a shortened version of the Drug Attitude Questionnaire, an instrument designed to measure the effects of the drug education program. A longer version than I've shown had excellent reliability (.93 to .97). You might want to examine the Drug Attitude Questionnaire to review some of the items. If you look closely, you'll note that this reliability came despite some items that I would change if I were to write them again. For instance, what about items 8, 9, and 17? Do they violate any guideline that we have learned in this chapter?

Self-Anchored Scales

Another option available to you when you are developing research instruments is to generate self-anchored, single-item scales for obtaining measurements (particularly about clients' problems). Self-anchored scales are especially valuable when you need to quickly estimate the magnitude or severity of a problem. A chief advantage is that they can be used to assess thoughts and feelings (such as security in a relationship, self-perceptions of stupidity or attractiveness to others) that may be unique to a client or group of clients and for which there may not exist a standardized measurement tool.

While many self-anchored scales are based on 10 equal intervals, it is not unusual to find scales based on 5, 7, 9, or even 100 points. The only thing tricky about designing these scales is keeping in mind that only one dimension of a concept should be presented. For instance, "angry" and "not angry" represent only one dimension and would be acceptable at opposite ends of a continuum. However, "angry" at one end and "happy" at the other involves two concepts instead of one and may make the scale less accurate because of different feelings associated with anger and happiness.

Self-anchored scales can also be used in single subject designs as a repeated measure to keep track of progress resulting from intervention. When self-anchored scales are designed for specific clients, their own actions and feelings—described in their own words—can be used to anchor the ends of the continuum. To demonstrate what self-anchored scales look like, I've created several examples shown in figure 7.5.

Figure 7.5 Examples of Self-Anchored Scales

The Amount of Anger I Felt Today

0	1	2	3	4	5	6	7	8	9	10

None
(Had pleasant
conversation)

Moderate
(Slammed the door
and walked away)

Extreme
(Shouted obscenities,
punched wall)

How Satisfied I Am with My Life

0	1	2	3	4	5	6	7	8	9	10

No Satifaction   *Average Satisfaction*   *Very Satisfied*

Community Involvement

0	1	2	3	4	5	6	7	8	9	10

Not Involved   *Medium Involvement*   *Very Involved*

Feelings of Emotional Intimacy with Loved One

0	1	2	3	4	5	6	7	8	9	10

*Not at All Close (Unhappy;
Not much sharing)*

*Very Close (Happy with
relationship; lots of sharing)*

While there is not a lot of empirical evidence attesting to the psychometric characteristics of self-anchored scales, Thyer et al. (1984) have reported data showing criterion validity of the Subjective Anxiety Scale. Hersen and Bellack (1988) have discussed the reliability and validity of the Fear Thermometer, and Nugent (1992) obtained a criterion validity index of .82 when he correlated a self-anchored depression scale with a standardized measure of nonpsychotic depression. However, although he found evidence for some convergent and discriminant validity for a self-anchored scale measuring self-esteem, the reliability was quite low, and Nugent (1993) recommended extreme caution when trying to use a single item to measure self-esteem. He concluded that some constructs may be well measured by self-anchored scales while others are not.

The Role of Questionnaires in Generalizing Results

Even if you have a strong sampling design that would ordinarily allow for generalizing your results, a poorly constructed questionnaire or scale can ruin your study. The expression "garbage in, garbage out" applies here. Minimize the inclusion of worthless items by ensuring that respondents understand each and every item as you intended it. Don't be afraid to circulate your drafts among those whose opinion you respect. Probably the best way to get feedback is by pilot testing the instrument. You could start with a small group of ten to fifteen respondents, revise, then pilot test again. It is not uncommon to go through five, six, or more revisions. Good questionnaires do not result from a single draft.

The items you develop for your study are the foundation for any knowledge that will be acquired. If you do a good job with the design of your questionnaire, respondents will not find it burdensome. In fact, it just might be possible to make it so interesting that respondents *enjoy* participating; when they are cooperative and honest, you will have much better data. Poorly designed questionnaires can generate worthless data when interviewers or raters get confused and enter data on the wrong line or in the wrong box. A well-designed questionnaire will not only be easy to complete, but also easy for the investigator to interpret responses and record data.

Although this chapter has placed a lot of importance on the wording and phrasing of individual items, there are other elements that can influence the responses you obtain. For instance, research subjects may need a line or two of directions on how to complete your questionnaire or scale. If the survey is being mailed, a cover letter is essential to provide a brief explanation of why the study is being conducted, who is being involved, and the extent to which confidentiality is afforded. It is also good practice to inform potential participants how much of their time the survey will take.

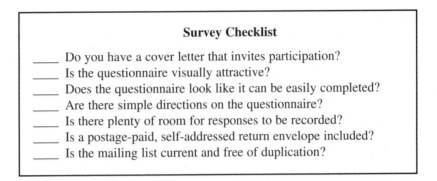

Finally, it is vital that your questions not only be technically correct but also provide you with the information you need to prepare a response to some problem. Each question should give you some essential information, and all of the questions taken together should help you conclude something about the topic of your investigation. Research is much more than formulating questions or devising questionnaires.

Perhaps my relating an actual experience will serve to reinforce this point: A group of local citizens once asked for my assistance in conducting a mental health needs assessment of their community. "Okay," I said, "tell me more." Their spokesperson indicated that they had found a book about needs assessment that included, in its appendix, a complete set of questions that could be photocopied and used with very little modification. As I looked at the needs assessment instrument, I saw a question that asked the respondents to list three problems in their neighborhood and another that asked for a ranking of the most serious problems in the community. In my mind, I saw respondents being concerned with street lights and potholes, police protection, and a great many other community concerns. I did not, however, believe the use of that particular questionnaire would produce much usable information about the mental health needs of the community. I asked the spokesperson, "What do you hope to learn from the community needs assessment?" "Well," she said, "we want to know about all the mental health needs in the community." Further questioning revealed that there wasn't anything more specific that they hoped to learn.

At that point I tactfully asked the group to meet together to determine what, exactly, they wanted to know about the mental health needs in the community. They met and discussed what they wanted to know, but to the best of my knowledge, that group never did conduct a community needs assessment. I strongly suspect that there was no agreement among them on what was important to learn about their community's mental health needs—or how the information would be used. As you can see, the point is not just to develop a set of questions—the questions we ask must have a clear focus and purpose.

Each question should add another increment to that sum of information that we require. The well-designed questionnaire asks no less and no more than is needed for our research. Anyone can develop a questionnaire or conduct a survey. The "test" of a good survey is whether it produces useful data. Genuinely useful information seldom comes about just because someone happens to find a set of already prepared questions.

Self-Review

(Answers at the end of the book)

1. T or F. Ideally closed-ended questions should communicate the same frame of reference to all persons.
2. T or F. With large samples, it is easier to analyze the data obtained from open-ended questions than from closed-ended questions.
3. T or F. Double-barreled questions are useful to researchers because they allow the respondent to supply twice as much information in a single answer.
4. What is wrong with asking a child this question: "When did you last see the principal?"
   a. Insensitive, inflammatory
   b. Prevents contingency mock-up
   c. Uses jargon
   d. Vague
5. What is wrong with this question: "Do you agree or disagree that EMDR contributes to resiliency among victims of PTSD?"
   a. Implies social desirability
   b. Uses jargon
   c. Is negatively constructed
   d. Creates acquiescence
6. What is wrong with this question: "How many times did you argue with your mother last summer?
   a. Implies social desirability
   b. Insensitive language
   c. Unavailable information
   d. Creates acquiescence
7. What is wrong with this question: "When you are punished by your parents, do you act like a jerk?"
   a. Leading question
   b. Insensitive language
   c. Unavailable information
   d. Uses loaded terms

8. What is wrong with this question: "Parents should not be so uncompromising and irrational."
   a. Negatively constructed
   b. Insensitive language
   c. Leading question
   d. Uses loaded terms

9. What is wrong with this question: "Do you always get your telephone privileges revoked when you don't clean up your room?"
   a. Negatively constructed
   b. Is all-inclusive
   c. Leading question
   d. Uses loaded terms

10. What is wrong with this question: "Do you regularly disagree with your parents' judgment on important issues?"
    a. Uses loaded terms
    b. Unavailable information
    c. Leading question
    d. Vague

11. What is wrong with this question: "Don't you think the city council should change the teen curfew to 2:00 A.M. on weekends?"
    a. Uses loaded terms
    b. Unavailable information
    c. Leading question
    d. Vague

12. Another name for a branching type question would be a _____ question.

Questions for Class Discussion

1. Why is it important that the questionnaire communicate the same frame of reference to all respondents?
2. What would be a good way to check questionnaire and scale items to make sure that they do not contain jargon or some other problem?
3. To what extent do the items we construct reflect our view of the world and our values?
4. From a research perspective, what is the advantage of self-anchored scales over single-item scales that do not contain "anchors"?
5. What bothers you most when you are asked to complete a questionnaire or instrument?
6. Why is it important to decide upon the survey methodology before designing the questionnaire to be used?

Mini-Projects for Experiencing Research Firsthand

1. Develop a set of questions to use to interview nursing home residents to find out about the quality of their lives.
   a. List the important dimensions to be covered.
   b. Construct five open-ended and five closed-ended questions along with the corresponding response set.
   c. As you reflect on the questions you would ask, what would you learn about life in a nursing home? What wouldn't you learn from this set of questions?
2. Conduct a twenty-minute interview with a neighbor, friend, grand-parent, or someone else you know. Explore a significant experience (such as, living through the Great Depression, recovery from major surgery, running for political office). Use only open-ended questions. Keep notes, and transcribe your interview. Be sure to include the questions that were asked of the respondents and any remarks (such as transitional statements) you made along the way. Share in class what you learned from the experience. Be sure to include a brief description of the person whom you interviewed (for example, female, eighty-three years of age, former journalist, and so on).
3. Develop a questionnaire that will help you learn why your fellow students have become social work majors.
   a. What hypothesis do you want to test?
   b. Develop ten to fifteen closed-ended questions and two open-ended questions.
   c. Interview ten social work majors.
   d. What did you learn from this experience? Did you learn more from the open-ended or the closed-ended questions?
4. Develop a self-esteem scale of about fifteen items. When you've finished, share it with a friend for constructive criticism. Then, compare it with one that has been published. How many of your items are similar to the one in print?

Resources and References

Bradburn, N. and Sudman, S. (1979). *Improving interview method and questionnaire design.* San Francisco, CA: Jossey-Bass.

DeVaus, D.A. (1986). *Surveys in social research.* London: George Allen and Unwin.

Dillman, D.A. (1978). *Mail and telephone surveys: The total design method.* New York: Wiley.

Fink, A. and Kosecoff, J. (1985). *How to conduct surveys: A step-by-step guide.* Beverly Hills, CA: Sage.

Gibbs, R.D. and Gibbs, P.H. (1987). Patient understanding of commonly used medical vocabulary. *Journal of Family Practice,* 25, 176–178.

Hersen, M. and Bellack, A. (1988). *Dictionary of behavioral assessment techniques.* Elmsford, NY: Pergamon Press.

Loftus, E.F. and Doyle, J.M. (1992) *Eyewitness testimony: Civil and criminal.* Charlottesville, VA: Michie Company.

Moore, D.W. and Gallup, A. (1994). The Holocaust: It happened. *Gallup Poll Monthly,* 340, 25–27.

Nugent, W.R. (1992). Psychometric characteristics of self-anchored scales in clinical application. *Journal of Social Service Research,* 15(3/4), 137–152.

Nugent, W.R. (1993). A validity study of a self-anchored scale for measuring self-esteem. *Research on Social Work Practice,* 3(3), 276–287.

Nugent, W.R. and Thomas, J.W. (1993). Validation of a clinical measure of self-esteem. *Research on Social Work Practice,* 3(2), 191–207.

Oppenheim, A.N. (1992). *Questionnaire design, interviewing, and attitude measurement.* New York: St. Martin's Press.

Rossi, P.F., Wright, J.D., and Anderson, A.B. (1983). *Handbook of survey research.* New York: Academic Press.

Schuman, H. and Presser, S. (1981). *Questions and answers in attitude surveys.* New York: Academic Press.

Sudman, S. and Bradburn, N.M. (1982). *Asking questions.* San Francisco: Jossey-Bass.

Sudman, S. and Bradburn, N.M., and Schwarz, N. (1995). *About answers: The application of cognitive processes to methodology.* San Francisco, CA: Jossey-Bass.

Thyer, B., Papsdorf, J., Davis, R., and Vallecorsa, S. (1984). Autonomic correlates of the subjective anxiety scale. *Journal of Behavior Theory and Experimental Psychiatry,* 15, 3–7.

CHAPTER 8

Unobtrusive Approaches to Data Collection: Secondary Data and Content Analysis

The research approaches we have discussed thus far have one thing in common—they involve interaction with respondents in order to collect the needed data. Unfortunately, any time interviewers interact with respondents there is the potential for producing unintended changes in them. For example, imagine that you are involved in presenting a workshop to your co-workers on the avoidance of sexist language. A week before the workshop you send each participant a small questionnaire that asks if he or she uses certain terms or phrases in conversation. Suppose Robert Doe reads the questionnaire, briefly considers how he will respond, and then indicates on the form that he does not use any of those terms in his normal conversation. However, driving home from work that night, he reflects back upon the questionnaire and realizes that there are several other ways in which his choice of words or phrasing might be considered sexist. As a result of thinking about the pretest, he resolves to eliminate these terms and phrases from his speech and writing.

Your workshop is conducted as scheduled, and you administer the posttest. An examination of the data reveals a decrease in the use of sexist language at the time of the posttest. But if others in the agency had the same experience as Robert Doe, how would you know which had the most impact, the workshop or the pretest? Perhaps any reduction in sexist language was merely the result of respondents' reactions to the questionnaire. It is conceivable that as mild an interaction as testing can bring about changes in attitudes, behavior, or knowledge.

Even if we are considerate and polite about it, asking respondents to give us information about themselves can be experienced as an invasion of privacy.

Researchers can gauge this by the number of respondents who refuse to cooperate with interviewers or to complete survey forms. And although people may agree to participate, there is still the possibility that merely asking certain questions may have an inadvertent effect upon the respondents.

In physics there is a principle, known as the Heisenberg Principle, which states that it is impossible to measure both the position and velocity of an electron in motion with a great deal of precision; the very act of trying to measure the position of an electron may change its velocity. Shouldn't those of us concerned with measurement in the social sciences be equally concerned that our tests and scales might somehow alter the very phenomena we are trying to define?

One of the more famous examples of an unanticipated effect on research subjects has come to be known as the **Hawthorne Effect**. Prior to World War II, researchers at a Western Electric plant in Chicago found that employees in the study raised their production—no matter what physical changes were made in their work environment (for example, the lighting was both increased and decreased). What researchers learned is that subjects may be significantly influenced by the knowledge that they are taking part in a research study. In fact, knowing that they have been chosen to participate in a research project had more influence on them than the independent variables.

One way to avoid problems with our measurements affecting that which we wish to study is to utilize data that already exist instead of collecting new data from respondents. The use of existing data that does not involve interaction with research subjects fits into the category called **unobtrusive research**. The classic work in this area is that of Webb, Campbell, Schwartz, and Sechrest (1966), *Unobtrusive Measures: Nonreactive Research in the Social Sciences.*

Whether they are aware of it or not, social workers in performing their routine tasks help collect mountains of data each year. The vast majority of these data come from the ordinary processing of clients into and out of service delivery systems. Each use of an admission form, evaluation form, progress note, or social history generates valuable information.

Data available for unobtrusive research are also contained in the records of institutionalized persons, in the portfolios of immigrants, and in the files of persons who've enrolled in community educational presentations. Sometimes these data are kept in "hard copy" form and stored in filing cabinets, or they may be contained in the electronic memory of a computer. These data are not collected with research purposes in mind. However, collections of such data represent a wealth of research opportunities for interested social workers.

Researchers who rely upon public documents, reports, and historical data are said to be engaged in a type of unobtrusive research called **archival research** or **secondary data analysis**. This type of research involves the analysis of an existing data set that results in knowledge, interpretations, and conclusions beyond those stated in the original study. The intent is not to find fault with another's study, but rather to test new hypotheses or explore questions not examined in the original report. While the original study may have collected data on the attitudes of a cross-section of Americans, a secondary analysis might examine only the attitudes of a minority subgroup.

Secondary analysis extends or goes beyond what the initial investigators reported. For instance, I once took coal production data from one state agency and matched up suicide data from another department. I had the hypothesis that coal tonnage and suicides would be inversely related—that as miners were laid off and fewer tons of coal were mined, suicides would increase. What I found was that there was virtually no correlation. However, I can't help but wonder what might have been uncovered if I had correlated homicides with coal tonnage. Secondary data analysis has a certain flexibility in that new hypotheses can be easily spun off and tested without a great deal of extra work. Investigators are not limited to a single data set or source document and may utilize several data sets from different sponsors or agencies.

In a fascinating article on the history of child protection efforts, Lindsey (1994) has used multiple sources of data to show that reports of child abuse in the United States have risen from approximately six thousand in 1963 to almost 3 million by 1992. During approximately the same period of time, child murder victims fifteen to nineteen years of age have increased from under five hundred per year in 1962 to more than twenty-five hundred by 1991. Increased reporting of abuse has not reduced child fatalities, and Lindsey speculates as to why this might be. One possibility could be that child welfare professionals are using inadequate technology to assess the risk faced by children. Another possibility is inadequate funding of child protective services. What other explanations might this secondary trend data suggest to you?

Secondary data analysis should not be considered as a research approach to be employed only when a researcher does not want to collect his or her own data. In fact, Stewart (1993) argues that

> it is hard to conceive of a research effort that does not begin with at least some secondary research. Existing information provides a foundation for problem formulation, for the design of new research, and for the analysis and interpretation of new information. There is little point in rediscovering that which is already known.

A good use of secondary data is to identify trends. For example, a student once approached me with some concern because she had heard from a relative that her home county had the highest suicide rate in the state. I was somewhat skeptical about this, but when I had the opportunity, I went to the Government Documents section of the library and examined several of the Department of Health's *Vital Statistics* annual reports. I found that in the most recent year the county in question, with a population of slightly more than 12,000, had 7 suicides. This gave it a rate of 52.5 suicides per 100,000 population. (This is a standard base for comparison so that urban counties can be compared with rural counties.) This was in fact one of the highest suicide rates in the state, as the overall average for the state was 14.3 suicides per 100,000 population.

This is the information the student had originally obtained for a specific county—it is easy to see why she was concerned:

	Number of Suicides	County Suicide Rate	State Suicide Rate
1986	7	52.5	14.3

Had the student gone to the library and looked at the previous year's data, this is what she would have found:

	Number of Suicides	County Suicide Rate	State Suicide Rate
1985	0	0	13.2
1986	7	52.5	14.3

Thus, the span of two years, the county had one of the lowest and one of the highest rates in the state. This is not uncommon when the actual number of events (such as suicides) is relatively small. This shows the inherent danger in selectively drawing a single year's statistic instead of examining a longer span of time. Depending on the year that was chosen to represent the county's problem with suicide, one might have come away with completely different impressions about the need for a suicide prevention program there.

When the secondary data are available, the good researcher wants to examine trends to have confidence that there is a real pattern one way or the other. And so, if we look at the period of time 1980 to 1995, we discover that Tobacco County's suicide rate exceeded the state's average in twelve of sixteen years. These data are much stronger than any one year in which something quite strange (remember the suicides that resulted from the Heaven's Gate cult) and out of character might have occurred. As you can tell by looking at table 8.1, there is a noticeable tendency for this one rural county to have higher suicide rates than one would expect. Over the span of time in the study period, its rate was 20.9 percent compared to the state average of 13.5 percent.

Advantages and Disadvantages of Unobtrusive Approaches

Right away, some exciting advantages of unobtrusive research are apparent. First, if you discover that someone else has already collected data that you can use for a study, you can save considerable time and effort in your data collection phase. Once an interesting data base has been identified, it is often pos-

Table 8.1 Suicide Rate in One Rural County

	Number of Suicides	County Rate	State Rate
1980	1	8.1	13.3
1981	2	15.7	12.1
1982	2	15.4	13.5
1983	4	31.0	13.2
1984	2	15.2	13.7
1985	0	0	13.2
1986	7	52.5	14.3
1987	5	38.1	13.8
1988	2	15.1	13.0
1989	3	22.4	13.2
1990	6	46.4	15.2
1991	1	7.8	13.9
1992	2	15.1	13.8
1993	4	29.7	14.1
1994	3	21.6	13.7
1995	0	0	12.5

sible to move rapidly into data analysis. Secondary data sources may already be held by the library or university, or you may be able to purchase them for a nominal fee.

Second, any bias associated with the collection of the data may be generally known and accepted. It may be known, for instance, that the data tend to underestimate the true incidence of a social problem (as in the case of suicide data). Other data sets may overestimate the incidence of a problem. For example, data on psychiatric hospital admissions that combined new patients with those who had previous admissions could overestimate incidence of the most severe form of mental illness. (**Incidence** is the number of *new* cases or events during a given period of time.) Since all studies have some limitations, the secondary data analyst may choose to use a data set even though it has several known problems. Problems with the data set are not a reflection upon the researcher using secondary data analysis. After all, the secondary data analyst is only borrowing the data set.

Third, since you are not interviewing clients or patients or interacting with them in any way, you need not worry that your inquiries will put them at risk or have any harmful effects. If the data are routinely collected, you may not need permission from institutional review boards or other research committees to conduct your research.

The final but best reason for conducting secondary data analysis is that it provides an opportunity to study social problems in terms of long-term change and enables comparative study. Secondary data analysts can make comparisons across localities, states, and nations (presuming, of course, that the data are available).

On the other hand, there are some disadvantages associated with relying upon secondary or archival data. Sometimes the important historical records you need have been destroyed by fire, flood, tornadoes, or rodents. Occasionally researchers, well into their projects, find gaps in the data because of changes in procedures or policies that affected the data collection. With the passage of time, it is quite possible for variables to change; categories can become more or less inclusive.

I once discovered that a set of child abuse archival data I wanted to explore was compartmentalized. The data were recorded in two different computers in two different formats because the data collection forms had been redesigned. There was no way to combine the data sets into one large file without going to the expense of hiring computer programmers to prepare the data in a more usable form. As a result, I did no research with that data.

If the data were reported more or less voluntarily (there was no penalty for not reporting), it may not be as reliable as when 100 percent of the units were required to report.

Several years ago I was examining one state's outpatient admissions to community mental health centers and found that not all centers were fully cooperating in returning their monthly reports. While the vast majority of these centers did, perhaps 5 percent didn't. These tended to be small, rural centers without a lot of staff.

While their failure to report on a timely basis didn't have a huge effect in terms of the total number of admissions in the state, it did raise questions about the reliability of the data set. Could there have been other, larger agencies that failed to report their admissions on occasion? Did anyone monitor the data to make sure there were twelve reports from each agency at the end of each year? Researchers using secondary data have to be concerned about the reliability of the data that they intend to analyze.

Finally, recent data may not be available as soon as the researcher may desire it. It is not unusual for some agencies or departments to take six to twelve months (or longer) to produce their most "current" annual report of the previous year's data.

In summary, while there are many advantages associated with secondary data analysis, the researcher should be alert to changes in the way the data items were defined, completeness of data, and the ease with which data can be manipulated.

State-Maintained Data Sets Are Useful for Secondary Analysis

Secondary analyses can be conducted in both private and public agencies. However, private agencies tend to be protective of their data. Even though researchers agree not to divulge personal data, private agencies often feel that

Table 8.2 Examples of Variables for Secondary Research

Indicator	Source
Marriages	Department of Health
Divorces	Department of Health
Suicides	Department of Health
Live births	Department of Health
Infant deaths	Department of Health
Deaths (all ages)	Department of Health
Deaths from cirrhosis of the liver	Department of Health
Inpatient admissions	Department of Mental Health
Outpatient admissions	Department of Mental Health
General relief cases	Department of Public Welfare
Aid to dependent children	Department of Public Welfare
Motor vehicle injury accidents	Department of Highway Safety
Motor vehicle deaths	Department of Highway Safety
Motor vehicle accidents	Department of Highway Safety
Dependency and neglect cases	Department of Child Welfare
Delinquency cases	Juvenile Court Statistics
Arraignments	Supreme Court Statistics
School dropouts	Department of Education
School enrollment	Department of Education
Unemployment	Bureau of Employment
Average weekly earnings	Bureau of Employment
Retail alcohol sales	Department of Liquor Control

any research within their agencies may endanger the privacy of individual clients. Another argument often heard from private agencies is that the proposed research will require too much clerical support to locate archival records or selected cases. Unlike private agencies, public agencies and departments are often required to keep certain statistics that are viewed as public information and available to all. While public agencies are not always as cooperative as many researchers would like, they generally do provide some form of aggregated data each year in the form of annual reports.

Table 8.2 contains examples of variables or **social indicators** (they tell us something about trends within social problems) that are commonly collected by all states. Generally these data are reported by county.

These examples are only some of the variables that are routinely collected and reported each month, quarter, or year. Public and university libraries often will be designated as state depositories and will have recent reports as well as more historical reports. You may also want to search the Internet. Or, contact the agency directly by phone.

Internet Resources

More than seventy federal government agencies that produce statistics can be located at a single web site (www.fedstats.gov) and have links to their own documents and reports. Some of these agencies are: Bureau of Labor Statistics, Bureau of Justice Statistics, Bureau of the Census, National Center for Health Statistics, Administration for Children and Families, Administration on Aging, Centers for Disease Control and Prevention, National Institute on Alcohol Abuse and Alcoholism, National Institute on Drug Abuse, Federal Bureau of Prisons, Indian Health Service, and so on.

A good many of these agencies provide their own search engines to make it easier for you to find the specific statistics you are seeking. Also, some provide links to private organizations such as the Annie E. Casey Foundation (www.aecf.org), which annually publishes the *KIDS COUNT Data Book*—state-by-state data on the educational, social, economic, and physical indicators of well-being of children in the United States.

Applications of Secondary Data Analysis

If information is power (Francis Bacon noted that "knowledge itself is power"), then the possibilities of being able to effect change are enormous when one has access to secondary data.

Example 1: Suppose you are a school social worker, and a number of children have been injured because there is no traffic light at a busy intersection they must cross before they can get to school. Let's further suppose that "officials" are dragging their feet, saying that a traffic light is not needed. You obtain a list of all the locations where vehicular and pedestrian-injury accidents have occurred in your city in the past year. What if the intersection that you feel needs a light was the site of more injury accidents than any other location in the city not only for the previous year, but also the past three years? Isn't that powerful information that you could use to help advocate for a traffic light?

Example 2: You are a state employee, the supervisor of a child abuse investigation team. You are painfully aware that your unit is understaffed. In talking with others, you sense that your unit may investigate more reported cases of abuse and neglect than any other unit in the state. Yet, when you talk to the agency director about this problem, he or she is not sympathetic about your need for additional staff. The director indicates that cases of abuse are increasing over the whole state—that it isn't just a problem in your county.

However, because you occasionally have the opportunity to talk to other social workers from across the state, you learn that some investigation units are adding staff, while your unit has added no new staff in three years. A research question forms in your mind. Which county has the highest incidence of child abuse/neglect cases in the state? When you look at the data you discover that while the more populous counties have significantly more cases of abuse and neglect, your county has more cases of child abuse and neglect *per thousand population* than any other county in the state. Would this information be enough to use for leverage to get some additional staff? If not, a next step might be to gather data on how many staff the other investigation units have and which units have the lowest ratio of cases to staff. If your county has the highest ratio (the most cases but fewest staff), this would be compelling objective information that could influence the decision to allocate additional staff to your unit.

This example could be carried further. If the data were available, you could examine the ratio of cases to child protective services staff in your state to those of surrounding states. This type of information might be used to influence your legislators to increase appropriations at the state level. You could also compare salaries of child protective workers in your state with those in other states. If workers in your state are paid below the average, lobby for increased pay.

Example 3: You become concerned about adolescents' use of illegal drugs in your community. You suspect that a new street drug is the cause of a rash of fatal overdoses, but you have no "hard" data to support this assumption. Since you want to conduct a drug education campaign for adolescents, you feel that local data are needed. You learn that the data are not obtainable from the state Health Department or from the police department. You find, however, that the hospital emergency room keeps this sort of data. Even if the hospital does not make these records available, you may find that the county's ambulance service keeps this data and would be happy to share it.

There is no shortage of ways that secondary data can be used. You could investigate whether the high school dropout rate has decreased within your community over the past five years. Has the dropout prevention program had an impact? Most school systems have good records on the number of dropouts. It would be relatively easy to determine if there has been a dramatic change in the dropout rate. Other uses of social indicators include examining how your state compares with other states in terms of unemployment, teen pregnancies, or some other social problem.

Additionally, you might want to formally test hypotheses—for example, that concern about AIDS will result in fewer divorces. You might want to conduct correlational studies to see if increases in unemployment are associated with increases in mental hospital admissions or if high school dropout rates are associated with juvenile delinquency rates. You could be interested, as Guyer, Miller, and Garfinkel (1996) were, in examining the state-by-state data on child support enforcement in order to understand the limitations of reporting measures employed by public officials and to design a better index of performance.

Social indicators can also be used to make national comparisons. How does the United States compare with other industrialized countries on such indicators as infant deaths or literacy rates? Have we made advances in the last five years, or have these indicators remained at about the same level?

There is virtually no end to social indicators that may be gleaned from state and federal departments, bureaus, agencies, and offices. And there are thousands of organizations that collect information on their membership and the services provided to members. Social service agencies across this nation have fascinating questions they would like explored—if only someone with the right combination of research skills and interest would come along.

As you have seen from these illustrations, secondary data analysis is versatile and can be used with problems that vary from those with a macro focus to those with a micro concern. One of the main strengths of secondary data analysis is that there are generally multiple sources of data relevant to the topic in which you are interested. If you cannot obtain data from one source, there is almost always another, sometimes better, data set.

Secondary Analysis of Survey Data

With the advent of computer processing has come a proliferation of large-scale surveys. These surveys, often with thousands of respondents, are generally available to a broad range of researchers because of the ease with which the data can be shared from one computer to another. These surveys differ in several ways from the occasional surveys conducted by social workers.

First of all, these surveys are designed so that they can be easily manipulated by computer processing. This greatly facilitates their use by researchers other than the original investigators. In fact, some of the surveys (for example, the General Social Survey) were designed particularly for secondary analysis.

Second, these surveys tend to use large, national, cross-sectional samples. Some of these surveys (or at least portions of their questions) are repeated at regular intervals, so that trends can be observed over time.

Finally, these surveys often are indexed, and usually even the entire data set can be purchased at nominal cost. Through the Internet, researchers can get a good idea of the data available before purchasing it.

Secondary analysis of survey data usually comes about in one of two ways: (1) a database is discovered that contains information not fully reported or examined; or (2) a hypothesis is generated and then a search is conducted to find an appropriate database. Normally, hypotheses occur before data collection; however, in the case of archival research and secondary survey analysis, the researcher needs to know beforehand that the type of data needed exists. He or she could spend several months requesting catalogs, reviewing existing databases, and contacting various research centers only to learn that the desired data are not available. Consequently, some researchers develop hypotheses *after* they come across (perhaps accidentally) a particularly exciting database. Hyman (1987) has written, "Among investigators with *broad* interests, serendipity is a likely occurrence. By chance, they are likely to find some of what they are seeking, and also to discover fortuitously in the course of one search valuable bodies of data that are strategic for the study of other problems" (p. 83).

The federal government funds and conducts hundreds of surveys every year. Perhaps the best known of these is the decennial Census of Population and Housing, but the various agencies of our government also provide for special purpose surveys that supply statistical information on different facets of our national character.

Many of these surveys provide researchers interested in secondary data analysis with exceptional opportunities to explore topics that might have been much more difficult to investigate without the availability of the large data sets. For instance, Corcoran and Kunz (1997) were interested in whether providing Aid to Families with Dependent Children to single African-American teen mothers leads to adult poverty and welfare dependency. They selected their sample from women who were part of a nationally representative survey of five thousand families in 1968 (the Panel Study of Income Dynamics) and who were children between the ages of four and fourteen at that time.

Detailed information on these families has been collected yearly since the first survey and constituted the data that the researchers analyzed—allowing Corcoran and Kunz to observe the entire welfare history of these women during adolescence. The authors found that when they controlled for background disadvantages, a woman who had an out-of-wedlock birth as a teen was 1.25 times more likely to be poor and 1.02 times more likely to receive welfare than a sister who avoided giving birth as a teenager. They concluded that prohibiting welfare payments to unmarried women under the age of eighteen would "likely do little to reduce adult poverty and welfare use" (p. 285).

You'll remember back in chapter 6 that several Internet addresses were provided to help you locate depositories of surveys such as the Louis Harris (http://www.irss.unc.edu:80/data_archive/pollsearch.html) and George Gallup (http://www.gallup.com/) public opinion data polls. One that was briefly mentioned then, the General Social Survey, deserves a bit more discussion.

The General Social Survey (GSS) first took place in 1972 and has been conducted almost annually since then by the National Opinion Research Center. Each survey is an independently drawn probability sample of persons eighteen years of age or over, not living in an institutional setting. Since 1972, more than thirty-five thousand respondents have been involved. Over the years, a broad range of variables (over twenty-seven hundred different questions) have been employed. The GSS is designed to allow replication, and more than nine hundred of the questions used have been replicated—some going back to 1972. This allows social scientists to observe social trends across the country, within subgroups, and since 1982, to make some cross-national comparisons with European countries. Whole survey data sets can be obtained from the Roper Center, or viewed via Internet (www.icpsi.umich.edu/GSS/search.htm).

Table 8.3 provides you with an example of the types of GSS questions that can be analyzed in great detail. For example, you could test the hypothesis that persons over sixty are more supportive of the death penalty than younger persons. Or, you could look at responses by level of education, race, geographic region, family income, and so on.

Notice how the questions have evolved over time. Question 81, for instance, has not been used since 1982. You'll understand why when you compare it to Question 82—which is more balanced. Question 82 also allows you to see that strongly held opinions tend to be maintained over time. Quickly compute the percentage of Americans who favor the death penalty for persons convicted of murder and you'll find that it was 72 percent of those surveyed in the years 1983–87, 72 percent in 1988–91, 72 percent in 1993, and 74 percent in 1994. In other words, there has been virtually no change in our national opinion about this topic. However, in Question 80.C there has been a noticeable decrease in the portion of Americans who responded that they "favor" removing certain books from public libraries. In the surveys conducted between 1972 and 1982, 41 percent replied that they favored removing these books, but that percentage has fallen through the years to 28 percent.

Content Analysis

Content analysis is another unobtrusive research process that objectively examines the content of communications. This objectivity is made possible by reliance upon quantification. Accordingly, content analysis involves searching for and counting key words, phrases, or concepts in communications. These may be counted (frequencies of occurrence), measured (for example, the size of a newspaper article in column inches or the amount of time allocated to a specific topic in a speech), or otherwise categorized in a manner that others could replicate. Content analysis can be used either retrospectively (to exam-

Table 8.3 Survey Data from the General Social Survey

80.C. If some people in your community suggested that a book he wrote in favor of homosexuality should be taken out of your public library, would you favor removing this book, or not?
(VAR: LIBHOMO)

Response	Punch	1972-82	1982B	1983-87	1987B	1988-91	1993	1994
				Year				
Favor	1	3,707	153	1,768	159	1,272	313	562
Not favor	2	4,987	162	2,567	182	2,512	713	1,366
Don't know	8	276	35	122	12	121	45	61
No answer	9	21	4	16	0	15	4	7
Not applicable	BK	4,635	0	3,069	0	1,987	531	996

81. Are you in favor of the death penalty for persons convicted of murder?
(VAR: CAPPUN2)

Response	Punch	1972-82	1982B	1983-87	1987B	1988-91	1993	1994
				Year				
Yes	1	1,750	0	0	0	0	0	0
No	2	1,151	0	0	0	0	0	0
Don't know	8	200	0	0	0	0	0	0
No answer	9	16	0	0	0	0	0	0
Not applicable	BK	10,509	354	7,542	353	5,907	1,606	2,992

82. Do you favor or oppose the death penalty for persons convicted of murder?
(VAR: CAPPUN)

Response	Punch	1972-82	1982B	1983-87	1987B	1988-91	1993	1994
				Year				
Favor	1	6,933	154	5,410	154	4,274	1,151	2,215
Oppose	2	2,936	165	1,696	165	1,242	337	580
Don't know	8	607	32	399	33	364	112	184
No answer	9	33	3	37	1	27	6	13
Not applicable	BK	3,117	0	0	0	0	0	0

DECK 5
COLS. 44-46
Qs. 88-90

90. In general, do you think the courts in this area deal too harshly or not harshly enough with criminals?
(VAR: COURTS)

Response	Punch	1972-82	1982B	1983-87	1987B	1988-91	1993	1994
				Year				
Too harshly	1	482	29	245	30	206	54	78
Not harshly enought	2	9,546	119	6,253	255	4,822	1,300	2,534
About right (Vol.)	3	1,227	17	694	43	573	156	226
Don't know	8	834	8	318	21	288	88	135
No answer	9	47	3	32	4	18	8	19
Not applicable	BK	1,490	178	0	0	0	0	0

ine materials already in existence) or prospectively (to analyze impending events or narratives). However, the major use of content analysis is to provide a framework so that a quantitative approach can be used to analyze communications after they have been spoken or printed.

Examples of materials that can be content analyzed include: newspapers, magazines, journals, books, television programs, audio and video tapes, minutes from agency board meetings, congressional records, presidential addresses, and historical documents such as letters, diaries, and so on.

While the first dictionary definition of content analysis appeared in 1961, its intellectual roots go back considerably further. In 1910, Max Weber proposed a large-scale content analysis of newspapers at the first meeting of the German Sociological Society. Also, around the turn of the century in this country, quantitative newspaper analyses (measuring the column inches devoted to specific subjects) were conducted because of concern that newspapers were not providing as much factual content as they were gossip, sports, and scandals (Krippendorff, 1980).

During World War II, content analysis was used to analyze propaganda. After the war, the value of content analysis as a research tool was widely recognized, and interest in it spread beyond the field of communications to the disciplines of political science, psychology, history, sociology, and literature.

Several interesting applications of content analysis have been made by social workers. Klein and Bloom (1994) used content analysis to look at selected social work publications in the one-hundred-twenty year period 1870 to 1990 and classified articles into one of five categories: empiricism, technology, conceptualization, valuation, and commentary.

Sutphen (1997) used content analysis to examine the amount of juvenile justice articles appearing in social work abstracts during the fifteen-year period 1980 to 1994. His main question was: "How much attention have social work journals paid to this field?" (p. 51). Reid, Bailey-Dempsey, and Viggiani (1996) applied content analysis to the tape recordings that students of a family service agency made of sessions with clients in order to compare field supervisors' ratings of students' performance with those of independent judges.

Moreover, undergraduate syllabi have been analyzed for minority content (Aguilar 1995), men's self-help groups on parenting have been examined for themes (Fagan and Stevenson, 1995), as have focus groups of foster parents (Wells and D'Angelo, 1994). Textbooks have been examined for their coverage on abortion and adoption (Stolley and Hall, 1994), and texts on human service management have been analyzed for their presentation of theory and knowledge development (Au, 1994). McMahon and Allen-Meares (1992) have asked, "Is social work racist?" and categorized articles in four major social work journals during the 1980s.

Content analysis lends itself well to other techniques employed by social

Practice Note: Policy Implications from Content Analysis

The Kaiser Family Foundation (www.kff.org) has funded several interesting research projects that provide valuable data for those concerned about the messages that adolescents in this country receive from the popular media about pregnancy, contraception, and sexually transmitted diseases. Researchers for the foundation have used content analysis to examine sexual health coverage in women's, men's, and teen specialty magazines; sexual content during television's family hour, and sexual behaviors during daytime soap operas. Their sponsored research has implications both nationally and worldwide.

Not only do American television programs affect our youth, but they are syndicated and seen around the world by young and impressionable people who view our TV lifestyle as the ideal—one they should emulate. Some health professionals who work in the areas of family planning and prevention of sexually transmitted diseases are concerned that while most soap operas feature frequent incidents of sexual intercourse, these programs rarely contain discussions about contraception or safer-sex practices. Should social workers in this country be concerned about sexual content on television?

workers. For instance, Barry (1988) has discussed the use of autobiographical writing with elderly adults. Content analysis could be used to show that this technique is successful in ameliorating depression, improving self-acceptance, and helping older adults focus on the present. As a research tool, content analysis would allow social workers to measure older adults' progress by quantifying the positive themes in their writings.

Include Martin Seligman (1990) among those researchers who have recognized the power of content analysis. Seligman has done some absolutely fascinating work, demonstrating from diaries that older adults kept as teenagers that explanatory styles for bad events are highly stable over forty and fifty years. Those who self-blame as teenagers (as opposed to finding other explanations) continue assuming responsibility for bad events in old age.

Further, his content analyses have shown that health at age sixty is strongly related to optimism at age twenty-five and that we Americans have elected the more optimistic-sounding candidate in eighteen of twenty-two presidential elections that he examined. Seligman believes that individuals who are depressed do a lot of self-blaming but that their depression can be reduced by teaching them to think more optimistically. Doesn't this again make the point that practice and research are vitally connected?

Examples of the use of content analysis abound. Morrow (1991) examined the explanations given by female adolescent incest victims for their molestation. It was found that those who attributed the molestation as due to something about self were more depressed and had lower self-esteem. Surprisingly, there was no significant association between time involved in group therapy and type of attribution (for example, external or internal).

Content analysis has even been used by parents' groups interested in documenting the amount of sex and violence on television and movies. Molitor and Sapolsky (1993) reviewed thirty "slasher" films and counted 1,573 violent acts, an average of 52.4 per movie. The hero of *Robocop II* massacres eighty-one people while 264 are killed in *Die Hard 2* (Giroux, 1995).

Advantages and Disadvantages of Content Analysis

Like secondary data analysis, content analysis has the advantages of being:

- Unobtrusive,
- Generally inexpensive to conduct, and
- Able to deal with large volumes of data.

No special training or expertise is required to conduct a content analysis—all that is needed is a research question or hypothesis and a set of communications or a body of materials from which to begin developing categories.

Probably the greatest disadvantage of content analysis is directly related to the methodology of counting individual words, expressions, or events—commonly known as the **manifest content**. As you know, often the actual choice of words we use is less important than *how* we say something, For instance, Wanda asks Renetta if she likes her new apartment, and Renetta responds sarcastically, "I *love* it, the tiny kitchen is especially appealing." Wanda realizes her friend is really *not* impressed with the apartment. As we read this dialogue, we could count the words *love* and *appealing* and conclude that *twice* something good was said about the apartment. Not being there, we miss Renetta's wry smile, the way she rolls her eyes to the ceiling right before she says disgustedly, "How on earth are you going to get your refrigerator in here?" The context in which something is said or done is often very important. In one study of TV violence the finding was that 73 percent of the time the perpetrators went unpunished. However, critics quickly argued that counting incidents of violence without looking at the context means very little. Thus, a police sniper could save a family held hostage by shooting a terrorist and become one of the "perpetrators" who got away (Gunther, 1996).

Besides the countable elements in the source material being analyzed, interpretative readings can be made of the **latent content**. While manifest content is comparable to the surface structure in a message, latent content refers to the deep structural meaning (Berg, 1998). Researchers concerned with latent content need to develop techniques that allow independent coders to corroborate the findings. Identifying three or more detailed excerpts to support each coder's interpretations is recommended (Berg, 1998).

A second disadvantage of content analysis is that it is like archival research in that it relies on material that already exists and therefore prevents the researcher from controlling influential extraneous variables. Unlike experiments, content analysis cannot be used to demonstrate cause and effect.

Steps in Conducting Content Analysis

Step 1: Framing a Research Question

When you want to employ content analysis you start with a research question or hypothesis. Perhaps you want to know when the term "clinical social worker" evolved in social work literature. Or perhaps you have a notion that the newspaper you most frequently read has a negative opinion of social workers or some other definite bias that you want to document. You may want to test the hypothesis that fewer articles on the topic of community development have been written in the past five years than on the topic of private practice. Some question or assumption that can be tested through an examination of written or spoken communications must be stated.

Step 2: Deciding upon Source Materials

From that hypothesis or research question, you begin to think about what materials would provide the best source of communications for the content analysis. Will you use a local newspaper, the *New York Times*, *Social Work*, *Social Service Review*, *Families in Society*, or some combination of journals or papers? Naturally, there are pragmatic decisions to be faced. The materials should be relatively easy to obtain. It is easier to conduct your study if your library has a complete collection of the materials you need than if you have to travel out of state to examine them. Familiarity with the source materials is also needed; some journals or newsletters may be less relevant to your topic than you originally thought. Newer journals may not have the historical record in which you are interested.

Step 3: Deciding upon Units of Analysis

You will need to decide what will constitute the **units of the analysis,** or the recording units. Depending upon the amount of data to be analyzed, you may choose to examine words or terms, entire paragraphs, or the whole item itself (for example, an entire article or speech).

The most common units of analysis are individual words or terms. However, if you search for selected key words, you may miss other terms that could also refer to the concept you are studying. Thus, if you instruct reviewers to search for the number of times "clinical social worker" is used in the newspaper, they might overlook references to "family services worker" or "mental health therapist"—both of which could require clinical social work skills. This problem is more likely to occur when computers are used to conduct the content analysis without the investigator pretesting categories on a sample of source materials. A good operational definition of categories or events to be counted is crucial (for example, does sexual behavior on TV include flirting? Are violent acts defined as threats of injury as well as physical harm?).

When determining units of analysis, think about what you intend to count or quantify. This generally leads to conceptualizing what categories will be needed. These categories should not be developed apart from the material being reviewed; your familiarity with the material will assist you in devising definitions and categories. As with questionnaire development, the use of a pilot test will assist you in refining the operational definitions of categories. Written rules, especially if more than one person is going to be involved in the content analysis, assist with the classifying and categorizing of data. It is important that categories be exhaustive and mutually exclusive.

The examination of themes from whole items can involve some complex decision rules. Take, for instance, the situation where you want to determine what newspaper editorials reveal about the president. Searching for a set of specific words or phrases (such as "the president is doing a good job in office") may not be of much help because there are so many ways to characterize the president's actions positively or negatively. Then there's the issue of balance—the editorial writers might like some of the president's policies but not others.

Step 4: Deciding upon Sampling Design

The researcher using content analysis needs to decide how much of the source material he or she can practically review. This is not a problem when the universe of materials is small enough that it is feasible to review all of it. However, if there are hundreds or thousands of items to be examined, then sampling is a logical decision. As discussed in the chapter on survey research, there are several ways to sample. With regard to content analysis, it makes the most sense to think of a random or systematic random design. Convenience samples, as with nonprobability opinion polls, could yield worthless data. For instance, there can be seasonal trends in the liquor advertisements found in magazines—more cognac and expensive alcoholic beverages highlighted in the winter months and more beer ads in the summer. And, too small a sample could also yield highly questionable data.

Step 5: Conducting Reliability Checks

As with other methods discussed in this book, investigators who are concerned with their results meeting the test of replication must concern themselves with issues of reliability in the classification of content categories. Of chief concern is intercoder reliability. If those who are coding the content don't agree with each other very often, the coding system will not be reliable. Particularly if multiple coders are used, it will be important to compute the reliability (consistency) of the categorization process. Reliability is strengthened when there is training for the raters with practice sessions and clear coding instructions and rules. If one person is doing all of the coding, reliability can still be tested by giving an independent rater the criteria and a sample of the source materials already reviewed. A simple approach would be to select ten samples and then see what percent of the time Rater A agreed with Rater B.

A Practical Application of Content Analysis

A serious problem for most mental health and social service agencies is public image. Bad publicity may affect agency admissions or the community's perception of the quality of care provided by an agency. What follows is a partially true (Royse and Wellons, 1988), partially fictionalized account of how content analysis has been used as a research tool to bring about needed change.

At one point in my career I was employed by a mental health system that was (so the administrators thought) too often in the local news. A newspaper reporter covered every board meeting, and much of the coverage had a negative slant to it. For instance, one editorial stated that the mental health system had "axed practically all hope of renewing the [mental health] levy with the construction of a $2.2 million building." Since the vote on the mental health levy was more than two years away, such a statement by the newspaper seemed to indicate a stance that was not supportive of the community mental health system's need for the county's property tax levy.

Our fear was that the newspaper had a powerful potential for influencing citizens of the community to vote against the renewal of the mental health levy. Since more than half of the revenue to operate the mental health system came from the tax levy, it became clear that effort should begin right away to counter negative perceptions held by the newspaper staff. Our strategy was to objectively demonstrate to them how the content of their articles and headlines was not balanced and could have a detrimental effect upon public opinion.

Every morning the director's secretary clipped articles from the local newspapers that referred to the mental health system. These were kept in a historical file. Clippings had been kept for about ten years and constituted an obvious source of material for a content analysis. Since reading ten years of newspaper clippings was a sizable task, we decided that reading headlines was much more manageable. A listing of all the headlines and captions above the news articles was made, and this constituted our units of analysis.

While our interest was in identifying the amount of negative coverage by the newspaper, this quickly became problematic. It was not difficult to identify those headlines we regarded as negative ("Hostility Erupts at Mental Health Board Meeting," "Mental Health Board in Dispute," "Mental Health Officials Squabble"). However, there were some headlines that we took to be negative, but that others who were not affiliated with the mental health system might not have interpreted that way. In addition, a headline might have been categorized as positive, but the article below it might have been negative. And some headlines were difficult to interpret ("Crisis Center May Resume Services" or "Judge Promises Fast Ruling") without reading the whole article. Consequently, it was decided to conduct the content analysis on selected key words.

It would not have been possible to anticipate every term or key word that indicated a negative reflection on the mental health system. Even clusters of negative words or phrases would have been very difficult to specify. Therefore, we decided to search for those key words that had something to do with the delivery of services or administrative issues.

Among our findings was that there were thirty-seven headlines, over the ten-year period, containing the key word *facility*. This number of appearances was larger than that of any problem-specific key word, such as *divorce, alcohol, stress, depression, addiction, domestic violence, incest, runaways, death,* and so on. It also occurred more times than population-specific terms, such as *aging, elderly, stepparent, families, teenagers, juveniles, children,* and *students*. Clearly, the newspaper was much more concerned with administrative issues (such as building a new facility) than with service delivery issues.

The number of square inches of newspaper coverage associated with each headline was also included in the study. We found that over 40 percent of all the coverage dealt with the mental health system's administrative board. The balance of the coverage was spread over the five local mental health agencies that actually delivered services to consumers. We also found that of the three local newspapers, the one perceived to be the most negative was providing about a third more coverage on the mental health system in terms of square inches of the articles than either of the two other papers.

When the study was finished, it was nicely typed and presented during a meeting of the agency staff and the editorial staff of the most negative newspaper. When confronted with the results of the study and examples of how the public could be interpreting their coverage, the editorial staff agreed to review their policies and coverage of the mental health system. Subsequent coverage was much more balanced and presented no opposition to the renewal of the mental health levy.

Final Thoughts on Unobtrusive Approaches

I have a file where I save articles and assorted items that I share with my research classes. One of my favorites is a newspaper account describing a "sick-out" staged by social workers in protective services. Twenty-three of them called in sick on the same day to protest a rise in their caseloads from an average of thirty-one to forty-three active cases while the child abuse investigation team's cases rose from 107 to 125 per year. At the same time, there were thirty-three vacant social work positions in their county. These social workers gathered their facts and used existing secondary data to advocate for themselves. As a result of this action, promises were made to begin filling the vacant positions.

Handgun Control, Inc. says on their web page, "In 1996, handguns were used to murder 2 people in New Zealand, 15 in Japan, 30 in Great Britain, 106 in Canada, 211 in Germany, and 9,390 in the United States." Other statistics are also compelling. "In 1995 alone, 35,957 Americans were killed with firearms in homicides, suicides, and accidents. In comparison, 33,651 Americans were killed in the Korean War, and 58,148 in the Vietnam War." (www.handguncontrol.org). Such facts as these help define the impact of guns in our society—a necessary step before we as a country can collectively realize the seriousness of the problem posed by guns.

This chapter provides only a few examples of secondary data sources and content analyses and illustrations of how they might be used. Unobtrusive methods provide a needed alternative for those situations where resources are lacking to conduct large-scale surveys or other more rigorous forms of investigation, or where the nature of the question or problem does not lend itself to first-hand data collection. Even if we could collect the data ourselves, often there is no need to because someone else has already compiled it.

Given the considerable wealth of information available in this society just for the asking, unobtrusive approaches ought to be considered first when research is required. Since unobtrusive methods do not require a lot of research expertise, even social workers who don't think of themselves as researchers can apply them. Finally, informed social workers need to be familiar with the social indicators available in the special fields in which they work. And where there is no good source of data about the problems with which we are concerned, then we need to advocate for and help establish mechanisms to collect needed data.

Self-Review

(Answers at the end of the book)

1. T or F.   Mailed surveys can be considered unobtrusive research.
2. How is a researcher who wants to conduct only secondary data analysis limited?
3. T or F.   The identification of trends is often an important focus of secondary data analysis.
4. Comparing social service expenditures in Sweden, Ireland, and South Africa with the United States and Canada would be an example of:
   a. content analysis
   b. deconstructionism
   c. secondary data analysis
   d. systematic random sampling
5. T or F.   In order to do secondary data analysis, the existing data set you examine must have been developed for a purpose identical to your own research interest.
6. T or F.   Content analysis can be used with any set of communications, whether they are written, spoken, or performed.
7. Besides being unobtrusive, what is another major advantage common to both secondary data analysis and content analysis?
8. What is a disadvantage common to both secondary data analysis and content analysis?
9. What is the term associated with content analysis that describes the context, subtle meanings, or nuances?
10. T or F.   Course syllabi from major universities could be content analyzed to determine if term papers are more common than exams or tests for evaluation of students' performance.

Questions for Class Discussion

1. On the chalkboard, list the social service agencies where students have worked or been placed in a practicum. In a separate column, list the types of social problems with which these agencies deal. Next, make a list of the social indicators that could be used by social workers in these agencies to determine if their programs are having an impact on the social problems.
2. Using the social indicators listed in table 8.2, discuss potential bias in terms of how each might under- or overestimate the extent of a social problem.

3. Among the social service agencies with which you are familiar, what local information do they report to the state capital each year? What should they report?
4. Identify a local issue or controversy in your community or on your campus. Discuss how content analysis might be used to provide some insight into how important this issue is compared to others.
5. Discuss ways that secondary data or content analyses could be used to advocate for clients or for the profession of social work. Suggest studies that need to be conducted.

Mini-Projects for Experiencing Research Firsthand

1. Think about the information collected by a social service agency with which you are familiar. List the different types of information that are available. Develop two hypotheses that could be tested using archival records from the agency.
2. Are higher rates of suicide found in rural counties or urban counties? Develop a hypothesis and test it using actual state data. (*Hint:* you will need to operationally define rural and urban counties by their population size.) How would you explain your findings?
3. Read all the past month's editorials in one daily newspaper. What consistent patterns or themes emerge? If this effort constituted a pilot study for a content analysis, what hypothesis could you develop? What kinds of categories or decision rules would you need to develop?
4. Skim through advertisements in a popular magazine such as *Newsweek, U.S. News & World Report, Time,* or *Better Homes and Gardens.* In terms of income and gender, to whom are the advertisements being pitched? Support your hypothesis by doing a content analysis.
5. Using the United Nations *Statistical Yearbook* or related materials, develop a hypothesis about some topic such as defense or social welfare expenditures. Test your hypothesis by looking at clusters of countries grouped by continent (for example, Africa, South America).

Resources and References

Aguilar, G.D. (1995). Minority content in undergraduate social work curricula. *The Journal of Baccalaureate Social Work*, 1, 55–69.
Au, C.F. (1994). The status of theory and knowledge development in social welfare administration. *Administration in Social Work*, 18, 27–57.
Barry, Joan. (1988). Autobiographical writing: An effective tool for practice with the oldest old. *Social Work*, 33(5), 449–451.

Berg, B.L. (1998). *Qualitative research methods for the social sciences*. Needham Heights, MA: Allyn and Bacon.

Corcoran, M.E. and Kunz, J.P. (1997). Do unmarried births among African-American teens lead to adult poverty? *Social Service Review*, 70, 274–287.

Davis, J.A. and Smith, T.W. (1991). *The NORC general social survey*. Newbury Park, CA: Sage.

Fagan, J. and Stevenson, H. (1995). Men as teachers: A self-help program on parenting for African-American men. *Social Work with Groups*, 17, 29–42.

Giroux, H. (1995). Pulp fiction and the culture of violence. *Harvard Educational Review*, 65, 299–314.

Gunther, M. (1996). Latest TV violence study seen as flawed, misread, distorted. *Lexington Herald-Leader*, February 16, A3+.

Guyer, J. Miller, C. and Garfinkel, I. (1996). Ranking states using child support data: A cautionary note. *Social Service Review*, 70, 635–652.

Hall, O. and Royse, D. (1987). Mental health needs assessment with social indicators: An empirical case study. *Administration in Mental Health*, 15(1), 36–46.

Harris, L. (1987). *Inside America: Public opinion expert Louis Harris looks at who we are, what we think, where we're headed*. New York: Vintage Books.

Hyman, H.H. (1987). *Secondary analysis of sample surveys*. Middletown, CT: Wesleyan Press.

Klein, W.C. and Bloom, M. (1994). Social work as applied social science: A historical analysis. *Social Work*, 39, 421–431.

Krippendorff, K. (1980). *Content analysis: An introduction to its methodology*. Beverly Hills, CA: Sage.

Kronick, J.C. and Silver, S. (1992). Using the computer for content analysis. *Journal of Social Service Research*, 16(1/2), 41–58.

Lindsey, D. (1994). Mandated reporting and child abuse fatalities: Requirements for a system to protect children. *Social Work Research*, 18(1), 41–54.

McMahon, A. and Allen-Meares, P. (1992). Is social work racist? A content analysis of recent literature. *Social Work*, 37(6), 533–539.

Molitor, F. and Sapolsky, B.S. (1993) Sex, violence, and victimization in slasher films. *Journal of Broadcasting and Electronic Media*, 37, 233–242.

Morrow, K.B. (1991). Attributions of female adolescent incest victims regarding their molestation. *Child Abuse and Neglect*, 15(4), 477–483.

Reid, W.J. and Bailey-Dempsey, C. (1994). Content analysis in design and development. *Research on Social Work Practice*, 4(1), 101–114.

Reid, W.J., Bailey-Dempsey, C., and Viggianai, P. (1996). Evaluating student field education: An empirical study. *Journal of Social Work Education*, 32, 45–52.

Royse, D. (1988). Voter support for human services: A case study. *Arete*, 13(2), 26–34.

_____. Newspaper coverage of a community mental health system: A descriptive study. *Journal of Marketing for Mental Health*, 1(1), 113–125.

Royse, D. and Wellons, K.W. (1988). Mental health coverage in newspaper headlines: A content analysis. *Journal of Marketing for Mental Health*, 1(2), 113–124.

Schulman, P., Castellon, C., and Seligman, M. (1989). Assessing explanatory style: The content analysis of verbatim explanations and the attributional style questionnaire. *Behavior Research and Therapy*, 27, 505–512.

Seligman, M. (1990). *Learned optimism.* New York: Random House.

State rankings. (1997). Lawrence, KS: Morgan Quitno Corp.

Stewart, D.W. (1993). *Secondary research: Information sources and methods.* Beverly Hills, CA: Sage.

Stolley, K.S. and Hall, E.J. (1994). The presentation of abortion and adoption in marriage and family textbooks. *Family Relations,* 43, 267–273.

Sutphen, R.D. (1997). Social work and juvenile justice: Is the literature trying to tell us something? *Arete,* 22, 50–57.

Webb, E.J., Campbell, D.T., Schwartz, R.D., and Sechrest, L. (1966). *Unobtrusive measures: Nonreactive research in the social sciences.* Chicago: Rand McNally.

Weber, R.P. (1990). *Basic content analysis.* Newbury Park, CA: Sage.

Wells, K. and D'Angelo L. (1994). Specialized foster care: Voices from the field. *Social Service Review,* 68, 127–144.

CHAPTER 9
Data Analysis

Most researchers enjoy data analysis. It is at this stage that the data begin to "come alive." Patterns emerge, trends are detected, and support either is or is not found for our pet hypotheses. We may come away with the smug feeling that we were right in our predictions all along and now have the data to prove it! Or, perhaps we did not learn as much as we had hoped but ideas and questions were generated that we can test in our next project.

The purpose of the data analysis is to take the **raw data** (the completed survey forms, scales, or questionnaires) produced in the data collection stage and summarize it. In a sense, the researcher is involved in a translation process. From a heap of raw data, the researcher hopes to wring something meaningful—patterns, trends, or relationships.

Analysis is not displaying all the responses that were given. Simply reporting the individual responses that seventy-five people gave to a specific question or questionnaire is not analysis. The researcher seeks order within the data and tests hypotheses that have "driven" the research.

There is no single way to go about analyzing a data set. The way you analyze your data will depend upon what you want to know. However, there are some basic techniques that are frequently used by all researchers. These techniques will not only introduce you to the topic of data analysis but also assist you in understanding your data.

Steps in Data Analysis

We start with the assumption that you have already administered some kind of data collection instrument to a sample of individuals or clients and are now in possession of the forms they have completed.

While small surveys can be manually tabulated, it is almost impossible to process large surveys this way. Tabulating by hand can be very time-consuming even with small projects if you want to know something other than how many responded one way or another. Consider how difficult it would be to examine a survey of 525 persons without a computer when you wanted to know if there were differences in the responses of low-income and middle-income persons or between young and old adults. Computers can analyze data a lot faster than you can, and they can conduct statistical tests more accurately than a person using a formula and a hand calculator.

Even if you don't have a very large data set, there is virtually no argument for not entering the data into a personal computer for processing. Statistical software like SPSS are widely available on college campuses and are so user-friendly with "help" features and statistical "coaches" that they make data processing almost painless. If you have a large data set (anything over fifty cases), it is essential that you use the power of the computer to look at your data.

Step 1: Cleaning and Editing the Data

Before data analysis can begin and before you enter the data into the computer, you need to examine the raw data for errors and missing data. You'll find that some individuals will have checked two responses for the same item because they forgot to erase one response, and that there will be a few cryptic markings where you'll wonder if the client had intended a 1 or a 7. Frequently, you find that a few individuals accidently overlooked some items, and others purposely provided no information (especially if you are asking about sensitive information like income, age, number of arrests). Most researchers want their data fields to be as complete as possible and may attempt to complete the missing items if it is convenient and feasible to do so. For instance, a client may have failed to give his age on the questionnaire at posttest but recorded it six weeks earlier on the pretest form. In other instances, it may be important to contact respondents again. Data are also edited for common mistakes, as when an interviewer transposes two numbers, like 94 instead of 49. When too much information is missing and cannot be reconstructed or obtained because clients contributed the data anonymously, these questionnaires or forms can be discarded. One set of responses, whether from a person randomly selected from the phone book or a client in a treatment group, is usually referred to as a **case**. All the cases together form the **data set**.

Step 2: Data Entry

There's not a great deal you have to know before plugging your data into the computer. When you open up SPSS for the personal computer, you will see a screen already set up and waiting for you to define your variables. It would be logical to number each respondent or client and, consequently, your first variable might be "client identifier." A second variable might be "marital status." With this variable you could enter the data from Joe Client as "single" or you could decide to **code** the various attributes of the variable, marital status. Coding simply means assigning a numeric value to the category as in the following example:

Coding Scheme for Marital Status

Category	Value
Single	1
Married	2
Divorced	3
Widowed	4

The coding scheme you use should be easy to remember. In the example, single is another way of saying one; it takes two to be married. However, you could have started with widowed persons being 1, and coded married persons as 2 and single persons as 3. There are no values you have to use. If you wanted to start with 5 and go through 8, that would work too, as long as you were consistent. The rule here is to make it as easy to remember as possible. Thus, having a certain status (like being employed) would usually be coded 1 and the absence of that same status (being unemployed) would be coded 0. Similarly, it is much easier to remember a rule as: "yes is always coded 1; no is always coded 0" than to try to remember exceptions.

Var 003 and Var 004 are coded so that the numeric values are associated with recognition of the problems caused by guns.

Coding Scheme for Var 003: Guns Are a Problem

Category	Value
Strongly Agree	5
Agree	4
Undecided	3
Disagree	2
Strongly Disagree	1

Coding Scheme for Var 004: Guns Are Easily Available

Category	Value
Strongly Agree	5
Agree	4
Undecided	3
Disagree	2
Strongly Disagree	1

The argument for coding opposed to typing in the client's marital status is that you can punch in a 1 faster than you can type "single." And, if you have two-hundred or three-hundred questionnaires to enter, you'll soon realize the benefit of coding. In SPSS you need to define each variable, which means you have to identify it as a numeric value or a "string"—describing categories using the alphabet instead of numbers (for example, "married").

If you employ coding, it is *important* that you write down your coding scheme on a reference sheet called a **codebook**. This will help you later if you get a printout of Var 017 and you can't remember whether the third category in V 017 represented "10–12 years of employment" or "13–15 years of employment." Sometimes in data analysis it becomes necessary to merge categories, and the codebook can keep track of the various way you transform your variables.

As you enter data into the computer and discover missing items (such as "age") that cannot be reconstructed, its often useful to define a value (such as "99") as the missing value. When you are editing your data for completeness, this lets you know, unlike leaving it blank, that nothing was missed. Blanks can also represent missing data that you know is missing, but unfortunately, blanks could also mean that someone was careless when entering the data. That's why it is a better practice to assign a unique number that informs the computer that data is missing.

If you employed one or more open-ended questions in your survey, it is highly likely you will want to code the responses. Take, for instance, individual answers to the question, "Why did you quit school?"

> Had no money.
> Couldn't pay my bills.
> Parents couldn't afford to send me.
> Loan didn't go through.
> Couldn't borrow any more.
> Didn't like it.
> Hated school.

A reading of the first five responses suggests that one possible motive for quitting school and, therefore, one category that ought to be recognized in the data analysis is "financial reasons." The last two responses suggest that respondents were disinterested in school. So, "financial reasons" could be coded "1" (since it was the first category we identified) and "disinterest" could be coded "2." Computers are not yet so powerful that they can read these six different replies and form discrete categories for you. But once you indicate which responses are similar, then the computer will be quick to allow you to count them by category.

I find it helpful to read through twenty to twenty-five of the open-ended responses to look for similarities in the kinds of things that are being reported. Sometimes it is easy to come up with four or five categories, and then place the remaining responses in a category called "other." Later on, I might subdivide the "other" explanations into different categories. I don't like "other" to represent much more than 10 percent of the data. If it grows to 25 or 30 percent of all your categorized responses, then this is good reason to examine the "other" responses more closely and possibly create new categories from them.

Step 3: Univariate Analysis

Even though you have checked the data prior to entering it into the computer, as a conscientious researcher you should still search for possible data entry error by asking the computer to create a **frequency distribution** for each variable. A frequency distribution is a listing of all the categories of numeric values associated with one variable. These values are arranged for low to high as in table 9.1.

Sometimes a little more cleaning is necessary before proceeding further. When entering a large amount of data into the computer, it is easy to lose one's place and make errors. But if you were careful, a quick look at the frequency distribution is often all that is needed to reassure you that the data are ready for analysis.

This advice applies even to faculty. I learned this lesson once again when the information coming from a questionnaire I had designed didn't provide me with the data I needed to know. One section of the questionnaire dealt with additional education that a group of mothers on welfare might have attained while participating in a project that provided them with intensive case management. The item went something like this:

Please Check the Educational Efforts You Have Made
Since Entering the Project
_____finished high school
_____attained a GED
_____completed vocational training
_____begun college (indicate hours completed_____)

This item appeared by itself at the top of the second page of the questionnaire. What's the problem? When all the questionnaires were returned, about half of the respondents did not check any categories on the top of page two. Did this mean that they didn't attain any additional education? Or did they just forget to fill out the second page? Since the questionnaires were completed anonymously, it's a question that I can never answer. A pilot test might have identified this problem for me and I could have fixed the item by providing a response choice for those who had not attained any additional schooling.

In table 9.1, there were four individuals twenty-three years of age and six who were twenty-seven. There were no teenagers. Had there been, the researcher would have known there was a problem because the sample consisted only of graduate students. Ages, quite appropriately, ranged from twenty-three to fifty-five. Further, there was only one fifty-five-year-old, but there were four persons twenty-three years of age. Frequencies are another way of saying "count" or "number of."

Note, too, that the 99 does not indicate a very old, almost-centenarian

Table 9.1 Frequency Distribution of AGE V0003

Value	Frequency	Percent	Valid Percent	Cumulative Percent
23	4	7.7	8.0	8.0
24	4	7.7	8.0	16.0
25	3	5.8	6.0	22.0
26	5	9.6	10.0	32.0
27	6	11.5	12.0	44.0
28	2	3.8	4.0	48.0
29	3	5.8	6.0	54.0
30	1	1.9	2.0	56.0
31	1	1.9	2.0	58.0
32	5	9.6	10.0	68.0
33	2	3.8	4.0	72.0
34	1	1.9	2.0	74.0
35	1	1.9	2.0	76.0
37	1	1.9	2.0	78.0
39	1	1.9	2.0	80.0
40	1	1.9	2.0	82.0
41	1	1.9	2.0	84.0
43	1	1.9	2.0	86.0
44	1	1.9	2.0	88.0
45	1	1.9	2.0	90.0
46	1	1.9	2.0	92.0
47	1	1.9	2.0	94.0
48	1	1.9	2.0	96.0
51	1	1.9	2.0	98.0
55	1	1.9	2.0	100.0
99	2	3.8	Missing	
Total	52	100.0	100.0	

completed a survey, but that two individuals did not report their age. Reading down the third column, we are informed that these two students represent 3.8 percent of all those surveyed. There's nothing remarkable about that, but had it been 38 percent, then we might wonder if there was something about the way the information was asked that generated such a large amount of missing data. Researchers don't like missing data.

The valid percent column removes the missing data from the calculations. These figures are computed by dividing each of the frequencies by a denominator of 50 (52 less the 2 missing cases).

You can use the cumulative percent column to partition the data into thirds, fourths, fifths, and so on. For instance, one-third of the students were twenty-six or younger; approximately two-thirds were thirty-two or younger.

By informing the computer that you want statistics to help you interpret the frequency distribution (in SPSS you would choose from the menu

"Statistics" then "Summarize" and "Frequencies"), you can obtain the following additional information for the variable "Age of Graduate Sample."

Range	Minimum	Maximum	Sum
32.00	23.00	55.00	1590.00

The first set of statistics provides us with the lowest (minimum) and highest value (maximum), the variable's range (the distance between the lowest and highest value plus one), as well as the sum of all the values added together.

The second set of statistics is often more useful. These **measures of central tendency** (the mean, median, and mode) allow us to understand the average response for that particular variable. We learn that the average (**mean**) age for our sample of graduate students is 31.8 years and that the most frequently reported age (the **mode**) is 27, because there were six students of that age.

Mean	Standard Error	Median	Mode	Standard Deviation
31.8000	1.1700	29.0000	27.00	8.2734

The **median** is the exact midpoint of all the values and is not affected by extreme maximum or minimum values. The median is computed by taking the number of valid cases and dividing by 2. In this example, fifty divided by two is twenty-five—so the midpoint is that place located either by counting down twenty-five cases from the lowest values of twenty-three or twenty-five cases up from the highest value of fifty-five. Try it. The twenty-fifth case is found within the group of three persons who were twenty-nine years of age.

The mean, median, and mode do not always align themselves perfectly on the same value. This is partly explained by the fact that the mean is pulled in the direction of extreme scores while the median is unaffected by them. And the job of the mode is to report the "most popular" response.

The frequency distribution in table 9.2 shows what happens when the original data are slightly altered. In this new example, there are no graduate students older than forty-five and there are a few more twenty-seven-year-olds. As a result, the median and mode are now the same. The mean is slightly lower, but still pulled in the direction of the oldest students. We can grasp this by realizing that 44 and 45 are quite a bit further from the median than the minimum of 23 and so they exert more numerical weight."

Note, too, that the **standard deviation** has grown smaller—from 8.27 in the first example to 5.7 in the second one. The standard deviation is an indicator of how much variation there is in the data; that is, how closely the individual scores cluster around the mean. The standard deviation represents the average distance between scores and the mean. The small the standard deviation, the less variability there is and the more similar the values are to each other.

Table 9.3 shows one of the many possible configurations of data that

Table 9.2 Distribution with No One Older Than 45

		Frequency	Percent	Valid Percent	Cumulative Percent
Valid	23.00	4	7.7	8.0	8.0
	24.00	4	7.7	8.0	16.0
	25.00	4	7.7	8.0	24.0
	26.00	5	9.6	10.0	34.0
	27.00	10	19.2	20.0	54.0
	28.00	2	3.8	4.0	68.0
	29.00	3	5.8	6.0	64.0
	30.00	1	1.9	2.0	66.0
	31.00	1	1.9	2.0	68.0
	32.00	5	9.6	10.0	78.0
	33.00	2	3.8	4.0	82.0
	34.00	1	1.9	2.0	84.0
	35.00	1	1.9	2.0	86.0
	37.00	1	1.9	2.0	88.0
	39.00	1	1.9	2.0	90.0
	40.00	1	1.9	2.0	92.0
	41.00	1	1.9	2.0	94.0
	43.00	1	1.9	2.0	96.0
	44.00	1	1.9	2.0	98.0
	45.00	1	1.9	2.0	100.0
	Total	50	96.2	100.0	
Missing	99.00	2	3.8		
	Total	2	3.8		
Total		52	100.0		

Statistics: Measures of Central Tendency for Table 9.2				
Mean	Standard Error	Median	Mode	Standard Deviation
29.5200	.8158	27.0000	27.00	5.7685

Range	Minimum	Maximum	Sum
22.0	23.00	45.00	1476.00

would result in the mean, median, and mode having the same numerical value. Observe that, once more, the standard deviation has become smaller as the extreme values were eliminated from the sample.

SPSS also produces other statistics that allow you to determine the extent to which your univariate data conform to or depart from the symmetrical bell-

Table 9.3 Frequency Distribution with No One Older Than 35

		Frequency	Percent	Valid Percent	Cumulative Percent
Valid	23.00	6	11.5	12.0	12.0
	24.00	6	11.5	12.0	24.0
	25.00	7	13.5	14.0	38.0
	26.00	5	9.6	10.0	48.0
	27.00	10	19.2	20.0	68.0
	28.00	2	3.8	4.0	72.0
	29.00	3	5.8	6.0	78.0
	30.00	1	1.9	2.0	80.0
	31.00	1	1.9	2.0	82.0
	32.00	5	9.6	10.0	92.0
	33.00	2	3.8	4.0	96.0
	34.00	1	1.9	2.0	98.0
	35.00	1	1.9	2.0	100.0
	Total	50	96.2	100.0	
Missing	99.00	2	3.8		
	Total	2	3.8		
Total		52	100.0		

Statistics: Measures of Central Tendency				
Mean	Standard Error	Median	Mode	Standard Deviation
27.1200	.4657	27.0000	27.00	3.2928

Range Statistic	Minimum Statistic	Maximum Statistic	Sum Statistic
12.00	23.00	35.00	1356.00

shaped curve of "normal" distribution. In a normal distribution, 95 percent of all cases fall within two standard deviations of the mean; 68 percent fall within one standard deviation of the mean. When your data fit the normal curve, the mean, median, and mode all coincide. The statistics supplied by SPSS to help you gauge the shape of your distribution are the measures of **skewness** and **kurtosis**. Kurtosis has to do with the flatness or "peakedness" of the data distribution. But since most small samples will not take the shape of a symmetrical bell-shaped curve, there is no need to worry a great deal about the interpretation of these statistics. When the mean is higher than the median, the distribution of values is positively skewed (the extreme scores are at the high end). When the mean is lower than the median, there are extreme scores at the low end (the distribution would have a negative skew).

Levels of Measurement

Variables are like most things in that they can be subdivided into different types. **Nominal variables** are easily identifiable because they are discrete, named categories. For instance, *male* and *female* are the attributes of the variable gender. Similarly, a student could be *full-time* or *part-time*; clients might be *first-time offenders* or *recidivists*. Symptoms might be understood in terms of whether the are *acute* or *chronic*. Another key feature of nominal data is that you can't average the categories. Thus, you wouldn't try to compute the mean of the males and females; it would make no sense. With nominal data we simply deal with percentages and might say something like, "52 percent of the sample were males, 48 percent were females" and that suffices. If there were multiple categories (like marital status) we might mention the modal category and say "Typically, clients were unmarried."

Variables like age, weight, height, income, and test or scale scores that are continuous with equal intervals in between each value are called **interval variables**. Measuring data at the interval level allows us to get accurate measurements—to measure change in small increments. For example, we might note that clients who participated in a bereavement group were 17 percent less depressed at posttest than a control group. Phobic individuals may have reduced their anxiety scores by 25 points after six weeks of intervention.

Researchers usually strive to obtain interval data because the more sophisticated statistical procedures require it. This is why it is important to give a great deal of thought to how you want to analyze your data as you are developing your research methodology and instrumentation. Suppose you design a questionnaire and ask your clients:

How many years of education have you completed?

a.) Eighth grade or less.
b.) Ninth to twelfth grade.
c.) Some college.

The problem with this scheme is that it is impossible to know exactly how many individuals finished the eleventh grade; further, you wouldn't have any idea as to the average number of years of education completed. This problem could have been avoided if you had asked the question this way:

How many years of education have you completed?_____years

By not supplying the categories but asking open-ended questions, you will obtain interval level data. The exception, of course, is that some variables (like gender) are always nominal variables. A rule of thumb is: interval data can be transformed into categorical data, but not vice versa.

Here's why you need to know the difference between interval and nominal data: the computer can, on occasion, supply you with garbage data if you

Table 9.4 Frequency Distribution for Gender

		Frequency	Percent	Valid Percent	Cumulative Percent
Valid	1.00	25	48.1	48.1	48.1
	2.00	27	51.9	51.9	100.0
	Total	52	100.0	100.0	
Total		52	100.0		

Statistics: Measures of Central Tendency				
Mean	Standard Error	Median	Mode	Standard Deviation
1.5192	6.996E-02	2.0000	2.00	.5045

don't know the differences between the two. Table 9.4 shows a frequency distribution for the variable *gender* when, to save time, I coded females as 1 and males as 2, and then asked the computer to furnish the mean, median, and mode. While the percentages are accurate, the mean in this instance has no real meaning. After all, what is the distance or interval between males and females? Would you think it appropriate to report that for this sample of fifty-two graduate students the average for the variable of gender was 1.52? Or would that be nonsense?

In table 9.5, the attributes of gender have been entered as "male" and "female." Note that there are no statistics other than percentages being reported even though I asked SPSS to supply mean, median, standard deviation, and so on. The software didn't supply these statistics because the data were entered as words ("male" and "female"), and you can't average words.

The **ordinal** level of measurement sometimes resembles nominal categories in that they are named categories. For instance, staff morale might be categorized as "good," "fair," or "poor"; clients might be designated as "highly motivated," "moderately motivated," slightly motivated," or "not at all motivated." Likert scales as in the following examples are also ordinal:

Overall, how satisfied are you with the services you received?

Very Satisfied	Mostly Satisfied	Mildly Dissatisfied	Quite Dissatisfied
3	2	1	0

How would you rate the quality of the services you received?

Excellent	Good	Fair	Poor
3	2	1	0

Table 9.5 Frequency Distribution for Gender

		Frequency	Percent	Valid Percent	Cumulative Percent
Valid	female	25	48.1	48.1	48.1
	male	27	51.9	51.9	100.0
	Total	52	100.0	100.0	
Total		52	100.0		

The secret of recognizing ordinal data is that there is a ranking, that some categories may be valued more than others. Another clue is that the scale is directional so that positions on the scale have a relative meaning associated with higher or lower values. With ordinal data there is a presumption that the distance between the categories are equal and that data from these scales can be treated as interval level.

The thing that's a little bit tricky about ordinal data is that sometimes the researcher may use the categories as if the data were nominal and at other times the data may be treated as if they were measured at the interval level. We'll talk more about this in the next section, but for now imagine that 129 clients have rated the quality of a respite service for families with Alzheimer's as 2.88 (mean). That suggests while the agency got a lot of "3" responses, they didn't get 100 percent agreement—which you wouldn't expect. The 2.88 would be even easier to interpret if we saw what percent of the families rated the services "excellent," "good," fair," and "poor"—or, if we could see improvment from lower ratings in prior years. Another rule of thumb that may help you: When you are trying to decide if data are being treated as if they were nominal or ordinal, see if percentages are being reported. If so, the data are probably treated as nominal data. If there are decimals, as in the example of mean satisfaction ratings of 2.88, then the data are being treated as if they were interval.

Realize, too, that items such as the two examples above are often combined to constitute a scale and what is important there is not the client's response to any one item but the combined or aggregate score. Thus, with a hypothetical ten-item client satisfaction questionnaire and a 0 to 3 rating scale, a respondent could rate the agency anywhere from 0 to 30—creating a dependent variable (overall satisfaction score) that could be analyzed as a continuous or interval level variable.

Whether your data are measured at the nominal, ordinal, or interval level, univariate analysis of data lends itself to graphic portrayals. Graphs, pie charts, histograms, and polygrams can be prepared almost effortlessly once you have entered your data into the computer and have access to a statistical software program. Figure 9.1 provides examples of the various ways data can be visually presented.

Figure 9.1 Graphic Portrayals of Univariate Analysis

A. Pie Chart

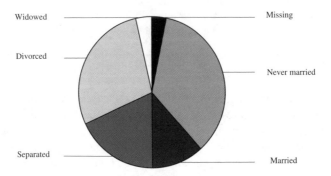

Marital Status of New Clients

B. Bar Chart

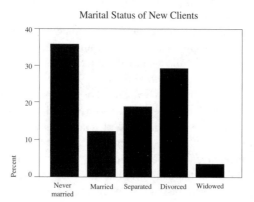

Marital Status of New Clients

C. Line Chart

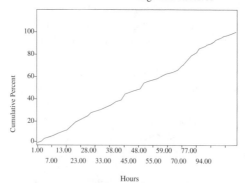

Hours of Case Management Received

Both the pie chart and bar chart give the viewer a quick way to assess the portions represented by the various categories associated with a nominal or ordinal variable. Notice that in the pie chart I included a missing data category (those who didn't report their marital status), but I removed those individuals from the bar chart. There's no real hard and fast rule here, however, the reader should be informed if there is a large number of cases with missing data.

Univariate analysis allows the researchers to become acquainted with patterns in the data—among other things, to understand who is included and who might have been excluded. Thus, if you were conducting a study within your agency and noticed that none of the clients in your samples were sixty-five or older, then you might want to hold off further analysis until data from a few of these clients could be added. In other words, univariate analysis could inform you when you might have experienced some sort of selection bias in your sampling procedures. Once you have examined your data one variable at a time and decided that the sample or data is adequate, then you are ready to begin to test hypotheses.

Step 4: Hypothesis Testing

Hypotheses can be either simple or complex. Hypothesizing that there may be more female clients than male clients in a certain program is too simplistic to be real research. The social work researcher would want to know why there might be differences in admissions by gender. And he or she might think of any number of relevant questions or hypotheses. For example, if there are more women than men clients, is this true for all income and educational levels? When men enter treatment, do they drop out sooner than women? Do they have more severe diagnoses upon admission? Are they more likely to have alcohol or drug histories?

Let's say you have an idea that, for whatever reason, men don't feel as welcome in the agency as women. You draw a sample of thirty-five clients and ask them the question, "If you were to need help again, would you return to our agency?" You discover that 67 percent of the women but only 60 percent of the men say that they would return. Is this a real difference? Can we say that it is a statistically significant difference?

By preparing a table like table 9.6, we can visually attempt to understand the data. However, it is impossible by simply "eyeballing" the numbers to know whether or not the differences are real or might have been produced by chance. If it is important for us to know whether males and females are significantly different in their responses about returning to the agency, then we need to compute a **chi square (X^2)**. We obtain this statistic either by calculating it by hand or by asking the computer to perform a **cross-tabulation**. The crosstabs procedure allows us to examine the dependent variable (willingness to return to the agency) by the independent variable of gender and is performed with categorical, not interval data.

Table 9.6 Cross-Tabulation of Willingness to Return to Agency by Gender

		Females	Males	Total
Would Return	Count	10	12	22
	%	66.7%	60.0%	62.9%
Wouldn't Return	Count	5	8	13
	%	33.3%	40.0%	37.1%
Total	Count	15	20	35
	%	100.0%	100.0%	100.0%

In our example, SPSS calculated the chi square and found it to be .16. That number won't mean a whole lot to you. In the days before computers, it meant a lot more. You would have had to consult a table in an appendix at the back of your book to learn whether or not the chi square was statistically significant. But today, the software program informs us that the probability (p) of the data falling into those cells the way they did by chance alone was .69—or many times larger than the five times in a hundred cutoff standard that social scientists most frequently use to determine statistical significance. Probabilities larger than .05 (p > .05) are not generally considered significant. So, even though there is about a 7 percent difference between men and women, that is not a real difference. In this example, males and females are more similar in their patterns of responding than they are dissimilar. One should not look at percentages and from them alone make a pronouncement about whether there are significant differences.

NOTE: even though p < .05 is the accepted standard, on occasions when it is critical to reduce the role of chance even more than what is normally tolerated investigators may adopt a more stringent criterion of accepting significance only if p < .01. This would be a conservative approach if there was some risk that the intervention might not be helpful or could have some adverse side-effects. Once in a while you'll also find that the standard is lowered—as when there is a report of exploratory research with a small sample. Under these conditions it is acceptable to raise the cutoff to p < .10.

What would a statistically significant difference look like? Using the same idea of a small survey of our clients, lets imagine that this time we find that only 30 percent of the males but 80 percent of the females indicated that they would return.

When we once again go to the computer and order crosstabs of the dependent variable ("would return to the agency") by gender, we find a much larger chi square (8.58) but, more importantly, a probability or significance level of .003 (see table 9.7). In other words, the tendency for women clients to indi-

Table 9.7 Cross-Tabulation of Willingness to Return to Agency by Gender

		Females	Males	Total
Would Return	Count	12	6	18
	% within	80.0%	30.0%	51.4%
Wouldn't Return	Count	3	14	17
	% within	20.0%	70.0%	48.6%
Total	Count	15	20	35
	% within	100.0%	100.0%	100.0%

cate they would return and for male clients to indicate that they probably wouldn't is a real finding that very likely did not occur by chance. Yes, it could be a fluke, but chance alone would explain the data falling this way only 3 times in 1,000. So, 997 times out of 1,000 independent samples with this population you would be safe in expecting women clients to indicate a greater likelihood of returning.

The simplest chi square table is the 2 x 2 (two variables each with two attributes). However, the crosstabs procedure will allow you to create tables which are 2 x 3, 3 x 3, 3 x 4, 4 x 4, and so on—you are not limited to a set of number of rows or columns. At the same time, if more than 20 percent of the cells in any one cross-tabulation have an expected frequency of five or less, the Pearson chi square produced by the computer will not be accurate, and you will need to combine or collapse categories so that there are fewer cells with more respondents in them. For example, if you were using a Likert scale with "Strongly Agree," "Agree," "Undecided," "Disagree," and "Strongly Disagree," then it would be logical to combine the "Strongly Agree" and "Agree" categories into one grouping (The "Agree" category) and then to combine the "Disagree" and "Strongly Disagree" into another (the "Disagree" category). Note that while we started with ordinal data, we end up treating it as discrete or categorical (nominal) data. Chi square is appropriate only for categorical data.

If there are few respondents in the "Undecided" category, another possibility would be to run crosstabs without the "Undecided" cases. In this situation, a 5 x 2 table (gender by a 5-point Likert Scale) could become a 2 x 2 (gender x agreement/disagreement) crosstab. Most statistical software programs will inform you of the number and percentage of cells that do not meet the minimum expected frequency.

Even with combining categories, it is still possible to have more than 20 percent of the cells not meeting the minimum expected frequency if you started with a very small sample. In such case, the best solution is to add to your sample. However, there is another chi square statistical procedure called Fischer's Exact Test that SPSS will produce for 2 x 2 tables when the expected value in one or more cells is small. Although it is somewhat more conservative, it is interpreted the same way as the basic chi square test (the Pearson chi square).

The T-Test

What are we to do if our questionnaire used a ten-point scale and we obtained the following data with this item: "How Would You Rate Our Program?" (Where 1 = Very Poor, 10 = Excellent)?

It wouldn't make sense to analyze the data in table 9.8 with the chi square procedure. For one thing, it's a toss-up as to whether or not the ratings constitute categories in the same way that we've learned to think about nominal data. Second, there's so many different "categories" or value positions that it's tempting to think of these being equal intervals between the values. And third, had we tried to conduct a chi square, the software program would have informed us that 100 percent of the cells failed to meet the minimum expected frequency—making the chi square statistic useless.

When we have a normally distributed dependent variable measured at the interval level, and a nominal level independent variable, we can look for differences between groups with the statistical procedure known as the **t-test**. This statistic compares the mean scores for the two different groups and provides a t-value and a probability statement. The t-test is appropriate even for small samples of about thirty individuals.

Using the data from the ten-point scale, our statistical software program produces several tables and informs us in the first one of the means for the two groups (table 9.9).

The next set of data provides an intermediate stage statistic that tells us which t-value to use in our research report. The Levene Test for Equality of Variances directs us to the best estimate for the standard error of the difference between the two means. When the significance level is less than .05 for the heading "Equal variances assumed," then the assumption is that the variances are not equal. In this case, p < .05 suggests that the variances are very different (as you might expect when the means appear very different) and so we go to the next table and look for the heading "Equal variances not assumed." Reading across, we learn that the significance for unequal variances is .012 (or p < .05). In other words, there is a real statistically significant difference in the way that men and women rank the program. Had the Levene's Test been p > .05 under "Equal variances assumed," that would have meant the variances were approximately equal and we could have used the t-value and probability associated with that estimate.

Table 9.8 Program Ratings by Gender of Clients

Ratings	Men	Women
1	1	0
2	2	0
3	2	0
4	4	0
5	2	3
6	3	1
7	1	6
8	2	3
9	2	1
10	1	1

Table 9.9 Initial Statistics Produced by the T-Test Procedure

VAR00001	N	Mean	Standard Deviation	Standard Error Mean
Women	15	7.0667	1.4376	.3712
Men	20	5.3000	2.5772	.5763

		Levene's Test for Equality of Variances	
		F	Significance
VAR00002	Equal variances assumed	7.124	.012

The t-test reported in table 9.10 requires a dependent variable measured at the interval level or ordinal data that can be treated as interval. Using the SPSS software, I clicked on "Statistics" then "Compare Means" and then informed the computer that we had **independent samples**—that is, the groups being used for the analysis were from different individuals (males and females). Had we wanted to compare, say pretest self-esteem scores with posttest self-esteem scores after an intervention for the group of thirty-five individuals, then we would have had to inform the computer that we wanted a **"paired samples" t-test**. This procedure would have matched the John Client's pretest with John Client's posttest, Susie Patient's pretest with her posttest, and so on. With the paired samples procedure, you are examining for the average change or improvement by comparing the individuals with themselves.

Table 9.10 Independent Samples T-Test

| | | | | T-Test for Equality of Means | | |
		t	df	Significance (2-tailed)	Mean Difference	Standard Error Difference
VAR00002	Equal variances assumed	2.386	33	.023	1.7667	.7406
	Equal variances not assumed	2.577	30.833	.015	1.7667	.6855

Both versions of the t-test are limited to only two groups at a time (either pretest scores versus posttest, or something like male versus female). If you want to compare three different groups and have interval level data, that procedure is called **one-way analysis of variance** (sometimes referred to as **ANOVA**). Instead of a t-value, this method of analysis provides the F-ratio. However, it is also computed from group means and interpreted much like the t-test, as can be seen in table 9.11.

In this example, we've broadened our agency study to include teenagers who are participating in an after-school program. The previous subjects were all men and women over the age of twenty-one; this new group consists of mostly male teens age thirteen to eighteen. When asked the same question, "If you were to need help again, would you return to our agency?" the teens had lower mean ratings than the other two groups.

The table produced by ANOVA informs us that the probability that these means occurred by chance was 3 times in 1,000 ($p = .003$). In other words, the three groups are not similar in their ratings of the agency. In fact, there are statistically significant differences in the way men, women, and teens view the agency. However, we cannot say from the one-way findings that there is a statistically significant difference between the way men and teens think about the agency. In order to be able to make that statement, we would need to compute a t-test for independent samples and compare the men's ratings against the teens' ratings. (In this case, it was not significant: $p > .05$). One-way analysis of variance simply allows you to test the hypothesis that the means of several groups are similar. Like the chi square statistic, one-way doesn't mind if you have three, four, five, or even more groups.

Correlation

Even though we've been discussing the differences among three or more groups, do not lose sight of the fact that we're still involved with bivariate analysis—we're employing two variables, one dependent and one indepen-

Table 9.11 One Way Analysis of Variance: Mean Ratings from Men, Women, and Teens

Group	Mean	SD	n
Women	7.07	1.44	15
Men	5.30	2.58	20
Teens	4.17	2.46	18

		Sum of Squares	df	Mean Square	F	Significance
VAR00002	Between Groups	69.235	2	34.617	6.718	.003
	Within Groups	257.633	50	5.153		
	Total	326.868	52			

dent. Still another way to analyze bivariate data is to examine the strength of relationships between variables using correlation coefficients. A **correlation coefficient** is a statistic that ranges between -1.00 and +1.00. In a perfect correlation, movement within one variable is matched by a corresponding movement in the other. In table 9.12, students' exam scores increased by ten points for every hour that they studied. Note that both variables would be measured at the interval level.

The closer the correlation coefficient is to one end or the other of the range, the stronger the relationship between the two variables. (This does not mean, however, that one variable was the cause of the other variable. A high correlation between the amount of street crime in a city and the number of social workers does not mean that the social workers cause the crime.)

Usually, however, it is not so easy to predict one variable from knowing the other. In table 9.13, the pattern of increasing scores with additional study time holds for only half of the students. For the other half, scores declined with more study time. In a sense, there were off-setting differences. Can you guess what the correlation will be? A correlation coefficient of 0 indicates that there is absolutely no relationship between the two variables—that it is not possible to make any kind of a prediction about one from knowing the other. In table 9.14, there is a slight tendency for grades to improve with additional study time for some students.

In these examples, the plus sign is understood. A plus sign indicates a positive direction—as one variable goes, so goes the other variable. If one variable tends to increase, so does the other. A negative sign in front of a correlation coefficient indicates an inverse relationship—the variables go in opposite directions. As one variable increases, the other decreases.

Table 9.12 Distribution of Data, a Perfect Correlation

	Hours of Studying for Exams	Exam Score
Edna	10 hours	100
Bill	9 hours	90
Wanita	8 hours	80
George	7 hours	70
Brooke	5 hours	50

Pearson correlation coefficient = 1.00

Table 9.13 Distribution of Data, Zero Correlation

	Hours of Studying for Exams	Exam Score
Martha	1	70
Micki	2	75
Waldo	3	80
Kenneth	4	85
Earl	5	90
Heather	6	90
Jennie	7	85
Bob	8	80
Nadine	9	75
Rondell	10	70

Pearson correlation coefficient = .00

Table 9.14 Distribution of Data, a Slight Correlation

	Hours of Studying for Exams	Exam Score
Rennie	1	70
Debra	2	75
Betty	3	80
James	4	85
Edward	5	90
Pam	6	90
Donald	7	100
Robin	8	90
Glenna	9	80
William	10	70

Pearson correlation coefficient = .24

By squaring the correlation coefficient (multiplying it by itself), it is possible to determine the strength of the relationship between two variables. This tells us how much of the variance in the two variables is shared. Thus, a coefficient of .24 allows us to explain or predict about 6 percent of the variances between the two variables. Saying this another way, knowing a value for one of the variables would allow us to predict the corresponding value on the other variable with only 6 percent accuracy.

$$
\begin{array}{r}
.24 \\
\times\ \underline{.24} \\
96 \\
\underline{48} \\
.0576\ (\text{or } 6\%)
\end{array}
$$

Correlations as high as .70 are rarely found in social science research, and, more typically, are .40 or less. There's something else you also need to know about correlations—they aren't always statistically significant. The earlier examples of a perfect 1.00 correlation with a sample of ten students produced a probability of .50. This means that we shouldn't place a lot of confidence in the finding because of the small sample. However, it is also true that you can ensure correlations will be significant if you make the sample large enough.

A **correlation matrix** is presented in table 9.15. This matrix resulted from correlating four scales—Homophobia, Empathy, Fear of AIDS, and Desired Social Distance from AIDS Victims—with each other. It produces some perfect correlations (when a scale is correlated with itself) as well as some positive and negative correlations. As you look at these correlations, do you understand why some have a negative sign in front of them while others do not? Why would Empathy correlate negatively with Fear of AIDS?

It is possible to obtain correlations that are statistically significant (meaning that they weren't likely caused by chance) but that do not suggest any implications for practitioners or policymakers. Because correlational studies do not allow us to control for extraneous variables that may be influencing the correlations that we are examining, we seldom make it the purpose of our research just to obtain correlations. They are appropriate, of course, in exploratory research designs.

Table 9.15 A Correlation Matrix with Four Scales

	Homophobia Scale	Empathy Scale	Fear Scale	Social Distance Scale
Homophobia Scale	1.00	-.63	.60	.66
Empathy Scale	-.63	1.00	-.55	-.68
Fear Scale	.60	-.55	1.00	.67
Social Distance Scale	.66	-.68	.67	1.00

Tip for Interpreting Correlations

Correlations smaller than .20 are often described as slight or inconsequential, those between .20 and .40 are small or low correlations, correlation coefficients between .40 and .70 are moderate correlations, and anything above .70 is said to be a strong correlation.

The Elaboration Model

Imagine that you have conducted a survey that produced the results in table 9.16. About a third of the respondents did not feel they were "well-informed about AIDS." At this point, you have conducted only a univariate analysis. But, suppose you introduce another variable. You ask: Is there a difference in how men and women view their knowledge about AIDS? Now you would conduct a bivariate analysis of the dependent variable (knowledge about AIDS) by the independence variable of gender. Table 9.17 shows virtually no difference between males and females (and there was no statistically significant difference either, p = .84) when a X^2 was computed.

Suppose there is a third variable that might have some explanatory power. Could knowledge of AIDS vary between men and women depending upon the community in which they live? We can tell from table 9.18 that male city dwellers rate their knowledge of AIDS higher than small town or rural dwellers and that this same pattern also holds for female respondents. Using the crosstabs procedure again, we could determine if there were statistically significant differences by community of residence when we control for gender. You would simply select which variable should be the row variable and which the column variable, and then indicate the control variable. In this case, two different chi squares would be produced: one for women respondents and one for male respondents.

In this case, there were no significant differences among the female respondents (p = .09). However, there were significant differences by community of residence for the male respondents (p = .009) (see table 9.18).

The elaboration model typically begins with the original findings from a survey and then explores relationships between two variables before introducing a third. The search is for causal explanations that, unlike laboratory experiments where the investigator has a greater ability to regulate the influence of extraneous variables, must be controlled by statistical procedures. This notion of controlling variables is the basis on which multivariate analysis rests.

Table 9.16 Frequency Distribution
           ("I am well informed about AIDS.")

Category Label	Absolute Frequency	Relative Frequency (Percent)	Adjusted Frequency (Percent)
Strongly disagree	18	2.4	2.4
Disagree	228	30.6	30.7
Undecided	36	4.8	4.9
Agree	386	51.7	52.0
Strongly agree	74	9.9	10.0
No answer/refused	4	0.5	Missing data
Total	746	100.0	100.0

Table 9.17 Cross-Tabulation of Knowledge about AIDS by Gender
           ("I am well-informed about AIDS.")

	Female	Male
Strongly agree/Agree	291	169
	(66%)	(65%)
Strongly disagree/Disagree	153	93
	(34%)	(35%)
Column totals	444	262

Table 9.18 Knowledge of AIDS by Community Type and Gender
           ("I am well-informed about AIDS.")

	Female respondents			Male respondents		
	Rural	Small town	City/ Suburb	Rural	Small town	City/ Suburb
Strongly agree/Agree	73	105	112	48	59	60
	(59%)	(65%)	(71%)	(53%)	(65%)	(76%)
Strongly disagree/Disagree	51	56	45	42	32	19
	(41%)	(35%)	(29%)	(47%)	(35%)	(24%)
Totals	124	161	157	90	91	79

Multivariate Analysis of Data

Multivariate analysis is any statistical procedure that involves several, sometimes many, independent variables and at least one dependent variable, although there may be more than one dependent variable as well. Typically, two or more independent variables are entered simultaneously (one at a time, as in bivariate analysis), and a computer is necessary to perform the complex statistical computations. These methods are usually considered "intermediate" or "advanced" and not generally covered in introductory textbooks. These procedures have names such as partial correlation, two-way analysis of variance, multivariate analysis of variance, path analysis, logistic regression, log-linear analysis, canonical correlation, exploratory factor analysis, and structural equation modeling. I'll explain two of them briefly to give you some idea of what the "higher order" techniques actually do.

- *Regression analysis. Multiple regression* is a term used when a researcher is interested in using an array of independent variables to find out which ones make the best predictors for a specified dependent variable measured at the interval level. Through complex statistical procedures, beta weights are computed and tested for significance. The researcher can choose to allow them to enter the regression equation simultaneously or one at a time. Often, researchers let the computer do the selecting of the best predictor variables based on those that have the highest correlation with the dependent variable. Multiple regression produces R^2, which reports on the percent of variation in the dependent variable explained by the predictor variables.
- *Discriminant analysis.* This procedure takes a set of independent variables and tries to find the best combination that will allow the researcher to classify groups of persons. For instance, suppose you want to know what characteristics distinguish clients who "dropped out" from those "succeeded" as a result of your program's interventions. You may find that race and gender are not useful for making differentiations but that whether the clients' parents had graduated from high school is useful. These variables are discussed in terms of those having the greatest discriminating power on the nominal or ordinal dependent variable.

There are many more statistical procedures and ways to go about analyzing data than there were twenty years ago. But the best news is that it is also a lot easier now that it has ever been. My goal in writing this chapter was not to tell you everything you need to know about data analysis but to help you understand how you might begin to go about looking for patterns and trends in the data you collect. Admittedly, it is a little scary when you don't know all of the vocabulary and may not know how to proceed at times, but dive in! There are useful guides (Norusis, 1997) to consult. Statistical software programs won't destroy your data or call you names, and often they have informative tutorials so that you can learn at your own convenience and pace.

Data analysis is at least as important as conceptualizing the study and collecting the data. Don't rely upon others who may not understand the data as well as you—or what you want to accomplish—to decide how your data should be examined or what constitutes your main findings.

A Final Note

Most of the techniques described in this chapter (for example, chi square, t-tests, one-way analysis of variance) are commonly used in **ex post facto** research. This is research that take place after the data have been gathered, generally when unexpected findings generate new hypotheses or research questions. Ex post facto research occurs frequently in analyzing the results of surveys when, for example, the investigator might wonder if individuals who differ on some attitudes are also different in terms of income level or education. Ex post facto research may involve the elaboration process.

A cautionary note: it is entirely possible to put too much importance on statistical significance. For instance, suppose you are running an after-school program for delinquent youth. At the end of the school year you find that those in the intervention group have seen their grade-point average rise from 1.40 to 1.65. A t-test reveals this to be statistically significant at $p < .05$. You feel good about this "important finding" until someone points out that practically speaking, there has been no major improvement—that most of the group is still having academic problems and in danger of seeing their Ds becoming failing grades. In the same way, a group of persons receiving intervention for depression might show some statistically significant reduction in symptoms but still be depressed and in need of treatment. The point here is that researchers should not be so swept away by the finding of significance that they forget about other considerations: Are the results also practically or clinically significant?

Finally, there is a strong bias in professional journals against publishing studies where there are *not* significant findings. This is unfortunate, particularly when studies are informative and well-conceptualized. For instance, imagine that you are comparing an expensive intervention with a cheaper one and obtain negative findings (no significant differences). This information has the potential for saving taxpayers and consumers a great deal of money, except for the fact that many, if not most, journal reviewers might not find your manuscript to be important enough to publish. Does this make sense? It doesn't and may change over time. I side with Kazdin (1992) who argues, "No-difference findings in a well-conceived and controlled study with adequate power (e.g., $< .80$) ought to be taken as seriously as any other finding" (p. 375).

Self-Review

(Answers at the end of the book)

1 Which measures of central tendency is affected by extreme scores?
a. median
b. mode
c. mean
d. stetactic harmony

2. Labeling clients' progress after intervention as "improved" or "not improved" would be using what level of measurement?

3. Labeling clients' progress after intervention as "major improvement," "slight improvement," or "no improvement" would be using what level of measurement?

4. A frequency distribution would be most useful to a researcher at what level of analysis?
a. multivariate
b. bivariate
c. univariate
d. trivariate

5. A cross-tabulation is associated with which level of analysis?
a. multivariate
b. bivariate
c. univariate
d. trivariate

6. Juanita runs an outpatient clinic for teens with a substance abuse problem. She claims that 60 percent of the clients are "improved" after six visits and that only 40 percent are "not improved." What statistical procedure would she use to see if males made more improvement than females?
a. chi square
b. t-test
c. one-way analysis of variance
d. frequency distribution

7. In a self-esteem group Sue was leading, the participants' mean score at pretest was 35.6 and posttest 41.1. She wants to know if this is a statistically significant improvement. With this interval data, Sue would use what statistical procedure?
a. chi square
b. t-test
c. one-way analysis of variance
d. normal distribution

8. Sue wants to examine her clients' improvement when she examines them by the variable of attendance. She divides her clients into three groups: those with "good" attendance, those with "average" attendance, and those with "poor" attendance. Using the same instrument as in 7 but with three groups instead of two, what statistical procedure should Sue employ?
   a. chi square
   b. t-test
   c. one-way analysis of variance
   d. standard deviation

9. How much variation between two variables does a correlation coefficient of .35 explain?
   a. about 30 percent
   b. about 20 percent
   c. about 12 percent
   d. less than 5 percent

10. T or F. using the appropriate statistical test, Carolyn obtained a probability of .90. This indicates that her findings are statistically significant.

11. What does p > .05 mean?
    a. a statistically significant difference
    b. differences between or among means was not statistically significant
    c. that the odds of obtaining approximately the same means could happen by chance more than 5 times in 100
    d. both b and c are correct
    e. none of the above are correct

Questions for Class Discussion

1. While charts or graphs can help readers grasp a study's findings, what is the problem with using charts and graphs solely to understand a study?

2. What are the limitations associated with doing correlational research?

3. What are the statistical software packages used at your college or university? What are students' experiences with these programs?

4. Why is it important for social work researchers to be able to conduct their own statistical analyses?

5. Is it possible to write a credible, professional evaluation of a program's effectiveness without using statistical analysis? Under what circumstances?

6. What facet of statistical analysis is most difficult to understand? Which is the easiest?

Mini-Project for Experiencing Research Firsthand

1. Using any of the instruments described in chapter 5, collect a small sample of data (for example, from fifteen to twenty students), and enter the data into a computer for statistical analysis. Report to the class your hypotheses, the statistical procedure you used, and your findings.

Resources and References

Benbenishty, R. and Ben-Zaken, A. (1988). Computer-aided process of monitoring task-centered family interventions. *Social Work Research and Abstracts,* 24(1), 7–9.

Clark, C.F. (1988). Computer applications in social work. *Social Work Research and Abstracts,* 24(1), 15–19.

Gibson, J.W. (1992). Compensating for missing data in social work research. *Social Work Research and Abstracts,* 28(2), 3–8.

Girden, E.R. (1996). *Evaluating research articles from start to finish.* Thousand Oaks, CA: Sage.

Kanji, G.P. (1993). *100 statistical tests.* Newbury Park, CA: Sage.

Kazdin, A. (1992) . *Research design in clinical psychology.* Boston: Allyn and Bacon.

Norusis, M.J. (1997). *SPSS 7.5: Guide to data analysis.* Upper Saddle River, NJ: Prentice-Hall.

Nunnally, J.M. (1994). *Psychometric theory.* New York: McGraw-Hill.

Pilcher, D.M. (1990). *Data analysis for the helping professions.* Newbury Park, CA: Sage.

Royse, D. and Birge, B. (1987). Homophobia and attitudes towards AIDS among medical, nursing, and paramedical students. *Psychological Reports,* 61, 867–870.

Royse, D., Dhooper, S., and Hatch, L.R. (1987). Undergraduate and graduate students' attitudes towards AIDS. *Psychological Reports,* 60, 1185–1186.

Weinbach, R. (1989). When is statistical significance meaningful? A practical perspective. *Journal of Sociology and Social Welfare.* 16(1), 31–37.

CHAPTER 10
Program Evaluation

Most often, program evaluation starts with a specific problem or question to be answered, such as: "Is our outpatient treatment program effective?" Or, "Are we as successful with our group counseling program as with our individual counseling?" Administrators, board members, and others may want to know if the program is a "good" program. If they decide that the program is not effective, then corrective action may be taken or funding may be cut off. Program evaluation, then, is an aid to program managers. It can improve program effectiveness and aid in decision making.

Program evaluation attempts to answer such general questions as:

1. Are clients being helped?
2. Is there a better (cheaper, faster) way of doing this?
3. How does this effort or level of activity compare with what was produced or accomplished last year? (Did we achieve our objectives?)
4. How does our success rate compare with those of other agencies?
5. Should this program be continued?
6. How can we improve our program?

Why do we need to conduct program evaluation? The best argument for evaluating social service programs comes from an analogy suggested by Martin Bloom: running a program without evaluating it is like driving a car blindfolded. You certainly are going places, but you don't know where you are or who you've endangered along the way. Program evaluation provides accountability. It can be used to assure the public, funders of programs, and even the clients themselves that a particular program works and that it deserves further financial support. Program evaluation can be used to ensure that certain expectations are met, that efforts are appropriately applied to the identified needs, and that the community is better off because the program is having a positive effect.

There are many other reasons for evaluating a program. In addition to providing a reassuring level of accountability to clients and the public, program evaluation may be used to meet accreditation standards, identify needs for staff and program development, and provide information for managing programs and monitoring their effects. Ultimately, program evaluation benefits clients. It tells us whether they are being helped, and, if they are not, it can indicate who they are and what is being done for them.

Program evaluation is an important phase in the development of a program. Ideally, every program should be examined, and what is learned from these efforts should go back to the managers and service providers to enable them to continually improve the effectiveness and efficiency of their activities.

Starting to Think about Conducting a Program Evaluation

Think about a social service program with which you have been associated. Perhaps it was an agency where you volunteered or were employed. Maybe you are currently there in a field practicum. Suppose that one day the agency director calls you into her office and says, "I've just got a letter from our principal funding source informing us that we must provide them with results of a program evaluation within the next ninety days or risk losing our funding. There's nobody here with that kind of expertise, but since you are taking that research course at the university, I'm hoping you'll agree to be the team leader on this. Let's meet again tomorrow and toss around some ideas about how to proceed. Can you sketch out a rough plan for us?"

Although this scenario may seem a bit unlikely to you now, over the years, I've had a number of phone calls from students who have described being in a similar situation and frantically have asked, "What do I do now?" What kind of an evaluation plan would you recommend if you were put in such a spot?

Considerations Before Beginning a Program Evaluation

Before you can realistically begin planning a program evaluation, there are a few questions that must be addressed:

1. How much *time* do you have to complete the evaluation?
2. What *resources* (staff, money, etc.) are at your disposal?
3. Who is the *audience* who will be reading the evaluation report? (Will they be consumers, lay individuals, or researchers?)

4. What is the *purpose* of the evaluation? (Are there certain questions that must be answered? How rigorous does it have to be?)

In this scenario, the expectation of a completed project within ninety days would certainly impose some limitations on the type of evaluation that could be conducted. There probably wouldn't be time to do a **prospective** (going forward into the future) **study** (for example, starting a new group or intervention and then capturing posttest data). You'd be more likely to do a **retrospective study** looking back over already collected, existing data. Generally, the more time that is available for planning, the more control and the more sophisticated the design can be.

Resources are a major consideration. If the student is informed that no funds are available for the evaluation, that situation will likely result in a simpler effort than one where standardized, copyrighted instruments might be purchased or consultants employed. If clerical help is offered, or even that of other social workers to form an evaluation committee, then more might be proposed than if the student has no other assistance.

It is important to know the audience when writing the evaluation report. A report being prepared for consumers and laypeople could be less complex and use a different writing style than a report going to the research staff of the funding source. Consumers may not want to read about t-tests and chi squares or at least would need help interpreting them; professionals with Ph.D.s may have different expectations and may expect you to address sampling design, sample size, the psychometrics of instruments, and so on. How you write the report is also closely associated with the purpose of the evaluation.

In the selection of an evaluation design, the factors of time, resources, audience, and purpose must be weighed simultaneously, insofar as that is possible. However, the purpose of the evaluation has an overarching influence for this reason: the results of an evaluation can be used to promote or to denigrate programs. If the required evaluation is viewed by your agency management as so much "busy work," then the effort and energy put into it will be minimal. On the other hand, if there is a perception that the principal funding source is looking for reasons to eliminate programs, your agency will want to do the best job possible given the constraints of time and resources. Sometimes agencies can, by demonstrating empirically the superior job they do, position themselves to receive *more* funding for continuing or special projects. And, of course, the extent of competition from other agencies or service providers also plays a role. The more competition there is for scarce funds, the more attention that will be given to the program evaluation.

Types of Program Evaluation

1. Patterns of Use

- Answers the question, "Whom are we serving?"
- Focuses on the characteristics of clients.
- Is descriptive.
- Allows for the monitoring of specific objectives.
- Allows agencies to target services precisely where needed.
- Helps to identify new patterns and trends.

Patterns of use (also known as client utilization) data is the most basic information that every agency and program should be able to report; it is a prerequisite before designing more elaborate evaluations. Every director of a program needs to have accessible such descriptive data as: How many clients were served in the past twelve months? How many were low-income? How many were males? How many were over the age of fifty-five? Who referred these clients? Where do they live? What are their problems? How many have dropped out? What is the average length of their stay with us?

As indicated in table 10.1, this type of data informs only about those clients who have expressed a need for the program by appearing at the agency. It does not tell us anything about those who *could* have benefited from the program but who did not request it. It does not allow us to conclude that the program is good, effective, or efficient. While the data informs us about the number of clients served and allows us to establish who the recipients of our services were; they tell us nothing about the quality of care clients were provided. We can reach no conclusion about whether the clients were better off as a result of being served by one of the agency's three programs. Even though many social service agencies report descriptive client utilization data in their annual reports, such information by itself does not constitute an evaluation of the agencies' activities or programs.

Patterns of use data are best used for indicating pockets of clients who are within the agency's target group for services but who are not being adequately served for some reason. For instance, in table 10.1 it is apparent that the Happy Healthy Thinking Project is serving women predominantly. Now, it may have been designed to serve this population, but if it was conceived for both genders then it is obviously underserving men. Similarly, the program is serving fewer minorities than their representation in the community and fewer children. Depending on the nature of the program, the small percentage of children being admitted may or may not be a problem. Also, we can tell that the program seems to be doing a great job of reaching older adults but not doing very well in bringing in low-income clients. In fact, the clients' median household income is quite a bit larger than the average for the community.

Table 10.1: Client Utilization Data from the Happy Healthy Thinking Project

	Clients Served	Census Parameters
Number of clients served this year	523	
Female clients	361 (69%)	52%
Minority admissions	115 (20%)	31%
Clients under 18	26 (5%)	26%
Clients 55 and older	209 (40%)	13%
Low-income households	99 (15%)	27%
Median household income	$27,232	$25,987
Prior mental health services	89 (17%)	
Dual diagnois	63 (12%)	
Self-referrals	507 (97%)	
Average number of treatment episodes	2.3	

Other possible areas of concern are the extremely low number of referrals that come from other professionals and organizations in the community and the fact that clients appear to drop out after only a few sessions. Such data should concern program managers.

Directors and managers of programs use patterns of use data for **program monitoring**—that is, measuring the extent to which a program reaches its target population with the intended intervention. Despite bright, capable staff, programs without guidance from management can wander aimlessly, like ships without rudders.

I once observed this firsthand with an agency that had drifted away from its primary mission of serving the whole community. At the time I encountered the agency, the vast majority of its clientele were white middle-class persons who were young, fairly articulate, and motivated to work on their problems. This public agency was serving a select group of clients, the bulk of whom could have obtained assistance from private practitioners. Since there were no other agencies in that area to serve low income families, these families simply were not being served. This situation came about because there was no program monitoring being done. Program managers ought to monitor who is being served and who is not. When done regularly and routinely, program monitoring can be considered a basic form of program evaluation. While it does not answer questions about quality, it does provide a foundation upon which to start a program evaluation.

With the data from table 10.1, it would be possible to develop concrete, measurable **objectives**. For example:

1. To increase minority admissions by 25 percent by December 31, 2003.

2. To increase admissions from low-income clients by 30 percent by December 31, 2004.

3. To decrease self-referrals to 75 percent by December 31, 2002.

4. To reduce the number of clients who don't return to 33 percent by June 30, 2002.

Notice that these objectives are:

- Specific—they state a desired result.
- Measurable—they are easily verified.
- Referenced to a date—they indicate when results can be expected.

Objectives are different from **goals**, which are broad, general statements of direction. For instance, the Happy Healthy Thinking Project might have the following goals: to diminish loneliness and isolation in the community and to improve the quality of life for persons who have lost a family member to suicide and, ultimately, to eradicate suicide. Note that goals may be idealistic, they may never be obtained during your lifetime—but that doesn't mean that they aren't worthwhile. Goals state what the program and its associated activities should be about, while objectives provide for pragmatic accountability. Once program objectives have been developed, program monitoring takes on a new importance.

The problem with reliance upon the program's own objectives to determine how the program is doing is that whoever developed the objectives may have made them so easy to accomplish that they are essentially worthless. For instance, if a program objective stated that 490 new clients would be served within the year, but for the past two years the agency has been serving 553 new clients, the objective will be met, but we would still have no idea about how "good" or effective the program was. Ideally, a program should have to stretch a bit in order to meet its objectives. Objectives should be attainable, but not be so easy to reach that no special effort is required.

If your boss thinks that the principal funding source would be happy with the kind of data provided in table 10.1, then there is no need to go further. But if the agency has a management information system in place and someone is already responsible for program monitoring, then we need to review some other types of program evaluation that you could propose.

2. Formative Evaluation

- Answers the question: What would make this a better program?
- Primarily narrative.
- Major use is with new programs still being developed.

Like program monitoring, **formative evaluation** is not specifically concerned with the worth of a program. As its name suggests, it focuses on improving programs and can often be accomplished quickly and cheaply. Formative evaluations are used to modify or shape programs that are still in development. They tend not to rely upon statistics or analysis of numerical data. In this sense, they are much more qualitative than quantitative and usually don't conclude whether a program is successful or not. However, they may describe the experiences of clients and staff.

There are several ways to go over conducting a formative evaluation. One avenue might be to *obtain expert consultation.* This could be a person with a national reputation in the field in which the program is based; it could be someone with a statewide or regional reputation. You could even use a social worker or agency director from a similar agency in the same town as long as his or her program had a "good" reputation. The person would visit the agency to review operating policies and procedures, interview clients and staff, tour the facility, and maybe even meet with board members and reflect on aspects of the program. Maybe the person will notice that staff have to share offices, that there aren't enough computers, that the agency is not in a location that is accessible to clients who have to rely upon public transportation. Depending upon the expert, his or her interest, and your instructions, the intervention might be closely scrutinized—or maybe the training or credentials of the staff, staff caseloads, or staff turnover rates. At a minimum, you would hope that this visit would result in some new ideas about how other programs operate. The best that could come from this approach would be a list of specific things that the agency needs to address immediately and in the long term in order to improve the program.

If money is not available for experts and no one can be found to do a formative evaluation for free, there are still two other avenues. A second idea would be to *locate model standards* from national accrediting or advocacy organizations. For instance, the Child Welfare League of America has prepared standards for those who are in the child care business. These standards are quite specific and address everything from the facility itself to the number of staff. Also, don't overlook the possibility of finding a relevant program evaluation from a literature search. While it is not uncommon to think that a "new" program is highly innovative, in actuality it is likely some other agency may already have written about their experiences in starting and running a program like yours. Such studies might provide rough guidelines for what your program might expect in terms of clients who drop out or relapse. You can be somewhat reassured if your rates match those reported in the journal articles and if they don't, then you have a strong argument that more evaluation is needed and, possibly, more resources to support the program.

A third approach to formative evaluation would be to *form an ad hoc committee*—sometimes known as a blue-ribbon committee. This task force could be composed of staff, clients, interested persons from the community, board members, and even university staff. The group could start by circulating a brief questionnaire to clients and staff soliciting their ideas on how the program could be improved. It would be important to use open-ended questions and to allow the respondents to be anonymous. However, the step might not be necessary. The group may already have some sound notions about needed improvements. They may want to visit other similar agencies to view their operations—maybe even talk with present or past consumers. When a blue-ribbon task force is carefully chosen, a richness of ideas can emerge as participants share their thinking, experiences, and hopes for the program.

Formative evaluation can also be known as **process evaluation**; however, not all process evaluations are formative. Sometimes, process evaluations are done at the conclusion of a project to get some idea of why the program did or did not work the way it was intended.

Like formative evaluation, process evaluations are also primarily narrative. They often describe the decisions and key events in the development of a new program. The federal government likes process evaluation—especially with research and demonstration projects—because this type of information is valuable to those who are interested in implementing or replicating a similar program in a different community. It makes sense: why reinvent the wheel? Unlike formative evaluation, process evaluation ought to address what has been learned in the launching and operating of a program, what mistakes should not be repeated, and advice for the next team.

Once again, note that the focus of process evaluation is not so much on the number of client successes that were experienced (although this can be a part of the evaluation report) but rather on what happened and why. In this sense, a process evaluator has a role not unlike that of an historian. However, the process evaluation can also include client utilization data, consumer feedback data, even client outcome data. You can see why it is important to have a clear understanding of the purpose of the evaluation.

3. Consumer Satisfaction

- Answers the question: "Are clients pleased with our services?"
- Easy to interpret.
- Inexpensive.
- Allows trends to be monitored.
- Client-centered.
- Can be implemented quickly.

When asked to plan a program evaluation, many students have a tendency to think first of client satisfaction surveys and for good reason. They are among the simplest and most frequently used of evaluation methodologies. These approaches do not require a lot of research expertise, expense, or planning, and once developed, the same instrument can be used over many years. What's more, obtaining client feedback is a democratic grass-roots approach that values input from those receiving the services. There is no assumption that staff or the administration know best. Every client is given the opportunity to comment negatively or positively about his or her experience within the agency.

At least one study has revealed that psychotherapy clients who show clinically significant change are more likely to report greater satisfaction and benefit from psychotherapy (Ankuta and Abeles, 1993). However, a subsequent study (Pekarik and Wolff, 1996) found no relationship between client satisfaction and clinical assessments (using the Brief Symptom Inventory). While the inconsistency between these two studies may be explained by methodological differences (the later study used stricter criteria of clinical significance), most would agree that client satisfaction approaches have strong face validity.

With these points in its favor, what's the argument against making consumer satisfaction the principal component of an agency program evaluation effort? Just this: in practically every study clients say that they are satisfied with services. The vast majority of published consumer satisfaction studies show that clients almost invariably report high levels of satisfaction (Royse, 1985).

Lebow (1982) reviewed twenty-six studies examining satisfaction with mental health treatment and found half of the studies reported satisfaction in the 80 to 100 percent range. More than three-quarters of the studies had satisfaction rates of higher than 70 percent in spite of the surveys being conducted of totally different programs in dissimilar settings and using various counseling approaches and assessment methods. As Lebow (1982) noted, these high satisfaction rates come from clients who "have little choice of facility, type of treatment, or practitioner" (p. 250).

High satisfaction rates are not found just in the United States. Deane (1993) has reported that 95 percent of a sample of psychotherapy outpatients in New Zealand indicated that they would return to the program if they needed help and would recommend the program to friends. Gaston and Sabourin (1992) found no differences in client satisfaction among Canadian patients receiving dynamic, eclectic, or cognitive/behavioral therapy in private psychotherapy. Perreault and Leichner (1993) found that satisfaction rates varied between 87.5 and 98 percent with French-speaking psychiatric outpatients in Montreal.

Satisfaction rates have remained high whether clients with persistent mental illness were interviewed by staff or by other clients (Polowczyk, Brutus, Orvieto, Vidal, and Cipriani, 1993). This is not to suggest that every client will give rave reviews. Most surveys will have a few unhappy and disgruntled clients, but usually there will be many more who indicate satisfaction.

There can be several reasons why this type of program evaluation tends to reveal positive findings. First of all, client feedback instruments are often "home made," and nothing is known about their reliability or validity. Second, they tend to have a selection bias—clients who are dissatisfied with services often drop out early and may not receive or participate in these studies. Further, clients are in a vulnerable position and may not want to risk saying something negative for fear that they might lose their social worker or therapist—or even services at a future point in time. This vulnerability can sometimes be experienced even when those being surveyed are not clients. I once conducted a survey of high school principals and guidance counselors and found that they were very hesitant to give negative feedback about an agency that they admitted "could be improved" because—and this is good logic—even a mediocre program was better than none at all. They feared that too much criticism might result in the funding agency "pulling the plug" and then this group of school administrators and guidance counselors would have one less resource in the community where they could refer high school students who needed outpatient services.

A problem with mailing client satisfaction forms is that often clients move frequently and do not leave a forwarding address. Also, clients with lower levels of educational achievement will not be as responsive to mailed questionnaires as those with higher levels of education. LaSala (1997) recently reported a response rate of less than 20 percent to a mail survey and a 53 percent response on samples who were telephoned. From a research perspective, one needs to be very cautious when interpreting data from surveys when response rates are under 50 percent. Just imagine that 85 percent of your clients respond that they are "very satisfied" with a certain program, but only 30 percent of those eligible return their survey forms. Wouldn't you wonder about the experiences of the 70 percent who did not respond?

Despite the generally positive bias and the problems associated with collecting representative samples of clients, there is much to recommend client satisfaction studies as one means of evaluating a program. Because we, the professionals, do not experience the agency in the same way as the clients, it is important that we ask them to share their experiences with us. The receptionist may be rude, a co-worker may be insensitive, inattentive, or engaged in questionable practices. We need to know if clients have been mistreated, if their problems have not been addressed, and if they feel they have received a benefit from the intervention at our agency. If we don't ask questions like those listed in figure 10.1, then we'll never know how clients might respond. Notice the use of both open-ended and closed-ended questions.

Client satisfaction studies should be used within agencies as one component of a comprehensive evaluation strategy. It is not recommended as the *only* means of evaluating a program, but as one way to gather supplemental information from the client's perspective.

If you and the agency decide to conduct a client satisfaction study, here are a few recommendations:

Figure 10.1: Examples of Client Satisfaction Questions

1. How would you rate the quality of the services you have received?
    Poor   Fair   Good   Excellent

2. How satisfied are you with the help you receive?
    Very Satisfied   Mostly Satisfied   Mildly Dissatisfied   Quite Satisfied

3. If a friend needed similar help, would you recommend our program?
    Yes, definitely   Not sure   No, definitely not

4. Did the staff treat you with courtesy and consideration?
    Always   Most of the time   Not very often   Not at all

5. Have the services you received helped you to deal more effectively with your problems?
    Yes, they helped a great deal.
    Yes, they helped somewhat.
    No, they really didn't help.
    No, they seemed to make things worse.

6. How could our agency's services be improved?

7. What did you like best about this program?

8. What did you like least about this program?

- Use a scale that has known reliability and validity. An example would be the Client Satisfaction Questionnaire developed by Larsen and his colleagues (1979). The use of such a scale will eliminate many of the problems found in hastily designed questionnaires.
- Use the same instrument on repeated occasions so that there will be a baseline and trend data from which periods of uncharacteristically low satisfaction can be noted. "Low" client satisfaction rates may differ somewhat from agency to agency, but rates where only 65 to 70 percent of clients are satisfied probably means the program needs close inspection.
- Encourage client satisfaction surveys to be conducted regularly to minimize "bugs" in the system and to routinize the evaluation process.
- To reduce the problem of selection bias, consider using a "ballot box" approach where one week every quarter or every six months each client coming into the agency is given a brief questionnaire and asked to complete it.
- Use at least one open-ended question to give consumers the opportunity to inform you about problems you did not suspect and could not anticipate.

4. Outcome Evaluation

- Answers the question: "Are clients being helped?"
- Often based on group research designs.

- The type of evaluation every program should conduct.
- Requires that indicators of "success" or "failure" are conceptualization.

Outcome evaluation, also known as impact or effectiveness evaluation, makes use of the more sophisticated group research designs—that is, the quasi-experimental and experimental designs. Typically, this approach will use a control group, random assignment of clients, and involve pre- and posttesting as a way to obtain hard objective data on the performance of a program. When rigorous designs are used, evaluation at this level builds knowledge and may result in publishable findings. Outcome evaluation attempts to demonstrate that a program did make a difference, that clients were helped and did improve.

Beutler (1993) has listed principles and Peterson and Bell-Dolan (1995) some "commandments" that not only make a good review of what we already have learned, but also suggest key considerations for when an outcome study is being planned.

1. *Employ a control or comparison group whenever possible.* The essence of program evaluation is comparison. How well did the program do? The comparison group provides the basis for answering this question by furnishing the contrast that allows the evaluator to observe for threats to the internal validity such as maturation, history, and effects of testing.
2. *Client samples should be representative.* Invalid conclusions can arise from convenience samples and those where the sampling procedures produce a selection bias.
3. *Random assignment to control and treatment groups is strongly recommended.* If random assignment is not possible, check pretreatment data to determine if there is group equivalence. Also, take steps to keep subjects from dropping out of the study (minimize the threat of mortality) because this can change the equivalence between groups. Start with a sufficient group size to support the statistical analyses you want to conduct and to protect against loss of subjects in the final stages of the evaluation.
4. *Outcome measures should have demonstrated reliability and validity.* If instruments are needed, it is recommended that only those with adequate reliability and validity be employed. It is not good research practice to use the same sample of clients to test an instrument's psychometrics and then to examine the pool for evidence of improvement. Additionally, multimodal measurement (using multiple instruments and measuring more than one domain) is more likely to detect an intervention's effects than a single instrument.

5. *Interventions need to be standardized and applied as evenly and uniformly as possible.* Therapists, even of the same theoretical persuasion, are notorious for improvising and deviating from the planned intervention. Developing treatment manuals may be useful for ensuring that clients with the same problems consistently receive the same treatment. To the extent that those providing treatment emphasize different themes or have different goals for their clients, the intervention will not be uniform and may produce inconsistent results.

6. *Samples of therapists providing the intervention need to be large enough to be representative.* While researchers often worry about whether they have large enough samples of clients, too few worry about whether they have an adequate sample of therapists who are providing the treatment being evaluated. Small, inadequate samples of therapists also limit the evaluator's ability to generalize. A single therapist, especially when one of the investigators is the provider of the intervention, can contribute experimenter bias to the study.

7. *Assessment of clinical meaningfulness should accompany computations of statistical significance.* It is entirely possible to obtain mean differences in scores that are statistically significant, but that have no real meaning clinically. In other words, clients' scores may improve but not so much that it would be noticeable to the client, to his or her family, or to the therapist. This makes more sense if you don't think about a particular client but about a large group of clients: within that group several may deteriorate, some may show no change, and some may report fewer symptoms. However, they all require an ongoing after care program because they have a chronic, persistent form of mental illness. To change the examples slightly, as a social worker you would still be concerned about a patient reporting suicidal thoughts even if his or her symptom scores indicated less depression than sixty days earlier. Also, realize that a major issue is whether treatment effects are maintained over time. All else being equal, the stronger study will contain follow-up data some months or weeks after clients have exited a program. Results that hold over time are more meaningful than those immediately observed at the conclusion of a program.

5. Cost Effectiveness and Cost Analysis

- Answers the question: "What does it cost to help a client?"
- Focuses on desired program outcome (success) indicators.
- Allows policymakers to look simultaneously at the expense of running a program (efficiency) and its success (effectiveness).

Cheaper is not always better. Some programs are inexpensive to operate but also, unfortunately, not very effective. More expensive programs may, in the long run, prove to be cheaper. For instance, Meltzer and colleagues (1993) demonstrated that there was a significant savings in hospitalization costs for psychiatric patients on the drug clozapine. It is very expensive and requires periodic blood testing to make sure the dosage is correct and not toxic. But those who remained on the drug for two years resulted in a cost-savings of $17,404 per patient, while those who discontinued its use experienced more hospitalizations and expense. Similarly, Buescher and colleagues (1993) have reported that the Special Supplemental Food Program for Women, Infants, and Children (WIC) saved Medicaid $2.91 for every dollar spent on WIC. Women receiving Medicaid but not WIC benefits were 1.45 times more likely to have a low-weight infant. Costs to Medicaid for newborn services beginning in the first sixty days of life were lower for infants born to women who participated in WIC during their pregnancies. Clearly, providing good nutrition to pregnant mothers is a good value and ultimately results in savings for taxpayers.

Cost-effectiveness and cost-analysis studies allow the evaluator not only to compare the success rates of two or more different programs but also to examine these rates in terms of their costs. These studies could be classified as a type of outcome evaluation but have been given their own category in this text to highlight their distinctive quality of factoring in program costs.

Steps in Conducting a Cost-Effectiveness Study

1. *Operationalizing program success.* Think, for example, of a program designed to provide supported employment for persons with severe disabilities due to mental illness. What would success be? Being employed at least twenty hours a week and at least forty weeks a year? Or, would you have a more stringent requirement?
2. *Preparing to gather program outcome data.* In a retrospective evaluation, this step involves identifying the clients to be included in the evaluation and deciding upon how many years to examine. If there are many clients, a random sampling strategy may be developed.
3. *Gathering client outcome data.* This step typically involves contacting former "graduates" of the program in order to determine how many meet the criteria of being successful.
4. *Computing the program costs.* The total costs for operating the program need to be computed. Costs include such items as personnel salaries and fringe benefits, facility rent and maintenance (heating, air conditioning, electricity, water, insurance, painting, office equipment repair, travel, publicity, telephones, and so on).

5. *Computing the cost-effectiveness ratio.* The cost effectiveness of a program is computed by dividing its total cost by the number of client successes. For instance, a program that expended $400,000 and had 125 "successes" costs $3,200 for each successful client.

As you can see, this type of evaluation supplies superior information for decision makers and enables them to choose the best programs. Those programs with substantial costs that produce few positive effects can be discontinued and the resulting cost savings can be applied to more effective interventions.

Other Models

Cost analysis is not limited to cost-effectiveness studies. There are cost-benefit analyses, cost-utility analyses, and cost-feasibility analyses, to name a few. Unlike cost-effectiveness studies, in cost-benefit analyses effort is made to measure both costs and benefits in monetary units. However, sometimes it is difficult to measure the absolute benefit of interventions. Since many benefits are intangible and cannot be easily converted to a dollar value (for example, improved self-esteem, the creation of a new park or playground), often those conducting these studies make estimates that you may or may not feel are defendable. Such findings should be viewed cautiously until you check their assumptions and methodology.

Although cost-analysis models can get very complex, social workers should not avoid them. The profession of social work will be enhanced to the extent to which we can show a skeptical public that costs to society are far greater when social services are inadequately funded than when sufficient funds are provided for prevention and remediation programs. Important programmatic decisions should not be made without evaluation data to guide us. To the extent that we can successfully identify the most efficient *and* effective programs, the prestige of the social work profession will be enhanced by a grateful and appreciative society.

There are numerous models from which to pattern a program evaluation. Some of the differences among these approaches are subtle, others are not. In planning an evaluation, you need to select a model that makes sense to you and with which you feel comfortable. In this chapter, my goal has been to familiarize you with just a few of many designs. The evaluation literature is replete with models, designs, and types. If you delve into this material you'll come across others terms that have not been discussed here. For instance, you may learn someone has conducted a summative evaluation (a final, concluding type—as opposed to formative) or has used the CIPP Model (an acronym for context, input, process, and product), and there's a host of others. Many of these have come from the field of education. However, you should be able to fit most of these models or designs into one of the broad types of evaluation that have been identified in this chapter.

Practical Considerations for Making the Evaluation Process Smooth

While the conceptualization of the evaluation design often seems like the most difficult part, any number of factors can influence the choice of a design—even the political climate within the agency. Ideally, it is helpful to know something about a program's history and its personnel before being asked to evaluate it. As a new staff person, student intern, or contract evaluator, however, you may not have the opportunity to gain "inside" information. So, what can you do?

First and foremost, the evaluator needs to keep in mind that all evaluation is inherently threatening. Practically all of us feel uncomfortable when we are being evaluated—especially when the evaluator is unknown to us. We are even more threatened when we think that person doesn't like us—or might want to eliminate our jobs. Therefore, the evaluator needs to be sensitive to the feelings of those who may be affected by the findings of the program evaluation. Try not to create anxiety within the staff. Communicate frequently with involved personnel. Avoid surprises. If at all possible, involve staff in the planning of the evaluation. Ask for their ideas. Remember that evaluations are a political activity. Someone may have a vested interest in making one program look good at the expense of another. Some policymakers may hope to use the program evaluation to justify firing staff or cutting a particular program's budget.

Second, expect obstacles and objections to the evaluation effort to arise. Even staff members who should be supportive may have strongly held but erroneous beliefs about the evaluation. There may be weird political alliances and defenders of the status quo who view the evaluation as terrifying because it will bring about change from the way things have "always been done." As a result, some staff may overtly not cooperate and others may conveniently "forget" to complete assignments or forms. Other staff will be too afraid to reply honestly and candidly for fear of being recognized.

Third, it is recommended that you develop a contract or, if that seems too formal, then a detailed memo describing your understanding of the following:

1. The *purpose* of the evaluation, including questions to be answered or hypotheses to be tested. You may also want to list the evaluation design to be used.

2. The *audience* for whom you will be writing the evaluation report. (Will it go only to the program director, the whole staff, the board of directors, the public?)
3. The *amount of time* you have to conduct the evaluation and write the final report.
4. The terms of your *reimbursement* or the amount of time that you will be released from your regular duties to conduct the evaluation.
5. The *budget* or amount that you can spend purchasing standardized instruments, visiting other programs, photocopying, and so on.

Don't be afraid to negotiate if you feel that you need more time or funds to do the job right. Put it all in writing, even the issue of who will have access to the data for purposes of publication. You may want to state that you will have first opportunity to use the data or ask for something like six months of exclusive use.

Reading Program Evaluation Reports

Even if you don't think you will ever be interested in conducting a program evaluation, at some point in your social work career you will come across a program evaluation report. It may be an evaluation of your program that has been conducted by some "outsider" or consultant. Or, you may be asked to read an evaluation of a program in order to determine if that program should be adopted by your agency. As a board member, administrator, or policymaker, you may attend a program evaluation presentation so that decisions can be made about whether a program should be continued, curtailed, or expanded. Some evaluations will be poorly done and have little merit, others will be thoughtfully conceptualized and well executed, providing substantive evaluative information for decision making. What are some of the criteria to help you distinguish the better from the poorer evaluations?

In the evaluation report you would expect to find the same components (the introduction, the literature review, the methodology, the results, and the discussion) as are found in most research reports and as described in detail in chapter 13. However, unlike a survey, content analysis, or secondary data analysis, with a program evaluation you would be interested in a detailed description of the target client population. Some of the questions you might want to see addressed about this group and the intervention they receive are as follows: Is the group who received the treatment clearly described? Do clients have a prior history or are they first-time offenders? Was random sampling used? If not, what steps were taken to try and create equivalence between the treatment group and the intervention group? To what extent do the subjects in the evaluation resemble clients with whom you are familiar?

Do you have enough information about them to conclude that they seem to be representative of clients with this particular problem?

In terms of design, if the evaluators don't use a control group, how convincing is their argument that the intervention is responsible for the desired changes in clients' behavior? Have they overlooked any other possible explanations?

Do the authors adequately describe the intervention with regard to its length, duration, frequency, and the efforts they made to ensure that it was implemented with fidelity? Did the staff receive special training? Are their credentials discussed?

How have the evaluators operationalized their dependent variables? Are the measurement procedures clear and objective? Are they verifiable? Are you convinced that the measures are reliable and valid? Have they provided you with enough information that you could replicate the study?

Are the data analyzed and interpreted properly? Do the authors overgeneralize or go beyond their data? Are the sample sizes adequate? Are the proper statistical tests used? Does the author confuse differences between groups with statistical significance?

Students who want even more information to help them read and professionally critique an evaluation report may wish to consult Blythe (1983) or Thyer (1991) for guidelines.

Self-Review

(Answers at the end of the book)

1. Which type of evaluation design answers the question: Whom are we serving?
2. Which type of evaluation design answers the question: What would make this a better program?
3. Process evaluations are primarily:
   a. narrative
   b. statistical
   c. hypothetical
4. Which type of evaluation design answers the question: How pleased are clients with our services?
5. Which type of evaluation design answers the question: Are clients being helped?
6. Which type of evaluation design answers the question: What does it cost to help a client?
7. T or F.   The focus of process evaluation is not so much on the number of client successes as on what happened during the intervention and why.

8. The main reason client satisfaction data can't be considered "proof" that a program is effective is_____.

9. Another name for an evaluation type that examines client utilization data is_____,

10. List four considerations when planning a program evaluation.

Questions for Class Discussion

1. The following could be called "Exemplars of Poor Evaluation Designs." What is wrong with each of the following plans for evaluating programs?

    a. The agency is a halfway house run by the Department of Corrections. Residents are all young men who have been in prison for the first time and are now on parole in a prerelease program. In this program evaluation, three new residents who have outward signs of depressions will be selected and compared with two other residents who are not depressed. The Zung Self-Rating Depression Inventory will be the instrument used to determine if a caring attitude by the program staff and conjugal visits can help with adjustment from prison to the larger community. A pretest-posttest design will be employed.

    b. A school has developed a latchkey program for students in the elementary grades. Parents who want to participate must contribute $50 a week for the program for each child enrolled. A pre-experimental (posttest-only with nonequivalent groups) design will be used to compare students enrolled in the program with other students who could benefit from it but whose parents can't pay the fee. At the end of the school year comparisons will be made on the variable of academic achievement. In order to show that the program is effective, the principal hand picks the students who will be in the control group based on low reading and math scores.

    c. A family preservation program wants to perform an outcome evaluation. A student intern is given the names and phone numbers for the last fifty closed cases. Success is defined as "no subsequent abuse." The student is instructed to call the fifty former clients and, after introducing herself, to ask if there has been any subsequent abuse in the families since the cases were closed. If she receives an affirmative response, there is another set of questions she is supposed to ask.

2. What conditions in an agency would make it "ripe" for evaluation?

3. What conditions in an agency would make it difficult to conduct evaluation there?

4. Does evaluation always have to be threatening? When would it not be?

Mini-Projects for Experiencing Research Firsthand

1. Locate an example of client utilization data from a social service agency. (Sometimes this information is printed in annual reports.) Examine this data to see if you can determine what groups the agency is primarily serving. Then, obtain census data for the same geographic region. Compare rates of key variables. For instance, if the percentage of older adults in the larger population is 10 percent, what percentage of older adults is the agency serving? How do the rates of minorities in the community and those being served compare? What other comparisons would be important to make?

2. For a real or fictitious agency, develop a program evaluation proposal that could realistically be implemented. Be sure to describe the program and then address:
   a. What questions do you want to investigate?
   b. Define your dependent and independent variables.
   c. Which design or methodology approach will you use?
   d. How will you collect your data?
   e. How will you analyze your data?
   f. What limitations will your study have?

Resources and References

Ankuta, G.Y. and Abeles, N. (1993). Client satisfaction, clinical significance, and meaningful change in psychotherapy. *Professional Psychology: Research and Practice*, 24, 70–74.

Beutler, L.E. (1993). Designing outcome studies: Treatment of adult victims of childhood sexual abuse. *Journal of Interpersonal Violence*, 8, 402–414.

Blythe, B.J. (1983). A critique of outcome evaluation in child abuse treatment. *Child Welfare*, 62, 325–335.

Buescher, P.A., Larson, L.C., Nelson, M.D., and Lenihan, A.J. (1993) Prenatal WIC participation can reduce low birth weight and newborn medical costs: A cost benefit analysis of WIC participation in North Carolina. *Journal of the American Dietetic Association*, 93, 163–166.

Deane, F.P. (1993). Client satisfaction with psychotherapy in two outpatient clinics in New Zealand. *Evaluation and Program Planning*, 16, 87–94.

Decker, J.T., Starrett, R., and Redhorse, J. (1986). Evaluating the cost-effectiveness of employee assistance programs *Social Work*, 31(5), 391–393.

Gaston, L., and Sabourin, S. (1992). Client satisfaction and social desirability in psychotherapy. *Evaluation and Program Planning*, 15, 227–231.

Greene, V.L., Lovely, M.E., and Ondrich, J.I. (1993). The cost-effectiveness of community services in a frail elderly population. *The Gerontologist*, 33(2), 177–189.

Larsen, D.L. Attkisson, C.C., Hargreaves, W.A., and Nguyen, T.D. (1979). Assessment of client/patient satisfaction: Development of a general scale. *Evaluation and Program Planning*, 2, 197–207.

LaSala, M.C. (1997). Client satisfaction: Consideration of correlates and response bias. *Families in Society*, 78, 54–64.

Lebow, J. (1982). Consumer satisfaction with mental health treatment. *Psychological Bulletin*, 91(2), 244–259.

Meltzer, H.Y., Cola, P., Way, L., Thompson, P.A., Basteni, B., Davies, M.A., and Snitz, B. (1993). Cost effectiveness of clozapine in neuroleptic-resistant schizophrenia. *American Journal of Psychiatry*, 150(11), 1630–1638.

O'Farrell, T.J., Choquette, K.A., Cutter, H.S., and Brown, E. (1996). Cost-benefit and cost-effectiveness analyses of behavioral marital therapy with and without relapse prevention sessions for alcoholics and their spouses. *Behavior Therapy*, 27, 7–24.

Pekarick, G., and Wolff, C.B. (1996). Relationship of satisfaction to symptom change, follow-up adjustment, and clinical significance. *Professional Psychology: Research and Practice*, 27, 202–208.

Perreault, M., and Leichner, P. (1993). Patient satisfaction with outpatient psychiatric services: Qualitative and quantitative assessments. *Evaluation and Program Planning*, 16, 109–118.

Peterson, L. and Bell-Dolan, D. (1995). Treatment outcome research in child psychology: Realistic coping with the "Ten Commandments of Methodology." *Journal of Clinical Child Psychology*, 24, 149–162.

Polowczyk, D., Brutus, M., Orvieto, A.A., Vidal, J., and Cipriana, D. (1993). Comparison of patient and staff surveys of consumer satisfaction. *Hospital and Community Psychiatry*, 44, 589–591.

Rogers, E.S. (1997). Cost-benefit studies in vocational services. *Psychiatric Rehabilitation Journal*, 20, 25–33.

Royse, D. (1985). Client satisfaction with the helping process: A review for the pastoral counselor. *Journal of Pastoral Care*, 39(1), 3–11.

Thyer, B. (1991). Guidelines for evaluating outcome studies on social work practice. *Research on Social Work Practice*, 1(1), 76–91.

Winegar, N., Bistline, J.L., and Sheridan, S. (1992). Implementing a group therapy program in a managed-care setting: Combining cost-effectiveness and quality care. *Families in Society*, 73(1): 56–58.

CHAPTER 11
Qualitative Research

You can observe a lot by just watching.

—Yogi Berra (1998)

One summer day I was driving through a rural part of Appalachia where years before the chief source of income had been the mining of coal. As the deep, rich veins of underground coal had been removed, high rates of unemployment caused many families to live in abject poverty in the midst of lush greenery of Daniel Boone National Forest. As we slowed to pass through one small town, I casually looked off to the side and immediately noticed a young man who was unlike any others I had ever seen. The left side of his face hung loose and sagged like a large deflated balloon, the skin hanging four or five inches below his chin. At first, I thought my eyes were playing tricks on me and that he was wearing a Halloween mask. But he wasn't, the right side of his face, as best I could determine, appeared perfectly ordinary. He was engaged in a conversation with two other fellows who, by their mannerisms, seemed to suggest that everything was quite normal.

I didn't stop the car and talk to the young man, although I burned with curiosity about him. Had he been told there was nothing medical science could do for him? Indeed, had he even sought medical attention—or had he merely assumed that nothing could be done?

Had he been sheltered, kept from school where children would have made fun? If he didn't go to school, did he work? Did he have many friends? What psychological defense mechanisms had he developed to protect him from the stares of strangers? Did he have an intimate partner? What was the quality of his life? How did he pass his time, what did he look forward to? What were his goals and aspirations?

Was he "normal" in intelligence? What was his personality like? Was he bitter and angry? Did he have a sense of humor? In short, who was this man? What was his world like?

If you find yourself reading these questions and almost automatically thinking that you, too, would like to have interviewed this young man in-depth, then you are probably thinking like a qualitative researcher. Even better than an interview would be to live in the same town with the subject for a while, perhaps interviewing his friends and family members, observing how he typically spent his day, who he talked with and about what topics. If the deformed young man kept a diary or journal, that would be of interest too, as would be any letters or documentation. In a sense, a qualitative researcher in this instance would be like a biographer, and the research report would be almost journalistic.

If, on the other hand, you found yourself thinking of hypotheses that involved groups (for example, do persons with profound facial deformities have lower self-esteem than a cross-section of eighteen-year-olds), then you are thinking like a quantitative researcher. Not that you have to choose sides and think one way or the other, but quantitative researchers will approach their topics quite differently than qualitative researchers.

Phillipe Berthelot once wrote, "If one man dies, it is a tragedy; if a thousand men die, it is a statistic." Sometimes when we are dealing with large numbers (for example, more than 465,000 children in substitute care, the Cook County, Illinois, public guardian represents 31,000 children), the problem is almost incomprehensible. But when our focus is on one family or a handful of children, then we experience the tragedy. This is, in my opinion, the value of qualitative research—its ability to help us understand social problems by focusing on a poignant few.

Qualitative researchers seek to understand the life experiences of those who may not be visible or well-known to "mainstream" society. They may, for instance, seek to describe the social worlds of drug addicts, prostitutes, the chronically mentally ill, illegal immigrants, persons dying of terminal illness, victims of abuse, or mothers who have put children up for adoption. But a subject doesn't have to be out of the mainstream to be of interest to a qualitative researcher.

This past summer I had some minor surgery. Right before I was wheeled into the operating room I heard one nurse turn to another, and in response to a question about me say, "Oh, he's healthy." While I was relieved to hear those three words, I immediately wondered what someone perhaps a little older than me or in more frail health might hear. An interesting qualitative research project might be to interview persons who have undergone surgery to discover what they learned about their illness or health status inadvertently from the conversations of medical personnel who were talking about them to each other. Do patients discover that they are not "healthy" from the over-heard conversations of others? Would they first receive the news that they were seriously ill by accident? Could they learn that the operation might not do any good, that they might not survive?

Characteristics of Qualitative Research

No intervention: There is no intervention, no control group, no experimental design or manipulation of the variables associated with the phenomenon under study.

Naturalistic: Unlike quantitative research, qualitative research (sometimes called field research because of its emphasis on conducting the study in the subjects' natural environment) is not as structured in the sense of knowing exactly what questions will be asked of whom and in what order. In fact, field researchers are quite comfortable with letting the study evolve and flow in unknown directions. Before going into the field, they may not have identified all of the persons they hope to interview or even all the questions they want to ask. Many rely upon a snowball methodology where one informant may lead them to another and so on.

Participant-observation: Researchers in the qualitative tradition rely primarily upon in-depth interviewing and observations. They might choose to observe only, but many qualitative researchers would be strong advocates for participant-observation—meaning that the investigator would try, as much as possible, to "walk in the shoes" of the subject being studied. Thus, social workers interested in the stigma associated with poverty might want to have the experience of shopping with food stamps to see if they are treated differently than when they use cash. The participant-observer could live for a while in a public housing project, shop for clothes at the Salvation Army Thrift Store, try to subsist on a poverty budget.

Small sample size: Qualitative researchers do not worry about obtaining large, representative sample sizes. For example, Davidson (1997) conducted a qualitative needs assessment of relatives providing care for children who might otherwise have gone into foster care. Although she randomly drew names from a list of 420 relative caregivers, Davidson's goal was to obtain ten interviews. She actually completed nine.

Little use of measurements: Unlike quantitative research, which deals with measurements and numerical values almost exclusively, qualitative researcher may use scales or questionnaires, but most don't. The investigator is the research tool; all data are filtered through his or her eyes and ears.

Journalistic narrative: The analyses produced by qualitative researchers most often are narratives and are based on the words used by informants to describe their life experiences. Jill Berrick (1995), for instance, learned enough as a participant-observer of five impoverished families to write a book entitled *Faces of Poverty: Portraits of Women and Children on Welfare*. Again, the emphasis is not on the quantity of subjects but on the rich details, the subtleties and interactions that may be overlooked by others.

Exploratory: Quantitative researchers explore problems and phenomena about which little is known. Unlike quantitative research, seldom is there any interest in testing a hypothesis or theory. While quantitative researchers tend to be *deductive* (using a specific theory to make predictions about a particular situation), qualitative research is basically *inductive*—generating new theory from the observation of a special phenomenon or situation.

Value-free: The researcher's position is that of learner, not expert or specialist; he or she wants to know, "What's going on here?" Assumptions and prior knowledge are held in abeyance until the latter stages of the analysis when they may then be compared to the findings (Morse and Field, 1995).

Qualitative researchers seek to understand the experiences of selected individuals—not to test hypotheses so much as to explore the question: What it is like? Have you ever wondered what it would be like to live in a nursing home? What would it be like to have a stroke, to lose the use of the left side of your body? How would your life change if you had to quit your job because of Alzheimer's disease? Qualitative researchers are interested in phenomena like this—topics that delve into the processes that shape and alter lives.

Qualitative approaches provide detail and add richness and depth to our understanding of any phenomenon being investigated and are similar to the "case studies" so familiar to social workers. Let's take the question "What is it like to live in a nursing home?" A story told to me by a former student provides an illustration of how one incident can tell much about the quality of life in a particular nursing home. In talking with a resident about what it was like living in the home, the student heard the following account: One day, several residents were in the back wing of the building watching television when two fellows, who didn't look like they belonged there, appeared. They announced that they were television repairmen and proceeded to cart away the television, which had been working perfectly. Being somewhat suspicious, one resident slipped away to her room and pressed her call button, which rang at the nurses' station. Meanwhile, the men loaded the television into a truck and left. Twenty minutes later, one of the staff strolled back to the resident's room to see why the call button had been used.

This incident raises several questions about the quality of care being provided in that nursing home. First, why did it take the staff so long to answer the call button? What would have happened if there had been a true emergency, such as a nursing home resident choking on a piece of food or falling out of bed? How good is the security in the facility—do residents fear that they will be robbed or their personal possessions stolen? If we were to informally interview other residents from this nursing home, we might find other equally alarming accounts. Such accounts provide a richer image of the quality of life in the nursing home than any objective scale that quantitatively measures such dimensions as the residents' satisfaction with life, or their loneliness and depression. The qualitative researcher is interested in what happens in the social world of nursing home residents. What is a typical day like?

Using a quantitative approach, we would begin by identifying some problem or by stating a testable hypothesis, for example, "Nursing home residents are more lonely or depressed than older adults who do not live in nursing homes." Even if we surveyed a large sample of older adults and gathered sufficient data, we still would have only a limited perspective on what life is like in a nursing home; the quality of the day-to-day life in the home would escape us.

Qualitative research is different from the type of research that has been discussed so far. In quantitative research, the investigator relies on counting, measuring, and analyzing numbers. In qualitative research, there is little or no use made of statistics. While counting may be employed, it is not the major emphasis. The qualitative researcher seeks to understand social relationships and patterns of interaction. Anecdotal accounts are used to describe the world of the persons being investigated.

The client or subject is acknowledged as the insider, the teacher, the expert concerning his or her world, and the qualitative researcher seeks to enter into the subjective reality, to discover that unique world. Unlike diagnostic or investigatory interviews that social workers may conduct, the qualitative interviewer does not try to maintain a formal distance or "objective" stance. The interview is conversational and the goal is to form a dialogue to facilitate the investigator's journey (Franklin and Jordan, 1995).

Qualitative researchers are flexible; their research goals or questions may be altered even while data are being collected. While they usually have a methodology in mind prior to starting their project, they do not require that the research design and methodology be rigidly and unalterably stated before they begin to collect data. There is nothing "wrong" with this fluidity, since many researchers feel that the purpose of qualitative research is to generate hypotheses for later testing. In this sense, qualitative research is commonly regarded as being exploratory.

For instance, Olson and Haynes (1993) set out to discover how successful single parents raised their children. Their data came from an exploratory study of twenty-six parents who were obtained by contacting psychologists, clergy, educators, and medical personnel who nominated individuals with positive attitudes toward their parental role and who also appeared competent in that role. From fifty nominations, twenty-six having the most traits associated with healthy families were personally interviewed for approximately two hours each. The transcripts from these interviews were read by the researchers and themes were identified. From these interviews seven themes emerged, such as: acceptance of the responsibility and challenges of being a single parent, prioritization of the parental role, and employment of consistent, nonpunitive discipline that provided structure and logical consequences for behaviors.

Qualitative and quantitative researchers have distinctive world views: "Quants" believe reality can be objectively determined, while "Quals" take the position that reality is subjective and is experienced differently by each speaker as he or she filters it through individual cognitions and conceptualizations. For the Quants, methodology is everything and rigidly guides their data collection and analysis. They generally have an easy time knowing when they are finished. For the Quals, methodology is not nearly as important. Since there is no hypothesis to "drive" the investigation, Quals may not know when they have collected sufficient data. One qualitative researcher aptly characterized the differences between the two traditions this way, "It is only at the point of closure to a qualitative research experience . . . that the complex, layered experience in which we engage begins to take shape as a sensible whole that can be—and indeed has been—organized, interpreted, and, perhaps, understood" (Meloy, 1994, p. 12). That quotation was from a chapter entitled, "Understanding by Finishing: The End Is the Beginning."

Among social scientists, cultural anthropologists and some sociologists are best known for their use of qualitative research methods. Sometimes these approaches are known as **ethnography** (folk description—describing a culture from a "native's" point of view) or **ethnomethodology** (the analysis of language and rules that underlie everyday events and social interactions).

Methods Used in Qualitative Research

Qualitative researchers use procedures that produce descriptive narrative data. These are:

- *Observation.* The observer locates him- or herself in an unobtrusive place in order to view the behavior, the social processes, or the individuals of interest. Blending into the setting is desirable, but it is not necessary for the observer to be hidden from sight. The observer's presence should not change the nature of the activities normally occurring.

- *Personal interviews.* Observers may employ in-depth interviewing of informants. Open-ended questions are asked that allow the subjects to talk about experiences, concerns, and views of their world.
- *Reading of personal documents.* Letters, diaries, autobiographies, and photographic albums may be used as sources of information providing "insider" views.
- *Participant-observation.* The qualitative researcher attempts to become fully immersed in the culture of those being observed by living alongside them and sharing their activities. The observer does what his or her subjects do (without violating personal or professional ethics, of course).

Let's return to the problem of trying to understand what life in a nursing home is like. What might you learn if all you did was observe? How would this compare to what you might discover if you were able to employ a little deception and have yourself admitted as a patient? (*Note:* You don't have to be eighty-five to be in a nursing home—younger individuals with fragile medical conditions can be found there, too.)

Although the research is quite dated now, some fascinating participant-observation was done by Rosenhan (1973). Eight sane "pseudopatients" sought admission at a variety of psychiatric hospitals. All were admitted when they complained of hearing voices and were kept an average of nineteen days (the range was from seven to fifty-two), although they ceased simulating any symptoms once they were admitted. None of them were detected as being sane, and most were discharged with a diagnosis of schizophrenia "in remission."

There are numerous other "classic" examples of this kind of research that might interest you. See, for example, Caudill, Redlich, Gilmore, and Brody (1952), Deane (1961), Ishiyama, Batman, and Hewitt (1967), Goldman, Bohr, and Steinberg (1970), and Estroff (1981).

For an extra-credit assignment one semester, an MSW student at my university attempted to find out how the public would view her if she were morbidly obese. She went to a thrift store and bought the largest sweater and the largest pants she could find and then used foam stuffing to make herself appear to weigh about 400 pounds. Once her disguise was in place, she went to a local mall and visited stores like Victoria's Secret. She said she was surprised that no clerks even asked if they could be of help when she was "fat," but they were eager to assist her when she went back without the padding.

You don't have to wear a disguise to be a participant-observer. Almost every semester a number of students borrow wheelchairs and spend a day learning about the obstacles and barriers than can make life difficult for those who have lost the use of their legs. What might you learn about your campus or your community if you spent eight hours in a wheelchair? What would you discover about the effects of stroke if you immobilized your right arm with a sling or elastic bandage?

Focus Groups

There has been growing use of qualitative focus groups, particularly by businesses. When compared to interviews, focus groups generate greater interaction among participants, which may then result in valuable suggestions for advertising, packaging, and product improvement. Focus groups are increasingly being adopted by nonprofit agencies because they are relatively inexpensive and do not require a large investment of time for development or analysis of findings.

In a recent report, social workers conducted focus groups with young adults who were former consumers of an independent-living program designed for youth in out-of-home care. The consumers were asked such questions as "What services helped you learn to live on your own?" and "What did you find helpful in the programs?" The audiotaped focus group sessions were transcribed and then themes were identified from a reading of the transcripts. The former consumers found that, among the nine themes that were identified, instruction in managing a budget was particularly valuable. The most dominant theme, however, was that participants appreciated the opportunity that the independent living program provided for meeting other young people who were in a similar situation. This helped to reduce their feelings of isolation and stigmatization (McMillen, Rideout, Fisher, and Tucker, 1997).

Steps in Doing Qualitative Research

Although qualitative researchers do not all go through a set of predetermined steps, it is still possible to talk generally about the process of beginning a qualitative investigation.

The first step involves the identification of a topic, a problem, a phenomenon, or a group of people of interest. Generally, an initial question or small set of questions has prompted the investigator's curiosity. Simultaneously, the investigator is probably also thinking about a field site where the study could or should be conducted. Generally, these would be locations where the researcher is not known.

Next, it is a good idea to become familiar with any literature relevant to your topic. Belcher (1994), for instance, reviewed the literature on homelessness before developing open-ended questions to be used with interviewing persons in the "homeless community" of Baltimore, Maryland. However, with qualitative research, there is no requirement that the literature review comes before beginning to collect data. Some qualitative researchers consult the literature during or after data collection. At least one (Agar, 1980) has taken the extreme position that literature reviews result in "clouding" the researcher's mind with the misconceptions and mistakes of others. He has noted that a thorough literature review "introduced a lot of unnecessary noise into my mind as I tried to learn about being a heroin addict from 'patients' in the institution" (p. 25). Qualitative researchers try to empty their minds of preconceptions and prejudices—to become "open" to alternative ways of thinking about and viewing the world.

The argument for diminishing the importance of the literature review is based on the belief that the ethnographer's role is "to give some sense of different lifestyles to people who either do not know about them, or who are so bogged down in their own stereotypes that they do not understand them" (Agar, 1980, pp. 26–27). Agar recommends that the investigator become familiar with the topic by talking with people who have worked with the group of interest, by reading novels that produce a "feel" for the lifestyle of the group, and by viewing existing literature with a skeptic's eye.

The third step involves gaining access to the field site and interacting with the people there, observing their activities, and possibly obtaining one or more informants to interpret events and help the researcher to gain further entry into private settings and activities. Informants are inside experts on the culture or group who are willing to share their everyday experiences and serve as translators—helping the qualitative researcher to acquire the necessary vocabulary to maneuver within that culture. Sometimes it is necessary to build rapport and long-term relationships with insiders before meaningful data collection can begin.

It is much easier to stress the importance of establishing rapport than it is to actually accomplish good rapport. Every culture or subculture is different. Rapport can be difficult to establish if the researcher is insensitive to local practices and patterns of communication. For instance, Thompson (1989), in writing about her experiences in Islamic countries, noted that indirect methods of communication and action are socially preferable to direct methods.

> If a person wants to raise an issue with another, he or she will visit the other, have tea, talk a great deal about generalities, and only at the end of the visit mention his or her real purpose in an offhanded way. . . . They couch negative responses in carefully selected terms so as not to offend or disappoint others. (P. 40)

The way one would go about building rapport with an informant in an Islamic country is very different from the approach one would use on the streets of New York.

Each researcher has a number of roles from which to choose. He or she may inform others about his or her student status or research project. Some researchers choose to go "under cover" and keep their true identities secret, allowing them to become full participants or participant-observers. Further, researchers can elect to be merely observers—whether they do it surreptitiously or not.

Data collection, step four, begins almost immediately and includes virtually everything the researcher sees, hears, or smells—information from all the senses as well as artifacts or objects of interest obtained from that culture. Interviews may be conducted and usually are unstructured—that is, not using predetermined questions. These interviews can occur on the street, in homes, or wherever the informants may be. Because the qualitative researcher is a learner, he or she does a lot of listening and writes a lot of field notes. These notes help the recall of important events and conversations. Unlike those investigators who are more interested in quantification, qualitative researchers can record feelings and interpretations in their field notes.

Questions about the culture or subgroup arise from observation of informants in different situations as they engage in various activities as well as from the need to confirm or consolidate newly acquired knowledge. Agar (1980) expressed his interest in predetermined questions this way:

> It's not necessarily that ethnographers don't want to test hypotheses. It's just that if they do, the variables and operationalizations and sample specifications must grow from an understanding of the group rather than from being hammered on top of it no matter how poor the fit. (Pp. 69–70)

Whether or not to record interviews on audio- or videotape is an issue with which researchers must wrestle. When you record (whether on the site or later, when you are at home) and how you record (tape-recorder or written notes) are up to you. Even with guarantees of anonymity, respondents often will not talk freely in the presence of a tape recorder or other such devices. Should you decide to record interviews, remember that you'll need to transcribe them or hire someone to make transcriptions. If you don't do the work yourself, it will be important to compare the written transcription against the tapes to make sure that they are accurate and that meaningful silences are reflected as well as false starts, nonlexicals like "uhm" and discourse markers like "y'know" (Riessman, 1993). In an effort to "clean up" the transcription, someone with good intentions could remove patterns of speech or hesitancies that characterize or indicate something of importance in the insider's world.

While informants may not be as threatened by note-taking, this will depend upon what they are saying and where they are at the time. In addition to interesting incidents, record the setting, the participants involved, and key words in conversations (if you are unable to record conversations verbatim). It is not crucial to have a perfect reproduction of what was said. Approximate wording and paraphrasing are acceptable. However, it is important to capture the meaning of any remarks. If you make sketchy notes in the field, expand them as soon afterwards as possible so that the details of important observations and incidents are not forgotten.

The last step in qualitative research is analyzing the data and writing the report. As with quantitative methods, the qualitative investigator is looking for patterns. As transcriptions and field notes are read, the researcher looks for categories that allow information to be organized into themes. For instance, if you had conducted interviews with street gang members, you might logically begin to group together relevant parts of their conversations on such topics as their views about police, girlfriends, guns, drugs, families, and school. Similarly, it makes sense to look for norms in their behavior—did they have predictable ways of responding in certain situations? Because this is "interpretive" research, there is no single cookbook approach for how the data ought to be sorted or analyzed.

Computer software (such as *Nudist*) exists to assist the researcher in finding key words and cataloguing text. Gilgun and Connor (1989) used the program *Ethnograph* to analyze life history interviews to understand how male sexual offenders viewed child sexual abuse.

Reports of qualitative research are, as noted earlier, most often narrative. A large portion of these reports are concerned with the events and conversations that occurred while the investigator was in the field. Characteristically, segments of conversations are often reproduced to illustrate the insiders' view of life.

Reliability and Validity in Qualitative Studies

Qualitative researchers approach the issues of reliability and validity of their findings somewhat differently than quantitative investigators. Belcher (1994) notes that three different strategies are used to establish trustworthiness or credibility, which "is analogous to establishing validity and reliability" (p. 128). These efforts involve:

1. *Prolonged engagement*—investing sufficient time to not only learn about the culture but also test one's understanding of it.
2. *Persistent observation*—to observe daily and keep records of the observations.
3. *Triangulation*—utilizing multiple sources of information to cross-check for inconsistencies or misinformation.

Qualitative researchers have numerous ways of checking for reliability. For instance, if an informant were to reveal something that the investigator didn't think was true, he or she may want to ask other informants, to get confirmation from the police or other officials, or to view records or reports, newspaper accounts, or other forms of evidence. The importance of certain observations can be verified with different respondents within the same culture or tested again at a later time with the initial informant. Because qualitative researchers do not rely upon a single source of information (such as a survey questionnaire or scale) but have "been there" themselves, they feel that qualitative research has greater validity than quantitative research.

Along these same lines, Meloy (1994) has identified six "thought-provoking questions" that make for fine principles for judging qualitative research:

1. *Verité*. Does it ring true? Are the findings consistent with generally accepted knowledge?
2. *Integrity*. Does it hang together? As a piece of research, is it logical, structurally sound?
3. *Rigor*. Is it superficial with simplistic reasoning?
4. *Utility*. Is it useful? Does it make a contribution?
5. *Vitality*. Does it communicate the excitement of discovery?
6. *Aesthetics*. Is it enriching, provide insight, touch your spirit?

If, after reading a piece of qualitative research, you can answer in the affirmative to all or almost all of these questions, then there would be little doubt that the work you have read meets the test of reliability (Could the same findings be produced again?) and validity (Are the findings real?).

Program Evaluation with Qualitative Approaches

Sometimes a qualitative approach is exactly what is needed to diagnose problems within a program or agency. Reflect on these questions: "How do clients experience your agency? Is the receptionist pleasant and courteous? Do staff treat clients with respect? What would it be like to be a client at your agency?

Over the years, I've heard stories of secretaries who wouldn't answer the phone because they were on a break, of receptionists who shouted at clients. I've observed counselors who would not see their clients early even if they were not busy and the clients were in the waiting room crying. I've been in buildings where the walls were so thin that voices from the next office traveled through the walls, where there wasn't enough parking, and where there were no handicapped-accessible facilities.

It could be interesting to pose as a client to see how you would be treated. What kinds of things go on that staff in the agency don't notice as problems? Perhaps the most vivid example that comes to my mind took place in a rural shelter for battered women. The shelter had a policy of requiring women residents who needed to make a phone call to go down the street and use a pay phone. The shelter's administrator did not seem to be concerned about the danger to these women each time one made a phone call from outside the shelter.

Books with Ethnographic Perspectives

The following books not only are interesting to read but also illustrate the qualitative approach to investigating various facets of society.

Bissinger, H.G. (1991). *Friday night lights: A town, and a dream.* New York: HarperCollins.

Bonazzi, R. (1997). *Man in the mirror: John Howard Griffin and the story of black like me.* Maryknoll, NY: Orbis Books.

Griffin, J.H. (1961, 1996). *Black like me.* New York: NAL/Dutton.

Kotlowitz, A. (1991). *There are no children here: The story of two boys growing up in the other America.* New York: Doubleday.

Liebow, E. (1993). *Tell them who I am: The lives of homeless women.* New York: Penguin Books.

Miner, H. (1993). *Body ritual among the Nacirema.* New York: Irvington.

Odzer, C. (1997). *Patpong sisters: An American woman's view of the Bangkok sex world.* New York: Arcade.

Ratner, M.S. (1993). *Crack pipe as pimp: An ethnographic investigation of sex-for-crack exchanges.* New York: Lexington Books.

Sikes, G. (1997). *8 Ball chicks: A year in the violent world of girl gangsters.* New York: Anchor Books.

Simon, D. (1997). *The corner: A year in the life of an inner-city neighborhood.* New York: Broadway Books.

Snow, D. and Anderson, L. (1993). *Down on their luck: A study of homeless street people.* Berkeley: University of California Press.

Taylor, S.J., Bogdan, R., and Lutfiyya, X. (1995). *The variety of community experience: Qualitative studies of family and community life.* Baltimore: Paul Brooks.

What do you think of a residential facility for teens that provided no food for a Sunday meal? And what if the only staff person on duty was a student in practicum who had to leave one teen in charge while she went to the grocery and bought supplies with her own money? Would you want to refer a client there?

Qualitative investigators conducting a program evaluation of an agency or program would not be counting successful clients or documenting how much clients had improved. Their interests would be in how clients' lives have changed as a result of the intervention they've received. The qualitative program evaluator would be looking for the values and benefits that the intervention provided for clients (Ruckdeschel, Earnshaw, and Firrek, 1994). As Goldstein (1997) has noted, "It is not how to count but what counts in peoples' lives that will begin to enlighten and shape the course and nature of our inquiries" (p. 452). And along this line, the qualitative investigator would address the program or agency's adequacy by examining the clients' experiences as they reported them in their own words.

Qualitative research approaches are superior to quantitative methods in some instances. For example, to test whether an apartment complex manager discriminates against nonwhites, an excellent way is to have a person of color make application and then, an hour or so later, a white person make application. If the first person was informed there were no vacancies, but the second person was shown a vacant apartment, then there is good evidence of discrimination—much better than conducting a survey of apartment managers and asking if they discriminate.

The Great Debate

Because of the enormous differences in the way that the research is conducted, quantitatively minded researchers are often suspicious of the findings of qualitative researchers. In the 1950s and 1960s, a debate began in professional journals regarding the relative virtues of quantitative and qualitative methodology. A continuation of this debate over appropriate research methods for social work has vigorously reappeared in recent social work journals. The debate appears to have surfaced once again because social work researchers are making greater use of the quantitative, empirical, scientific (sometimes known as the logical positivist) approach. Advocates for the use of quantitative methods believe that qualitative methods will not produce the knowledge needed to document effectiveness and to guide practice.

On the other hand, those who advocate for greater use of qualitative approaches argue that the trend toward empiricism results in research that is too restrictive and superficial, because of the tendency to investigate only those aspects that can be operationally defined and measured and for which data can be collected. Instead of looking at the whole situation, empiricists fragment a situation and focus on what they can easily count. In the empiricists' quest for "objectivity," important interactions between participants and other details are often overlooked.

Which viewpoint is right? What is the most appropriate research method for social work? Actually, both sides are right. There are limitations associated with both quantitative and qualitative approaches to learning about a phenomenon. As researchers-in-training, you should learn how to use both approaches. Both methodologies can be used profitably by social workers in their practice. Each approach can be used to enrich the findings of the other.

Madey (1982) has addressed the benefits of integrating qualitative and quantitative methods in program evaluation. Some of the ways each approach enriches the other are as follows: Qualitative approaches can assist with the selection of survey items to be used in instrument construction. They can provide external validation of empirically generated constructs. From the field notes of qualitative researchers come real-life examples that can be used to help illustrate the findings of a quantitative study. Quantitative procedures benefit the qualitative researcher by: identifying representative and unrepresentative (overlooked) informants/cases; providing leads for later interviews and observations; correcting "elite bias" (the tendency to interview primarily the elite or gatekeepers in a social system) in the collection of data; and verifying the findings of a qualitative study by systematically collecting data on a larger scale.

A number of other writers have called for qualitative and quantitative approaches to be used together. Kidder and Judd (1986), for instance, note that participant observation can involve quantitative measures. They cite a qualitative study of parole officers in which the investigator used a quantitative approach to investigate a hypothesis dealing with the amount of paperwork performed by each parole officer. The investigator analyzed the number of copies made by each parole officer on the office's photocopying machine as a quantitative (and unobtrusive) measure of parole violations.

Finally, a noted qualitative researcher, William Foote Whyte (1984), said this about the integration of qualitative and quantitative methods:

> Reliance upon a single research method is bound to impede the progress of science. If we use the survey alone, we may gather highly quantitative data measuring the subjective states of respondents, in relation to certain demographic characteristics. ... Some apparently objective questions may yield answers of doubtful validity. ... In any case, the survey yields a snapshot of responses at a particular time. We can fill in this dimension partially with a resurvey, but this by itself only provides evidence of the direction and magnitude of change. Without the use of other methods, we can only speculate on the dynamics of change. (P. 149)

The Problem with Qualitative Research

Qualitative researchers are probably at a disadvantage when it comes to having their research funded and published. This is a serious problem for the social work professional who may be working toward either of those two goals. Here's a couple of excerpts from qualitative researchers who make these same points. "Quantitative research has become the normative mode of inquiry taught in universities, and quantitative researchers have tended to dominate review panels of funding agencies and the editorial boards of prestigious research journals" (Morse and Field, 1995, p. 3).

Marshall and Rossman (1995) have noted: "Reviewers for funding agencies, as well as dissertation committees, sometimes look askance at qualitative research proposals. Too often, proposers speak vaguely of their project research; it seems an unfocused, unplanned desire to go out in the world and 'hang out' or 'muck around' " (p. 5).

Qualitative research is sometimes viewed as not being "serious" research because it does not produce generalizable knowledge. As a result, many academics question its value; funding agencies usually prefer to allocate their monies on projects that will create "hard" rather than "soft" data.

A fierce controversy in the social sciences has been ranging for several years over Margaret Mead's 1928 book, *Coming of Age in Samoa,* which illustrates the problematic nature of qualitative research. Briefly, Mead did not speak Samoan but relied on teenage interpreters. When interviewed in adulthood long after Mead's death, one revealed that they "fibbed and fibbed"— possibly out of embarrassment because of Mead's questions about sexual activity. Did she know when her informants were honest and when they weren't? Further, there are suggestions that Mead was not objective but guilty of presenting only the evidence that supported her view of Samoan village life (Orans, 1996; Cote, 1994; Gardiner, 1993).

The very characteristics of qualitative research (for example, little structure, few guidelines) that make it exciting and innovative may also make it difficult for the qualitative investigator to compete against the quantitatively oriented project for resources. This is not to say that this situation is right or fair, but simply to inform the reader that qualitative research might not always be viewed with the same amount of respect as quantitative research.

There are, undoubtedly, situations where qualitative methods are superior to quantitative approaches. However, the decision to use qualitative methods should not be made quickly. Certainly, there are wrong reasons to choose qualitative approaches: because they seem easier, because they don't require knowledge of statistical procedures and sampling designs, because one doesn't have to be overly concerned with reviewing all the relevant literature.

But the biggest caution has to be that subjective impressions may not square with reality. Gilham, Lucas, and Sivewright (1997), while evaluating two drug education and prevention programs, found a major disparity between impressionistic and empirical assessments. On the one hand, the staff rendered qualitative judgments that the programs were successful and had distinct effects on the youth. Yet results derived from empirical assessments did not support the staff's impressions—the prevention programs did not reduce the proportion of participants reporting recent use of drugs or increase prohibitive attitudes toward drug use. Gilham, Lucas, and Sivewright offer a partial explanation: impressionistic evaluations tend not to focus on the larger group receiving the intervention, but on a small number of individual problem cases that were identified as "successes."

For my money, I think the old maxim is correct, there *is* safety in numbers. And the more numbers, the better.

Final Thoughts on the Quantitative-Qualitative Controversy

Sometimes it seems easy to divide all the world into two parts. Under such a schema, we may identify those who think like we do and those who do not. For example, you may be sympathetic to the qualitative perspective, while your best friend may recognize only research that uses quantitative procedures. Like disagreements over politics and religion, you may become frustrated if you try to convert your friend to your viewpoint. In my opinion, it is more important to recognize the strengths and advantages that each perspective brings to the understanding of a problem or phenomenon than it is to insist upon the superiority of one approach over another.

The findings of qualitative research can be rich and comprehensive, providing insight into poorly understood behaviors or cultures through the use of accounts of actual dialogue and graphic descriptions. Qualitative research vividly brings out perspectives that may be quite different from those with which we started.

Some will feel attracted to qualitative approaches because of the flexibility in determining research designs (and ease of modifying them once data collection has begun) and data collection techniques. Qualitative researchers do not need extensive planning, nor do they need to be too concerned about instruments, sampling, computers, or statistical procedures. Qualitative research can be relatively inexpensive to do if you choose subjects or a culture close by. But, if you must travel quite a distance and have no means to support yourself in that setting, the research could be quite expensive.

It could be said that a qualitative researcher is always prepared when an interesting topic comes across his or her path. No scrambling to find a control group or representative sample is necessary, and there is no need to spend hours in the library trying to find the most psychometrically sound instrument(s) to measure the dependent variables. Most quantitatively oriented researchers could not begin their work so easily.

Qualitative approaches can use procedures to minimize the likelihood that findings are the product of a single misguided observer. A large number of informants and a variety of sources can be used to confirm observations. Since researchers devote an extended period of time to observing and studying the group, there are multiple occasions to "check out" new insights. Open-ended questions may be asked in order to understand other points of view without predetermining them through prior selection of questionnaire items. Then, other participant observers can be brought in to verify findings. The qualitative researcher can even use small group or informal surveys to test hypotheses.

Although I think of myself as more of a Quant than a Qual, I would be the first to admit that on occasion the qualitative researcher learns a great deal more than the quantitative investigator. I also believe that the nature of the study and the questions you want to ask also suggest the most relevant strategy. When I wanted to know about emotional abuse, I didn't try to find an abuser who would allow me to live in his or her household—participant observation would not have been appropriate—but I did locate about a dozen individuals who allowed me to interview them in-depth (Royse, 1994). Their stories tugged at my heart and involved me in a way that would not have occurred if questionnaires had been mailed to them. "Cindy," one of my informants, still drops by to talk to me from time to time to keep me abreast of developments in her life. She is no longer suicidal and seems to be progressing well in her healing.

It would be short-sighted to dismiss qualitative research (or quantitative, for that matter) simply because it might not conform to some notion we hold about the world. Each of these approaches has its place, and the contributions of both have been highlighted in a way that is succinct and profound:

> The methods are analogous to zooming in and zooming out with a lens. To the extent that they are reproduced objectively, wide-angle, telephoto, and microscopic views must be simultaneously valid, and zooming from different directions merely focuses attention on different facets of the same phenomenon.... There are no grounds, logical or otherwise, for calling any view simple. We can start anywhere and zoom in to infinite detail or zoom out to indefinite scope. (Madley, 1982, pp. 83–83)

While I have a great deal of faith in quantitative approaches, it is still possible for me to recognize the value of something other than a standardized measurement. A good example of this is found in Irving Yalom's 1989 book, *Love's Executioner*. A psychiatrist, Yalom scheduled one-year follow-up sessions with his clients after completion of therapy to judge the success of his intervention. Playing back a ten-minute recording made of the initial interview, one of Yalom's clients jokingly remarked upon hearing himself, "Who is that jerk, anyway?" (p. 269). Yalom notes that the client was indicating that he was a different person now—that he was not like that any more. Yalom then remarks, "These are no minor adjustments: they represent basic modifications in personhood. Yet they are so subtle in character that *they generally elude most research outcome questionnaires*" (p. 269, emphasis added).

Qualitative approaches are valuable tools for helping us to understand our clients and the world in which they live. There are plenty of social problems that need investigation by social workers—whether we are qualitatively or quantitatively oriented, or, more accurately, mostly one or the other.

Self-Review

(Answers at the end of the book)

1. Which group believes the world can be objectively determined?
   a. quantitatively oriented researchers
   b. qualitatively oriented researchers
   c. ethnomethodologists
2. Which of these characteristics does not describe qualitative research?
   a. no intervention
   b. use of participant-observation
   c. large sample sizes
   d. journalistic narrative
3. Which of these characteristics does not describe qualitative research?
   a. diminished importance of literature review
   b. in-depth interviewing
   c. exploratory
   d. concern with instruments and measurement
4. For each of the research questions below, indicate the most appropriate research approach:
   a. You want to know how much time the average felon spends in prison.
   b. You want to know how prisoners experience the power wielded by their prison guards. You convince the warden to let you go "under cover" as a prisoner for two weeks.
   c. To understand the influences that shaped criminal behavior, you develop a survey and administer it to five-hundred prisoners in one maximum security prison.
   d. To understand the influences that shaped their criminal behavior, you interview in-depth five prisoners awaiting execution on death-row.
   e. After advocating to get college classes offered in a nearby prison, you follow the first sixty prisoners to complete one class and leave prison. You want to know if they are less likely to be rearrested than other prisoners.

Questions for Class Discussion

1. Suppose you want to know what it is like to live in poverty, so you interview an impoverished person in-depth one Saturday afternoon. Compare and contrast a lengthy interview with an ethnographic study of impoverished persons. In what ways would they be similar? How would they differ?

2. Which research approach has the greatest potential for advancing social work practice? (List arguments for and against qualitative and quantitative approaches.)

3. What are the pros and cons associated with not doing a thorough literature search before beginning an ethnographic study?

4. Discuss any books, movies, or plays that recently may have helped you better understand the life of a unique group of persons.

5. Share your life experiences that have given you insight into other cultures. What special world views or vocabularies were discovered?

6. Into what situations or settings would you like to go in disguise? What would you learn that you couldn't learn without disguise?

7. Discuss how qualitative research is different from research employing a single system design.

Mini-Projects for Experiencing Research Firsthand

1. Spend no less that eight hours observing (it can be on separate occasions) one of the following persons. Try to discover what problems they encounter, their coping or survival strategies, and any special terms or vocabulary that they use. Write a report summarizing what you learned.
   a. An impoverished person
   b. An elderly person
   c. A person with physical handicaps
   d. A social worker with a child-abuse protection team

2. Arrange to spend the night in a shelter for homeless persons. Keep a notebook with you and record your impressions and significant events. Share your observations with the class. If more than one person in your class engages in this activity, what patterns or themes emerge from the observations?

3. Consider a problem common to many persons who receive some form of welfare payment or food stamps. Since the amount of support is inadequate to their needs, they run out of food toward the end of the month. How do they survive? Do they borrow money to buy groceries? Do they go without food? Do they pool their supplies with neighbors or other family members? Do they go to soup kitchens? Draft a design for an ethnographic study of impoverished families that could provide some answers to these questions. Assume that you have received a grant that will allow you to take up to six months to live with or observe these families. Where would you go to begin your study? How would you find informants? What kinds of ques-

tions would you start with? How would you ensure that your findings weren't fabrications of your observed family or a product of your own presuppositions about poverty?

4. Interview in-depth a recent immigrant to this country. Obtain a life history or autobiography. Try to capture the experiences that would assist your fellow classmates in understanding both the quality of life in the home culture and the experiences the immigrant has had in adjusting to the new culture.

5. To understand a little more the kinds of problems experienced by certain individuals in our society, spend at least twelve hours with one of the following simulated disabilities:

   a. paraplegia (borrow or rent a wheelchair and spend a day in it)

   b. cataracts (smear Vaseline on a pair of eyeglasses)

   c. hearing impairment (wear ear plugs)

   d. birth defect or stroke (immobilize your right hand or arm with a splint, bandage, or sling)

   e. aphasia (try to go the whole day without speech)

Resources and References

Agar, M. (1980). *The professional stranger: An informal introduction to ethnography.* New York: Academic Press.

Agar, M. (1986). *Speaking of ethnography.* Beverly Hills, CA: Sage.

Becker, D.G., Blumenfield, S., and Gordon, N. (1984). Voices from the eighties and beyond: Reminiscences of nursing home residents. *Journal of Gerontological Social Work,* 8(1,2), 83–100.

Belcher, J.R. (1994). Understanding the process of social drift among the homeless: A qualitative analysis. In Edmund Sherman and William J. Reid (eds.), *Qualitative research in social work.* New York: Columbia University Press.

Berg, B.L. (1998). *Qualitative research methods for the social sciences.* Needham Heights, MA: Allyn and Bacon.

Berra, Yogi, (1998). *The Yogi book: I really didn't say everything I said.* New York: Workman.

Berrick, J.D. (1995). *Faces of poverty: Portraits of women and children on welfare.* Cary, NC: Oxford University Press.

Bogdan, R. (1974). *Being different: The autobiography of Jane Fry.* New York: Wiley.

Bogdan, R. (1992). *Qualitative research for education: An introduction to theory and methods.* Boston: Allyn and Bacon.

Brannen, J. (1995). *Mixing methods: Qualitative and quantitative research.* Brookfield, MA: Avebury.

Caudill, W., Redlich, F.C., Gilmore, H.R., and Brody, E.B. (1952). Social structure and interaction processes on a psychiatric ward. *American Journal of Orthopsychiatry,* 22, 314–334.

Conover, T. (1987). *Coyotes: A journey through the secret world of America's illegal aliens.* New York: Random House.

Cote, J.E. (1994). *Adolescent storm and stress: An evaluation of the Mead-Freeman controversy.* Hillsdale, NJ: Lawrence Erlbaum.

Davidson, B. (1997). Service needs of relative caregivers: A qualitative analysis. *Families in Society*, 78, 502–510.

Deane, W.N. (1961). The reactions of a nonpatient to a stay on a mental hospital ward. *Psychiatry,* 24, 61–68.

Denzin, N. and Lincoln, Y. (1994). *Handbook of qualitative research.* Thousand Oaks, CA: Sage.

Estroff, S. (1981). *Making it crazy: An ethnography of psychiatric clients in an American community.* Berkeley: University of California Press.

Fetterman, D. M. (1989). *Ethnography: Step by step.* Beverly Hills, CA: Sage.

Fielding, N.G. (1991). *Using computers in qualitative research.* Newbury Park, CA: Sage.

Franklin, C. and Jordan, C. (1995). Qualitative assessment; A methodological review. *Families in Society.* 76, 281–295.

Gardiner, M. (1993). The great Samoan hoax. *Skeptical Inquirer*, Winter, 131–135.

Gilgun, J.F. (1995). The moral discourse of incest perpetrators. *Journal of Marriage and the Family,* 57, 265–282.

Gilgun, J.F. and Connor, T.M. (1989). How perpetrators view child sexual abuse. *Social Work,* 34(3), 249–251.

Gilham, S.A., Lucas, L.W., and Sivewright, D. (1997). The impact of drug education and prevention programs: Disparity between impressionistic and empirical assessments. *Evaluation Review*, 21, 589–613.

Goldman, A.R., Bohr, R.H., and Steinberg, T.A. (1970). On posing as mental patients: Reminiscences and recommendations. *Professional Psychology,* 1(5), 427–434.

Goldstein, H. (1991). Qualitative research and social work practice: Partners in discovery. *Journal of Sociology and Social Welfare,* 18(4), 101–119.

Goldstein, H. (1997). Shaping our inquiries into foster and kinship care: Editorial note. *Families in Society*, 78, 451–452.

Inciardi, J.A. (1995). Crack, crack house sex, and HIV risk. *Archives of Sexual Behavior*, 24, 249–269.

Ishiyama, T., Batman, R., and Hewitt, E. (1967). Let's be patients. *American Journal of Nursing,* 67, 569–571.

Jacobsen, G.M. (1988). Rural social work: A case for qualitative methods. *Human Services in the Rural Environment,* 11(3), 22–28.

Johnson, J.C. (1990). *Selecting ethnographic informants.* Newbury Park, CA: Sage.

Keigher, S.M. (1992). Rediscovering the asylum. *Journal of Sociology and Social Welfare,* 19(4), 177–197.

Kidder, L.H. and Judd, C.M. (1986). *Research methods in social relations.* New York: Holt, Rinehart and Winston.

Loftland, J. (1995). Analytic ethnography: Features, failings, and futures. *Journal of Contemporary Ethnography*, 24 (1), 30–67.

Loftland, J. and Loftland, L.H. (1995). *Analyzing social settings.* Belmont, CA: Wadsworth.

Madey, D.L. (1982). Some benefits of integrating qualitative and quantitative methods in program evaluation, with illustrations. *Educational Evaluation,* 4(2), 223–236.

Marshall, C. and Rossman, G.B. (1989). *Designing qualitative research.* Beverly Hills, CA: Sage.

Marshall, C. and Rossman, G.B. (1995). *Designing qualitative research.* Thousand Oaks, CA: Sage.

McMillen, J.C., Rideout, G.B., Fisher, R.H., and Tucker, J. (1997). Independent-living services: The views of former foster youth. *Families in Society,* 78, 471–479.

Meloy, J.M. (1994). *Writing the qualitative dissertation: Understanding by doing.* Hillsdale, NJ: Lawrence Erlbaum.

Miles, M.B. and Huberman, A.M. (1984). *Qualitative data analysis.* Newbury Park, CA: Sage.

Moore, P. and Conn, P. (1985). *Disguised.* Waco, TX: Word Books.

Morgan, D.L. (1997). *Focus groups as qualitative research.* Thousand Oaks, CA: Sage.

Morse, J.M. and Field, P.A. (1995). *Qualitative research methods for health professionals.* Thousand Oaks, CA: Sage.

Olson, M.R. and Haynes, J.A. (1993). Successful single parents. *Families in Society,* 74(5), 259–267.

Orans, M. (1996). *Not even wrong: Margaret Mead, Derek Freeman, and the Samoans.* Novato, CA: Chandler and Sharp.

Patton, M.Q. (1990). *Qualitative evaluation methods.* Newbury Park, CA: Sage.

Riessman, C.K. (1993). *Narrative analysis.* Newbury Park, CA: Sage.

Riessman, C.K. (1993). *Qualitative studies in social work research.* Newbury Park, CA: Sage.

Rosenhan, D.L. (1973). Being sane in insane places. *Science,* 179 (Jan.), 250–258.

Royse, D. (1994). *How do I know it's abuse? Identifying and countering emotional mistreatment.* Springfield, IL: Charles C. Thomas.

Ruckdeschel, R.A., Earnshaw, P. and Firrek, A. (1994). The qualitative case study and evaluation: Issues, methods, and examples. In Edmund Sherman and William J. Reid (eds.), *Qualitative research in social work.* New York: Columbia University Press.

Sherman, E. and Reid, W.J. (1994). *Qualitative research in social work.* New York: Columbia University Press.

Sander, J. (1991). *Before their time: Four generations of teenage mothers.* New York: Harcourt Brace Jovanovich.

Shaffir, W.B. and Stebbins, R.A. (1991). *Experiencing fieldwork: An inside view of qualitative research.* Newbury Park, CA: Sage.

Silverman, D. (1993). *Interpreting qualitative data.* Newbury Park, CA: Sage.

Skoll, G.R. (1992). *Walk the walk and talk the talk: An ethnography of a drug abuse treatment facility.* Philadelphia, PA: Temple University Press.

Steffensmeier, D.J. (1986). *The fence: In the shadow of two worlds.* Totowa, NJ: Rowman and Littlefield.

Strauss, A. and Corbin, J. (1990). *Basics of qualitative research.* Newbury Park, CA: Sage.

Thompson, R.J. (1989). Evaluator as power broker: Issues in the Maghreb. International innovations in evaluation methodology. *New Directions for Program Evaluation,* 42 (Summer), 39–48.

Van Maanen, J. (1988). *Tales of the field: On writing ethnography.* Chicago: University of Chicago Press.

Weiss, R.S. (1995). *Learning from strangers: The art and method of qualitative interview studies.* New York: Free Press.

Whyte, W.F. (1984). *Learning from the field: A guide from experience.* Beverly Hills, CA: Sage.

Yalom, I. (1989). *Love's executioner and other tales of psychotherapy.* New York: Basic Books.

CHAPTER 12
Ethical Thinking and Research

Most social workers would never do something that they knew would be viewed by others as unethical. The problem comes when we assume that others think like we do—and they don't. An ethical dilemma arises anytime you have to choose—not between a right and a wrong but between two arguably correct but conflicting courses of action. Thus, while we all know that it is wrong to lie and believe that the ethical researcher would always want to inform his or her research subjects about the nature of the study, does this means that we can never deceive in the interest of research? Let's think about several possible ethical dilemmas:

- Maria wants to learn experientially how society treats our senior citizens. She has a friend who can create latex wrinkles and folds on her skin and they've found clothing and a wig that guarantee that she'll look like an eighty-year-old. Is Maria being unethical if she doesn't tell the people she encounters that she is really only twenty-three years old?
- Conover's (1987) interest was in illegal immigrants: what plans and decisions they made, how they survived, and what they experienced. He crossed the U.S.–Mexican border with a group of Mexicans and was later arrested in the United States for driving a car for the immigrants (they didn't have driver licenses). While aiding and abetting these temporary workers may have been illegal, was it unethical?
- Wellons (1973) engaged in some brilliant, creative research. Knowing about the powerful effect of negative labeling (sometimes known as the self-fulfilling prophecy), Wellons gave workshop supervisors positive but untruthful labels for a group of trainees with mental retardation. He told the supervisors that certain of their supervisees could be expected to "blossom" in intelligence and workshop performance. And sure enough, one month later the experimental group of adult trainees not only had a higher level of productivity but also showed gains in intel-

ligence. There were no changes in the control group. Even though deception was used, was this research unethical?

You begin to see the problem. Ethical dilemmas thrive in those gray areas in between totally right and totally wrong. Sometimes research cannot be conducted without deception. The purist might argue that deception should never be used, but what if the research could benefit society? Even if there would be no direct benefit to society, should we prevent research where subjects are not informed precisely of the study's purpose and whether they would be in the control group or the experimental group? And before you answer that, must we inform even those participating in medical research that they will be receiving the placebo—not the new experimental drug?

Heated controversies occasionally arise because of disagreements over what constitutes an unethical act. My final example involves a researcher who submitted a fabricated study of the benefits of temporarily separating asthmatic children from their parents to 146 journals in social work and related fields (Coughlin, 1988). One version of the article claimed that social work intervention benefited the children. A second version indicated that the intervention had no effect. Upon acceptance or rejection of the manuscript, the study's investigator notified the journal of the real purpose of his study—to collect data on whether there was a tendency among journals to accept articles that confirm the value of social work intervention.

The controversy arose when an editor of the *Social Service Review* lodged a formal complaint against the author with the National Association of Social Workers. The author's position is that the review procedures of journals ought to be investigated because of their potential influence in determining what will be printed in professional journals. Some argue that the author should not have initiated such a large-scale deception of journals, but how does one investigate the hypothesis that professional journals have a bias that constitutes "prior censorship" without using a little deception? In many instances of unethical research, some harm results. Who was harmed in this example?

Historical Context

Guidelines to protect the subjects of research originated with the Nuremberg trials after World War II, which, among other areas of concern, examined the Nazis' medical experiments upon involuntary prisoners. Nazi physicians conducted cruel and harmful experiments on human subjects. Some of their experiments, for example, were designed to determine how long it was possible for human subjects to live in ice water. Prisoners were subjected to conditions that literally froze them. Female prisoners were ordered to warm the frozen subjects with their naked bodies in order to determine if more subjects lived with slow thawing than with quick thawing.

Other prisoners (including children) were injected with diseases such as typhus, malaria, and epidemic jaundice in order to test vaccines. To test antibiotics, human beings were wounded and had limbs amputated. Grass, dirt, gangrene cultures, and other debris were rubbed into the wounds so that the injuries would simulate those received on the battlefield. To simulate the problems of high altitude flying, test chambers were created where oxygen was removed and the effect of oxygen starvation on humans studied. Other prisoners of the Nazis were given intravenous injections of gasoline or various forms of poison to study how long it would take them to die. These involuntary subjects experienced extreme pain, and of those few who lived, most suffered permanent injury or mutilation.

These and other atrocities resulted in what became known as the Nuremberg Code—a set of ethical standards by which research with human subjects can be judged. Organizations such as the World Medical Association subsequently developed their own guidelines (The Declaration of Helsinki) for distinguishing ethical from unethical clinical research. The American Medical Association and other groups endorsed the Declaration or developed similar guidelines.

Despite awareness of the Nazi atrocities and the development of ethical guidelines for research by a number of organizations and professional associations, there have been unfortunate incidents in this country in which subjects were experimented upon without their permission. In late 1996 our newspapers began carrying headlines such as "Families of Radiation Victims to Get Settlement." The U.S. Department of Energy had just acknowledged that, between 1945 and 1947, twelve individuals were involved in government sponsored human radiation experiments without their permission. The government will pay the one survivor and the eleven other families $400,000 each to settle a lawsuit brought because plutonium injections were given without the recipient's knowledge or consent. In some instances, more than 600 rads of radiation were given—enough to cause bone cancer. Although not all of the relevant documents have been made public, it has been revealed that prisoners in Washington and Oregon were also irradiated between 1963 and 1971. Hundreds, if not thousands, of unsuspecting charity patients at university hospitals may have received radiation in secret experiments during the early days of our atomic era. These experiments violated the first principle of the Nuremberg Code:

> Before the acceptance of an affirmative decision by the experimental subject there should be made known to him the nature, duration, and purpose of the experiment; the method and means by which it is to be conducted; all inconveniences and hazards reasonably to be expected; and the effects upon his health or person which may possibly come from his participation.

The National Commission for the Protection of Human Subjects in Biomedical and Behavioral Research (*The Belmont Report*) identified these three ethical principles for research on humans in 1978:

- Beneficence—maximizing good outcomes for humanity and research subjects while minimizing or avoiding risk or harm.
- Respect—protecting the autonomy of all persons, treating them with courtesy and respect including those who are not completely autonomous (for example, children, the mentally incompetent).
- Justice—ensuring reasonable, nonexploitative, and well-considered procedures administered fairly; the fair distribution of costs and benefits (for example, those bearing the risks of research should receive the benefit). (Sieber, 1992, p. 18)

In the 1960s in New York, a physician injected cancer cells into twenty-two geriatric patients. Some were informed orally that they were involved in an experiment, but were not told that they were being given injections of cancer cells. No written consent was acquired, and some patients were incompetent to give informed consent. Later it was learned that the study had not been presented to the hospital's research committee and that several physicians directly responsible for the care of the patients involved in the study had not been consulted (Faden and Beauchamp, 1986).

Another notorious case involved a sample of men with syphilis. In 1932 four hundred mostly poor and illiterate black males with tertiary stage syphilis were informed that they would receive free treatment for their "bad blood." In actuality, these men received no treatment for syphilis. They received free physical exams, periodic blood testing, hot meals on examination days, free treatment for minor disorders, and a modest burial fee for cooperating with the investigators. The researchers (supported by the Public Health Service) were interested only in tracing the pathological evolution of syphilis. Although the study was reviewed several times by Public Health Service officials and was reported in thirteen articles in prestigious medical and public health journals, it continued uninterrupted until 1972, when a reporter exposed the study in the *New York Times*. The survivors were given treatment for their disease only after this publicity. After the story broke, the Department of Health, Education and Welfare appointed an advisory panel to review the study. Not until 1975 did the government extend treatment to subjects' wives who had contracted syphilis and their children born with congenital syphilis (Jones, 1981).

Public outcry over the Tuskegee Syphilis Study and other abuses led Congress in 1974 to pass the National Research Act (Public Law 93–348), which requires any organization involved in the conduct of biomedical or behavioral research involving human subjects to establish an Institutional Review Board (IRB) to review the research to be conducted or sponsored. This act also created the National Commission for the Protection of Human Subjects of Biomedical and Behavioral Research. In October 1978, this commission produced recommendations for public comment. The Department of Health, Education and Welfare (HEW) refined the recommendations and, in

1981, issued them as regulations for research being conducted with its funds. In 1983, specific regulations protecting children were incorporated.

The impact of these standards was that colleges, universities, hospitals, and other organizations engaging in research and receiving federal funds from HEW (now the Department of Health and Human Services) and selected other departments established institutional review boards (sometimes called human subjects committees) to review and oversee research conducted by investigators affiliated with their organizations. Under some circumstances, the IRBs review students' proposed research as well. These review boards have the authority to approve, disapprove, or modify research activities covered by the regulations, to conduct a continuing review of research involving human subjects, to ensure that there is an informed consent process, and to suspend or terminate the approval of any research.

Institutional Review Boards

Institutional review boards are now firmly established as our society's "watchdogs" protecting human subjects from risky or harmful research. This does not mean that IRBs prevent all unethical research practices. They cannot monitor research that is covert or not brought to their attention. However, there is much greater monitoring of research today than there was twenty or so years ago. Currently, organizations that receive federal funding and conduct research (such as universities and hospitals) are required to have IRBs to review proposed studies of human subjects.

Researchers begin the process of getting IRB approval by obtaining an application and preparing a description of their project. This narrative containing the research methods and procedures, the benefits and risks, the hypotheses, the recruitment of the subjects, the consent form, and so forth is called the **protocol**. Protocols vary in length and format depending upon the planned research and the procedures established by the local IRB. There are several levels of review, from the most cursory (the exempt status) to full review. Federal regulations allow for some kinds of research to be exempted from a full review by the IRB. Those activities most applicable to social work are:

1. Research conducted in educational settings, such as research on normal educational practices involving instructional strategies or effectiveness of instructional techniques, curricula, or classroom management methods.

2. Research involving the use of educational tests (cognitive, diagnostic, aptitude, achievement) if information taken from these sources is recorded in such a manner that subjects cannot be identified, directly or through identifiers and if any disclosure of the subjects' responses

outside the research would not place the subjects at risk of criminal or civil liability or be damaging to the subjects' financial standing, employability, or reputation.

3. Research involving survey or interview procedures and observation of public behavior is exempted when meeting the conditions specified in item 2.

4. Research involving the collection or study of existing data, documents, or records if these sources are publicly available or if the information is recorded by the investigator in such a manner that subjects cannot be identified directly or through identifiers linked to the subjects.

5. Research and demonstration projects approved by the federal department that examines public benefit of service programs.

6. Research involving survey or interview procedures when the respondents are elected or appointed public officials or candidates for public office.

Exemptions may not always be available from IRBs. In such an instance, the researcher will complete a lengthier application and usually is required to appear before the IRB to make a presentation or to respond to questions. Most IRBs will not grant exemptions to research involving certain vulnerable populations (children, prisoners, the mentally disabled, and economically or educationally disadvantaged persons), or when there is deception of subjects or use of techniques that expose the subject to discomfort or harassment beyond levels normally encountered in daily life. Further, exemption is not usually available when the information obtained from medical records is recorded in such a way that subjects can be identified directly or through identifiers linked to the subjects. However, some local IRBs may be more lenient than others.

Generally speaking, students are not required to seek approval from institutional review boards when their research projects are primarily for educational purposes (for example, an assignment to interview a small sample of people in order to learn about interviewing, recording data, or other aspects of the research). However, if the project involves living human subjects and is likely to contribute to generalizable knowledge (that is, research that is likely to be of publishable quality), students ought to seek IRB approval. Normally, student projects with the greatest potential for generating generalizable knowledge are doctoral dissertations and some master's theses.

General Guidelines for Ethical Research

Social workers do not, as a rule, get involved in biomedical or other research where invasive procedures or physical harm to subjects is likely to occur. Research conducted by social workers involves surveys and interviews that require a certain amount of cooperation from the participants in the study. The risks to the subjects of social work research derive from the possibility that a third party will violate confidentiality and cause the subject physical, psychological, social, or economic harm. This threat is particularly acute for those subjects engaged in or with past histories of illegal acts.

When questionnaires are used or interviews are conducted with adults who are not in a vulnerable population, the principle of "implied consent" is applied. The act of participation is seen as giving informed consent. In these instances, IRBs do not require written documentation that subjects gave their consent. However, a problem arises when potential subjects feel that they cannot refuse to participate. If these subjects are clients (for example, persons on probation or parole, or recipients of some form of public assistance), they may not feel free to refuse without putting themselves in some jeopardy. This is when consultation with an institutional review board can come in handy. The IRB may suggest alternative ways to collect data or to reduce any implied coercion by informing potential subjects of their rights in writing. (A written consent form as in figure 12.1, is often required that specifies clearly that the potential subject has the right to refuse participation without any penalty or loss of service.) Social workers must be alert to the possibility that encouraging their clients to participate in research could be perceived as coercion. Since social workers are often "gatekeepers" of services, clients could feel pressured into participating in order to gain access to or continue receiving services.

If you are employed at a small agency that does not have its own IRB and you have questions about a proposed research or evaluation project, you might try contacting the IRB at the nearest university for consultation. To help you understand how they make their decisions in weighing risks against benefits, the following guidelines are presented.

Guideline 1: Research Subjects Must Be Volunteers

Social work research is not something imposed upon involuntary subjects. All of those participating in a research effort should freely decide to participate. No coercion of any kind should be used to secure participants for a study.

All subjects must be competent enough to understand their choice. If they are not able to fully comprehend (for example, individuals under the age of majority), then their legal caretakers must give permission, and the subjects also must assent. Even if parents give permission for their children to participate in a research project, the children may still refuse to participate. The subject's right to self-determination is respected, and any research subject is free to withdraw from a study at any time.

The use of written consent forms helps assure that research subjects know that they are volunteers. These forms provide brief, general information about the nature of the research, the procedures to be followed, and any foreseeable risks,

Figure 12.1 Consent to Participate in a Research Study

Outpatient Drug Treatment Program After-Care Study

Investigator:

Ellen Samovar, MSW, Principal Investigator, (231) 323-5760

I _____ have been asked to participate in a research study under the direction of Ms. Samovar.

Purpose:

I understand that the purpose of this study is to examine the success of the Outpatient Drug Treatment Program in which I am participating–to learn why clients start and stop using drugs and what factors may influence these decisions.

Duration and Location:

I understand the study will take place at the ODTP offices on 717 South First Street. Further, I understand that the study will take about 60 minutes of my time.

Procedures:

I will be asked to answer questions about my social and psychological well-being, relationships, employment, drug use, and illegal activities. In addition, I will be asked to provide a urine sample to test for evidence of drugs in my system and will be given a breathalyzer to test for alcohol.

Risks/Discomforts:

It has been explained to me that some of the interview questions are very personal, involving drug and criminal behavior and may cause some discomfort in answering them.

Benefits:

I understand that the benefits from participating in this study may be to help researchers and those involved in public policy better understand the factors that lead to the starting and stopping of drug use.

Confidentiality:

I understand that a research code number will be used to identify my responses from those of other clients and that my name, address, and other identifying information will not be directly associated with any information obtained from me. A master listing of persons participating in the study and their identifying information will be kept in a secure location under lock and key except when being used by select staff. Further, I understand that a certificate of confidentiality has been obtained from the Department of Health and Human Services (DHHS) that protects investigators from being forced to release any of my data, even under a court order or a subpoena. When results of this study are published, my name or other identifying information will not be used.

Payments:

I will be paid $50 for my time and cooperation. If I stop early, I understand that I will be paid an amount appropriate to the time I have spent.

Right to Withdraw:

I understand that I do not have to take part in this study, and my refusal to participate will involve no penalty or loss of rights to which I am entitled. I may withdraw from the study at any time without fear of losing any services or benefits to which I am entitled.

Signatures:

I have read this entire consent form and completely understand my rights as a potential research subject. I voluntarily consent to participate in this research. I have been informed that I will receive a copy of this consent should questions arise and I wish to contact Ms. Samovar or the University of Somewhere's Institutional Review Board (231-323-4949) to discuss my rights as a research subject.

_____	_____
Signature of Research Subject	Date
_____	_____
Signature of Witness	Date
_____	_____
Signature of Investigator	Date

Practice Note: Anonymity and Confidentiality

Anonymous responding means that the research participant cannot be identified by any means or by any person. When anonymity is promised, not even the researcher should be able to associate a response with a particular individual. Researchers need to be sensitive to the issue that participants can sometimes be recognized not from their personal identifiers like addresses and social security numbers but from sociodemographic information. For instance, a small agency might employ one female Asian American or only one Ph.D. fifty years of age. With small samples of research subjects, researchers might want to use broad categories for such variables as age, education, ethnic groupings, and years of experience in order to keep from identifying persons with unique characteristics.

Confidentiality means that the potentially sensitive or private information is being supplied with the understanding that the research participant's identity, although known to the researcher, will be protected. Clients participating in an agency's focus group discussing suggestions for improving services may not want their comments linked in any way to them. Sometimes it is necessary to know a research participant's name, address, phone number, or social security number in order to match current information with medical records, prior offenses, or even when pre- and posttesting of an intervention are being done. Where it is necessary to know the identities of research subjects, investigators routinely use a coding scheme so that personally identifying information is not contained on clients' survey forms, assessment forms, and so on. The listing that links code numbers with individuals' names is always kept in a secure, locked area except when being used.

---

discomforts, or benefits, and they indicate that the research subject is free to withdraw consent and to discontinue participation in the project at any time without penalty or loss of benefits. Consent forms generally contain the name of someone to contact should there be questions about the research or the subject's rights.

Guideline 2: Potential Research Subjects Should Be Given Sufficient Information about the Study to Determine Any Possible Risks or Discomforts as Well as Benefits

"Sufficient information" includes an explanation of the purpose of the research, the expected duration of the subject's participation, the procedures to be followed, and the identification of those procedures that might be experimental. The exact hypothesis does not have to be given away; it can be stated generally. However, the researcher must be specific about procedures that will involve the research subjects. If there are potential risks, these must be identified. Subjects should be given the opportunity to raise and have answered any questions about the study or procedures that will be used. Subjects must also be allowed to inquire at any time about procedures and have their questions answered.

Types of risks resulting from social work research might be psychological, physical, legal, and economic. Psychological risks could result from those procedures that cause research subjects to leave with lowered self-esteem and a sense that they aren't as smart as others (for example, that they were "stupid" to have been a victim of abuse). A problem could arise if a subject became depressed because a researcher's questions awakened long-dormant and painful memories.

Physical risks might occur to research subjects. For instance, if questionnaires were mailed to the homes of women who had surreptitiously attended a support group for battered spouses, their violent partners may discover this and take exception to their efforts to get help.

Legal risks are those associated with illegal behaviors—drug use, child abuse, stealing, or other illegal activities. Just as a social worker would do in beginning treatment, researchers must inform adults that if they reveal child abuse in an interview, the investigator is obligated to report it to the appropriate authorities. The most common risk here, however, is that a subject's confidentiality may be compromised if the researcher receives a subpoena or if personal identifiers are used and an assistant identifies a prominent individual and talks about sensitive material outside of the project.

Economic risks could occur when, for example, employees reveal that they are taking drugs or when they are surveyed about the work climate within their agency. Sometimes there are social costs for speaking the truth, and one's co-workers could make the workplace environment so unpleasant that the employee might have to quit his or her job. The IRB's job is to think not only about the direct risks but also about the indirect or remote possibilities.

Benefits may be conceptualized as those that obviously reward the subject (such as cash payment, small incentives), those that result in subjects acquiring some type of insight or learning, and those that provide some worthwhile information for a service-providing organization or community in which the subject lives. Researchers quite often appeal to subjects' altruism and state that the project will advance scientific knowledge. Sometimes a final report of the project is offered to those subjects who voluntarily participated.

Finally, note that informed consent means that language used to inform the prospective research subjects should be not only age appropriate (an especially important consideration with children) but also free of jargon and technical/professional terms that an average person might not understand. Some

---

Practice Note: Research and Persons with Alzheimer's Disease

Research involving patients with Alzheimer's disease is fraught with ethical problems. Because their illness destroys cognitive abilities, most lack the capacity to understand an informed consent process, and even if they do, they may forget that they have given consent. Further, there are no well accepted standards for determining when individuals with Alzheimer's disease have lost the capacity to give consent. Even mildly cognitively impaired older subjects experience difficulty in understanding consent information (High, 1992).

If the patient with Alzheimer's disease is unable to understand the consent process, informed consent is generally obtained from the next-of-kin or legal guardian. In any case, assent from the subject is still sought (High, Whitehouse, Post, and Berg, 1994).

---

word processing programs can provide a readability level on typed text. A good guide might be to try not to exceed a ninth or tenth grade reading level with adult client populations. Further, using "I" language seems to make the informed consent easier to understand than use of the second or third person.

Guideline 3: No Harm Shall Result as a Consequence of Participation in the Research

Social work researchers are not likely to propose research that would result in evident harm to their subjects. But one's perspective on harmful effects should not be limited to the active participants in a study. Punch (1986) related a dilemma that he faced. A group of female students wanted to study the reactions of policemen to reports of rape. In order to conduct this study they would have had to fabricate stories. While policemen might have been quite insensitive in their dealings with rape victims, Punch objected to the study on several grounds. First, there could have been legal repercussions for filing false police reports. Second, subsequent disclosure might have made the police distrustful of researchers. But most important, it might have led police to be skeptical of legitimate claims of sexually assaulted women. The benefits did not seem to outweigh the risks and the potential harm to others that could result.

Unethical research can result in harm to succeeding generations. For instance, the Tuskegee Study has been offered as one of the reasons why few blacks participate in research trials (Gamble, 1993) and may help explain why African Americans frequently delay getting needed medical attention. One of the jobs of the IRB is to look for any potential exploitation of subjects.

Researchers have a responsibility to identify and to minimize harm or risk of harm that might befall the research subjects. And researchers should constantly monitor the subjects for harmful effects of the research. Subjects should not go away from a study feeling that they possess undesirable traits. Often, debriefings are used to inform subjects about the study and to neutralize negative feelings once participation in a project has concluded. Sometimes it is useful to point out that "most subjects" responded in a certain way.

Guideline 4: Sensitive Information Shall Be Protected

This guideline suggests that no harm to research subjects should result from improper handling of information. The privacy of research subjects may be protected in the following ways:

- Allowing subjects to respond anonymously.
- Separating identifying information from the research data by using special coding and keeping the master list under lock and key.
- Stressing the importance of protecting confidential material.

It is not always possible for subjects to respond anonymously, as in the situation when you have administered both pretests and posttests and need to match individuals' scores to check for improvement. However, it is often convenient to invent a special code that is easy for subjects to remember and still provides a good measure of anonymity. Such a code might consist of the first four letters of the subject's mother's maiden name and the last four digits of the subject's social security number. Even a code this simple will help guard against unauthorized persons accidentally recognizing or identifying your subjects.

Quantitative researchers report their research findings in the aggregate (group means and totals), which offers a great deal of protection to subjects who would not want to be connected to their responses. However, sometimes researchers wish to use a particularly apt comment (especially when open-ended questions have been employed) to summarize or illustrate the sentiments of the respondents. The caution here is to never report anything from which an individual subject could be identified. For instance, it would be a serious mistake to use the following quote in showing the depth of employees' feelings about a new director in a study of job satisfaction at a county-run social service agency.

> I've been working abuse investigation longer than anyone else here—twenty-two years—and I can say, without any doubt in my mind, that our new executive director is all fluff and no substance. He doesn't have a clue about how to do his job; I'm not sure he would even recognize an abused child if he saw one.

Another protection for clients when an "outside" researcher makes a request to collect information beyond what may be available from agency files is for the agency to contact the former or present clients. Then, if they give permission, client names, addresses, or phone numbers might be released to the researcher. Finally, agencies sometimes ask researchers and those working with privileged communications to sign a written pledge of confidentiality.

Potential Ethical Problems in Research

Deception

One of the thorniest ethical problems facing researchers in the social sciences has to do with deception. Generally speaking, deception should not be employed unless there is no other way to collect the necessary data or to study the phenomenon. Thus, deception might be acceptable if without it respondents would be too embarrassed, ashamed, or defensive to respond truthfully.

Some researchers can avoid risky deception of clients or vulnerable populations by the creative use of simulations in which subjects (such as college students) are asked to imagine themselves in a particular role or setting—and then to respond as if the situation were real. In a study of the qualities that make someone a "good" therapist, subjects might, for instance, be shown video clips of three persons from different walks of life and then asked to choose the "therapist" they would want if they had a problem that could benefit from counseling. It could be concealed from the subjects that none of the choices were actual therapists, because the simulation is somewhat contrived anyway and the subjects were not real clients.

At times, the informed consent that subjects must read and sign alerts them that some deception may be involved. At other times, the IRB can decide to waive the right of subjects to be fully informed until a full debriefing after data has been obtained from the subject(s). When deception is used, most commonly subjects are not informed or are given misleading information about the nature of the project. IRBs generally require debriefing of subjects whenever any deception is employed. Because it is important that the deception does not cause subjects to lose confidence in science or the scientific process, IRBs also expect that subjects should be given ample opportunity to have their questions answered about the project at the time of the debriefing, and, if they choose to do so, subjects should be allowed to withdraw their own data from the study.

Should you involve a deception? Clearly, you should not if someone could be harmed—could go away from the study with a feeling of having been degraded or exploited. For this reason, the decision to use deception should not be made without consultation with others. As part of this process, alternative methodologies for studying the problem should be considered. But, as indicated earlier, sometimes the best way to study a problem depends upon deception. An example comes to mind: Suppose you want to study racism but you know that if you approach the topic directly, most individuals would see your intent and construct their answers to minimize their racist opinions. However, suppose you inform your subjects that you are conducting a study on humor and you will be giving them fifty different jokes to see which ones they thought were the funniest. Couldn't this mild deception allow you to investigate racist values without alerting subjects to your real intent? The answer, of course, is yes. It is important that we not quickly label the use of deception as unethical. Deception, of course, may be unethical, but it may also be handed responsibly and ethically.

Denial of Treatment

Another problem is that sometimes social workers who contemplate research think that the use of a control group may be unethical because clients would be denied services. It would indeed be unethical to deny beneficial services to clients strictly for the purpose of research.

But there are ways to obtain control groups without being unethical. For instance, if we wanted to evaluate a new program or intervention, we could compare clients receiving the new or experimental intervention against those who receive the usual set of services. In this scenario, there would be no denial of services. Some clients would get a slightly different intervention or set of services from those clients normally receive. This could be to their advantage.

In those agencies or programs where there is a long waiting list, researchers might consider as a control group those clients in line for services. For instance, if a wait of six weeks or longer is inevitable before those on the waiting list could begin receiving services, there is no denial of benefits. In fact, clients on a waiting list might appreciate a periodic contact with an agency representative (even if it is limited to the administration of a pretest and posttest), because it would constitute evidence that they have not been forgotten by the agency and that they are still actively queued for services. If these clients had similar problems (such as, alcoholism), it might be possible to distribute educational pamphlets or materials to them while they were waiting for service. This group of clients could be considered to be receiving an educational intervention. While it may be a weaker or milder intervention than they would later receive, it would be better than nothing at all and may help the researcher feel better about gathering data from them. Comparisons could be made to the waiting-list clients (the control group) and those who received the new intervention (the experimental group).

Another way to obtain a control group would be to compare your program participants with the clientele of a similar program or agency. While the groups would not be equivalent (since random assignment wasn't possible), at least you would have beginning evaluative data. Still another "natural" comparison group could be found in that group of clients who keep one or two appointments, then drop out of treatment. This group could be compared with those individuals who complete the intervention. These are only some of the ways in which control groups can be identified without denying treatment.

Should Some Research Questions Not Be Investigated?

Living in an open society as we do, the suggestion that we should not investigate some research questions sounds strange indeed. However, remember that research results can be used for purposes other than those for which they were intended. Research could be conducted to support stereotypes or prejudices. For example, one research question that should not be investigated is: "Are there racial differences in intelligence?" (Sieber and Stanley, 1988). While it is conceivable that some interest groups could make funds or grants available for the conduct of such research, the ethical social work researcher has a responsibility to not engage in research that could be used to denigrate or harm a group of individuals.

Not too long ago I attended an IRB meeting where an undergraduate proposed a survey of prisoners. The protocol wasn't particularly creative, and I found myself wondering if the student would get sufficient information from her research for a publication. Several other members wondered the same thing and were opposed to giving the student permission to go forward with her project. IRBs have a responsibility to weigh the scientific merit of the proposed research and can block or stop a plan which doesn't seem like it would add to our knowledge base. But unlike the example of questions that should not be investigated (Are there racial differences in intelligence?), I found myself advocating for the student. I simply did not feel that I or the committee should "censor" proposed research—which might, after all, end up producing some unexpected finding that could merit publication or a presentation at a regional psychological or sociological meeting. Ultimately, the committee decided to approve the subject.

In this survey, there was no risk of harm to prisoners, although they might have missed an hour or two of pay if called away from their work. But could there have been some "harm" if the prison decided against allowing the next legitimate researcher access to prisoners on the grounds that the prison had already allowed "too much" of this kind of thing? In essence, could the student's project jeopardize the prison as a future research site? It was a risk we had to take. I share this story with you to illustrate how difficult ethical decisions are—the outcome could just as easily have been a disapproval. However, had the student's research been turned down, she could have received some consultation, revised her protocol, and sought approval again.

Compensation

Is paying respondents or research subjects unethical? While reimbursing subjects for costs incurred (such as, baby-sitting, time away from work, transportation) seems reasonable and is not offensive to most, questions are raised when there is a large financial incentive for participation. The guideline here is avoid giving incentives that are so large or excessive that they constitute "undue inducement." When large financial rewards are offered for research subjects, there is a risk that some individuals may fabricate information in order to become eligible for money. Could you reimburse subjects for time lost from work and their time for commuting to the agency to participate in research? Generally, this level of compensation would not be viewed as excessive. Sometimes when subjects are followed over several years (longitudinal design), an incentive is built in (for example, a $50 bonus) if they participate in all of the scheduled follow-ups. Increasingly, lotteries have become popular as incentives. Typically, there is a cash prize that every respondent/participant becomes eligible to win.

Existing Data—Research Without Clients' Consent

Although many community mental health centers and other such agencies routinely request clients to sign consent forms at intake in the event that a researcher or program evaluator will need to look at their records some day, many agencies do not use consent forms unless their clients are involved in a specific study.

Suppose you wanted to do research within a state psychiatric hospital to determine if more personality disorders were being diagnosed in a recent year than ten years ago. In such a situation, would you be prevented from conducting your research because clients did not give their permission for you to perform archival research involving their records? Probably not—if you are a legitimate researcher and have the approval of an institutional review board.

As an official student or faculty member, you would go first to your own university's institutional review board, stating your research objectives, how you would collect the data, and so forth. Once you received their approval, you'd be in a stronger position with the state hospital's human subjects committee. Your study has a greater likelihood of being approved if it has the potential for making a contribution to our knowledge base or if it would be useful to the hospital.

Archival research of this type is not generally viewed as having any real potential for harming subjects. Further, in some localities the information you want might even be a matter of public record. Even so, some agencies may have you sign an agreement of confidentiality before allowing you access to their records.

Final Thoughts

Some might argue that going through an institutional review board is a waste of time for the knowledgeable and ethical researcher who will not be doing any harm with a simple survey. However, to bypass review boards entails a certain risk as revealed in the case of a university-based investigator who did not get approval for a controversial questionnaire administered within a school district. To avoid hostile parental reaction and a possible lawsuit, a school official shredded several hundred already completed questionnaires (Schilling, Schinke, Kirkham, Meltzer, and Norelius, 1988). You can imagine how much time was lost—to say nothing about the likely fate of that research project. Consulting with a review board and having a general demeanor of openness about research is better than going it alone. Ultimately, however, it is the researcher who is responsible for the ethics of the research effort. Even with the approval of an institutional review board or other advi-

---

Practice Note: Conducting Research with Children

Federal legislation has been proposed (The Family Privacy Act) that would require explicit written consent from parents (active consent) before minors could participate in any research containing sensitive questions including: sexual behavior; illegal, antisocial, or self-incriminating behavior; and psychological problems. Presently, IRBs can waive active parental consent by requiring researchers to send home information to parents giving them the option to refuse their child's participation.

The new legislation would prevent IRBs from allowing passive consent. This could present a problem for researchers as typically 40 to 50 percent of parents fail to respond to mailed or student-delivered active consent forms; and further, minority students and those from single-parent households are underrepresented in samples requiring active parental consent (Dent, Sussman, and Stacy, 1997).

There can be a host of ethical problems associated with conducting research with children. Gensheimer, Ayers, and Roosa (1993) have identified several of these in discussing a prevention program designed for children of alcoholics. They point out that the very act of recruiting these children, whether by teacher referral or child self-selection after viewing a special film, places them in a situation where "labeling is almost assured." Another problem is that requiring informed consent from parents may prevent at-risk children from entering the program, because they might fear being harmed by a parent who would be opposed to their participation. Still another question is: How much coaching or prompting is ethical? Could children even with parental permission truly feel that they could choose not to participate when teachers and other adults in the school were encouraging them to be involved?

---

sory group, the researcher must constantly be vigilant and stop any research project in which harmful effects may be occurring.

While the thought of preparing a research protocol or appearing before an institutional review board might be somewhat intimidating, another way to see the process is as a review by concerned peers—individuals who really want good research to be produced. Their suggestions and comments may well improve your project.

As social workers, we really don't have an option *not* to engage in research and evaluation activities. The National Association of Social Worker's Code of Ethics requires us to evaluate our policies, programs, and interventions—to develop professional knowledge while protecting our research participants. A relevant section of the code addressing ethics in research and evaluation is reproduced in figure 12.2.

Figure 12.2 NASW Code of Ethics

5.02 Evaluation and Research

(a) Social workers should monitor and evaluate policies, the implementation of programs, and practice interventions.

(b) Social workers should promote and facilitate evaluation and research to contribute to the development of knowledge.

(c) Social workers should critically examine and keep current with emerging knowledge relevant to social work and fully use evaluation and research evidence in their professional practice.

(d) Social workers engaged in evaluation or research should carefully consider possible consequences and should follow guidelines developed for the protection of evaluation and research participants. Appropriate institutional review boards should be consulted.

(e) Social workers engaged in evaluation or research should obtain voluntary and written informed consent from participants, when appropriate, without any implied or actual deprivation or penalty for refusal to participate; without undue inducement to participate; and with due regard for participants' well-being, privacy, and dignity. Informed consent should include information about the nature, extent, and duration of the participation requested and disclosure of the risks and benefits of participation in the research.

(f) When evaluation or research participants are incapable of giving informed consent, social workers should provide an appropriate explanation to the participants, obtain the participants' assent to the extent they are able, and obtain written consent from an appropriate proxy.

(g) Social workers should never design or conduct evaluation or research that does not use consent procedures, such as certain forms of naturalistic observation and archival research, unless rigorous and responsible review of the research has found it to be justified because of its prospective scientific, educational, or applied value and unless equally effective alternative procedures that do not involve waiver of consent are not feasible.

(h) Social workers should inform participants of their right to withdraw from evaluation and research at any time without penalty.

(i) Social workers should take appropriate steps to ensure that participants in evaluation and research have access to appropriate supportive services.

(j) Social workers engaged in evaluation or research should protect participants from unwarranted physical or mental distress, harm, danger, or deprivation.

(k) Social workers engaged in the evaluation of services should discuss collected information only for professional purposes and only with people professionally concerned with this information.

(1) Social workers engaged in evaluation or research should ensure the anonymity or confidentiality of participants and of the data obtained from them. Social workers should inform participants of any limits of confidentiality, the measures that will be taken to ensure confidentiality, and when any records containing research data will be destroyed.

(m) Social workers who report evaluation and research results should protect participants' confidentiality by omitting identifying information unless proper consent has been obtained authorizing disclosure.

(n) Social workers should report evaluation and research findings accurately. They should not fabricate or falsify results and should take steps to correct any errors later found in published data using standard publication methods.

(o) Social workers engaged in evaluation or research should be alert to and avoid conflicts of interest and dual relationships with participants, should inform participants when a real or potential conflict of interest arises, and should take steps to resolve the issue in a manner that makes participants' interests primary.

(p) Social workers should educate themselves, their students, and their colleagues about responsible research practices.

Practice Note: Unethical Use of Evaluation

Almost all of the social workers I have known have struck me as being ethical. For the most part, they have been concerned with such issues as protecting clients' confidentiality and privacy. However, even social workers can engage in unethical behavior when they allow their ambition to run unchecked.

Earlier in my career I was the director of research and evaluation for an agency that funded contract agencies to provide mental health services. As part of my job, I was asked to evaluate a particular agency and its director. There were rumors that the director was playing too much tennis during business hours and that he wasn't managing the agency well.

I went about the evaluation by contacting key professionals in the community who either had been or should have been making referrals to the agency. I obtained a mixed bag of comments. While it was evident that the agency could have done better in some areas, it also did some things reasonably well. I knew that the way the results were presented could affect whether or not the director continued in that position. Since the instructions to me had been vague, I chose to present the findings in a formative manner rather than in a summative style. I attempted to make a balanced presentation and, in so far as possible, to let the data speak for itself. I did not feel comfortable concluding what the policymakers should do in this situation. Had they been kindly disposed toward the agency director, some of the findings from the evaluation would have been seen as providing constructive suggestions for change. Other statements would have provided positive strokes for the agency and its staff. However, there were political shenanigans going on.

The director of the counseling agency felt that the evaluation of the agency was an undeserved and unwarranted affront and soon resigned. At the funding agency, the individual who had been the strongest critic of the outgoing director, the one who pushed the hardest for an evaluation of the agency, applied for the director's position and was subsequently hired.

I came away with a firm sense of having been used to oust the former agency director. The new agency director (the individual who had advocated for an evaluation of the outgoing director) had a master's degree in social work and would have been incensed if anyone suggested that something "unethical" had been done. What do you think? Is the act of causing an evaluation to be conducted unethical? At what point was something unethical done?

I do not want to conclude this chapter with you feeling worried that you or your proposed research will be viewed as unethical because there is a likelihood that a client could be hurt during the course of an empirical investigation. If you have sought IRB approval and been open and honest about how the study will be conducted, there should be nothing to fear. While it is true that asking for sensitive information could be traumatic for some clients, rarely is that a problem. When a protocol involves a vulnerable population, for example, interviewing sexual assault victims, IRBs may ask that researchers provide their subjects with the phone numbers and addresses of counseling agencies or rape crisis centers. Most researchers do not worry about the ethics of their investigations, because their interviews, surveys, or studies are so innocuous and pose little risk.

Besides that, being a research subject can have positive effects. In clinical interventions, subjects may gain from new therapeutic procedures. Even if that doesn't occur, subjects may feel that the research is important and that they have made a contribution that will be of help to others. Participants may experience an increase in self-worth because they feel honored to have been selected to participate in "research." Sometimes participants receive some form of remuneration, and they appreciate it—even if it is inconsequential. Another consideration is that some research projects are interesting. Participants don't mind giving their opinions or sharing their insights. These are just some of the benefits to research participants.

Self-Review

(Answers at the end of the book)

1. T or F.   Legitimate researchers using archival or existing data pose very little risk of causing harm.
2. T or F.   Social workers are required by their Code of Ethics to evaluate programs and interventions.
3. T or F.   When parents grant permission for their children to be interviewed or tested in a research project, these children cannot refuse to participate.
4. T or F.   Institutional Review Boards cannot refuse to grant permission for researchers if there is no harm to participants and also no scientific merit.
5. T or F.   Deception can never be used in a research study involving participants under the age of twenty-one.
6. T or F.   Separate signed informed consent statements are usually not used with mailed surveys.
7. The research proposal describing the methods and procedures, recruitment of subjects, the consent form, and so forth is called the _____.

8. _____ means the research participant cannot be identified by any means or any person.

9. _____ means that sensitive or private information may be linked to personally identifying information but is supplied with the understanding that the participant's identity will be protected.

10. T or F. *Every* potential research subject has the right to refuse to participate and may even choose to quit in the middle of a project without being assessed any penalty or losing any benefits.

Questions for Class Discussion

1. Discuss situations in which it would be acceptable to involve people in research without their knowledge.

2. A researcher wants to interview children in families where there has been a hospitalization for mental illness within the past three years. Discuss the potential ethical issues that will have to be addressed.

3. A researcher is interested in observing family functioning in families that have experienced a recent suicide. What precautions would the researcher need to take to ensure that no psychological or emotional harm resulted from the interviews?

4. A doctoral student studying terminally ill patients of a hospice program finds that 15 percent of the subjects are contemplating suicide. Discuss what you would do with this information.

5. A researcher wants to investigate the emotional consequences associated with abortion. Because of the difficulty in getting access to the names and addresses of women who have had abortions, the researcher proposes a snowball sampling design. What are the ethical issues involved in the use of this design?

Mini-Projects for Experiencing Research Firsthand

1. Obtain a copy of the exemption certification form used by the institutional review board at your college or university. Think of some research that you would like to conduct. Develop this idea, sketch out a research design, and then complete the exemption form. Bring these to class and exchange forms with a fellow student. Critique each other's effort.

2. In the late 1960s, a sociologist, Laud Humphreys, reported his study of homosexual activity occurring in "tearooms" or public restrooms. He volunteered to be a "watchqueen"—that is, to serve as a lookout for

the individuals engaged in this form of sexual activity. In order to obtain additional demographic information about homosexual men, Humphreys recorded the license numbers of their cars and traced the men to their homes. A year later, he posed as a health service interviewer and collected personal information from them. It could be argued that his research was important for its contributions to our understanding of this type of behavior. He found, for instance, that only a small percentage of his subjects were members of the gay community. Many were married men. Humphreys certainly was guilty of deception and invading the private lives of the subjects. Do you feel that the benefits of such research outweigh the methods that he used? Read Laud Humphreys' *Tearoom Trade* (1970) and other commentaries on his book, and write a paper defending your position.

3. Stanley Milgram, a social psychologist at Yale University, began a series of studies on obedience in the 1960s. His experiments involved an elaborate deception. He led subjects to believe that they were giving a dangerous level of electrical shocks to other subjects who had not learned a list of words. Those who thought they were administering the shocks believed that the study was of the effects of punishment on learning (therefore justifying the electrical shock). The "learner" did not actually receive any electrical shock, but was instructed to feign discomfort upon receipt of the shock. In actuality, Milgram was interested in the extent to which subjects obeyed authority and would administer apparently dangerous levels of electricity to other participants in the research. It could be argued that Milgram's experiments constitute important findings on how ordinary people can be led to engage in the inhuman treatment of others. Milgram's report of his findings was met with much controversy. Do you feel that the benefits of such research outweigh any potentially unethical practices involved in the use of deception? He did, after all, debrief his subjects so that they knew no electrical shock had really been administered. Read Stanley Milgram's *Obedience to Authority* (New York: Harper and Row, 1974) in order to write a paper defending your position.

4. In the late 1950s, a series of experiments were conducted to confirm the usefulness of gamma globulin to immunize against hepatitis. The researchers went to a residential school, the Willowbrook State School, where a hepatitis epidemic was in progress. Researchers obtained the consent of the parents and divided the children into experimental and control groups that received hepatitis virus at various levels of infectiousness and gamma globulin inoculations at various strengths. Some of the gamma globulin was given below the strength known to be effective. When the results were published in the professional literature, they produced a storm of controversy (Harris, 1986).

Why? Because all of the children in the Willowbrook State School were children with mental retardation. Even though all the children who contracted the disease recovered, and the researchers argued that valuable medical knowledge was gained from the experiments, do you believe that this research should have been allowed? Try to find some of the arguments for and against this research and write a paper defending your position. The original articles reporting the experiment were: Ward, R., Krugman, S., Giles, J.P., Jacobs, A.M., and Bodansky, O. (1958), Infectious hepatitis: Studies of its natural history and prevention, *New England Journal of Medicine,* 258(9) (Feb. 27), 407–416; and Krugman, S., Ward, R., Giles, J.P., Bodansky, O., and Jacobs, A.M. (1959), Infectious hepatitis: Detection of the virus during the incubation period and clinically inapparent infection, *New England Journal of Medicine,* 261(15) (Oct. 8), 729–734.

Resources and References

Annas, G.J. and Grodin, M.A. (1992). *The Nazi doctors and the Nuremberg code: Human rights in human experimentation.* New York: Oxford University Press.

Baumrind, D. (1985). Research using intentional deception: Ethical issues revisited. *American Psychologist,* 40(2), 165–174.

Caplan, A.L. (1992). Twenty years after, the legacy of the Tuskegee syphilis study: When evil intrudes. *Hastings Center Report,* 22(6), 29–32.

Conover, T. (1987). *Coyotes: A journey through the secret world of America's illegal aliens.* New York: Random House.

Coughlin, E.K. (1988). Scholar who submitted bogus article to journals may be disciplined. *Chronicle of Higher Education,* Nov. 2, p. A7.

Dent, C.W., Sussman, S.Y., and Stacy, A.W. (1997). The impact of a written parental consent policy on estimates from a school-based drug use survey. *Evaluation Review,* 21, 698–712.

Edgar, H. (1992). Twenty years after, the legacy of the Tuskegee syphilis study: Outside the community. *Hastings Center Report,* 22(6), 32–35.

Faden, R.R. and Beauchamp, T.L. (1986). *A history and theory of informed consent.* New York: Oxford University Press.

Gamble, V. (1993). A legacy of district: African Americans and medical research. *American Journal of Preventive Medicine,* 9, 35–38.

Gensheimer, L.K., Ayers, T.S., and Roosa, M.W. (1993). School-based prevention interventions for at-risk populations. *Evaluation and Program Planning,* 16, 159–167.

Harris, E.E., Jr. (1986). *Applying moral theories.* Belmont, CA: Wadsworth.

High, D.M. (1992). Research with Alzheimer's disease subjects: Informed consent and proxy decision-making. *Journal of the American Geriatrics Society*, 40, 950–957.

High, D.M., Whitehouse, P.J., Post, S.G., and Berg, L. (1994). Guidelines for addressing ethical and legal issues in Alzheimer's disease research: A position paper. *Alzheimer Disease and Associated Disorders*, 8, 66–74.

Humphreys, L. (1970). *Tearoom trade: Impersonal sex in public places.* Chicago: Aldine.

Jones, J.H. (1981). *Bad blood: The Tuskegee syphilis experiment.* New York: Free Press.

Kimmel, A.J. (1988). *Ethics and values in applied social research.* Beverly Hills, CA: Sage.

King, P.A. (1992). Twenty years after, the legacy of the Tuskegee syphilis study: The dangers of difference. *Hastings Center Report,* 22(6), 35–38.

Marshall, G.D. and Zimbardo, P.G. (1979). Affective consequences of inadequately explained physiological arousal. *Journal of Personality and Social Psychology,* 37, 970–988.

Milgram, S. (1977). Ethical issues in the study of obedience. In S. Milgram (Ed.), *The individual in a social world.* Reading, MA: Addison-Wesley.

Morris, M. and Cohn, R. (1993). Program evaluators and ethical challenges. *Evaluation Review*, 17(6), 621–642.

Newman, D.L. (1996). *Applied ethics for program evaluation.* Thousand Oaks, CA: Sage.

Punch, M. (1986). *The politics and ethics of fieldwork.* Beverly Hills, CA: Sage.

Reamer, F.G. (1990). *Ethical dilemmas in social service.* 2d ed.. New York: Columbia University Press.

Schilling, R.F., Schinke, S.P., Kirkham, M.A., Meltzer, N.J., and Norelius, K.L. (1988). Social work research in social service agencies: Issues and guidelines. *Journal of Social Service Research,* 11(4), 75–87.

Sieber, J.E. (1992). *Planning ethically responsible research: A guide for students and internal review boards.* Newbury Park, CA: Sage.

Sieber, J.E. and Stanley, B. (1988). Ethical and professional dimensions of socially sensitive research. *American Psychologist,* 43(1), 49–55.

Wellons, K. (1973). The expectancy component in mental retardation. Ph.D. diss., University of California, Berkeley.

Zimbardo, P.G., Andersen, S.M., and Kabat, L.G. (1981). Induced hearing deficit generates experimental paranoia. *Science,* 212 (June), 1529–1531.

CHAPTER 13

Writing Research Reports and Journal Articles

You have conducted some exciting research and now you want (or have been asked) to communicate your findings in writing. You might be prompted to write about your research because:

- The clinical director or agency executive asks you to draft a report on your project.
- The grant or funding source requires an evaluation.
- You want to try writing for publication in a professional journal.
- You are involved in writing your thesis or dissertation.

Each of these writing projects shares certain similarities even though your audience may run the gamut from coworkers inside your agency to nitpicking professors and journal editors. The purpose of this chapter is to show you how to conceptualize and prepare a report of research findings.

Publication as a Practice Goal

Williams and Hopps (1987) noted that while few social workers "achieve comfort or familiarity with publishing," one of the hallmarks of a mature profession is that verifiable knowledge derived from practice is used to increase the quality, effectiveness, and efficiency of all practice. But where does verifiable knowledge come from? It does not flow automatically from the conduct of research, but is dependent upon the reporting or communication of the research. All too often, good applied social work research is never "written up," but remains in file folders or on someone's desk until it becomes outdated or is thrown away. For the results of research to guide practice, the findings must be disseminated to colleagues and other professionals.

Writing about the successes and failures of interventions and about the problems of clients is clearly a responsibility of professional social workers.

Indeed, the following passage is found in the National Association of Social Workers' Code of Ethics (1996):

> 5.01 (d) Social workers should contribute to the knowledge base of social work and share with colleagues their knowledge related to practice, research, and ethics. Social workers should seek to contribute to the profession's literature and to share their knowledge at professional meetings and conferences.

Writing for professional audiences can also provide a great deal of personal satisfaction as well as recognition.

The basic structure and key elements needed to report research findings are the same whether one is writing a thesis, an evaluation report, or a journal article. Of course, there are some observable differences when we compare these three types of reports. For one thing, academic committees expect the literature review section of a thesis or dissertation to be longer than that of most journal articles.

Manuscripts for journal articles must often be between sixteen and twenty pages; research reports written for internal agency consumption may have no set limit on the number of pages. However, the basic components of the research report, journal article, and thesis or dissertation are generally expected to include the following sections:

Components of a Research Report

1. Introduction
   a. Description of problem
   b. Statement of research question or hypothesis
   c. Significance of problem and rationale for studying it
2. Literature Review
   a. Theoretical and historical perspectives
   b. Identified gaps in literature
   c. Reiteration of purpose of study
3. Methodology
   a. Research design and data collection procedures
   b. Characteristics of subjects
   c. Sampling design
   d. Description of instrumentation
   e. Data analysis procedures
4. Findings (results)
   a. Factual information presented
   b. Statistical and practical significance discussed
   c. Tables, charts
5. Discussion
   a. Brief summary of findings

   b. Explanation of unexpected findings
   c. Applications to practice
   d. Weaknesses or limitations of research
   e. Suggestions for future research
 6. References
 7. Appendices

Introduction

The purpose of the Introduction is to present the research question or problem and to place it within some context or frame of reference. This generally entails describing the problem and its extent. For instance, in an article on adolescent parents, a logical starting place would be recent estimates of the number of teenaged girls who become pregnant each year. Is it 100,000 or 1,000,000? Has it been increasing lately or falling off?

After this background has been presented to help the reader understand the scope of the problem, the author needs to begin discussing the kinds of problems experienced by teen parents and, more particularly, to focus on the specific problem that will be the topic of the research report or article.

In an article entitled "The Effects of Anger Control Training on Adolescent Antisocial Behavior," this is how the authors began:

> Some estimates suggest that one-third to one-half of all referrals of children and adolescents to outpatient clinics are for antisocial behavior problems (Kazdin, 1987). Adolescent antisocial behavior is one of America's most costly social problems, partly because these adolescents frequently remain in continued contact with both the mental health and criminal justice systems well into adulthood (Farrington, 1991). The monetary costs associated with antisocial behavior are exorbitant (Ziglar, Taussig, and Black, 1992). And as Kazdin (1987) points out, discussions of adolescent antisocial behavior frequently neglect the personal tragedies, for both adolescents and their victims, associated with adolescent antisocial behavior. Among the intervention procedures that have shown promise for positively influencing adolescent antisocial behavior is anger control training (ACT). (Nugent, Champlin, and Winimaki, 1997, p. 446)

There are many different ways to begin an article, and the nature of your topic may suggest an approach. In a content analysis of social work literature, Sutphen (1997) opened with a question:

> How involved is social work in the juvenile justice field? Several social work scholars have questioned the extent of the profession's involvement in this field (Roberts, 1983; Spake, 1987) and have suggested that it is less involved today that it has been in the past (Corcoran and Shireman, 1996; Ezell, 1996). A 1991 survey of more than 87,000 NASW members seems to provide some substance to these claims. The survey revealed that merely 1,025 (1.2 percent) social workers were working in the justice area, and only 500 listed it as a secondary area of practice. These are results that are virtually unchanged from 1972, and they stand in

contrast to a field such as mental health that attracts one out of three NASW members (Gibelman and Schervish, 1993; McNeece, 1996).

The Introduction should be viewed as an opportunity to stimulate the readers' interest in your topic. Tell readers how your research or theoretical perspective is different and why innovative methods are needed. You might start with what is known about a problem and then move to what is not known about it. Controversies work, too. Briefly present the debate as it serves as the stage from which your research emerges. Note that in the previous two examples, both of the authors succinctly summarize other studies and articles. You must learn to do this for journal publication.

When you have finished writing the Introduction, read it over to make sure that you have:

1. articulated some problem or issue that would interest the professional community;
2. identified your specific research question or hypothesis; and
3. offered a rationale for your study.

The easiest research reports to read are those that engage your interest. Williams and Hopps (1988) have noted, "Getting off to a good start truly is three-quarters of the battle" (p. 456). One way to do this is to present the problem early in the Introduction instead of burying it toward the end. Material discussed in your Introduction makes more sense when the reader has a clear understanding of the problem prompting your investigation.

Review of the Literature

The Literature Review section of a report or journal article is where the notable and relevant theoretical explanations of the social problem or phenomenon of interest are summarized. You need not describe every study that has ever been conducted on your topic. Cite only those pertinent to the issues with which you are dealing. Inform your readers about the major findings from other research. For example, consider the following fictitious excerpt:

> While relatively little has been written in the literature of criminology about shoplifting, it is a topic of interest to those who work in the criminal justice system because of the seemingly complex dynamics involved. Financial need does not appear to be a significant factor. Almost all of the studies have shown that poverty is not a major explanation for shoplifting (Mills, 1996). Shoplifters tend to come from all economic classes (Hunt, 1994), and the overwhelming majority of persons caught shoplifting do not intend to resell the item (Book and Vurm, 1997). It has also been noted that in only a minority of cases is shoplifting associated with mental illness, and the majority of arrested shoplifters do not have any psychotic features (Doktor, 1995). Recent studies have shown that shoplifters are not apprehended differentially by race, sex, or age when control variables are employed (Mills, 1996; Vurm, 1996).

From this brief example we can learn that theories based upon economic deprivation or mental illness have not been found to explain shoplifting. Further, explanations involving a greater level of absent-mindedness among the elderly do not seem to be viable. Since these theories have been tested and then discarded, the way is open for a new theoretical explanation—perhaps that shoplifting is a help-seeking activity unconsciously motivated by high levels of stress.

This passage also demonstrates how quite a few studies can be summarized in a short amount of space. This is necessary when writing for journals as most do not want long manuscripts. Many times students provide too much irrelevant information in the literature review. It is, for example, usually inconsequential whether the studies were conducted in Idaho or Missouri, or whether very large or medium-sized survey samples were used. It is more important that the literature review show trends in the major findings of these studies. The location, methodology, sample size, and other facets of the earlier research take on more importance only when you describe your study as being different from or similar to that research. In this instance, you may want to go into more detail in describing the study you are departing from or replicating. Why is it important to replicate or depart from another study? There may be legitimate reasons. You may want to correct for problems the previous study had with internal validity. Otherwise, it is not important to go into great detail regarding the methodology and each finding in all of the prior studies mentioned in your review of the literature.

Another common mistake authors make is to cite lengthy passages of background material. This is done either because the writer does not know how to paraphrase or summarize or because these passages provide "proof" that the writer actually read the background material. Actually, there is seldom a need to reproduce quotes verbatim when writing for professional audiences.

After you have thoroughly reviewed the material available on your topic, this information must be organized in some fashion. Generally, the reviews can be organized in one of two schemes: by chronological order or by theoretical orientation. A chronological organization involves an overview of the problem—mention the classic or pioneering studies, then move on to more recent studies that are most like the research you have conducted.

The other approach, organizing by major theoretical orientation, is illustrated by the following example from an article entitled "Group Work Intervention with Female Survivors of Childhood Sexual Abuse." The authors' theoretical rationale for a group work approach with survivors drew heavily upon Yalom's work and then was developed this way:

> Short-term groups, which typically range in length from ten to fifteen sessions, are often preferred to group interventions of longer duration for work with survivors (Alexander et al., 1989; Fowler, Burns, and Roehl, 1983; Herman and Schatzow, 1984). In addition to their being less costly, the therapeutic benefits of opting for time-limited work are threefold: (a) Agency resources may be more

efficiently used to provide services to more people; (b) it is easier for the survivor, on both an emotional and practical level, to commit to a short-term group; and (c) group members' work toward individual as well as group goals is facilitated by their cognizance of the time-factor (Gil, 1988; Goodwin and Talwar, 1989; Hansen, Warner, and Smith, 1980; Knight, 1990; Kreidler and Hassan, 1992). (Richter, Snider, and Gorey, 1997, p. 55)

In reviewing the literature, you may find a number of competing theories. Even though you may not subscribe to all of them, you still owe it to your readers to give a balanced presentation and to acknowledge rival theories or explanations. This helps provide some of the controversy or interest that can make reading your article or report more enjoyable. Unless the theories are currently in vogue or important for some other reason, you are not obligated to give them a large amount of space or detailed coverage.

Since new research is usually conducted on those topics about which there is not much literature, the review of the literature section helps justify your research by pointing out gaps in the knowledge base. Unless you are replicating someone's study, you are likely to be conducting research in an area where not much is known. This gap in knowledge provides a major impetus for research.

There has been little investigation of the effectiveness of efforts to engage first-time blood donors more substantially in the process of maintaining the community's blood supply and thus produce more committed donors. Similarly, there has been no research on how incentives or efforts designed to increase self-identity as a blood donor actually affect subsequent donations. This research was planned to test the effectiveness of an incentive and two different foot-in-the-door techniques designed to foster greater self-attribution as a blood donor as measured by the number of units donated by first-time donors. (Royse, 1998)

After you have reviewed the relevant literature and noted the gaps in knowledge on a particular problem or topic, it is helpful to restate the purpose of your study. The reader may not be as familiar with the problem area as you are, and restating your hypothesis or research question will assist the reader in assimilating the potpourri of literature to which he or she has just been exposed.

When you have finished writing your review of the literature section, look it over to make sure that you have:

1. covered all of the major (sometimes the first or classical) studies in the field;
2. included the most recent studies (there shouldn't be a large period of time without any studies; if you discover that all of your references are dated between 1978 and 1990, then you probably need to look a little further); and

3. summarized what is *not* known about the problem you have been studying and reminded the reader of your specific interest.

When you have done these things, then you are ready to begin the methodology section.

The Methods Section

The Methods section of the report describes in detail how the study was done. In this section, the reader learns the procedures for and things you did when collecting the data. Typically, the following are described:

1. *The research design.* Explain whether it was a one-group pretest-posttest design, an experiment, a nonequivalent control group design, or a survey of some sort.
2. *The subjects.* How were they recruited or selected? Random or convenience sampling? What was special or unique about them?
3. *Data collection procedures.* Did you use mailed questionnaires or personally interview the respondents?
4. *The instrumentation.* What instruments did you use? Have the instruments been used in a similar application before? What is known about reliability and validity?
5. *Data analysis.* What statistical procedures will be employed?

You should give sufficient information in this section to allow another investigator to replicate the study. Commonly, subsections and subheadings are used to differentiate the various components of the methodology. This is an example of how one author described her research design:

Study Design
The research design was quasi-experimental, which has been found to be appropriate for "natural social settings" (Campbell and Stanley, 1963). The design was a derivative of Campbell and Stanley's research design 5. An experimental group was pretested, received the intervention, and was posttested. A comparison group was pretested as a comparison measure for the experimental group. For ethical reasons, including the risk of dropout related to the emotional stress of a waiting period in exploring personal issues related to coming out, the control group received an intervention similar to the experimental group after the pretests without being required to undergo a waiting period for the sake of posttesting. Thus, the pretesting of the control group served as the comparison measure for the experimental group. Additional measurements included within-group comparison of experimental pretest and posttest means on each of the dependent variables. (Morrow, 1996, pp. 649–650)

Morrow went into a little more detail than many authors. Here's an example of a briefer description:

Research Design
This correlational study explored whether any significant relationships existed between child, family, and service characteristics with service outcome for clients of the Family Initiatives program. The study's major focus was to determine whether having knowledge about child, family, and service variables could help to predict the service outcome a family experienced at three and six months after Family Initiatives ended. (Unrau, 1997, p. 204)

You will see somewhat different approaches in the way authors present their subjects. Often they provide minimal detail in the Methods section and more about the subjects' characteristics in the Results section. Your readers will typically be interested in how many subjects there were, how they were obtained, and something about their personal characteristics. This is the way Paris, Tebow, Dahr, and Cooper (1997) described their subjects under the heading "Patients and Methods":

All patients (n = 60) were from the Oklahoma Transplantation Institute and had undergone heart transplantation since 1989. Each patient was informed of the purpose of the study and asked to complete a questionnaire. Demographic, occupational, and attitudinal data were gathered. This was combined with the physician assessment of the patient's work ability and status vis-à-vis social security guidelines for disability. The assumption was that a completed survey constituted consent for participation. (P. 372)

Nugent, Champlin, and Wiinimaki (1997) handled it this way:

Sample
The subjects involved in this study were 102 male adolescents between 12 and 18 years of age. The mean age of the males in this study was 14.7 years (SD = 3). Only about 14 percent of the sample were minorities. All subjects were in custody of the state of Tennessee Department of Youth Development for delinquent and/or unruly behavior. One group of males, nine of whom agreed to participate in this study, was living in a group home (Group Home A) in which ACT was implemented. A second group of males, four of whom agreed to participate in this study, was living in a second group home (Group Home B) in which ACT was not conducted. The four males in Group Home B made up one comparison group. A total of 89 other males in state custody for delinquent and unruly behavior were a random sample drawn as part of a previous study (Glisson, 1994, 1996) and were used as a second comparison group. (p. 448)

Readers will also be interested in the instruments or measures used in the study. Typically, the author identifies the source reference for the instrument and discusses its reliability and validity, as in the following example:

The Maslach Burnout Inventory was used to measure burnout (Maslach and Jackson, 1981). This instrument measures three components of burnout: emotional exhaustion, depersonalization ("loss of concern and feelings for clients") and (lack of) personal accomplishment ("a negative self-concept and negative job attitudes") (Pines and Maslach, 1978, p. 233). The original instrument measured each area for frequency and intensity; however, the instrument's authors have stated that the frequency scale can be used alone, as was done in this study, with acceptable results (Maslach, 1987). The instrument has twenty-two items, and each is answered in terms of how frequently the feeling is experienced.

Test-retest reliability is reported by Maslach and Jackson (1981) as follows: emotional exhaustion, .82; depersonalization, .60; and personal accomplishment, .80. Internal consistency (alpha) for these subscales is .90, .79, and .71, respectively. Maslach and Jackson also tested the instrument for discriminant and confirmatory validity, with satisfactory results. More recent analyses of the MBI using factor analysis confirm its validity (Koeske and Koeske, 1989). (Oktay, 1992, p. 434)

Usually only a paragraph or two is needed to inform the reader about the way in which the data were analyzed. Here's the first of two paragraphs on the data analysis from an article about adult children with mental illness serving as supports to their mothers in later life (Greenberg, 1995).

Analysis

Descriptive statistics address the first purpose of this study: to investigate the amount of help that adult children with mental illness provided to their mothers. Hierarchical multiple regression was used to test the major research hypothesis: whether the social support provided by the adult child was associated with a lower level of maternal subjective burden. The study used a hierarchical regression strategy to determine the amount of additional variance the adult child's support explained in subjective burden after controlling for background variables and sources of stress. The control variables were entered in step 2 of the hierarchical regression model. In step 3, the measure of the adult child's support and assistance to his or her mother was entered. (P. 418)

When you have described the research design, the subjects, the data collection procedures, and how the data are to be analyzed, you are ready to begin writing the results section.

The Results

This section of the report or article contains what you actually discovered from conducting your research. The Results section summarizes the data. It does not present the raw data; it reports aggregate or average scores. Up to this point, you have not revealed your findings. Now it is time to exhibit your findings. Your task in this section is to present the results factually, without opinion. The facts must stand by themselves.

You can organize your findings in many ways. The most common practice is to present the major findings first. If you have used several hypotheses, report your findings relative to the first hypothesis, then move to the second hypothesis, and so on.

Many researchers and would-be authors often feel overwhelmed because there appears to be too much information for a single research report. This can happen when they have lots of hypotheses or as a result of doing data analysis to the point that their shelves sag from the weight of computer printouts. Thinking that findings are all equally important contributes to a feeling of drowning in data.

I find it helpful to get a blank sheet of paper and write down what I would report if I were limited to one major point. I then ask myself, "What is the second most important finding coming from this study?" This process continues until all of the important points have been identified. Once the important findings have been noted, I begin thinking about how I will present them. Tables are helpful in that they visually break up the narrative while providing precise information that makes pretty dry reading if it is incorporated into the text.

Most research reports contain tables as a way of reducing verbiage. You should develop at least one or two tables for your research report, particularly if you have gone beyond univariate analysis. However, having too many tables is almost as bad as not having enough. Because of space limitations and the expense required to reproduce tables, you will seldom see journal articles with more than four or five. When too many tables are employed, it is hard for a reader or reviewer to keep all of the main points in mind; the information tends to run together.

In the Results section you will also report the outcomes of the statistical tests you have conducted. For example, if your studies found that BSW social workers received higher quality assurance ratings than MSW social workers, it will be important to determine if the difference in ratings is statistically significant. Do not allow your readers to conclude that a difference of three points, for example, makes BSW social workers superior to MSW social workers if a t-test or other appropriate statistical test reveals no statistically significant difference in their scores. Report the average scores, the results of statistical tests, and the associated probability.

If you are thinking about submitting a manuscript for publication, take the time to prepare the tables in such a way that the data displayed can be "digested." Don't throw some numbers together and think you are done, as in the following example:

Scale	Pretest Mean	Posttest Mean	t-value	Significance
A	5.308	4.809	2.15	.04
B	4.339	5.900	4.11	.001
C	6.663	5.323	2.84	.01
D	5.777	4.990	1.57	.13
E	6.191	7.42	1.92	.07
F	5.901	6.02	1.85	.80

Although this table might look neat and tidy, notice that it has no heading or caption. The reader has no idea what is being presented or what scales have been selected for tabular presentation. Do lower posttest mean scores suggest client improvement or do they indicate that clients have gotten worse? The reader should not have to guess whether Scale A represents social maladjustment or if that concept is represented by Scale E.

If you are in doubt about how to present your findings in tabular form, consult the American Psychological Association's *Publication Manual.* It is being widely used even by social work journals. The manual also demonstrates how to portray statistical data within the text. For instance, chi square is shown this way:

> There were no statistically significant differences among the four groups by race X^2 (6, $N = 1003$) = 4.41, $p = .62$, gender X^2 (3, $N = 1003$) = 1.33, $p = .72$, or age F (3, 1002) = .40, $p = .75$.

And one-way analysis of variance is expressed in this manner:

> There were no statistically significant differences in the number of deferrals by group F (3, 1002) = .75, $p = .53$.

Previously it was mentioned that some authors prefer to inform readers about the characteristics of the sample in the first section of their results instead of describing it under Methodology. Here is the way Hudson and McMurtry (1997) handled it in their Results section:

> *Respondents*
>
> All 311 respondents were either undergraduate or masters-level students in research courses in the seven schools of social work that participated in the study. Demographic information gathered via the background questionnaire is summarized in the second column in Table 1. As the information shows, the respondents were predominantly female (79%), White (80%), and unmarried (59%). The mean age of the sample was 32.4 years, the mean number of years of schooling completed was 16.4, and the mean annual family income of the respondents was about $40,000. The mean number of times married was less than one (0.7), and for those currently married, the mean number of years with the current spouse was 6.1. The average total family size of the respondents was 1.8, and the mean number of children was 0.9. (Pp. 87–88)

If you read a number of professional journals, you'll realize that there are many variations and stylistic differences among them. Study the journal to which you are considering submitting a manuscript so that you can conform, as much as possible, to the journal editors' expectations. Find an article from that journal and then model your manuscript after it.

When you have presented all of the results that merit reporting, then it is time to move on to the Discussion section.

The Discussion

The Discussion section often begins with a brief summary of your findings. It is not necessary to go into a lot of detail—this information was just exhibited in the Results. Just address the major findings or the highlights of your study. Once that is done, you can begin to expound on the findings. Perhaps you were surprised to find that the BSWs in your study performed better than the MSW employees; here is the place to elaborate the reasons for your surprise. You can reveal any unexpected findings—as well as what didn't go as planned.

Most importantly, the Discussion section should interpret the findings for the reader and address the relevance of these findings for practice. What do the findings mean or suggest to you? Are you recommending that social service agencies hire BSWs rather than persons with other undergraduate degrees? Does additional training seem to be indicated for the type of employee covered in your study? Do social work educators need to re-examine and possibly revise the curricula at their institutions? What implications does your study have for practice or policy? Discuss findings that have practical significance—even if there was no statistical significance. As Reid (1988) has indicated, our findings do not always "prove," "establish," or make a point so strongly that there can be no other interpretation. Usually, Discussion sections contain what he calls "appropriately qualified language"—phrases that indicate that the findings "provide evidence for," "suggest the possibility that," or "raise questions about."

The part of the Discussion section that many researchers do not like to write is the description of what did not go according to the research design. Sometimes secretaries forget to administer questionnaires. Clients drop out of studies or forget to bring needed documentation. Questionnaires may not be mailed on time. These glitches are normal in applied social science research. Social workers don't have the same degree of control that laboratory scientists have. So, admit any major departures from planned research procedures. The problems you encountered in collecting your data may well explain why you got the results that you did. For instance, someone forgetting to mail reminder postcards could have caused you to have a lower response rate for one group than for another. A change in agency policies during the middle of your study could have changed staff morale or increased the proportion of employees who felt "burned out"—which in turn could have affected the quality of their work. Also, recognize biases that may have crept into your study or that you discovered too late to do anything about.

Your study may have significant limitations. Perhaps you had hoped for a representative sampling of social workers from all educational backgrounds, but you heard from 75 percent of the BSWs, and only 8 percent of the MSWs. In this section you can discuss the extent to which it is possible to generalize your research.

Almost every study has some limitations—perhaps the most common one is some sort of selection bias. If it is hard for you to think of limitations, you may want to review the section on internal and external threats to the validity of a study.

Many authors conclude their research reports and journal articles by indicating areas for future research. As a result of their experiences, they may have suggestions for other researchers about procedures, instruments, the operationalization of variables, sampling techniques, and so on. This is done for altruistic reasons—a researcher may not plan on further work in that area but wishes others to benefit from what has been learned in the process of conducting the present research.

Here are two examples of how some authors addressed limitations:

> The study design was limited in the use of a matched comparison group, rather than a control group. However, a variety of measures indicated that the GAP (Growth and Achievement Program) clients did have consistent gains toward self-sufficiency over time compared with a similar group. Other studies have not examined similar outcomes in terms of progress towards self-sufficiency, focusing instead on indicators of mental health. The sample studied was similar to the SRO populations described in much of the literature (that is, it had low income and mental and physical health problems). (Shepard, 1997, p. 591)

> Finally, a weakness of this study lies in the relatively small clinical sample as well as the uncertainties regarding general application of the findings. Further research is needed to determine whether the results reported here may be replicated with different samples. Future research on the test-retest reliability of the scale is also important to make sure the scale does not suffer from response decay when used repeatedly on many occasions. These cautions notwithstanding, the evidence in this article provides a strong initial basis for recommending use of the IDI (Index of Drug Involvement) in clinical and research applications concerned with drug abuse. (Faul and Hudson, 1997, p. 572)

Some professional journals may require a separate section called "Conclusion." Whether you write a Conclusion section separate from your discussion section is a matter of individual preference—unless, of course, the journal requires one. It is important, however, that you have conclusions. Did the intervention work as expected? Were clients helped? Be careful not to become too exuberant and make claims that go beyond your data.

References, Appendices, and Abstracts

Whenever other written documents have been cited in your research reporting, they need to be listed in the Reference section at the end of the report or manuscript. References are usually listed alphabetically by authors' names, and there are various styles or ways in which the titles can appear. The reference style that you use is likely to be more important to academic committees and journals than it will be to funding sources. Some journals have their own style. When preparing your Reference section, look for examples or ask a person in authority which style you should use. The APA style is both convenient and widely used in professional journals. You may want to adopt this style unless told to use another.

The Appendix is where you place a copy of instruments, written instructions given to subjects, or important materials that may have been used during the course of your study. Research reports (especially those prepared for academic committees) are not complete without a copy of your instrument. However, most journals do not require or expect you to submit a manuscript with an appendix. Journals seldom have the space to publish instruments used in research reports.

Abstracts are brief summaries of reports or manuscripts. Generally, they average one-hundred to one-hundred-fifty words (although some journals may want a twenty-five to fifty word abstract). Abstracts are prepared to help readers decide whether they want to read a journal article, to help those who are attending national or regional conferences decide which presentations they will go to, and to help those who are categorizing research know which subject headings to use. Abstracts are almost always difficult to write because of the need to compress a complex manuscript into one paragraph or less. When you write an abstract, limit yourself to two or three sentences to introduce the study and two or three sentences to present your major findings. If you get stumped, look at several abstracts in a recent issue of *Social Work Abstracts* for ideas on how to be succinct.

Writing for Professional Journals

When you prepare a manuscript, have a specific journal in mind. Become familiar with that journal. Are its articles written for the practitioner or for the scholar? Journals have different audiences. Those oriented more toward practitioners may expect case examples, vignettes, or suggestions for working with a particular type of client. Other journals expect sophisticated analytical procedures. Some journals want a very detailed literature review, while others don't. You will have more success placing articles in a journal when you become well acquainted with it (for example, know the style, format, and type of article that the journal tends to publish).

Practically all journals carry a statement informing readers and prospective authors of the type of content with which they are concerned. By reading such statements, prospective authors determine if their manuscripts would be appropriate for the journals. For instance, this statement is found in *Social Work:*

> Social Work is a professional journal committed to improving practice and extending knowledge in social work and social welfare. The Editorial Board wel-

comes manuscripts that yield new insights into established practices, evaluate new techniques and research, examine current social problems, or bring serious critical analysis to bear on the problems of the profession itself.

Research on Social Work Practice defines its interest as

> devoted to the publication of empirical research concerning the methods and outcomes of social work practice. Social work practice is broadly interpreted to refer to the application of intentionally designed social work intervention programs to problems of societal and/or interpersonal importance, including behavior analysis or psychotherapy involving individuals; case management; practice involving couples, families, and small groups; community practice and the development, implementation, and evaluation of social policies.
>
> The journal will serve as an outlet for the publication of original reports of quantitatively oriented evaluation studies on the outcomes of social work practice; reports on the development and validation of new methods of assessment for use in social work practice; and empirically based reviews of the practice literature that provide direction applications to social work practice.

Journals want original manuscripts that are clearly written, of timely interest, appropriate to the journal, of the right length, and in the correct style. Journal reviewers look for an adequate literature review, reasonable research design, and the correct use of statistical techniques. But beyond those considerations, reviewers must decide whether or not your manuscript makes a "contribution" to the knowledge base. Reviewers may decide that your manuscript makes no contribution because of severe limitations in its generalizability, or because a more thorough literature review would have revealed the existence of studies similar to the one being reported. A manuscript might even be judged "interesting" but not relevant to social work practice.

You will probably increase your chances of publication if you find a journal that, in the last six years or so, has published similar (or somewhat related) articles to the one you are preparing. While this is no guarantee that the journal will publish your article, at least it indicates that the reviewers have had an interest in your topic. Study the articles that have recently appeared in the journal. Observe the reference style, the use of tables, the length of the literature review, and the general level at which the article is written. Keep in mind that the entire manuscript (including references) should not exceed sixteen to twenty double-spaced pages.

When you have narrowed down your choice of journals to one or two, it is time to look for their "Information for Authors." Sometimes the instructions about manuscript preparation and the types of manuscripts that journals are seeking are found in the back of selected issues. Or, you may want to look for that journal on the Internet. Information about the NASW Journals (*Social Work, Health & Social Work, Social Work in Education,* and *Social Work Research*) can be found at www.naswpress.org.

After you revise and polish your manuscript to the point where you think it is finished, set it aside. After several days, reread it. Make necessary revisions, and prepare a clean copy. Share that with two or three persons whose opinions you respect. Find someone who can give you constructive criticism without battering your ego. If you know that you are weak in the grammar department, seek a reviewer who knows that area.

One thing that you should *not* do is send your manuscript to more than one journal at a time. Most journals are not interested in manuscripts being reviewed by another journal. If your manuscript is rejected by the first journal you choose, do not be discouraged. A rejection does not necessarily mean that your manuscript is poorly conceptualized or written. It could be that the journal just accepted a similar article on the same topic last week. Or, it may mean that the journal is planning special issues, and your manuscript does not fit their needs. You may have submitted your article to an inappropriate journal. Sometimes, reviewers may not completely understand your approach. Reviews are conducted "blind"—that is, you will not know who read your manuscript and will have no way of knowing whether the reviewer knew as much about your topic or your methodology as you do. So, even good articles can be rejected. If your first effort is rejected, dust off your pride and try to objectively read your manuscript again. Revise it if necessary, and submit it to the second journal of your choice.

Journal reviewers usually make one of three decisions: they accept it as is; they accept it if the author makes certain changes; or they reject it. Don't let your ego deflate if you are asked to make certain modifications and resubmit. Often articles are strengthened by the additional information that a reviewer might request. Even if the manuscript is rejected, the reviewers' comments are forwarded to the author and these contain valuable comments that will be useful in revising the manuscript so that it can be sent to another journal.

Should your manuscript be rejected twice, it still may have a chance at publication. You may want to get Mendelsohn's (1997) *Author's Guide to Social Work Journals* for suggestions of additional journals that might be interested in your manuscript. Some journals accept proportionately a much larger percentage of manuscripts than others.

If your manuscript has been rejected three times, should you continue trying to get it published? This is the point at which I become frustrated and tired of working with one manuscript, and I quit. However, if you feel that yours is basically a good manuscript, and some of the reviewers have encouraged revision, then you should try it again.

Getting a manuscript published is like most other things in life that require practice. The more you practice, the better you will become at this activity. Carlton (1988) says that it is like learning to ride a bicycle. The way to learn is by trying again!

Reading and Critiquing Research Manuscripts

Students have a tendency to believe that any research that manages to appear in print is "good" research. I wish that this were so. Unfortunately, some pretty shoddy research can be found in journals without too much difficulty. As I stated in the beginning of this book, one reason you are required to enroll in a research methods course is to help you recognize poor or inadequate research. Flawed research (if unrecognized) could lead you to conclusions that are not warranted and could be dangerous to your clients.

Using the major content areas of research reports, we can construct a set of criteria to use in evaluating research reports, journal articles, or manuscripts. (These criteria can also be used to double-check your manuscripts.) I'm indebted to Garfield (1984) for his observations and guidelines on this topic.

1. Does the Introduction provide a clear notion of (a) the problem, (b) the purpose of the research, and (c) its significance?
2. Are the stated hypotheses reasonable? Do they appear to logically follow from the review of the literature?
3. Is the literature review (a) relevant to the study, (b) thorough, and (c) current?
4. Is a research design stated? Do the subjects appear to have been selected without overt bias? If there is a control group, does it seem to be an appropriate group for comparison? Is the number of subjects sufficient?
5. Is there a discussion of the reliability and validity of the instruments that are used?
6. Is there enough information on (a) the procedures and (b) the instruments and the operational definitions of the variables to allow you to replicate this study?
7. Are statistical tests present when needed? If statistical tests are used, are they the appropriate tests?
8. Are the findings discussed in terms of their implications and practical significance? Are the conclusions supported by and do they logically follow from the data that have been presented? Is the author guilty of overgeneralizing? Has actual or potential bias been recognized?

When evaluating a report of research, you should find yourself answering "yes" to most of these questions. Strong research articles will elicit a greater number of affirmative responses. Weak articles will receive a larger number of negative responses. You can use these criteria not only to evaluate the research reports prepared by others, but also to check your own report or manuscript to ensure that you have included all of the crucial elements.

This chapter has attempted to provide you with instruction in the key components in research report writing. Three points cannot be emphasized enough: (1) the importance of studying examples of other research reports and literature; (2) the importance of social workers' publishing their research results; and (3) the need to have perseverance when first efforts are rejected by journal reviewers.

When you publish your research, you contribute to the knowledge base of social work and allow others to build upon your research. Knowledge is an incremental process; it moves forward in small steps rather than large leaps. Any movement toward the goal of advancing social work knowledge starts with understanding the research process. Knowledge tends to become obsolete with the passage of time, so it is necessary that social workers not only read research as a way of keeping up with new developments in the field but also engage in research and seek professional outlets for the dissemination of research efforts. Otherwise, as Williams and Hopps (1987) have noted, "the profession does not advance, clients cannot thrive, and practice does not improve" (p. 376).

Writing Grant Proposals

It is very likely that at some point in your career as a social worker you will want to apply to a funding source for monies to allow you to develop some new intervention or to evaluate it. The larger the scale of the effort you have in mind, the greater the likelihood that you could benefit from external funding.

Most research grant proposals require that you address in your application the various components of a research report that we have discussed in this chapter. Not only do you need good written communication skills to write a "persuasive" grant application, but you also need to understand the roles of the principal investigator and how to prepare timetables, work plans, and budget justifications. A useful guide is *Applying for Research Fundings* by Joanne Ries and Carl Leukefeld (1995) and *Research Funding Guidebook: Getting It, Managing It and Renewing It* (1997) by the same authors.

An Internet resource you might want to check out is (www.nih.gov/grants). The National Institutes of Health maintains this page, and from it you can obtain program announcements and information about applying for NIH grants and fellowships as well as learn about those that have been awarded. The site also contains a search engine to facilitate locating relevant material.

Self-Review

(Answers at the end of the book)

1. T or F.   The Discussion section of a research report is where the notable theoretical explanations of the problem are summarized.
2. Why are tables included in research reports?
3. T or F.   The Results section of a research report contains only the findings the investigator has obtained; this is not the place for speculation or implications.
4. T or F.   The study's limitations are presented in the Methodology section.
5. T or F.   The Introduction is where a clear statement of the research problem is addressed so that the reader understands the study's purpose.
6. T or F.   The usual length of manuscripts submitted to professional journals is twenty-five to thirty pages, exclusive of tables and references.

Questions for Class Discussion

1. Discuss the ways in which a research report is similar to and different from the customary term paper.
2. Discuss what it is about a "good" journal article that makes it interesting or fun to read and what it is about some journal articles that make them dull and uninteresting.
3. How is writing for professional audiences different from writing to relatives or friends?
4. Think about the various sections of the research report. Tell the class what you think would be the most difficult section to write and your reasons for thinking this.

Mini-Projects for Experiencing Research Firsthand

1. Select a term paper that you wrote recently. Prepare it as if you were going to submit it to a social work journal. If you do not have real data, use fictitious data for the Results section and for the purpose of preparing a table or two. If you are feeling especially brave, exchange this effort with a classmate for friendly criticism concerning your writing style and understanding of this chapter.

2. Go to the library and locate several dissertations on topics of interest to you. Select one and summarize the important points made under each of the major sections of the dissertation. Briefly discuss what you learned from this project.

3. Interview one or more faculty members about their experiences with professional writing. What have been their joys and frustrations? What advice do they have for you?

4. Find an evaluation report or some research reported in a journal article. Using the criteria suggested in this chapter, evaluate the research. What did you learn in the process?

Resources and References

American Psychological Association. (1994). *Publication manual of the American Psychological Association.* 4th ed. Washington, DC: APA.

Beaver, M., Gottlieb, N., and Rosenblatt, A. (1983). Dilemmas in manuscript evaluations. *Social Work,* 28(4), 326.

Beebe, L. (1993). *Professional writing for the human services.* Washington, DC: NASW Press.

Carlton, T.O. (1987). Who are our authors? *Health and Social Work,* 12(Spring), 82–84.

Carlton, T.O. (1988). Publishing as a professional activity. *Health and Social Work,* 13(Spring), 85–89.

Faul, A.C. and Hudson, W.W. (1997). The index of drug involvement: A partial validation. *Social Work,* 42, 565–572.

Garfield, S.L. (1984). The evaluation of research: An editorial perspective. In A.S. Bellack and M. Hersen (Eds.), *Research Methods in Clinical Psychology.* New York: Pergamon Press.

Geever, J.C. (1997). *The Foundation's Center's guide to proposal writing.* New York: Foundation Center.

Greenberg, J.S. (1995). The other side of caring: Adult children with mental illness as supports to their mothers in later life. *Social Work,* 40, 414–423.

Hudson, W.W. and McMurtry, S.L. (1997). Comprehensive assessment in social work practice. *Research on Social Work Practice,* 7, 79–98.

Johnson, H.C. (1988). Drugs, dialogue, or diet: Diagnosing and treating the hyperactive child. *Social Work,* 33(4), 349–355.

Leukefeld, C.G. and Ries, J.B. (1993). Strategies to compete for federal grant funding for research on social work practice. *Research on Social Work Practice,* 3(2), 208–218.

Mendelsohn, H. (1997). *An author's guide to social work journals.* Silver Spring, MD: National Association of Social Workers.

Morrow, D.F. (1996). Coming-out issues for adult lesbians: A group intervention. *Social Work,* 41, 647–656.

Nugent, W.R., Champlin, D.N. and Wiinimaki, L. (1997). The effects of anger control training on adolescent antisocial behavior. *Research on Social Work Practice,* 7 (4), 446–462.

Oktay, J.S. (1992). Burnout in hospital social workers who work with AIDS patients. *Social Work,* 37, 432–439.

Paris, W., Tebow, S., Dahr, A.S., and Cooper, D.K.C. (1997). Returning to work after heart transplantation: A replication. *Research on Social Work Practice*, 7, 350–369.

Richter, N.L., Snider, E., and Gorey, K.M. (1997). Group work intervention with female survivors of childhood sexual abuse. *Research on Social Work Practice*, 7 (1), 53–69.

Reid, W.J. (1988). Writing research reports. In R.M. Grinnell (Ed.), *Social work research and evaluation.* Itasca, IL: Peacock.

Ries, J.B. and Leukefeld, C.G. (1995). *Applying for research funding: Getting started and getting funded.* Thousand Oaks, CA: Sage.

Ries, J.B. and Leukefeld, C.B. (1997). *Research funding guidebook: Getting it, managing it and renewing it.* Thousand Oaks, CA: Sage.

Royse, D. (1998). Exploring ways to retain first-time volunteer donors: A test of interventions. *Research on Social Work Practice* (in press).

Ruskin, K.B. (1995). *Grantwriting, fundraising, and partnerships: Strategies that work!* Thousand Oaks, CA: Corwin Press.

Shepard, M. (1997). Site-based services for residents of single-room occupancy hotels. *Social Work*, 42, 585–594.

Sutphen, R.D. (1997). Social work and juvenile justice: Is the literature trying to tell us something? *Arete*, 22 (1), 50–57.

Unrau, Y.A. (1997). Predicting use of child welfare services after intensive family preservation services. *Research on Social Work Practice*, 7, 202–215.

Williams, L.F. and Hopps, J.G. (1987). Publication as a practice goal: Enhancing opportunities for social workers. *Social Work,* 32(5), 373–376.

Williams, L.F. and Hopps, J.G. (1988). On the nature of professional communications: Publication for practitioners. *Social Work,* 33(5), 453–459.

Appendices

Appendix A: Spearman-Brown Prophesy Formula

The Spearman-Brown Prophesy Formula for estimating new reliability coefficients when increasing or decreasing the length of the original scale.
Where:

k = the factor by which the scale will be increased or decreased

r_0 = present (original) reliability coefficient

r_N = reliability coefficient (alpha) of the new scale

$$r_N = \frac{k \times r_0}{1 + (k-1) \times r_0}$$

Using this formula, the following reliabilities can be computed:

Original Alpha	.25	.33	.50	2	3	4
.50	.20	.25	.33	.67	.75	.80
.60	.25	.33	.43	.75	.82	.86
.70	.37	.44	.54	.82	.88	.90
.80	.50	.57	.67	.89	.92	.94
.90	.69	.75	.82	.95	.96	.97

Appendix B: Attitudes about Research Courses (Instrument)

1. Check the following courses that you successfully completed in *high school*:

   Algebra I _____   Geometry _____
   Algebra II _____   Calculus _____

2. What is your age? _____

3. What is your gender? Male _____   Female _____

4. Consider for a moment the extent (if any) of your fear of research courses. Indicate your fear on the scale below:

No fear				*Some fear*				*Lots of fear*	
1	2	3	4	5	6	7	8	9	10

5. On the following scale, rate your perception of how useful you think research courses will be to you.

Not very useful				*Some use*				*Very useful*	
1	2	3	4	5	6	7	8	9	10

6. On the following scale, rate your interest in taking research courses.

No interest				*Some interest*				*Lots of interest*	
1	2	3	4	5	6	7	8	9	10

continued

In order to better understand your feelings about research, indicate whether the following statements are true or false.

7. T or F   I dread speaking before a large group of people more than taking a research course.

8. T or F   I would rather take a research course than ask a waitress to return an improperly cooked meal to the chef.

9. T or F   My fear of snakes is greater than my fear of taking a research course.

10. T or F   My fear of spiders is less than my fear of taking a research course.

11. T or F   I would rather take a research course than ask a total stranger to do a favor for me.

12. T or F   My fear of research is such that I would rather the university require an additional two courses of my choosing than take one research course.

13. T or F   I dread going to the dentist more than taking a research course.

14. T or F   I fear a statistics course more than a research methodology course.

15. T or F   I have always "hated math."

The following symbols frequently appear in research studies that utilize statistical analyses. To the best of your ability, identify the statistical symbols. If unknown, write "unknown." (Example: the symbol + means addition.)

16. F

17. df

18. t

19. r

20. X^2

21. p < .05

22. $\bar{X}$, M

23. SD, S

Appendix C: Drug Attitude Questionnaire (Instrument)

Please read each of the following items carefully and rate your agreement or disagreement by checking the appropriate blank to the right of the question.

	Strongly Agree	Agree	Undecided	Disagree	Strongly Disagree
1. Using marijuana or beer often leads to becoming addicted to more harmful drugs.	——	——	——	——	——
2. Drugs are basically an "unnatural" way to enjoy life.	——	——	——	——	——
3. I see nothing wrong with getting drunk occasionally.	——	——	——	——	——
4. Too many of society's problems are blamed on kids who use alcohol or drugs regularly.	——	——	——	——	——
5. Even if my best friend gave me some drugs, I probably wouldn't use them.	——	——	——	——	——
6. If I become a parent, I don't intend to hassle my kids about their use of drugs or alcohol.	——	——	——	——	——
7. Certain drugs like marijuana are all right to use because you can't become addicted.	——	——	——	——	——
8. It is not difficult for me to turn down an opportunity to get high.	——	——	——	——	——
9. Marijuana should not be legalized.	——	——	——	——	——
10. It is not OK with me if my friends get high or drunk.	——	——	——	——	——
11. I would rather occasionally use drugs or alcohol with my friends than lose this set of friends.	——	——	——	——	——
12. Someone who regularly uses drugs or alcohol may be considered a sick person.	——	——	——	——	——

continued

	Strongly Agree	Agree	Undecided	Disagree	Strongly Disagree
13. Most of my friends have experimented with drugs.	___	___	___	___	___
14. Personally, use of alcohol is more acceptable than use of drugs.	___	___	___	___	___
15. Any addict with willpower should be able to give up drugs on his/her own.	___	___	___	___	___
16. Either drug addiction or alcoholism leads to family problems.	___	___	___	___	___
17. Most Americans do not heavily rely on drugs.	___	___	___	___	___
18. Some experience with drugs or alcohol is important for a teenager in today's society.	___	___	___	___	___
19. Kids who use drugs are less popular than kids who do not.	___	___	___	___	___
20. Drugs or alcohol provide a good way to "get away from it all."	___	___	___	___	___
21. I think the legal drinking age should be lowered.	___	___	___	___	___
22. Teachers should place more emphasis on teaching American ideals and values.	___	___	___	___	___
23. It is all right to get around the law if you don't actually break it.	___	___	___	___	___

Source: Royse, D., Keller, S., and Schwartz, J.L. (1982), Lesson learned: The evaluation of a drug education program, *Journal of Drug Education*, 12, 181–190.

Appendix D: How to Use a Table of Random Numbers

Assume that you have 500 clients and you need to select a random sample of 25 from that population. You have already made a list of these persons and accurately counted or numbered them from 1 to 500. In order to draw a random sample, you will need to get a random starting place on the Table of Random Numbers. Before you do this, you need to think about a way to encompass every numerical possibility that will occur within your population. If you choose a single digit number—for example, 9—as the starting place, any number larger than one digit (the numbers 10 through 99, and 100 through 500) would be excluded. There is no possibility of their being chosen. If you choose a two-digit number, you would still exclude the three-digit numbers. Therefore, you have to look at the numbers in the Random Number Table in groups of three—numbers such as 009, 147, 935, and so on. This will allow the lowest possible number (001) and the highest possible number (500) in your population (as well as all the numbers in between) to have an equal chance of being chosen.

Now you are ready to draw a sample from the Random Number Table. Since the values on the table are arranged in no particular order, it makes no difference where or how you start. You could, for instance, roll a pair of dice. The number of dots on one could direct you to a particular column and the value on the other would direct you to a particular row of random numbers. You can start from the top or bottom of the table and from the left or right side. You could also shuffle a deck of cards and select two cards—again letting the value of the first indicate a specific column and the value of the second, a particular row.

A third way to find a random starting place would be to shut your eyes and, holding a pencil or pen, let your hand come down somewhere on the page. Start from that point and take the next twenty-five three-digit numbers. Of course, if you select a number like 947 or 515, you will have to discard them as they fall outside of the range (1–500).

As you look at the Table of Random Numbers, you will notice that they are grouped in sets of six. It makes no difference if you ignore the first three digits and use the last three of each set or vice versa. When you have selected twenty-five three-digit numbers falling between 1 and 500, you have your random sample! For your convenience, six-digit random numbers have been provided, as well as two-digit numbers. All of the random numbers appearing in these tables were created using StatPac (Walonick Associates, Minneapolis, MN), a computer software program for IBM personal computers.

Table of Random Numbers

```
360062  190148  438921  828610  137813  597216  745136  848373  980702  292403
934762  289048  055252  239359  049231  215708  828323  995602  968653  358123
316630  308216  845177  333584  306213  537904  849376  571680  527394  587341
827749  459314  277743  328793  589905  452433  234203  534213  474746  301166
103359  918057  943330  745098  125601  036980  264454  594793  641501  882535
375215  397377  256691  478121  756814  210058  534319  441724  852186  016678
711032  882621  934206  136008  254288  288709  678536  919749  453691  818526
804845  256068  781681  476628  926897  721293  885133  841857  170057  958707
597462  768354  455724  262587  204958  059064  129034  774120  391834  283950
383424  363439  565399  148896  123675  712072  996343  282454  249228  733297
845446  785274  471471  718267  294703  952780  751216  614147  457324  357589
171037  236626  116308  872015  117031  393199  195654  417915  018433  885064
663704  963322  005562  992787  948421  510794  503441  139789  965668  766346
523120  499512  649587  503120  800718  621563  607424  665129  444721  989526
943685  339626  172547  475197  315309  814281  493565  095760  286835  187233
558632  445148  561021  599971  695121  839266  279515  263519  094626  630463
688812  481716  366194  887525  382441  049265  372731  024735  983979  595913
432063  938512  127163  196425  190817  044621  282333  700128  923578  279450
616425  385590  995664  296416  700414  148695  772517  274528  450435  312249
177081  382698  762128  096542  471251  085339  773561  531650  371110  232144
530653  007347  034621  130744  819405  044061  723251  190820  948230  420664
859438  714944  839905  399521  403420  389841  865691  925150  534086  261256
478363  028813  179916  334684  484782  273687  169375  159339  855149  501638
179879  858717  458259  662477  496169  146879  054723  012672  049258  883983
197394  745101  457920  776831  870531  729547  653602  451897  126884  288820
864168  863472  759723  713886  954710  314435  427718  136254  608664  820371
289783  139474  443702  674947  482657  948359  675381  826215  567342  320576
453771  612352  964705  584665  576308  021767  131857  121105  116437  586709
771929  432675  678846  540545  261755  722765  349004  558358  061999  470437
438957  456465  462582  436340  439747  995892  780771  086956  331691  334670
423067  313598  952164  288314  368104  215367  758617  797918  015908  268229
635581  071294  187198  997320  028534  678312  990718  802314  896228  742233
469967  251190  422673  372251  056526  859375  364695  542428  278938  354415
229743  588774  943979  332417  965270  655637  884089  696910  950841  324693
191392  506200  244620  456768  704170  114582  215714  082047  211036  557119
694263  645228  571122  404316  476840  552599  105398  446706  612208  069318
351932  442182  850948  841429  173236  187547  552477  131697  916519  029457
558148  431434  478713  007287  886565  575708  286567  724930  298812  943466
038521  199608  271446  416385  236335  462221  229815  538351  988086  718374
864765  228339  185429  574355  140673  021209  909292  244733  669420  291568
974542  569344  959914  700605  782962  169014  973246  671660  192281  661616
264162  109862  867096  687032  598209  665463  066929  722172  590366  238613
445488  309098  421077  946418  127374  286528  764465  273529  294707  920736
467002  286904  132511  993433  649861  827461  222143  556678  432181  456489
986860  978646  111117  024382  603227  377658  573793  128952  716583  775441
169511  226369  780706  930881  685925  294012  262731  544159  377025  570185
308173  625996  969762  979549  664350  012532  512684  588049  318207  564618
878811  783706  910275  112341  218124  652945  171602  527991  229607  815838
278763  297234  048362  308910  187519  185283  364950  433522  704987  059778
```

530363 171119 888942 167106 088337 519772 911971 607160 913710 779405
866869 688575 126713 737843 574003 216753 721812 813626 255670 771795
891861 442215 376581 850219 389477 925962 585869 161312 936721 760627
322786 491593 429552 836224 607442 327051 112775 664766 725967 795476
076249 431363 462194 445651 805690 228695 133676 011440 587539 484783
874146 718672 417301 913406 186209 028230 580430 488330 156319 472929
104513 534446 071772 923958 277696 438183 363891 736907 792323 033881
272359 342335 479491 752199 439043 135940 177676 489942 823149 389964
837251 449346 990749 232106 849040 246120 915151 046574 086474 951102
300239 526082 275425 864644 255618 586659 586779 634811 760206 651101
326919 522280 135116 633716 242288 394810 469045 913214 872541 623147
286540 344675 688627 747112 218430 889465 713441 164061 743321 129213
562576 417784 123878 615964 731064 206033 649060 029306 462497 898382
147167 122636 428552 479679 677090 334296 418436 971886 821828 209413
315649 417693 433447 275273 904126 206837 305433 749136 239819 340865
648650 778748 858718 907534 373539 203721 640184 172232 611261 695838
834730 325729 777355 126053 304084 159225 329256 882337 370627 413617
987275 175087 613310 441852 625687 662889 133838 518255 276538 821307
251799 323724 543163 013816 700677 155137 326035 491384 273298 032312
753162 993738 040435 680578 852692 539350 267744 294590 782261 034416
784092 496125 541474 182310 976291 621721 230184 471211 841234 930067
841844 938184 109491 957664 477333 847088 913504 515006 077653 126463
545078 063366 627602 995358 264044 544670 882557 476983 389775 456239
164724 120527 179080 309514 047799 061393 645651 769262 163020 459569
761433 081901 050561 360229 561105 175595 713613 669764 123888 087305
902684 551644 837068 171911 627997 674947 239108 661286 731266 497194
261632 555061 730594 275155 828748 240707 615985 267413 621999 374517
958988 356182 869666 864566 413596 101896 333437 354502 938975 863428
748569 455584 418153 160238 095463 330085 258035 676887 492603 251398
995430 641294 427426 455163 943985 384488 136526 964447 746515 708724
956215 830348 525163 609376 455178 737630 152265 501178 703582 295828
511139 546370 855892 789137 746091 842430 607468 087634 739539 400568
189068 404796 138075 639059 919469 252411 707994 210365 141856 495632
589571 313497 071962 517638 720857 612681 382192 322761 077542 828422
984835 822396 659712 589836 271442 033396 303404 613157 532634 037025
845293 981683 615881 219591 527250 452723 708748 830794 564915 434747
124531 129637 652386 578694 131967 450529 117483 486800 816065 227018
384639 949459 093621 295163 276654 473410 491026 594617 795927 569888
243543 695889 922952 881611 877041 352198 915765 396644 081382 975151
622302 483201 644443 967914 390779 151218 644301 899950 062328 025854
857471 031119 165942 167312 924395 321514 366357 392558 956718 249373
178286 684356 809681 131210 176870 448290 609916 973228 379069 791758
443008 158904 779758 189283 350316 979783 587586 374269 589338 968024
598940 868212 983014 378833 826406 891028 734779 456553 288100 592301
370939 841968 182186 454701 230046 045351 844519 428438 950725 112235
398881 185248 365169 472322 751988 275591 454914 904038 886313 776566
156138 853547 912549 723498 325563 964226 493813 063187 617240 290437
408062 150806 152468 739663 981826 202206 698117 590745 814507 112806
721228 112073 056712 264597 451561 147033 100817 535994 326176 614676
721190 399214 293671 353228 931598 325218 335996 935316 867382 373235
154787 240715 535107 689927 762804 321127 775267 792724 467721 155978
532643 369843 798877 608447 172582 429622 143483 417422 287601 057343

```
154144  691289  519238  863037  622625  197219  371853  899947  595789  309547
746845  478417  342906  350916  514353  088278  507124  685727  594705  656146
001035  537965  927346  685597  076802  730995  592412  870556  090309  634497
377141  615820  622926  964942  143322  550171  325874  362046  561667  626383
135918  415509  545895  146601  144155  929658  071321  203839  814732  952532
670012  611934  878476  206920  071128  566623  775407  723438  125868  362163
735642  074829  697719  112493  206493  228157  680488  816144  307254  101267
694556  165996  438329  225530  689537  928896  492600  869972  615567  786554
484205  333404  735725  462430  474932  391296  794264  192903  849922  147401
862537  675645  905221  283924  694956  264651  187131  111245  153893  168577
610323  954314  499918  203838  622421  964812  658753  258581  440881  827922
824517  677577  142000  853789  327631  005242  575257  611859  586983  997421
425936  475266  965271  630342  811155  290622  282301  529180  961431  071887
249194  821913  226211  214979  142871  323025  866573  239377  196238  124983
624517  718822  914510  807246  287277  222788  972259  101272  368951  145111
588724  622573  651468  149139  210402  561132  473894  713883  034079  333652
444542  120017  512157  242871  815654  472193  531818  303038  159597  463842
```

```
24  05  35  72  53  97  56  04  97  75  15  12  35  23  94  96  95  70  37  44
65  94  98  51  65  60  65  87  05  91  71  54  45  83  31  42  41  93  89  98
83  38  35  06  01  82  53  67  24  04  43  39  20  47  70  46  28  65  09  56
98  38  94  52  86  06  90  94  11  88  31  37  29  51  15  54  71  70  10  66
97  21  59  36  07  87  22  45  01  22  90  50  20  11  74  44  71  55  31  40
63  27  69  38  17  77  35  69  83  43  67  07  50  17  65  45  75  88  27  20
84  45  52  45  65  70  82  89  91  24  94  47  59  75  14  78  87  24  27  09
52  23  62  72  26  36  55  79  77  76  85  28  52  04  51  82  32  40  52  64
32  96  64  53  63  97  30  99  35  21  78  89  22  35  90  08  93  32  72  44
50  78  88  85  42  88  20  86  38  63  76  09  37  83  74  74  24  37  09  51
06  19  39  97  91  28  94  16  65  94  62  25  61  63  86  87  38  13  53  80
12  03  03  27  74  80  60  68  06  51  94  73  80  15  76  04  09  07  43  00
82  24  80  04  12  00  91  52  55  96  50  25  18  54  03  47  40  84  32  98
30  94  19  05  63  21  06  51  42  51  80  24  19  92  90  59  87  75  25  69
83  37  12  32  42  20  55  14  01  38  74  51  13  37  89  32  63  88  28  46
85  66  88  13  37  09  77  11  40  09  15  03  85  35  04  75  79  86  51  62
92  00  87  93  88  04  36  59  69  14  51  75  83  78  39  12  10  22  82  41
60  51  55  79  56  39  49  59  96  62  75  76  84  09  93  15  48  90  14  13
48  32  19  35  57  26  79  52  53  26  18  00  58  38  18  64  68  14  38  24
94  67  67  56  46  12  99  94  97  08  77  25  34  85  91  49  54  80  78  92
45  76  36  57  05  45  64  95  21  54  34  97  64  43  44  19  23  95  54  33
65  31  88  44  29  07  58  43  93  20  74  61  73  97  23  43  96  73  18  55
88  87  40  47  88  35  29  50  32  16  13  81  68  64  83  53  10  57  31  51
67  71  02  31  99  68  34  88  92  86  18  38  91  11  80  97  39  88  13  14
68  93  02  45  95  71  99  11  54  26  27  33  18  09  66  80  45  55  42  81
58  49  16  33  18  97  53  97  11  55  74  94  65  66  39  74  82  65  42  09
15  72  97  85  77  39  64  67  87  66  28  92  82  07  34  38  57  81  48  64
44  94  80  90  78  45  83  34  45  18  60  71  73  51  27  76  85  51  29  94
32  83  21  38  47  87  23  97  38  89  83  72  44  66  18  67  72  46  97  38
07  69  16  09  94  51  35  18  69  27  96  15  54  47  81  69  73  12  37  64
54  40  07  75  21  35  68  94  75  85  46  90  68  97  87  91  03  16  00  53
86  95  66  28  20  22  16  18  98  93  83  43  25  58  10  80  99  90  94  15
35  64  89  69  82  87  46  12  25  59  29  48  46  88  01  67  64  13  31  13
94  80  15  98  90  06  66  91  95  64  17  81  69  47  80  93  67  71  38  11
```

66	08	77	92	77	01	06	18	28	63	98	78	18	84	14	73	11	53	93	40
28	73	84	96	78	21	86	12	99	57	90	51	51	74	19	25	30	54	83	34
46	15	42	79	55	04	53	08	36	64	62	04	09	37	99	23	56	76	79	99
79	56	67	84	28	57	81	39	71	08	38	23	26	59	41	74	68	15	57	58
95	24	40	38	32	39	25	63	96	49	04	20	29	04	93	98	83	47	90	30
25	53	02	01	38	07	87	04	86	93	38	78	85	31	22	42	37	56	44	86
82	95	94	98	92	95	41	35	45	12	51	41	72	99	90	20	22	63	85	37
22	91	86	32	55	63	36	67	77	72	91	00	56	07	51	45	62	39	75	43
63	23	41	94	82	83	83	78	40	71	15	09	70	63	88	23	00	18	03	52
01	86	03	55	74	15	86	21	88	03	36	81	39	09	83	95	83	57	50	57
64	85	26	07	27	50	94	09	43	31	06	77	38	59	17	33	60	24	87	71
20	37	72	07	32	82	94	44	77	74	38	96	35	71	27	09	49	94	86	36
71	32	19	72	38	69	35	49	56	45	59	96	66	87	53	79	69	43	46	96
47	92	32	73	45	59	45	94	43	05	66	98	53	25	35	35	21	62	92	95
36	98	50	11	94	50	52	41	11	64	26	48	68	90	26	54	84	24	81	36
50	61	17	98	18	35	64	71	31	53	03	41	30	96	55	51	28	04	07	48
49	38	52	47	68	02	89	66	49	88	25	65	66	34	83	89	73	84	30	04
63	10	89	95	52	26	86	28	76	07	66	70	19	51	88	11	99	20	56	41
94	52	53	53	73	91	76	55	54	77	54	83	08	70	32	01	22	96	99	38
63	64	04	59	43	30	66	98	46	97	51	61	73	34	16	45	24	20	76	86
89	21	74	95	68	47	07	01	17	52	81	37	19	24	24	26	38	89	87	79
45	60	17	16	09	78	76	45	89	01	98	55	28	52	09	95	62	43	89	47
45	49	53	33	11	95	34	17	96	60	67	99	13	42	21	04	27	63	54	90

Answers to Self-Review Questions

Chapter 1

1. Psychology
2. a. To be an informed consumer
   b. To maintain accountability
   c. To meet CSWE standards
   d. To be an ethical practitioner
   e. To contribute fully to the profession
3. To accredit social work programs; to make sure BSW and MSW programs meet standards
4. True
5. Empirically based practice means to rely upon research to guide assessments, the choice of interventions, and to gauge the effectiveness of those efforts. In every facet of practice, to call upon and use research as a tool.
6. Social work research is applied. We use it to improve the quality of out clients' lives.
7. Research starts with us and with the questions we have about the world around us.

Chapter 2

1. Step 1: Posing a question or stating a hypothesis
   Step 2: Reviewing the literature
   Step 3: Developing a research design
   Step 4: Operationalizing key variables
   Step 5: Collecting necessary data
   Step 6: Analyzing and interpreting the data
   Step 7: Writing the report

2. True. The hypothesis states there is no difference between the two groups.
3. Impulsivity is the dependent variable.
4. They are large-scale efforts that attempt to speak definitely about a population of client group. Usually explorative studies will have been done first and the descriptive study follows because of flaws or problems with the earlier samples or methodology.
5. There are many ways you could have gone about this. Here are a few examples:
   - Students with at least a 3.5 GPA
   - Students with perfect attendance
   - Students who study at least three hours a night
   - Students who take notes and ask questions in class
   - Students who turn in all their assignments
   - Students who make A's on all their tests
6. Independent variables could include age, race, income, other prior arrests, marital status, employment status, alcohol/drug use history, and so on.
7. Concept or construct
8. True
9. c. Bias
10. True
11. This is a correct interpretation.

Chapter 3

1. True
2. False. Time goes on the horizontal axis.
3. Two
4. ABAB
5. c. $A_1A_2A_3B$
6. Many peaks and valleys, not a straight linear line.
7. a. They lend themselves to clinical practice.
   b. They are not burdensome and complement practice.
   c. They are primarily visual and do not require statistical expertise.
8. The major problem is one of generalization. Success with one client doesn't mean, for example, that the social worker is successful with all or most of her clients.
9. The baselines for subjects 2 and 3 are longer than for the first subject; intervention with the second subject is not started until it is shown to be effective with the first subject. Intervention with the third subject is not started until intervention with the second subject has also shown to be effective.
10. To determine if clients are making progress.

Chapter 4

1. No, it would be much more labor-intensive for Marsha to construct eighty different single system graphs and then have the possible problem of not being able to interpret them in a conclusive sense. Her focus is not on an individual client, but should be on whether the majority of the clients as a group received benefit from the intervention. Does she need to assess their depression weekly? Probably not. In a situation like this, the investigator would normally administer just pretests and posttests.
2. A control group and random assignment.
3. Extraneous variables.
4. True. It would be an experiment even without pretests.
5. True. In twelve months or more children grow up, bodies change, even our thinking about various topics can move one way or the other.
6. False. This would be the threat of testing or practice.
7. True
8. True
9. False. This is a quasi-experimental design.
10. The time series design or the time series with control groups.
11. True.
12. Because it has no immunity to any of the threats of internal validity, it is susceptible to all of them. This makes generalization very difficult.

Chapter 5

1. b. Test-retest reliability.
2. She would want to keep it; if it correlates with the other items, it will add to/improve the scale's internal consistency.
3. Computing interrater reliability
4. Validity
5. False
6. False
7. False
8. False
9. False
10. True

Chapter 6

1. b. Personal interview
2. True
3. True
4. True
5. True
6. Convenience or nonprobability
7. Sampling frame
8. a. Less than 3 percent
9. True. Three hundred in a sample of 1,200 client population equals every fourth client.
10. Stratified random sample
11. True
12. True
13. False
14. Availability and accidental samples.
15. False. It is a type of nonprobability sampling.
16. True
17. No, this is a quota sample—a nonprobability design.
18. The interviewer can probe, draw out the respondent. Also, you could have mentioned the ability to observe body language or client's living situation and to monitor the situation (for example, the house is too noisy, client is too intoxicated to give reliable data).
19. Small sample size. Few people have investigated this topic before.
20. True

Chapter 7

1. True
2. False
3. False
4. d. It is vague.
5. b. It uses jargon.
6. c. It asks for unavailable information.
7. d. It uses inflammatory or loaded terms
8. a. It is negatively constructed.
9. b. It is all-inclusive.
10. d. It is vague.
11. c. It is leading.
12. Contingency question.

Chapter 8

1. False
2. He or she is limited by the fact that the data may not exist, or if it does, it may not be available for the years or locations in which the researcher is interested. There could be incomplete or sloppy records, or data that has questionable reliability. The researcher using archival data is limited by not being able to create new, original data.
3. True
4. c. Secondary data analysis
5. False
6. True
7. They tend to be relatively inexpensive.
8. Lack of control over the source material/data—because it already exists. The researcher cannot reword questionnaire items to make them less vague or insensitive, and cannot probe like an interviewer to achieve greater clarification. The researcher also cannot introduce new variables.
9. Latent content
10. True

Chapter 9

1. c. The mean
2. Nominal
3. Ordinal (because there is directionality from high to low)
4. c. Univariate analysis
5. b. Bivariate
6. a. Chi square
7. b. The t-test
8. c. One-way analysis (because there are more than two groups and interval data
9. c. About 12 percent
10. False (anything less than .05 would be significant)
11. d. (both b and c are correct)

Chapter 10

1. Patterns of use
2. Formative evaluation
3. Narrative

4. Consumer satisfaction
5. Outcome evaluation
6. Cost-effectiveness
7. True
8. Client satisfaction studies invariably produce high satisfaction ratings.
9. Patterns of use
10. Time, resources, audience, purpose

Chapter 11

1. a. Quantitatively oriented researchers
2. c. Large sample sizes
3. d. Concern with instruments and measurement
4. a. Quantitative—could be secondary data analysis or survey
   b. Qualitative
   c. Quantitative
   d. Qualitative
   e. Quantitative

Chapter 12

1. True
2. True
3. False. Minors must still assent to participate.
4. False. If there is no scientific merit, IRBs may refuse to grant permission for research.
5. False. Although IRBs will review these proposals much more closely to ensure there is no possibility of harm and that the research cannot be conducted any other way.
6. True
7. Protocol
8. Anonymity
9. Confidential
10. True

Chapter 13

1. False
2. To cut down on the amount of verbiage in a paper
3. True
4. False
5. True
6. False

Index